Drugs, Alcohol, and Society
Social Structure, Process, and Policy

R O N A L D   L .   A K E R S

University of Florida

Wadsworth Publishing Company
Belmont, California
A Division of Wadsworth, Inc.

Sociology Editor: *Serina Beauparlant*
Editorial Assistant: *Marla Nowick*
Production Editor: *Donna Linden*
Designer: *Carolyn Deacy*
Print Buyer: *Barbara Britton*
Permissions Editor: *Peggy Meehan*
Copy Editor: *Margaret Moore*
Signing Representative: *Leo Simcock*
Compositor: *Bookends, Ashland, Oregon*
Printer: *Maple Press*

*This book is printed on acid-free paper that meets
Environmental Protection Agency standards for recycled paper.*

2 3 4 5 6 7 8 9 10—96 95 94 93 92

Library of Congress Cataloging-in-Publication Data

Akers, Ronald L.
   Drugs, alcohol, and society : social structure, process, and
policy / Ronald L. Akers.
      p.   cm.
   Includes bibliographical references and index.
   ISBN 0-534-16806-X
   1. Drug abuse—Social aspects—United States.   2. Alcoholism—
Social aspects—United States.   I. Title.
HV5825.A676   1991
362.29'0973—dc20   91-22721

Contents

CHAPTER EIGHT
Social Control and Public Policy on Drugs: Law Enforcement 134

CHAPTER NINE
Social Control and Public Policy on Drugs: Treatment and Prevention 162

PART III

Legal Drugs   185

Preface

PURPOSES AND ORIENTATION OF THE BOOK

Drug and alcohol use and abuse constitute an enormous social problem in American society and in other societies around the world. They are the focus of legislation, law enforcement, treatment, prevention, and other actions that make up public policy as well as the efforts of private groups and individuals to deal with individual and interpersonal problems associated with substance use and abuse. They are also the subjects of intense social scientific, medical, pharmacological, and neurophysiological research to understand and explain drug and alcohol behavior.

The primary purpose of this book is to introduce the body of knowledge and practice that has accumulated from these scientific and policy efforts to readers who are in the beginning stages of learning about them. It was written for use as a classroom text—either as a central text in a course on alcohol and drugs or as supplemental reading to other texts. At the same time, there should be aspects of the theoretical approach, research, and discussions of issues that researchers and professionals already active and knowledgeable in the field will find of interest. A second purpose is to further disseminate *social learning theory* as an explanation of alcohol and drug behavior, not only to students, but to researchers and professionals in the field who may not be familiar with this approach.

I have written with the student, or the professional newly embarking on the study of drugs and alcohol, in mind. I have tried not to compromise complex issues by oversimplifying them; I do try to state them simply and clearly. The interested and motivated student should find the book challenging without being incomprehensible, understandable without being intellectually condescending. Technical terms are used where needed, but jargon has been avoided wherever possible. Although an extensive range of topics is included, the book is not intended to be exhaustive or comprehensive.

The major features of this book are contained in the subtitle—a sociological and social psychological orientation to drugs and alcohol that focuses on social *structure, process,* and *policy.* The classroom materials most widely available for adoption in courses on alcohol and drugs lean very heavily toward pharmacological, medical, and psychological approaches. There are very few textbooks available with primarily a social science or sociological orientation. *Drugs, Alcohol, and Society* is, to the best of my knowledge, the only one that applies a social learning theory of substance use, linking the social learning process to social structure. Policy refers to legislation, law enforcement, treatment, and prevention policies and programs on alcohol and drugs and these are described and evaluated.

Other approaches are presented, but I do not attempt to review or apply all of the perspectives on drugs and alcohol. I do review the major sociological theories of drug and alcohol behavior in the first chapter. Where appropriate in subsequent chapters, medical and genetic approaches are also addressed.

The social learning theory by which I analyze drug and alcohol behavior is a social behaviorist's approach drawing from both sociology and behavioral psychology which I have been developing and testing for many years. I have applied it to a wide range of criminal and deviant behavior in three editions of *Deviant Behavior: A Social Learning Approach,* also published by Wadsworth. (Indeed, those familiar with that book will recognize that significant parts of the drugs and alcohol chapters are incorporated into the present book.)

This social learning approach recognizes the importance of social structure as indicated by variations in drug behavior by society, region, community, and group and by location of users and abstainers in the social structure indicated by sex, age, race, and social class (social epidemiology). Social learning is proposed as the social psychological process, operating at the micro level, by which these social structural factors, operating at the macro level, have an impact on individual behavior.

As I have stated, one of the objectives of this book is to make social learning theory more visible in the field of alcohol and drug use studies. Sociologists and criminologists may be familiar with the social learning approach to deviance and crime, but are likely to be less familiar with the ways in which it has been applied to alcohol and drugs. The study of alcohol and drugs is a multidisciplinary field (including knowledge from pharmacology, medicine, psychology, political science, psychiatry, social work, and law) and the goal is to communicate to these other disciplines as well. The social learning approach to substance use and abuse taken here, and the research on drugs and alcohol supporting it, have been published in journal articles and book chapters over several years. Presenting the theory and research here makes them more accessible to those not familiar with the other sources.

PLAN OF THE BOOK

Part I analyzes major concepts, issues, and problems related to substance use and abuse. Chapter 1 introduces social learning theory and other theories of drug behavior and defines the issues of social structure, process, and policy. In Chapter 2, we review all of the major categories of drugs that have been implicated in problems of abuse in this country and their short-term and long-term physical and behavioral effects. Chapter 3 provides a thorough examination of patterns and trends in drug and alcohol behavior in American society, and Chapter 4 looks at the problems of drugs related to work, sports, and crime.

Part II examines structure, process, and policy with regard to three major types of illegal drugs. Marijuana and related drugs are discussed in Chapter 5, heroin in Chapter 6, and cocaine in Chapter 7. Law enforcement policies and their effectiveness are evaluated in Chapter 8, and drug treatment and prevention programs and their outcomes are reviewed in Chapter 9.

In Part III, these same themes are explored regarding legal drugs: alcohol and tobacco. In Chapter 10, the physiological, psychological, and social factors in drinking and alcoholism are reviewed, and then Chapter 11 looks particularly at social structure and social learning in alcohol behavior. Chapter 12 reviews enforcement of the legal regulation of alcohol and the approaches to treatment and prevention of alcohol problems. An overview of tobacco use, public opinion, and legal regulation of tobacco is found in Chapter 13, which also offers an evaluation of smoking cessation and prevention approaches.

ACKNOWLEDGMENTS

I draw on my own research and publications in several chapters. In particular, the text and tables in the section on drugs and crime in Chapter 3 are taken from my article, "Delinquent Behavior, Drugs, and Alcohol: What Is the Relationship?," originally published in *Today's Delinquent* (1984), and

permission of the National Center for Juvenile Justice is gratefully acknowledged. Also, the section on the concept of addiction in Chapter 2 and
the section on cocaine as an addictive drug in Chapter 7, are taken from my
article, "Addiction: The Troublesome Concept," originally published in the
Journal of Drug Issues (1991); permission of that journal is also gratefully
acknowledged.

I acknowledge the great help of the Wadsworth editorial staff in beginning and completing this project. Serina Beauparlant, sociology editor, helped
shape the vision of what the book would be, and Donna Linden, production
editor, played a key role in moving the project along once the draft manuscript
was completed. I appreciate very much the keen eye and competence of
Margaret Moore, who did an excellent job of copyediting the manuscript. I
take this opportunity to thank Marilyn Carroll, Rockhurst College; James
Hawdon, University of Virginia; Craig Reinarman, University of California,
Santa Cruz; and David Rudy, Morehead State University for their insightful
reviews of the manuscript and many helpful suggestions for improving it. I
want to thank my colleague, Leonard Beeghley, who shared many ideas with
me regarding drug policy, and offered cogent and helpful comments on
Chapter 8. I am especially pleased to acknowledge the assistance of my son,
Levi, in doing the indexing. My gratitude for the assistance of these people
does not, of course, deflect onto them any of the shortcomings of the book,
which remain my responsibility alone.

Finally, I am proud to have the chance once again to acknowledge in
print the affectionate support and encouragement of my wife, Caroline, who
makes it all possible.

About the Author

RONALD L. AKERS is professor of sociology and graduate coordinator, and the former chairman of the Department of Sociology at the University of Florida. He is also senior research associate of the university's Center for Studies in Criminology and Law.

He received his Ph.D. in sociology from the University of Kentucky in 1966 and is the recipient of that institution's Distinguished Doctoral Alumnus Award in sociology. The American Society of Criminology has awarded him the Edwin H. Sutherland Award for outstanding contributions to criminological theory and research. He is currently president of the Southern Sociological Society and is past president of the American Society of Criminology.

Dr. Akers has directed numerous research projects and has published many research and theoretical papers on drinking, drug use, delinquency, law, and crime. He has served as consultant to private, state, and federal agencies that fund research and action programs in these same areas.

His previous books include *Deviant Behavior: A Social Learning Approach*, Third Edition (Wadsworth) and *Law and Control in Society* (Prentice-Hall).

Major Concepts and Issues in Substance Abuse

The Problem of Alcohol and Drugs in Society: Social Structure, Process, and Policy

I N T R O D U C T I O N

We live in a drug-saturated society. The different kinds of drugs available in this country number in the hundreds, the number of drug takers are counted in the millions, and the doses taken every year number in the billions. Some of these drugs are difficult to obtain, whereas others are as handy as the over-the-counter shelves of the local drugstore. Some drugs put you to sleep; others wake you up. If you are underactive, depressed, too relaxed, lethargic, too tired, or not assertive enough, there are drugs available to bring you out of it. There are also drugs for the person who is too active, overanxious, overaggressive, or tension ridden. There are pills, capsules, or liquids for losing or gaining weight, for alleviating pain, or for just feeling good. Want to relax, enjoy others' company, have a party, have some recreation? Alcohol and a range of other substances are available with the promise to do just that.

Most of this use of drugs is legitimate use of legitimate substances. There are positive social functions of drugs, and the availability of certain substances provides social and personal benefits and contributions to society. Drugs provide alleviation of both physical and mental illness. They can be life-saving. Both

3

prescribed and self-administered medications can ease pain and enable people to function who otherwise would not be able to do so. Alcohol has been integrated into the social and recreational life of society.

However, much drug use is not legitimate. It is deviant, violates laws, contravenes social norms, and is disapproved of by most people. It presents society with enormous costs and problems. Even medically beneficial drugs can be misused and abused. The litany of drug-related problems and damage to persons and society seems endless.

Damaged health, injury, and death result. People die of overdoses. Drugs (and drug–alcohol combinations) are the second leading method of suicide. At least one-half of highway fatalities are alcohol or drug related. Four out of five cases of lung cancer are related to smoking. Alcohol consumption is implicated in heart disease, cancer, high blood pressure, and circulatory diseases and about half of the murders, suicides, and accidental deaths. Intravenous drug use is the second leading route of AIDS infection. Lives are disrupted and destroyed by drug abuse. Relationships, careers, families, and whole neighborhoods and communities suffer from the ravages of drug and alcohol abuse.

The direct and indirect economic costs of substance use and abuse in law enforcement, health care, treatment, crime, loss of employment, and lowered productivity apparently are difficult to estimate accurately, but they are enormous. A family with an alcoholic member has medical costs that are twice those of nonalcoholic families. In 1990 the federal antidrug budget was $9.5 billion, and that is just a fraction of the total direct costs of containing drugs through law enforcement, treatment, and prevention at all levels, federal, state, and local. The National Institute on Alcohol Abuse and Alcoholism estimates that the total direct economic cost to American society from alcohol abuse alone is $117 billion per year (from premature deaths, reduced productivity, and treatment costs) (NIAAA 1987). Heien and Pittman (1989) seriously question these estimates and find them flawed by many problems of methods of gathering the information and techniques of estimating from that information. The governmental figures probably overestimate the cost, but there can be little doubt that the economic consequences of alcohol and drug abuse are a significant drain on the American economy. The size of the underground drug economy rivals that of many of our major legitimate industries (Goode 1989a).

PERSPECTIVE ON ALCOHOL AND DRUGS

It is this deviant drug use with harmful consequences for individuals and society on which this book focuses. The problem of drugs and alcohol in American society will be viewed in this book primarily from a sociological and social psychological perspective. From this point of view, the principal issues regarding the problem of alcohol and drugs in society fall into two broad categories:

1. Social Structure and Process in Alcohol and Drug Behavior
   a. sociocultural (structural) and social psychological (processual) factors, as well as other factors, in explaining drug and alcohol use and abuse
   b. prevalence of and trends in use and abuse in society
   c. group variations and individual differences in drinking and drug behavior
2. Public Policy and Social Control of Alcohol and Drugs
   a. the social and legal acceptance or disapproval of alcohol and drugs (social norms)
   b. the social/legal regulations and control of alcohol and drugs in society
   c. efforts to change or limit drinking and drug behavior (informal sanctions, law enforcement, treatment, and prevention)

In Part I, theories of drug use are reviewed and basic concepts are discussed and defined. The major types and effects of drugs are outlined, and the overall extent, historical and recent trends, and epidemiology of substance use are presented. In addition, some major special issues such as drugs and crime, sports and drugs, and drugs and alcohol on the job are discussed. The extent, distribution, and explanation of the major types of illegal and socially deviant drugs—marijuana, heroin, and cocaine/crack—are the subjects of Part II. The history, current status, effectiveness, and prospects of public policy on drugs, law enforcement, treatment, and prevention are also reviewed in Part II. Alcohol use and tobacco use, considered in Part III, are legally acceptable for adults, but they are also major substances of abuse and deviant use. Alcohol consumption in moderation is socially acceptable, but excessive or abusive use of alcohol is deviant in American society. Tobacco use, particularly smoking tobacco, has come increasingly to be socially defined as unacceptable and legally regulated. Purchase of alcohol and tobacco by minors is legally prohibited, socially unacceptable to a large segment of society, and actively discouraged by public policy. Also in Part III, the nature of this public policy, treatment, and prevention programs for alcohol and tobacco are reviewed and evaluated.

THEORIES OF DRUG BEHAVIOR

A wide range of theories have been offered to explain drug and alcohol use in general or for specific drugs. One collection of a large number of these grouped them into theories on one's relationship to self, to others, to society, and to nature (Lettieri, Sayers, and Pearson 1980). A common classification identifies theories as biological, psychological, personality, sociological, or anthropological. (For the best review of these see Goode 1989a.) The physiological and pharmacological factors in drug effects and the disease concept of drug addiction are presented in Chapter 2. The disease concept of alcoholism and genetic theories of alcoholism are discussed in Chapter 10. However, no general overview of all theories of drug use and abuse will be presented. Rather, *sociological and social psychological* theories of deviant behavior (for a review see Akers 1985) as applied to substance use will be briefly reviewed. Then a **social learning** theory of drug behavior will be presented in brief form. This is the social psychological approach that serves as the unifying perspective of the book.

Although there are differences in the ways in which these sociological theories explain drug use, they share common features. All agree that the effects of drugs on behavior are the result not just of the pharmacological properties of drugs or their impact on the nervous system but also of what Zinberg and Harding (1979) refer to as the "set" and "setting." That is, the effects of the drug are conditioned by the mental and emotional set that the individual brings to the drug-using episode and both the immediate and larger social setting in which the drug taking occurs.

When ingested, alcohol and drugs affect the central nervous system and have other direct physiological effects on the body. The way people actually behave while or after drinking or taking drugs, however, is only partly a function of these direct physical effects. Overt behavior while under the influence of drugs depends also on how persons have learned to behave while drinking in the setting and with whom they are drinking at the time. Variations in individual experience, group and societal customs, and the social setting produce variations in observable drug and drinking behavior. Some actions reflect impairment of coordination and perception as direct physical effects of drugs on the body. Cross-cultural studies, surveys, and social psychological experiments have shown that behavior while "under the influence" is more a function of sociocultural and individual expectations and attitudes than of the purely physiological effects of the substances taken (Lang and Michalec 1990).

Sociological theories share this emphasis on social, cultural, and social psychological variables not only in understanding the way people act when they are under, or think they are under, the influence of drugs and alcohol but also in understanding differences in drinking and drug-taking patterns at both the group and individual levels. Sociologists see all such behavior as socially patterned, from abstinence, to moderate use, to abuse. Alcohol and drug behavior vary systematically across societies, and variations in group rates within a society indicate that persons are subject to different group and cultural influences, depending on the communities in which they reside, their group memberships, and their location in the social structure as defined by their age, sex, class, religion, ethnic background, race, and other statuses in society. Whatever other biological or personality factors and mechanisms may be involved, both conforming and deviant substance use are explained sociologically as products of the general social structure and culture and the more immediate groups and social situations with which individuals are confronted. Differences in rates of drinking and alcoholism across groups in the same society and cross-nationally reflect the varied cultural traditions regarding the functions alcohol serves and the extent to which it is integrated into eating, ceremonial, leisure, and other social contexts. No other substance has become as integrated into a range of societies across time as has alcohol. But both societal and subgroup practices and settings provide learning and control that affect cross-cultural and group variations in the use and abuse of other substances as well.

Anomie/Strain Theory

Anomie refers to a condition of society or some part of society in which there is disequilibrium, disorder, social disorganization, lack of social integration, or lack of normative consensus. Under conditions of anomie, higher rates of drug abuse and other forms of deviant behavior are expected; under conditions of strong social integration, lower rates are predicted.

The lower-class slum areas of large cities are described as anomic or socially disorganized because of lack of neighborhood cohesion, breakdown of informal social controls, incomplete and broken families, physical decay, poor housing, and unstable, shifting populations of various and often conflicting groups. Whole communities may be described as being more or less anomic or socially disorganized. And societies may be seen as having differing conditions of anomie. These conditions may result from rapid social change, urbanization, and industrialization.

The best-known theory in the anomie tradition was originally stated by Robert Merton (1938, 1957) and is often referred to as strain theory. In strain theory, the form of anomie that produces deviant behavior results from the malintegration of cultural ends (goals) and societal means. The theory views all of American society as overstressing high achievement and material success while underemphasizing that this success should be attained through socially approved educational and occupational means. In addition to this disjuncture between means and ends that permeates all of American society, anomie affects certain segments of society more than others. This results from the fact that while all are taught to aspire to the American dream of success, those at the bottom of the social-class structure and members of disadvantaged minority groups have unequal access to the legitimate educational and occupational opportunities and means to fulfill those aspirations. This places disproportionate strain on lower-class and ethnic minorities to make use of deviant means to get ahead. Anomie theory expects higher rates of deviant drug use in the lower class than in the middle or upper classes.

This strain does not always result in utilizing criminal or deviant means, and some individuals will adapt to the strain in other ways. One of these, according to Merton, is a "retreatist" adaptation in which the person gives up on success goals, as well as the socially approved means, and retreats or escapes into drug abuse or alcoholism. Merton's theory has been modified by Cloward and Ohlin (1961) to apply to lower-class delinquent gangs and subcultures. They view delinquent gangs as developing collective solutions to problems of access to both legitimate and illegitimate opportunities in lower-class and minority neighborhoods. The type of delinquent subculture that develops depends on the extent to which the neighborhoods are socially integrated, even if this integration is around criminal and deviant values. Adolescents in neighborhoods in which both conventional and criminal opportunities are unavailable will become involved in retreatist or escapist gangs in which the principal activity is getting high on drugs and maintaining drug habits.

Anomie theory explains the high rates of drug use and abuse in the United States and the high rates of use and abuse in certain segments of American society, then, by reference to social malintegration and disorganization. This same perspective has also been applied to cross-cultural and ethnic-group differences in rates of alcoholism as well as high rates of alcoholics in lower-class urban areas. Socially integrated societies and groups are predicted to have low rates of alcoholism, whereas those which have nonintegrated cultures with conflicting and ambivalent drinking norms experience high rates of alcohol abuse. At the individual level, those who are under stress or experience alienation, whether from a social condition of anomie or other cause, are felt to be more likely to develop drinking problems (Ullman 1958; Snyder 1964; Seeman and Anderson 1983).

Social Control/Bonding Theory

In social control theory, drug use and abuse can be expected to the extent that social controls break down or are weakened. The individual who has been inadequately socialized into conformity in the family so that internal control is weak and who is subject to weak external controls is the one who is most likely to begin drug use and develop patterns of abuse.

The major version of control theory is *social bonding* (Hirschi 1969). There are four main elements in social bonding theory. "Attachment" refers to the affective and emotional ties that one has with others in the family, peer groups, school, and elsewhere. "Commitment" refers to the individual's investment of time, energy, and ambitions in conventional activities and pursuits. Engaging in deviant acts such as drug or alcohol abuse would jeopardize that investment, and the risk or costs of doing so would forestall or prevent such acts. "Involvement" refers to engagement in conventional activities so that one (especially in adolescence) is caught up in them enough that time and opportunity for deviant activities are reduced. "Beliefs" refers to the individual's internalization of the general moral beliefs, norms, and values of society, respect for the law, and sharing the principles and standards of parents, family, and other groups. The stronger these bonds, the more the individual's behavior will be controlled in the direction of conformity. The weaker they are, the more likely the person is to commit deviant acts such as taking up illegal drugs or abusing legal drugs.

A principal mechanism of social control—adequate socialization so that individuals develop strong internal or self controls—is not given much attention in Hirschi's social bonding theory, although other versions of control theory have incorporated it. In later developments of control theory, however, Michael Gottfredson and Travis Hirschi (1990) have made self-control the central factor in the tendency for persons to maintain conformity or commit deviance under a variety of circumstances. In this theory, the person with strong self-control will not succumb to the temptations, rewards, and opportunities for deviant drug and alcohol use. The person who has low self-control will be more likely to use alcohol and drugs. This difference in individuals' level of self-control is essentially established early in life and remains throughout life.

Labeling Theory

The unique feature of labeling theory is the proposition that when stigmatizing legal or social labels are applied to persons believed to have committed deviant acts they may contribute to the causation of the very behavior they are meant to control. That is, defining certain drug use as deviant and labeling users as "addicts," "alcoholics," or "junkies" often results, paradoxically, in those so labeled becoming even more committed to the deviant role of substance abuser. Society's attempt to control drug use, then, may have the unintended consequence of making matters worse rather than successfully controlling drug use. There are at least two ways in which labeling theory states that this may happen.

First, this approach views deviance as essentially an interactive process between those who commit or are believed to have committed deviant acts and others who define and react to the acts and people as deviant (Becker 1963). Some individuals accept the right of others to enforce the norms, become ashamed of their actions, and respond to the punishing reactions such that they are less likely to repeat their actions. But the key point in labeling theory is that the disgrace of people who are labeled as deviant often furthers rather than discourages their deviant behavior (Schur 1965). The stigmatized persons may come to adopt a stabilized deviant role and self-identity and may begin to see themselves as others have labeled them, as irrevocably deviant. Thus, labeling someone a junkie may operate as a self-fulfilling prophecy in which people become as others expect them to be, dependent on drugs. This may induce continued deviance and various forms of "secondary deviance," motivating individuals to become involved in drug subcultures that support their drug life-style (Schur 1965, 1971; Lemert 1967).

Braithwaite's (1989) theory is that these deviance-enhancing effects of stigmatization are more likely to occur in societies or communities that are not "communitarian." Under communitarian conditions in which individuals are integrated and there is a social atmosphere of continuing acceptance of the individual, the stigmatizing label induces feelings of shame and remorse that will lead to reformation, not furtherance of deviance. This is "reintegrative shaming." Stigmatization, shaming which ostracizes and brands the individual in a social context that is hostile and nonintegrative, tends to produce more rather than less drug use.

Second, social control can have the unintended consequences of promoting additional secondary deviance by prohibiting goods or services for which there continues to be demand, such as gambling, drug use, or prostitution. This prohibition sets up the conditions for the development of a black market, such as drug trafficking, to supply the illegal demand. Organized crime and freelance groups are attracted to this black market where the prices and profits are inflated enough to make it worth the risk of legal penalty. For those, such as addicts, for whom the demand for drugs is fairly inelastic, the demand does not lessen much with a reduction in supply, and addicts may step up their commission of property crimes or become drug dealers to get money for their drug habits. Illegal drug traffic is one of those prohibited activities that have been called "crimes without victims" (Schur 1965). That is, they are acts for which there is a consensual exchange of money for goods or services or in which the persons may themselves be the victims so that it is difficult to find a complaining victim. This does not mean that drug abuse and the drug trade do not have real victims, society and other individuals, who are harmed. It means only that both parties to the transaction are breaking the law without one being a clearly unwilling victim as in the case of rape, violence, or property offenses.

Self-Esteem/Derogation Theory

Howard B. Kaplan views deviance and drug use as one result of an attempt by adolescents to deal with attitudes of self-rejection and self-derogation (Kaplan 1975; Kaplan, Martin, and Robbins 1982; Kaplan et al. 1986). Experiences in conforming membership groups produce in some individuals loss of self-esteem and development of self-rejection. The "self-esteem motive" refers to individuals' attempts to minimize negative self-attitudes and maximize positive self-attitudes (perceptions of self and one's own behavior). If one's experiences with family, school, and peer membership groups are such that the person is unable to adapt to self-devaluing reactions of others, the motivation to conform to the group norms is lessened and motivation to deviate from the normative patterns with which the distress is associated is increased. The social control of conforming groups that the individual associates with rejection becomes less effective.

As the person becomes increasingly aware of deviant alternatives and of the possibility that self-esteem might be enhanced by these alternatives, he or she will seek out membership in drug-using or other deviant groups if these groups are perceived as offering positive, self-enhancing substitutes for the patterns previously associated with self-derogation. Thus, self-derogation will lead to drug use and abuse to the extent that such behavior and affiliation with drug-using peers are perceived as resulting in countering negative self-attitudes and increasing self-esteem. Escalation of drug use will occur to the extent that it satisfies the need for positive self-evaluation. The deviant activity promotes self-esteem by allowing the person to get around conventional expectations by which he or she has failed, positively conforming to the standards of a new reference group, and making drug use and a deviant identity acceptable.

Selective Interaction/Socialization Theory

Selective interaction/socialization is an elaboration on the notion of drug use as the result of participation and socialization in a drug subculture. According to Erich Goode, "'Selective interaction' refers to the fact that potential drug users do not randomly 'fall into' social circles of users; they are *attracted to* certain individuals and circles—subcultural groups—because their own values and activities are compatible with those of current users" (1989a:71). That is, there is anticipatory socialization in which a person attains a certain readiness to indulge in drugs prior to involvement with drug subcultures. A process of "selective recruitment" brings him or her into contact with and under the influence of drug users. The values which the recruit shares with the subcultural users are not confined to similar views and use of drugs; indeed, these values precede drug use. They include religious alienation, leftist political opinions, and sexual permissiveness. Once in the group, the person is further socialized through interaction with group members into drug use and values supportive of drug use.

Continued socialization in these groups, through imitation and reinforcement of drug use and values, produces further involvement in such drugs as heroin and advanced stages of drug abuse. However, at these stages other factors that were previously less important come into play, such as alienation from the family, psychological distress, and closer relationships with only one specific drug-using and abusing friend.

Social Learning Theory

Each of the theories of drug use reviewed here has value and has received some empirical support. These perspectives (as well as the genetic and disease approaches discussed in later chapters) are presented to provide an overview of other theories. In this book, I take a social learning approach to drug behavior (see Chapters 5, 6, 11, and 13). Social learning theory has been used to account for a wide range of deviant and criminal behavior and has received extensive empirical support (Akers 1985). The theory is compatible with the general sociological emphasis on social structure and the other theories (indeed, it overlaps with them—especially the selective interaction/socialization, self-derogation, and social bonding theories—in many ways). It is also consistent with the general social learning approach of Albert Bandura (1977, 1986) as well as other variations on social learning explanations of drug use (Jessor and Jessor 1977; Stumphauzer 1983) or combinations and integrations of social learning with other theories such as control theory (Kandel and Adler 1982; Elliott, Huizinga, and Ageton 1985; White, Bates, and Johnson 1990).

The version of social learning theory used in this book can be summarized as follows. Drug and alcohol behavior are viewed as socially influenced behavior of individuals acquired and sustained through a learning process. Behavior is learned by instrumental conditioning and by imitation or modeling of others' behavior. The probability that behavior will occur is increased by actual or anticipated reward or positive consequences (positive reinforcement) and avoidance of punishment or negative consequences (negative reinforcement) and is decreased by aversive consequences (positive or direct punishment) and lack of reward (negative punishment). Whether individuals will abstain from or take drugs (and whether they will continue or desist) depends on the past, present, and anticipated future rewards and punishments perceived to be attached to abstinence and use (differential reinforcement). The person learns attitudes, orientations, and evaluative knowledge that are favorable or unfavorable to using drugs (definitions). These are themselves verbal and cognitive behavior that can be directly reinforced and can also act as cue stimuli for drug use. The more individuals define drug behavior as good or at least as justified or excusable rather than holding to general beliefs or specific attitudes counter to a drug, the more likely they are to use that drug.

The reinforcers and punishers can be nonsocial, as in the direct physical effects of drugs and alcohol. The principal behavioral effects, however, come from interaction in or being under the influence of those groups (primary groups of family and friends but also secondary groups and the media) with which one is in differential association. These groups provide reinforcement and exposure to norms and behavioral models. Drug use is predicted to the extent that it has been differentially reinforced over abstinence and is defined by the individual as desirable or justified when he or she is in a situation discriminative for the behavior. Although all the behavioral and cognitive mechanisms of learning are recognized in the theory, the application of the theory in this book focuses on the processes mentioned here: differential association, favorable and unfavorable definitions, imitation, and differential reinforcement.

Social Structure and the Social Learning Process

In Chapter 3, general trends in drug use, with special attention to trends in marijuana use, and social characteristics of drug users are described. In following chapters, the social epidemiology (variations in social characteristics of users), group rates, and trends are presented for each of the major types of drugs included in this book (see Chapters 5, 6, 7, 11, and 13). These are seen as reflecting social structure—the general sociocultural context and the more specific groups, subcultures, and environments in which individuals are located. I view social learning theory as providing the connection between social structure (macro-level factors) and the behavior of individuals (micro level). See the diagram of the overall theory on page 14. Social learning provides the process through which social structure has an impact on individual behavior. Society and particular groups and social situations provide environments in which the social learning variables of association, definitions, reinforcement, and imitation operate.

The positive and negative sanctions applied to behavior sustain or discourage certain drinking and drug behavior and socialize individuals to exercise self-control. This does not mean that socialization is perfect, either toward conforming or deviant behavior, or that only social reinforcement shapes behavior. It does not imply that individuals learn nothing outside of what they are taught by socializing groups. It does mean that group influences on learning to use and abuse drugs are central to the process. The most significant groups through which the general cultural, religious, and community orientations toward drinking and drugs have an impact on the individual are family, peers, and friendship groups, but secondary groups and the media also have an impact. This connection between social structure and social process is, for the most part, implicit in the discussion of the rates and distribution of alcohol and drug use, but specific research support for it is offered in Chapter 5 regarding adolescent drinking and marijuana use and in Chapter 11 regarding patterns of elderly drinking.

Social Learning Theory of Drug Behavior

Whether the individual's behavior will be drug abstinence, use, or abuse is the result of a social learning process involving principally differential association, differential reinforcement, definitions, and imitation. The effects of social structure at the macro level are mediated by this social learning process at the individual, or micro, level. Social structure refers to the society and community and to the person's location in the age, sex, race, social class, and religious and other sociodemographic groupings in society. Differences in rates of drug and alcohol behavior by group or society reflect the extent to which the group's or society's cultural traditions, norms, and social control systems provide different socialization and learning environments conducive to abstinence, use, or abuse. Primary groups such as family and peer groups, as well as school and other groups, provide the most important immediate environments in which the social learning process operates.

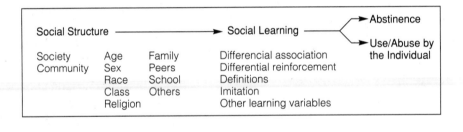

Drugs, Drug Effects, and Drug Behavior

CONCEPTS AND DEFINITIONS OF DRUGS AND DRUG BEHAVIOR

A *drug* is any substance that has a psychoactive, chemical, or medicinal effect when ingested and which is socially defined as a drug. The inclusion of a social dimension to the definition of drug is necessary because there is no common pharmacological property distinguishing drugs from other substances; the distinction is social (Goode 1989a:22–26). All of the substances included here have been socially defined as a drug by the majority of the population, common culture, or by segments of society powerful enough to have their drug definitions prevail in public policy. *Drug use* is the general term used to refer to both legitimate and illegitimate use of substances and the full range of use patterns from the lightest to the most habitual. *Drug abuse* means the misuse of legal and illegal drugs. Use of substances that are legally and/or socially disapproved is referred to as *deviant drug use*. Drug use here almost always refers to deviant drug use. *Abstinence* means no use at all of a particular substance. There are three major phases of drug-using behavior: (1) initial/occasional, (2) habitual use, of which addiction is a subtype, and (3) relapse. Usually, *drug behavior* is used as a general term encompassing nonuse and all phases of use.

Initial use includes experimental, occasional, and light irregular consumption of a drug by someone without a prior history of sustained use. It is prehabitual or nonhabitual use by someone who was previously an abstainer. The person may initiate use, never use more than sporadically or occasionally, and then return to abstinence. Thus, there is no inevitability about going to the next stage of use. However, it is self-evidently true that one cannot become a habitual user without first trying a drug.

Habitual use is the regular use of a drug continued over time. A sustained or increasing substantial dosage of a drug taken every day is the clearest indication of a habit. But there may be great variability in the size and frequency of a habit. Habituation may be to small dosages and the time between doses could be fairly long. Therefore, light or moderate nonhabitual use of some substance often shades into or overlaps habitual use.

Addiction is a subtype of habituation, but no term relating to drug use has caused as much misunderstanding and has been as misused. It has been applied in popular discussion and the media, and often in the professional and research literature, in a vague and unsystematic way to a wide range of behavior.

Relapse is the return to the habitual use of a drug after one who has had the habit stops taking the drug for a period of time significantly longer than the customary or average period between doses while he or she was habituated. Thus, persons who regularly smoke two or three marijuana cigarettes a week cannot be said to have given up the habit and then relapsed if they do not smoke again until the next week. Because complete withdrawal and relapse involve a definite period of abstinence sickness, they are more easily identified in cases of heroin or other opiate addiction. But relapse to opiates after one undergoes the symptoms of withdrawal and sheds the physiological dependence is just one subtype of relapse. The same behavioral sequence occurs when marijuana, tobacco, alcohol, or coffee habitues stop for a while and then resume their habits.

ADDICTION:
THE TROUBLESOME CONCEPT

Persons are said to be addicted to television, to chocolate, to work, to sports, to candy, to gambling, to soft drinks, to coffee, to food, to exercise, to shopping, to sex, and a seemingly endless list of other consumables and activities. One writer has even written that all sinful behavior (including all other addictions) is really an "addiction to selfishness" (Miller 1987). Virtually anything that some people do with regularity, dedication, commitment, single-mindedness, or "compulsion" has been called addiction.

There is no one common denominator in all of these "addictions." But in most cases, calling them addiction is a nontechnical analogy to drug addiction. If one wants to underscore it, the addiction is said to be "just like heroin addiction." Sometimes the analogy is drawn to alcoholism (itself seen as an addiction) and persons are labeled as, for example, work-a-holics, sex-a-holics, and choc-a-holics. The addiction metaphor is apt to be applied to any hard-to-stop undesirable habit, especially if the person applying the term wants to show how serious the problem is. That is, addiction is widely used as a stigmatizing label to condemn those who have the habit and justify the need to do something about it, rather than an accurate description or explanation of the behavior. Anything addictive is bad; if it is not addictive, it is all right. A smoking habit is bad enough, but it is even worse when one thinks of it as an addiction. To argue that a particular drug is not addictive is interpreted as arguing that the drug is harmless and endorsing its use.

While addiction is a negative label, it is also taken to mean that the person is suffering from an illness caused by the chemical action of the drug on the physiological processes of the body. That is, addiction is often viewed as a property of the drug taken which renders the user powerless, or nearly so, to stop voluntarily or as an act of will. Every substance discussed in this book has at one time or another been labeled an addictive drug. When he was U.S. Surgeon General, C. Everett Koop declared nicotine in tobacco to be addicting, and all the advertisements for stop-smoking programs and packages have repeated this over and over. Very often the ones identifying the addiction are those who have a cure or a service to offer. If nicotine is addictive, obviously the person cannot stop without help of the product or program.

Sometimes the substance is believed to be so potently addictive that anyone trying it even once will become hooked and will give up everything (family, friends, job) to get more of the drug (Smith and Gay 1972). The most recent example of this is "crack" cocaine (see Chapter 7), which is almost never mentioned in the popular press without the modifying phrase "highly addictive" attached to it. It is claimed that many persons become addicted on the first use, and cocaine addiction has been called nearly impossible to kick (*New York Times*, June 25, 1988). The craving produced by crack addiction is said to be unconrollable, and the user will do virtually anything to obtain the drug (Rosecan, Spitz, and Gross 1987:299).

William Wilbanks (1988a) calls this view the "monkey model of addiction":

> The monkey model asserts that those who take such drugs as heroin and cocaine will inevitably increase their intake until they reach a point where the craving for the drug . . . causes them to "lose control" . . . evidenced by the willingness to sacrifice all—to the point of self-destruction—to ingest the drug.
>
> This popular belief . . . is buttressed by animal research that allegedly shows that monkeys will press a lever to get more cocaine until

they kill themselves. The monkeys cannot help themselves because the addictive power of cocaine is so great. (1988a:1)

Wilbanks (1988b) refers to the application of this model to a proliferating number of habits as the "new obscenity," a four-word philosophy of "I can't help myself," which denies the very quality that separates humans from animals.

The label is usually mistaken for an explanation. That is, the label of addiction is attached to the behavior because the person is assumed to have lost control of the substance use; when asked why the person has lost control, the answer is that he or she is addicted. Another troublesome aspect of the concept of addiction is that it is very widely used to label habitual behavior as a *disease*, induced by ingestion of the drug and maintained by the power of the drug to overcome one's efforts to quit. As we shall see in Chapter 9, most treatment programs rely on this model of addiction as a disease in which the person with the disease is essentially unable to control its progress without treatment intervention (Peele 1988a). The addict is encouraged to recognize this helplessness and admit that he or she has no control over the addiction. Paradoxically, this admission is seen as the prerequisite for cure and recovery, over which the person is now supposed to have control. Almost all of the programs rest on the assumption that, while the addict is not responsible for the addiction, he or she is responsible for the cure (with of course the help of the treatment program).

All drugs to which some individuals become addicted have been controlled and used nonhabitually by most of those who have tried them. Even for the seemingly most addictive drugs, the majority of persons who try them do not progress to addiction. The research on animals does not support the assumption that certain drugs will inevitably lead to addiction (Peele 1985, 1988b). Thus, the term *addiction* may be a misleading label or metaphor for habitual behavior (Marlatt and Fromme 1988).

There is great confusion about just what is addiction. So many different definitions and diffuse meanings have become attached to it that addiction is a "muddy term" which "has passed into that group of terms that elude precise definition" (Ray and Ksir 1987:24, 26). There is no way to bring final clarity to it, but the concept of addiction has a technical meaning in the research literature which, although it has undergone some change, has more precision than the meanings wrapped up in public discourse.

The Traditional Concept of Addiction

The habitual use of some substances, such as heroin, seems to be more readily acquired, and once acquired, the habit is more "compulsive" and harder to quit than with other drugs, such as marijuana. Generally, the less enjoyment the habit holds, the fewer the unpleasant consequences of quitting are, and the harsher the outcome of continuation is, the more readily one is able to give up the drug. Although these consequences are partly a function of the "habit-forming" or "addictive" properties of the drug itself, they always depend on other factors as well. The usual setting in which drugs are taken, the reliability of supply, variations in personal background, and societal definitions are all important in determining how compulsive habituation to drugs is.

Tolerance to a drug means that the body becomes progressively immune to the toxic effects of the drug; hence there must be an increase in the dosage to achieve the same results. *Physiological dependence* refers to the actual tissue or cellular changes that take place in the process of adaptation to the chemicals introduced into the body by the drug. Physiological dependence means that the body must have periodic doses of the drug to function normally and to maintain physiological homeostasis. The absence of the drug upsets the drug-adapted bodily equilibrium, and malfunctioning or sickness—the physiological *withdrawal symptoms*—sets in. The dependence and the withdrawal symptoms are not just a product of drug effects on the central nervous system and the brain; they also involve cellular adaptation in the autonomic nervous system. All drugs have physiological effects by producing (electrochemical) changes in the nervous system. (See the box "How Drugs Affect the Nervous System" on page 21 and the discussion of types and effects of drugs which follows.) However, the production of this physiological dependence occurs with some drugs and not with others, and it is this dependence which plays a key role in habituation to certain drugs. In the traditional (Goode 1989a calls it the "classic") meaning, it is *only* when these physiological qualities of tolerance and dependence are present that the term *addiction* is used (Ausubel 1958; Blum 1967; Lindesmith 1968). Habituation is the general concept referring to all drug habits; addiction is a subtype of habituation with distinguishable properties of physiological tolerance and dependence.

During the time that people are addicted to a drug, they have the ability to refrain under certain conditions. Moreover, for all substances to which persons have become habituated or addicted, some portion (often a very high portion) will give up the drug on their own for periods of time and eventually become totally abstinent. The fact that habituation cannot be solely based on pharmacological action of the drug is underscored by the phenomena of persons withdrawing for long enough periods so that the physiological dependence is removed and yet they begin taking the drug again and become readdicted.

The term *psychological dependence* came into use in the traditional concept as a not very precise term to refer to the psychosocial adaptation and craving for the drug. Psychological dependence may develop with or without physiological dependence. But it was (and still is) used mainly as a residual or contrasting category for compulsive, habitual drug behavior when physiological dependence could not be shown. For these reasons, psychological dependence can develop on all of the drugs discussed here.

Newer Concepts of Addiction

Ray and Ksir (1987), among others, argue that the generally accepted technical definition of addiction has changed during the past two decades. The newer concepts incorporate both physiological and psychological dependence. Some drug experts see the distinction between physical dependence and psychological/behavioral dependence in addiction as either impossible or irrelevant to make (Goode 1989a). To Ray and Ksir (1987), physiological dependence refers only to negative reinforcement whereas psychological dependence refers to strong positive reinforcement. Although, as I have noted earlier, no drug can produce physiological dependence on the first use, it is possible that a strong positive response to the drug effects on the first try motivates an individual to take it again at the next opportunity.

Without saying that one concept is right and the other is wrong or attempting to redefine addiction, Ray and Ksir (1987) recognize that the older view was based mainly on experience with heroin and other narcotics. Physical dependence was defined as "true addiction"; psychological dependence was seen as "merely mental" whereas addiction is a true bodily process subject to biochemical analysis. The newer view stresses that the physical dependence may play less of a role. The actual withdrawal may not be severe; psychological reinforcement rather than physical changes sustain the addiction.

> Psychological dependence, based on reinforcement, is apparently the real driving force behind even narcotic addiction, and tolerance and physiological dependence are less important contributors to the basic problem. (Ray and Ksir 1987:26)

Although Ray and Ksir are correct that recent analyses of addiction recognize that behavior referred to as addiction is not a unitary pattern involving only physiological dimensions (see Peele 1985), theirs is not an entirely accurate description of changing views of addiction. First, neither newer nor traditional views of psychological dependence see it as only a function of positive reinforcement. Unpleasant psychological or psychosomatic withdrawal symptoms are included in the concept of psychological dependence. Second, newer conceptions of addiction refer to the strong positive reinforcement from the physiological effects of the drug, not just psychological reinforcement (McAuliffe and Gordon 1980). Thus, newer concepts continue to include physiological effects (both positive and negative), but the stress is on the displacement of naturally occurring endorphins and enkephalins in the receptor sites in nerve cells by the externally induced drugs. (See the box "How Drugs Affect the Nervous System.") Withdrawal may be a function of the nervous system readjusting to natural production of these neurotransmitters after cessation of drug use. (See Corry and Cimbolic 1985; Schlaadt and Shannon 1986; Goode 1989a.)

How Drugs Affect the Nervous System

The basic unit of the nervous system is the *neuron*. There are billions of neurons in the human system. Each neuron is composed of receptors (dendrites) at one end connected to transmitters at the other end by an axon. Sensory information is passed along through the system by moving from the receptor end of the cell to the transmitter end. The transmitter end releases *neurotransmitters* out into the microscopic space (synapse) between neurons and carries messages to the receptor end of the next cell.

When drugs are ingested, they enter the bloodstream and are carried to the central nervous system, where they affect the release and action of the neurotransmitters in the synapse. Certain drugs, such as alcohol, opiates, marijuana, and depressants, affect some neurotransmitters, which produces the lowered level of activity associated with taking these drugs at sufficient dosage levels. Other drugs, such as cocaine and amphetamines, stimulate electrochemical activity, which produces the excitation associated with taking these drugs (Girdano and Girdano 1980; Ray and Ksir 1987).

The neurotransmitters include *neurophormones*, such as norepinephrine, serotonin, acetylcholine, and dopamine, and strings of protein molecules known as peptides. Apparently, each neurotransmitter requires a specific *receptor site* into which it fits with a "lock and key" action. It is this fitting of the neurotransmitter to the receptor site that produces the effect on the cell.

When opiates, such as heroin and morphine, are externally injected into the bloodstream, they assume a peptide structure that enables them to act as the "key" that fits into the "locks" of the opiate peptide receptors in the body's nerve cells. Thus, they bind the receptor sites and perform the same function as, and replace, the body's own opiate peptides (endorphins and enkephalins). Repeated doses may cause the body to reduce its own production of endorphins to such an extent that the artificially induced opiates become physiologically necessary to fill the role of the endorphins. It appears that other drugs besides the opiates may work in a similar way. When ingested into the body, they bind themselves to receptor sites in cells that are located there to receive naturally occurring neurotransmitters. (See Goldstein 1979; Simon 1980; Edelson 1981; Snyder 1984; Corry and Cimbolic 1985.)

However precisely it is defined, addiction is a label, a term applied to behavior. It is not, itself, an explanation for that behavior. The definition of addiction is often confused with its explanation. We label excessive involvement in a drug that the person cannot seem to give up as addiction, and think we have explained the excessive, hard-to-stop drug behavior by saying that the person is suffering from an addiction. This says that addiction causes addiction.

A Useful Resolution: Stay with the Traditional Concept

I suggest that the most precise concept of addiction is a strictly behavioral/physiological definition in line with the traditional concept. *Addiction is the habitual daily use of a drug over time on which the person has developed physiological dependence.* This leaves open the question of whether that daily use is a function only of that physiological dependence or involves other physiological, psychological, sociological, or other causes. This definition avoids the problem of circular reasoning in which habitual use is described as addiction and then addiction in turn is used to explain the fact that the person is using a substance habitually. In this concept, the physiological dependence is a necessary but not sufficient condition for addictive behavior. As we shall see in the chapter on heroin, it is possible for persons to develop physical dependence on a drug but get off of that dependence without ever developing a habitual pattern of use.

Addiction does not mean that there is some irresistible force or inherent property of the drug or bodily process enslaving individuals so that they cannot on their own avoid taking up a drug habit or give up the habit once it has been acquired. In fact, for every drug discussed here, even those which are the most potent and most "addictive," the majority of persons who have been addicted to them and then given them up have done so on their own. Since 1965 millions of people have given up smoking cigarettes; 95 percent of them have done so on their own with only their self-control and perhaps the informal help of family and friends. They have not been under treatment.

At the same time, habitual users of drugs that do not produce physiological dependence often become as heavily involved in their drug-using behavior and find it as difficult to quit as do those using addictive drugs. Although physical dependence adds an extra element of motivation to continue taking a drug, inability to give up the habit is not by itself an indication of addiction. Habituation without addiction may be as harmful and destructive to the person and relationships as addiction is.

To say that a drug has not been shown to be addictive, therefore, is not to condone it or to argue that it may be used with impunity. It is not to say that habituation to drugs which do not produce physical dependence is "all in the mind" or that such drugs do not have physiological effects and can be easily quit. Free of the emotional and condemnatory connotations, the concept of addiction can be used as an objective term to describe a specific type of habituation.

T Y P E S   A N D   E F F E C T S
O F   D R U G S

Table 2.1 shows one common way of classifying drugs (see Corry and Cimbolic 1985; Ray and Ksir 1987; Goode 1989a for similar classifications). The classification of these drugs is based on their demonstrated primary effects on the central nervous system through their impact on the neurotransmitters and on particular centers in the brain. However, it should be remembered that the same drug may have multiple effects. Moreover, as stated in Chapter 1, the actual effects experienced subjectively, as well the overt behavior of persons under the influence of a substance, are the result of a combination of factors of the pharmacological effects, the cognitive "set" or expectations that the user has, and the social "setting" in which he or she is located at the time of taking the drug (Zinberg and Harding 1979; Zinberg 1984; Goode 1989a). If a pregnant woman ingests any of the drugs listed in Table 2.1, they may have harmful effects on the unborn baby that will be visible after birth. Fetal alcohol syndrome and fetal drug syndrome refer to the physiological effects on the baby including low birth weight, slow development, and possibly permanent mental disability, and physical deformities. The more potent the drug the more severe the effects on the baby. If the mother is addicted, the baby will be born physically dependent on the drug and will suffer withdrawal sickness at birth.

The drugs listed under each heading in the table do not exhaust the possibilities—only the major ones are included. The drugs listed include only those which have been implicated in nonmedicinal, recreational use and abuse. Many are legally produced and used as medication by prescription, but have been diverted from the legal distribution system into the illicit market or have been grown, processed, and produced specifically for deviant use. Some have no legal production and distribution and any use is illegal, whereas alcohol and tobacco are legal substances (for adults) that have been abused.

Heroin and Other Opiates

Opiates are the "hard" narcotics; heroin in particular forms the standard against which the addicting properties of other drugs are judged. All natural opiates are products of *opium*, which is the purified juice of the green, unripened seed of the white opium poppy, grown principally in Southeast Asia and the Middle East. It has been known since antiquity as a painkiller. Mixed with other substances it can be eaten, and dried further it can be smoked. Eating and smoking opium were the common practices of confirmed addicts until the first part of the twentieth century (see Eldridge 1962:4–7). *Laudanum* is opium tinctured with alcohol, and *paregoric* is a camphorated

T A B L E   2 . 1   *Major types of drugs*

1. Opiates
   a. *Opium*
      Pure opium
      Laudanum
      Paregoric
   b. *Opium derivatives*
      Morphine
      Codeine
      Narcotine
      Papaverine
   c. *Morphine derivatives*
      Heroin
      Hydromorphine (Dilaudid)
   d. *Synthetic opiates*
      Methadone (Dolophine)
      Meperidine (Demerol)
      Pentazocine (Talwin)
      Fentanyl (Sublimaze)
      Oxycodone (Percodan)

2. Hallucinogens
   a. *Modified and synthetic*
      LSD (lysergic acid
         diethylamide)
      Psilocybin
      DMT (dimethyltryptamine)
      Mescaline
      PCP (phencyclidine)
      MDMA (methylenedioxy-
         methamphetamine)
   b. *Other natural hallucinogens*
      Belladonna
      Peyote
      Psilocybe mushrooms
   c. *Cannabis*
      Marijuana
      Bhang
      Ganja
      Hashish
      THC (tetrahydrocannabinol)

3. Depressants
   a. *Barbiturates*
      Pentobarbital (Nembutal)
      Secobarbital (Seconal)
      Amobarbital (Amytal)
      Butabarbital (Butisol)
      Phenobarbital (Luminal)
   b. *Tranquilizers*
      Diazepam (Valium)
      Chlordiazepoxide (Librium)
      Chlorpromazine
      Meprobamate (Miltown)
   c. *Other*
      Bromides
      Chloral hydrate (Somnos)
      Methaqualone (Quaalude)
   d. *Alcohol*

4. Stimulants
   a. *Amphetamines*
      Amphetamine (Benzedrine)
      Dextroamphetamine
         (Dexedrine)
      Methamphetamine (Methedrine)
   b. *Strong nonamine stimulants*
      Cocaine
   c. *Mild nonamine stimulants*
      Nicotine
      Caffeine

5. Solvents and inhalants
   Airplane glue
   Aerosol sprays
   Paint thinners
   Amyl nitrite
   Butyl nitrite

Note: Trade names are in parentheses following generic names. Where acronyms are given, generic names follow in parentheses.

tincture of opium. Both of these were common drugstore remedies for pain in the nineteenth century and the first part of this century. Opium solutions were also often the active ingredients in nineteenth-century patent medicines taken for a variety of illnesses.

Pure opium and soluble opium gave way to *morphine* and *heroin* as drugs of choice by addicts. Morphine is a refined alkaloid derived directly from opium and is several times more potent than pure opium. It is probably the most effective painkiller in medical practice and is the standard against which other painkillers are judged. *Codeine* (along with the other drugs listed under 1b in Table 2.1) is also a direct derivative of natural opium used in medical practice. Morphine was first extracted from opium in 1804, and because it satisfied the "opium appetite" it was regarded as a cure for opium addiction. Morphine came into wider use during the Civil War. The hypodermic needle was invented shortly before the Civil War, and morphine injections became the standard treatment for pain from wounds and disease on both sides of the conflict. Because it was believed that one acquired the opium appetite only by eating opium, injections were not believed to be habit forming, although many physicians knew by that time that morphine taken orally produced a more avid appetite than opium did (Lindesmith 1967:129–130). Morphine subsequently became the preferred drug of female addicts and was used almost as frequently as opium by men. By the twentieth century, it was the most commonly used opiate by both men and women. Earlier it was sniffed or mixed with other substances and eaten, but injections became and remain the preferred method of administration.

Heroin is about seven times more potent than morphine and 400 times more potent than codeine. It is known in the drug subculture as "junk," "smack," "H," "skag," and other terms. Heroin cannot be directly extracted from opium but must be synthesized from morphine, and when ingested, heroin is metabolized into morphine (opium alkaloid). Heroin was first refined from morphine in 1898, and because it took smaller dosages than morphine to achieve the same effect, heroin was also hailed for a while as a cure for the morphine or opium addiction. After the turn of the century, heroin became known on the streets and was sniffed in powdered form ("snorting"). While one may begin use by snorting, the common method of taking heroin by addicts is to dissolve it in water under low heat and inject it directly into the veins (intravenous), known as "mainlining," often preceded by a period of skin (subcutaneous) injections ("skin-popping"). American soldiers in Vietnam (from the mid-1960s to 1975) resurrected the practice of smoking opium and heroin (often mixed in tobacco or marijuana cigarettes). They also practiced snorting opium in the belief that only injection, not smoking or snorting, is addicting (an ironic twist on the earlier belief that oral ingestion but not injection was addicting). "Black tar" or "tootsie roll" heroin, a gummy partially processed heroin that can be smoked, became noticeable in the illegal trade in the 1980s. Heroin remains the most commonly ingested illegal opiate. Because heroin is not legally produced or used in medical practice, all heroin in the United States is illegal and must be smuggled in.

Methadone (Dolophine) and *meperidine* (Demerol) are synthetic opiates developed during World War II in a search for nonopiate analgesics. Although they are not derived from natural opiates, they have the same effects, including the same physical dependence and addiction potential. However, methadone and meperidine tend to have somewhat less severe withdrawal symptoms than heroin or morphine have, and they were pressed into service in the treatment of addicts. Switching addiction to one of the synthetics and then gradually lowering the dosage to the point where withdrawal would produce only mild reactions became a standard treatment procedure during the time (up to 1974) when the federal narcotics hospitals were operating. Pentazocine (Talwin) is a synthetic opiate developed in the mid-1960s that is about one-third as potent as morphine. Fentanyl is a powerful synthetic analgesic that has been sold on the street in several variants as a sort of fake heroin. It is one of the so-called designer drugs first seen in the mid-1980s that are the result of slight modifications in the molecular structure of opiates and other drugs by private chemists (see Chapter 3).

Although they vary in potency, the natural opiates and their synthetic analogs are analgesics and depressants. They help to reduce the effects of pain and decrease sensitivity to pain, and they lower body activity. All are cross-tolerant and cross-dependent. First doses may result in nausea, vomiting, itching, and other unpleasant effects, but they also may produce pleasant feelings, contentment, or euphoria. They are reported to give an initial "kick" or "rush," followed by ease and lethargy. Physical tolerance and dependence develop rapidly (use three to four times a day for a week will likely result in dependence) and almost invariably with frequent use (although it is possible to use irregularly without dependence).

When addicts are under the influence of a strong dose of the drug, they tend to be subdued, nonaggressive, and withdrawn. There is no organic deterioration directly attributed to the toxic effects of opiates; however, an overdose can cause a comatose condition or death.

Long-term addiction can be debilitating. Loss of appetite, emaciation, susceptibility to infectious disease, accident proneness, chronic constipation, and infection from the needle, cuts, and burns all plague the addict. Long-time street addicts are often haggard, thin, run-down, and generally in poor health. However, addicts who have a more certain supply at reasonable expense and who watch their diets can maintain habits, hold down jobs, and keep in fairly good shape, although never in as good a condition as when they are not addicted. This principle has been applied in methadone maintenance programs, in which addicts are admitted to the program as outpatients. The goal is not to take the individual off opiates; rather, it is to substitute methadone addiction for heroin addiction. Addicts are supplied with a regular dosage of methadone at nominal cost. The aim is to allow addicts to have a sure and inexpensive supply of opiates so that they may keep jobs, spend their money on things other than drugs, and negate the necessity of procuring illegal heroin and committing crimes to support the habit. The extravagant claims that have been made for the success of these programs, and the claims that methadone blocks the effects of heroin without producing a high, are unsubstantiated, however, and research has shown that the connection between addiction and crime cannot be assumed. (See the discussion of methadone maintenance programs in Chapter 9.)

Once physical dependence on opiates is acquired, cessation of the drug produces characteristic *withdrawal symptoms*. These symptoms begin within 6 hours after the last dose, reach a peak within 24 to 36 hours, and disappear in 7 to 10 days. Uncontrolled yawning, itchy, running nose and watering eyes, restlessness, nervousness, and nausea are among the early symptoms of opiate withdrawal distress. The eye pupils, "pinned" or constricted while on the drug, become dilated. Head pains, stomach cramps, muscular pains in the back, legs, and arms develop. The person sweats profusely, vomits, gets the "dry heaves," diarrhea and dehydration, alternate hot and cold chills, goose flesh ("cold turkey"), and jerks arms and legs ("kicking the habit").

This distress is always present with opiate withdrawal, which at its worst can be a terrible physical ordeal. But withdrawal may be mild. The severity of withdrawal depends on the strength and purity of the drugs the addict has been using and how long the addiction has lasted, the dosage size, the setting and situation (in a jail cell, at home, in a hospital room, and so on), who is present at the time, and the expectations the addict brings to the experience.

AIDS and Intravenous Drug Use.   The gravest danger connected with heroin addiction and other injected drugs today, however, has nothing to do with the effects of the drug itself or of addiction. Rather, it is exposure to *AIDS* (acquired immune deficiency syndrome). The AIDS epidemic has plagued the United States and the rest of the world since 1980, and the number of cases and deaths continues to increase yearly. With AIDS the body is unable to resist infection and becomes highly susceptible to cancer, pneumonia, and other life-threatening diseases. There is no cure, and it is almost invariably fatal. AIDS is highly contagious through transmission of the AIDS virus in blood from an infected person to another person.

Addicts stand at high risk of AIDS infection because they tend to share needles without cleaning or disinfecting them. Intravenous drug injection involves sucking blood up into the syringe and then pushing it back into the vein. If an addict infected with the AIDS virus shoots up this way, the AIDS virus will be in the needle when it is passed to another user. When that person shoots up, the AIDS virus is injected along with the drug. This sharing of "dirty" needles has long posed a health threat because of the spread of infectious hepatitis, which is itself a serious disease. AIDS is infinitely more threatening than hepatitis and has become the scourge of intravenous users. The risk is the same whether it is heroin, cocaine, or some other drug that is being injected with a shared needle and whether one is an addict or a first-time intravenous user. But addicts are more susceptible because of the frequency of injection and the tendency to be careless in using infected needles. Although the highest risk group for AIDS remains homosexual males, in New York the number of new cases attributable to intravenous drug use is about equal to the new cases of AIDS in homosexuals.

LSD and Other Hallucinogens

LSD and other *hallucinogens* are so called because of the changes in sensory perception and sometimes mind-altering hallucinations they produce. The actual effects depend not only on the potency and size of the dosage taken but also on the social and physical setting and the individual's expectations. The more potent hallucinogens may produce complex alterations in perceptions of taste, odor, color, light, and sound. These and other visual and auditory effects can be interpreted as either a sought-after expansion of one's sensory universe or as a frightening psychosis. Although LSD has often been charged with causing chromosomal damage, genetic mutations, and cancer, there is no reliable evidence at this time for these effects in humans (see Corry and Cimbolic 1985; Abadinsky 1989; Goode 1989a).

None of the hallucinogenic drugs produce physical dependence and cannot be said to be addictive in the traditional sense. The physiological effects they have on the brain come from their action on neurohormones. *LSD, psilocybin, and DMT* affect the transmission of serotonin in the synaptic spaces. *Mescaline* and similar substances affect the neurotransmitter norepinephrine (Corry and Cimbolic 1985). LSD is a lysergic acid first synthesized from ergot, a wheat and rye fungus, in 1943. Psilocybin is derived from the psilocybe mushroom. Mescaline is the active agent in the buttons of the peyote cactus.

PCP was originally produced as an animal tranquilizer and anesthetic. It affects a number of different neurotransmitters and may function variously as a stimulant, a depressant, or an analgesic. PCP is a powerful substance that can produce irrational and disoriented reactions, hallucinations, feelings of loss of sensory control, speech difficulty, and frightening "death" feelings. In high dosages, psychosis, convulsions, coma, and death have been reported. The actual effects, especially with controlled dosages, are very much influenced by the user's expectations and drug-related life-style and experience. However, PCP is most often classified as a hallucinogen, and the most frequently self-reported effects are hallucinogenic (Petersen and Stillman 1978; Feldman, Agar, and Beschner 1979; Johnston, O'Malley, and Bachman 1988; Goode 1989a:220, classify it as a sedative). *MDMA* ("Ecstasy") is one of the designer drugs that was originally developed as a diet aid. It came to be used by some psychiatrists in therapy (similar to the early use of LSD) and was not illegal until 1985. MDMA is an amphetamine derivative and therefore produces insomnia and loss of appetite in addition to its hallucinogenic effects. (PCP and MDMA will be discussed in Chapter 3.)

Marijuana

The principal active chemical ingredient in cannabis products is a powerful hallucinogen (THC), and at one time all drug typologies included marijuana as a hallucinogen. However, marijuana in the typical dosages taken has a milder hallucinogenic effect, and today many experts do not classify it as a hallucinogen at all, placing it in a class of its own (see Ray and Ksir 1987; Abadinsky 1989; Goode 1989a). Nevertheless, the presence of THC in marijuana and its sensory distortion effects make its classification as a hallucinogen appropriate.

The flowering and top parts of the female Indian hemp plant (*Cannabis sativa*) contain the most *cannabinol*, the basic ingredient in marijuana and hashish ("hash"—the resin extract). Cannabis products have been consumed by mixing with food and eating them, making tea and drinking them, and smoking them. In this part of the world, marijuana is smoked in the form of leaves hand-rolled in commercial cigarette paper in "joint" form. Both marijuana and hashish are also smoked in a pipe. The marijuana cigarette is the most common form of smoking, but it is common for an array of "hit" paraphernalia such as hash pipe, bhongs, and other dry- and water-smoking devices to be used. In the 1920s and 1930s, marijuana was known as "reefer," "muggles," "tea," "gauge," "Mary Jane," "weed," and many other street names. In the 1960s, it picked up the names of "grass" and "pot." The most common term today is pot, but some of the earlier terms are still heard.

There are sixty-one known cannabinoids in cannabis, but the main one is *tetrahydrocannabinol* (THC). The marijuana that has typically been used in the United States, Canada, Mexico, Central and South America, and the Caribbean has low potency (about 1 to 6 percent THC content). However, much of the marijuana yield from plants grown in increasing abundance in Florida, California, Oregon, and other parts of the United States (especially *sensimilla*—a seedless hybrid) has considerably enhanced potency (8 to 16 percent THC in smoked marijuana and 15 to 29 percent in "hash oil"). The cannabinoids are absorbed into the fatty tissues, and although THC leaves the blood fairly quickly, its metabolites remain in low levels in those tissues until slowly eliminated from the body (mainly in the feces). Laboratory techniques for precise measurement of cannabinoid level in the blood and urine have been developed. Simpler, more routine techniques for detecting cannabinoid levels have not yet been perfected for testing at the scene of a driving citation or treatment program (Petersen 1980; Mann 1980b).

The immediate effects of marijuana on the smoker are probably best described as a form of intoxication, light-headedness, or a "high." The overall effect is as a depressant rather than a stimulant, resulting in drowsiness, lower nervous system activity, and slower stimulus reaction time. For some first-time users there may be negative reactions such as vomiting and dizziness. More dramatic physiological reactions are likely to occur with higher dosages of THC content including sensory distortion. Clear physiological reactions at the time of smoking marijuana are an initial increase in blood pressure, pulse rate, and respiration rate. Neither physical tolerance nor dependence develops, and it is not accurate to speak of marijuana addiction. These effects are well established (Hollister 1971; Petersen 1980; Ray and Ksir 1987), and there seems to be little controversy about them. However, marijuana has been charged with much more harmful and disastrous effects than these, and at the same time has been described as a completely harmless substance. The long- and short-term health effects of marijuana will be discussed in Chapter 5.

Depressants

All of the drugs listed as depressants in Table 2.1 are so called because they depress central nervous system activity. They are taken orally and by injection. When absorbed into the system, they inhibit a number of different regions of the brain, depress respiration, and decrease neurotransmitter action (Corry and Cimbolic 1985).

Barbiturates are regularly prescribed in medical practice as sedative, hypnotic, or sleep-inducing medication to fight insomnia and to encourage relaxation. Pentobarbital and secobarbital are quick-acting, amobarbital and butabartial are intermediate-acting, and phenobarbital is slow-acting (one hour) and long-lasting (up to ten hours) (Corry and Cimbolic 1985; Ray and Ksir 1987).

Overdosage can be lethal, and even prescribed dosages can produce ill effects such as coma and even death when taken in combination with alcohol. (The effects of alcohol are discussed in detail in Chapter 10.) Since both barbiturates and alcohol are depressants, they have a synergistic effect amplifying their separate effects. Taking overdoses of barbiturates is a common form of suicide, and barbiturates are implicated in accidental deaths and poisonings of those who, after a night of heavy drinking, unwittingly take too many pills to help them sleep. Some traffic accidents are also attributable to loss of control while under the influence of barbiturates.

Moreover, not only do many people develop a tolerance and become habituated to barbiturates, but this type of drug produces physical dependence, complete with severe withdrawal symptoms. One may not only form the habit of relying on sleeping pills to get to sleep because they can be addicting, chronic abuse may also mean that one comes to rely on the drugs just to keep from getting sick. Addiction does not occur with small prescription-level dosages but is very likely to occur with high dosages. While on the drug, the barbiturate addict suffers extreme drowsiness, disorientation, depression, and speech, motor, and judgment impairment. Withdrawal from barbiturates is likely to be more severe than withdrawal from opiates. Within hours after cessation, the addict becomes increasingly agitated and often suffers hallucinations, delirium, and convulsions. The person may become comatose or die (Smith, Seymour, and Wasson 1979).

Barbiturates are used recreationally and are involved in the illicit supply–demand market, where they are known by several street names: "barbs," "nimbies," or "seccys" (taken from brand names); "yellow jackets," "red devils," "blue heavens," "rainbows" (after the color of the pills and capsules); or "goofballs," "downers" (after the effects). Barbiturates seem to be used more in rotation or combination with alcohol or amphetamines and other drugs rather than alone to the exclusion of other drugs.

Methaqualone is chemically different from barbiturates but has similar sedative–hypnotic effects (drowsiness, motor/speech dysfunction) along with local anesthetic and muscle-relaxant effects. Although it tends not to have as strong of a knockout effect as barbiturates have, it produces a "drunken" intoxication and its effect becomes dangerously enhanced when combined with alcohol. Its use has been implicated in highway accidents and hazardous driving. It was first believed to be nonaddictive, but it has the same or higher risk of tolerance and addiction as barbiturates have, and the margin between a safe prescription-level dosage and an unsafe overdosage is very small. Overdoses produce internal bleeding, convulsions, stupor, and coma (Corry and Cimbolic 1985; Ray and Ksir 1987).

Tranquilizers were developed primarily as medicinal adjuncts to psychotherapy with mental patients. The larger dosages and more potent tranquilizers are still used in this way, whereas the benzodiazepines (Valium and Librium) are prescribed by physicians for general use as antianxiety, antidepression, and "nerve" medicine. Although tranquilizers are not much implicated in the illicit drug traffic, some are diverted from the prescription-drug industry, the pharmacy, and family medicine chest for sale and use along with other illegal drugs. They are used as part of a polydrug pattern and sometimes as "downers" to help counteract the strong effects of hallucinogens or stimulants (barbiturates, too, are used for this purpose). Even when not diverted into the illicit market, tranquilizers are subject to serious abuse as prescription drugs, and strong dependence on them has come to be recognized as the probable outcome of the overuse of tranquilizers. It should be noted, however, that addiction potential for such drugs as Valium is high only for large dosages taken for a long time. There is some evidence that both illicit use and the overprescribing of tranquilizers have subsided somewhat in the past decade, as both physicians and users have become more aware of their abuse potential (Corry and Cimbolic 1985; Goode 1989a).

Stimulants

Amphetamines have exactly the opposite effects of barbiturates. Barbiturates are "downers," whereas amphetamines are "uppers." That is, amphetamines have a stimulating effect on the central nervous system which increases wakefulness and alertness and masks the symptoms of fatigue. Tolerance develops rapidly and larger dosages are needed for the same effect, but physiological dependence and addiction do not occur. Overdosages cause delusions, hallucinations, dizziness, and sometimes death.

In addition to medical use, all of the amphetamines are part of the illicit drug traffic. They are both diverted from the legal prescription market and illegally manufactured specifically for street use. At least three patterns of deviant amphetamine use are discernible. First, Benzedrine has long been used by truck drivers, writers, and others to keep awake and alert for long periods of time without sleep. Benzedrine (bennies), Dexedrine (dexies), and other "pep pills" are used by students for cram studying and term-paper writing. Second, amphetamines are used and abused, without prescription or medical supervision, as short-cuts to dieting because of their appetite-depressant effects. Third, amphetamines are used both by themselves and in combination with other drugs for recreational purposes to get high. Sometimes they are taken in addition to hallucinogens, sometimes in combination with barbiturates and opiates. Any of these patterns may lead to habituation.

Staying high on any amphetamine for long periods of time leads to chronic insomnia interspersed with periods of deep exhaustion, fatigue, and depression. Users become overly nervous and agitated. They are skittish and ill at ease all the time and are unable to sit still for even a short time. The habitual high-level use of any amphetamine will produce these results. At one time, methamphetamine (Methedrine) was the drug most used by "speed freaks" and "meth monsters"—those who display all of these symptoms in extreme form. Although the term "speed" may be applied to virtually any amphetamine, it is most apt to refer to methedrine crystals.

These negative side effects of amphetamines must also be viewed in the context of how effective stimulants are in weight loss, staying awake, fighting fatigue, and enhancing mental alertness. These effects have either not been clinically established or have proven to be severely limited. Amphetamines can have a marginal effect on controlling food intake above placebos, but the effects are uncertain and short-term. They are ineffective in long-term weight control. When compared to following designed diets, the clinical effects are trivial and the Food and Drug Administration has for a long time approved prescription amphetamines only for limited-time weight-control programs. Similarly, while performance on simple, short tasks can be enhanced by stimulants, the evidence is clear that mental alertness and the performance of complex tasks are impaired, not heightened, by taking amphetamines (Ray and Ksir 1987).

Cocaine comes from the South American coca plant. For a short time, in the nineteenth century, it enjoyed a favorable reputation in medical and psychiatric circles as a beneficial drug for combating opiate addiction and other uses without adverse effects. Until just after the turn of the century, it was the stimulant ingredient in and source of the trade name for Coca-Cola and other over-the-counter preparations and drinks. Cocaine's medical applications today are very limited and confined largely to its use as a local anesthetic in nose and throat specialties. In the twentieth century and especially in the past two decades, it has become a major drug of abuse and central to the smuggling and illegal drug trade.

Cocaine stimulates the central nervous system (in addition to its local anesthetic effects) and produces a euphoric high. Thus, although not chemically related to amphetamines, its effects are very similar. Its ingestion increases the heart rate, blood pressure, and metabolic rate. Chronic, heavy use with high dosages has a number of very harmful effects, including disruption of eating and sleeping patterns, irritability, and damage to the liver and nasal septum. Acute overdosages can produce convulsions and death through cardiac and respiratory arrest. Indeed, in some persons (including some who have previously used cocaine) even small amounts can produce death in this manner.

Cocaine in the powder form (cocaine hydrochloride) is ingested by "snorting" or sniffing it through the nose. It is this form and method from which cocaine, most commonly called "coke," derives its other slang appellations such as "snow," "gold dust," "toot," "flake," and "blow." It may also be cooked up and dissolved for intravenous injection and is often mixed with heroin in "speedballs." "Freebasing" involves dissolving and boiling the cocaine powder in an alkaline solution, purified with ether and solvent, and then smoked (typically in a water pipe). The volatile chemicals and high heat in freebasing present a high risk of starting an explosive fire. "Crack" cocaine, which became the cocaine scourge of the 1980s, is made from mixing the powder with water and baking soda. As the lumps of the mixture float to the top, they are removed and dried. These "rocks" can be cracked and sliced into very small portions and are smoked in pipes or rigged-up beer or soft-drink cans. The heat vaporizes the crack, and the fumes are inhaled. Freebase and crack cocaine act much more quickly than the powder. When smoked, crack produces a very intense, but short lived, high which users report is highly pleasurable. Another smokable form of cocaine that has surfaced in illicit use in the 1980s is "basuco," the partially processed cocaine paste (see Inciardi 1986:81).

Tolerance at low dosages is not common with cocaine but does develop with higher dosages. In the traditional view, physical dependence does not develop even with high dosages, and cocaine was classified as a nonaddicting drug. Many have come to dispute this view and to hold that cocaine does produce physical dependence. Crack especially is seen as not only addictive but also "highly addictive." But whether or not cocaine produces addiction in the traditional sense is still not a settled issue. Crack is cocaine and contains no more active ingredients than powdered cocaine contains. It is unclear, then, how crack can be more addictive than other forms of cocaine. This issue will be discussed more fully in Chapter 7.

Inhalants

A number of common household solvents, cleaners, and aerosols have been inhaled by young teenagers who are not regularly part of the illegal drug trade. At one time, the most frequent practice of this type was glue sniffing— placing ordinary airplane or plastic-model glue in a bag or sock and inhaling the fumes. Glue sniffing appears to have been significantly reduced by more secure control and display of model glue in retail outlets and by the development of "sniffproof" glue either by the addition of ingredients in the glue or by removing toxic ingredients such as toluol or toluene from the glue. Inhalation of solvents or glue produces intoxication, drowsiness, slurred speech, delirium, and sometimes unconsciousness. One does not develop physical dependence on inhalants, but they are extremely toxic, and even moderately long exposure can produce irreparable damage to the liver, kidneys, bone marrow, and brain. Use of all of these common inhalants appears to have declined somewhat in the United States, although in some countries (such as Taiwan) glue sniffing is the leading drug problem among adolescents.

Today there is some evidence that the most commonly abused inhalants are *amyl* and *butyl nitrites* (called "poppers" and "snappers"), which are ingredients in nasal-inhalant ampules (e.g., Aspirol). Because they quickly dilate the blood vessels in the brain, they can produce a subjective feeling of extending orgasm if inhaled during or right before sexual intercourse. This effect forms the basis for the sale of liquid nitrites in sex and pornography stores (apparently, especially those catering to a homosexual clientele), specifically for prolonging orgasm, under such trade names as Locker Room and Rush (Cohen 1979; Goode 1989a).

Drug Use and Abuse in American Society: Social Patterns and Trends

SCARY DRUG OF THE YEAR: MYTHS AND REALITIES

Drugs that have been around for a long time, such as cocaine, can suddenly take on new and different use patterns and acquire faddish status in the drug world. A drug can take on new forms, such as crack, and sweep through a segment of society in a way that catches law enforcement, treatment agencies, and researchers off guard. Similarly, as new drugs are discovered or compounded from known substances, abuse of them on the streets often follows shortly. There is a seemingly endless supply of substances to be used and abused. It seems that virtually anything which has some psychoactive effects, and which does not immediately kill anyone who tries it, is a candidate for use on the street. At least for a while, such a drug may even be the center of an epidemic or widespread use.

Whenever a new pattern or form of drug abuse happens, there is usually a strong reaction and concern on the part of the public, the media, law enforcement, and treatment/prevention agencies. Often there is an overreaction, a fearful response that distorts the reality. The new drug is seen as more dangerous, more threatening, more harmful than any substance that has preceded it.

35

Each substance, at least for a while, is called, as cocaine is now believed to be, the "most addicting substance known to man" (*Reader's Digest*, Jan. 1987:32). Each has in turn been described as an irresistible temptation to young people. The admonishment has been, "It's so good, don't even try it once" (Smith and Gay 1972). Horror stories quickly circulate about the devastation that the new drug has wreaked on individuals and society. Many of these anecdotes are accurate, but others are more in the nature of rumors or hoaxes. Often, careful research following the initial media and political attention substantiates the dangers of the drug, but many times it shows the problem to have been overstated. After a time, the epidemic subsides or a new drug comes along to capture the headlines; then another fad spreads among users. This has happened so many times that it almost seems as if there is a new drug scare every year.

Heroin, marijuana, LSD, and speed (methamphetamine) have in succession been seen as the principal drug menace. Methaqualone, PCP (phencyclidine), pentazocine (Talwin), MDMA (Ecstasy), fentanyl, and most recently powdered cocaine, crack, and crank or ice (methamphetamine again) have each had a turn as the scary drug of the year. (For descriptions of these drugs and their effects, see Chapter 2.)

> When TV's Mike Hammer, actor Stacy Keach, appeared before a government committee in 1985 to confess his problems with cocaine, some observers referred to the drug as "the most dangerous substance on earth." But wait, there seems to be a contradiction here. Earlier, heroin was reportedly the "most dangerous" of all. But then, at different times and in various media such drugs as marijuana, LSD, PCP, the amphetamines, Quaalude, and Ecstasy have each been designated as the world's most dangerous substance. (Inciardi 1986:71)

Quaaludes and PCP

Methaqualone was first placed on the legal prescription market as a nonbarbituric sedative in the mid-1960s (see Chapter 2). By the early to mid-1970s, methaqualone was being diverted to the black market where it was called "sopers" (after the trade name Sopor) and now most frequently "ludes" (after the trade name Quaalude). Its legal manufacture and distribution declined while illegal production, sale, and consumption increased, reaching a peak around 1981. By the late 1970s, methaqualone was being branded as the latest "killer" drug, more addictive and deadly than heroin, PCP, or any other drug (see *Reader's Digest*, May 1982:161–166). It was placed on the federal government's controlled-substance list in the early 1970s and has not been produced legally as a prescription drug in the United States since 1985. Use of methaqualone steadily declined in the 1980s so that only about 3 percent of adolescents have had any experience with it by the time of high school graduation, and current usage (in the last thirty days) among teenagers and young adults in essentially zero (Johnston, O'Malley, and Bachman 1988; Johnston 1989). Emergency room admissions for methaqualone have declined by 95 percent since 1980, and deaths attributed to Quaaludes have virtually ended (NIDA 1988b; Goode 1989a:216).

PCP (phencyclidine) first appeared in various forms on the streets in several cities in the mid-1960s, but it was not until a decade later that it began to be used by a significant number of people. By 1975, PCP had jumped into media attention as a new drug of abuse, and treatment and law enforcement agencies reported it as the major new drug threat. Much of this attention emphasized the "grave dangers" and "horrors" of PCP and tied it directly to bizarre and violent behavior reminiscent of the early stories on marijuana and LSD (see for example *Time*, Dec. 19, 1975:53; *People*, Sept. 4, 1978:46–48).

Television specials on such programs as "60 Minutes" showed horrific street scenes of "spaced out" and uncontrollable abusers of this potent new drug. Its use was the subject of congressional hearings, and it came to be viewed as the most serious and damaging form of drug abuse in history. Many of the more horrible stories about PCP, especially its connection to violent behavior, have been discounted by some (Feldman, Agar, and Beschner 1979; Inciardi 1980).

Ingestion of PCP quickly spread. Between 1976 and 1977, its use nearly doubled among adolescents and young adults. By this time it had acquired over thirty street names, varying by section of the country and the form in which it was sold, such as "PeaCe Pills," "crystal," "rocket fuel," and "tic." It was most often called "angel dust," however, and this is the street name by which it is almost exclusively known today. This name comes from the white powder of the drug in its pure form, but it is also sold and consumed in liquid, tablet, and crystal form. It is often passed off as mescaline, LSD, cocaine, and THC. It is often snorted, but the most common technique of ingestion is by sprinkling the powder on marijuana and smoking it, which produces hallucinogenic effects more quickly.

Following the initial burst of use in the mid-1970s, PCP use stabilized and declined. No more than a tiny fraction of 1 percent of adolescents have ever used PCP daily, and by 1980 the levels of PCP use had dropped down to less than use of methaqualone—virtually zero daily usage and 1 to 3 percent current (in the past month) usage (Petersen and Stillman 1978; Johnston, Bachman, and O'Malley 1980; Fishburne, Abelson, and Cisin 1980). By the end of the 1980s, monthly PCP use had virtually disappeared, and lifetime use among graduating high school students had dropped below 3 percent (Johnston 1989). As with other drugs, PCP did not turn out to be the horrendous threat to the youth of society that it was originally thought to be. However, as with the other drugs, its dangers were and remain real enough. While overall prevalence has declined, emergency room episodes and deaths have remained high (NIDA 1988b).

The practice of lacing marijuana with PCP and smoking it seemed for a while as if it would broaden to include treating marijuana with a variety of chemicals, formaldehyde, rat poison, and insecticides. Such chemically treated marijuana was dubbed a *WAC* joint and getting WAC'd out threatened to become the drug fad of 1986. Youngsters who had smoked WAC joints turned up in emergency rooms with hallucinogenic symptoms and with behavior that the treating physicians interpreted as severe psychosis. They also thought that the combination of marijuana and poison produced "heroin-like" highs and addiction. Fortunately, the fad did not become widespread, the evidence of psychosis and addiction remained unconvincing, and little has been heard about getting WAC'd since 1986 (*Newsweek*, Jan. 20, 1986:25).

Pentazocine, Fentanyl, and Designer Drugs

Pentazocine is an opiate-like analgesic that has been available for medical applications since 1967, and its effects of euphoria, tolerance, and physical dependence have been known from its first introduction (Inciardi and Chambers 1971). It was given life as a street drug, however, by its combination with an over-the-counter antihistamine. The combination known as "T's and Blues" or "T's and B's" (after Talwin, the trade name for pentazocine, and the blue color of the antihistamine tablets) is injected as a relatively inexpensive substitute for heroin. Although first used this way some years before, T's and B's appeared noticeably on the street in 1979 and came into significant enough use for agency and media attention between 1980 and 1981, principally in New Orleans, St. Louis, and Chicago (*Time*, July 20, 1981:26). In the late 1980s, local police began noticing use of another street combination known as "T and R speedballs." This is pentazocine mixed with Ritalin, a stimulant prescribed for hyperactive children (Stewart 1989). Apparently it has the same function as a poor man's speedball as does T's and B's, but I have not seen any more reports on it.

In addition to synthetic opiates such as pentazocine, new forms of heroin and other opiates continue to show up in street use (see fentanyl below). *Black tar*, or *tootsie roll*, is a semiprocessed dark brown or black heroin from Mexico (with a purity of about 40 to 60 percent). It can be sold in very small quantities, which can be further processed to produce powdered heroin, cut to 10 percent purity. It began to show up in sizable quantities in 1984 on the streets of Seattle, San Francisco, San Diego, Phoenix, Denver, and other western cities. Black tar is not a new drug, but it is a new form of crudely processed heroin that previously was not sold in the illegal drug market. Its higher purity and combination with cocaine (speedballing) produced an increase in emergency room episodes in the mid-1980s and caused some concern that it might portend a new heroin epidemic (NIDA 1985). Since neither pentazocine nor black tar is reported as a separate category in the national surveys, it is difficult to know how widespread their use was or is. As opiates, however, they have probably followed the trend of decreasing prevalence that heroin and other drugs in the opiate class have followed in the past decade (Johnston, O'Malley, and Bachman 1988; Johnston 1989).

At about the same time as black tar appeared in the illicit drug trade in this country, *basuco*, a coca paste, also was coming into use in Miami and New York. Just as black tar heroin is a form of partially or incompletely processed heroin, basuco is a form of partially processed cocaine. It has a high cocaine content (at least 40 percent) and is smoked by mixing with marijuana or tobacco. Basuco has been smoked in South America since the early 1970s, and by the mid-1980s had come to this country where it was sometimes known as "bubble gum" (NIDA 1985; Inciardi 1986).

Designer drugs are synthetic chemical substances that are analogs to existing illicit drugs. These drugs, which began appearing on the streets in the early 1980s, are "designed" by slightly altering the molecular structure while retaining or enhancing the effects of the drugs that they are intended to mimic. The major ones which achieved media and official attention are analogs of fentanyl and other synthetic heroins, MPTP, an analog of the opiate meperidine, and Ecstasy (MDMA), a hallucinogenic/amphetamine analog (see *Time*, Apr. 8, 1985:61–62; Associated Press, Feb. 16, 1986; Ray and Ksir 1987; Gallagher 1989b; Straus 1989).

Since the DEA's dangerous and controlled-substance schedules were specific as to the chemical makeup of banned or controlled substances, the slight modification made the designer drugs legal. As the newly designed drug was placed on the schedule, another modification bypassing the prohibited molecular structure would appear. From media coverage, it appeared for a while as if designer drugs would sweep the country displacing heroin, LSD, cocaine, and other illegal drugs with just as dangerous but now legal drugs. As one DEA official put it, "Millions of doses could be placed in the general drug traffic, people would die—and no crime would have been committed" (Straus 1989:94). One writer predicted that "the flood of designer drugs portends that in the not-too-distant future there may no longer be any demand for botanical narcotics" (Gallagher 1989b:97). That did not materialize, partly because the production of the designer drugs did not turn out to be as widespread or as easily accomplished as the drug authorities had first believed, but also because of a change in the law. The Anti-Drug Abuse Act of 1986 placed any present or future designer analogs on the schedules that were "substantially similar" to existing controlled substances.

Designer *fentanyl* was first discovered in the illicit drug trade in 1979 in California where it was being sold as heroin, and by 1985 at least six fentanyl-like drugs were known to be implicated in illicit drug use. Fentanyl analogs have produced a number of overdose deaths since their toxicity is many times that of heroin. They also produce physical addiction, apparently as quickly or more quickly than heroin, although it is an obvious case of hyperbole to claim, as one "addiction specialist" has, that one can become addicted from "one shot [of] fentanyl" (Gallagher 1989b:96). This "one shot and you're addicted" label has been applied to many of the scary drugs. Although these types of designer drugs have spread beyond California to New York and elsewhere, they have not become the plague that many feared.

MPTP is also an opiate analog dating from 1982, which resulted from a failed attempt to produce MPPP (similar to meperidine). MPTP is a neurotoxin that creates symptoms which look like advanced stages of Parkinson's disease. The original episode of MPTP usage occurred in California, and a few cases turned up in South Florida about a year later (Associated Press, Feb. 16, 1986). But thus far it has not become a continuing part of street drug use. Ironically, the MPTP episode may ultimately provide some clues in the treatment of Parkinson's disease (*Time,* Apr. 8, 1985:62).

Ecstasy (MDMA) is a synthetic amphetamine that was first synthesized in 1914 but was not manufactured for market distribution. It began to be used in psychiatric practice as a substitute for LSD in the 1970s, but by 1985 its street use in designer forms caught the attention of the media. It was called the "LSD of the 1980s" and was predicted to become the "psychedelic drug of the 1990s." Reported instances of recreational use and abuse caused enough concern at DEA that ecstasy was temporarily placed on the schedule of controlled substances. As an amphetamine, ecstasy has stimulant effects, but more notably it also has pronounced hallucinogenic effects. Beyond these, little is known about MDMA's long-term physiological or psychological effects. Psychiatrists and others defended MDMA as a fairly safe substance useful in therapy and resisted its listing as a dangerous substance without medical use. But DEA was sufficiently convinced by animal studies showing abuse potential that MDMA was permanently given controlled-substance status in 1986 (*Gainesville Sun,* Nov. 8, 1985; Ray and Ksir 1987; Goode 1989a:182–184). Street use of ecstasy has not become widespread, and one seldom hears any more predictions of how it will be the drug of the 1990s.

Cocaine: Crack and Otherwise

All of these instances of the waxing and waning of drug scares pale in comparison to cocaine in the 1980s. First powdered cocaine (cocaine hydrochloride) and then a little later *crack* cocaine became *the scariest drug of the latter part of the twentieth century.* Cocaine has been a significant part of the drug subculture seriously implicated in drug abuse in ghetto areas at least since the 1930s both used alone and in combination with heroin.

However, snorting, freebasing, and injecting cocaine became prominent among affluent sectors of society in the early 1980s. Not only rock music stars, but movie actors, producers, writers, executives, and others of the "yuppie generation" took up cocaine use. This created a storm of magazine and newspaper coverage, television news, documentaries, and movies and TV dramas about cocaine. In 1985 crack burst into public consciousness as the "most dangerous substance" of all and quickly became the major drug problem in the lower-class black community. It became *the* drug menace of the 1980s and continues as a priority of drug control and media attention today.

Even as the public attention was white-hot, cocaine use had already been in decline for several years. There was a time when crack use was raging in the black community and was making some inroads in the white population. However, the prevalence of crack use never reached the national epidemic levels feared, and almost as soon as its prevalence began to be measured in careful surveys, it started to decrease. Heavy cocaine use, cocaine deaths, and other indicators of abuse continued upward for a while, but by 1990 these, too, had come down. Disruption in the coca-growing countries and interdiction of smuggling in the United States have begun to show some effects. Both demand for and supplies of cocaine hydrochloride and crack cocaine have been on a downward slope. The threat of cocaine in all its forms is real and not to be underestimated, but apparently its days as scary drug of the year are numbered. (Cocaine will be discussed in more detail in Chapter 7.)

Ice-Hot

As each current scare wanes, another will come along to take its place. History teaches us that the same will happen with crack. Indeed, at the end of the 1980s and in the early 1990s, there were reports that as adolescents and others are getting frightened away from crack cocaine, speed may be making a comeback as *crank* or *ice*, the newer terms for methamphetamine. The crystals can be smoked, snorted, or cooked up and injected. Illegal methamphetamine sales and production in clandestine laboratories have been most noticeable in southern California, where it has spread beyond use by bikers and truckers. But crank use reportedly has been growing in Texas, Oklahoma, Florida, and elsewhere (*Time*, Apr. 17 1989:10–12; *USA Today*, July 26, 1989:3A).

From the beginning of reported seizures of crank and discovery of crank laboratories in 1989, newscasters and news reporters have described crank as "more potent and just as addictive as crack." Some describe it as the "poor man's cocaine" that "could become the crack of the 1990s" (*USA Today*, July 26, 1989:3A). Later in 1989 the term *ice* became the more frequently used designation for methamphetamine in general or to designate a stronger and more crystalline form of crank. It was also increasingly referred to as simply the latest and most destructive designer drug and was hailed as a "new, hallucinogenic, highly addictive drug" (*Gainesville Sun*, Sept. 26, 1989). Ice definitely has qualified as scary drug of the year.

Smoking ice was reported as having reached major proportion in Hawaii and heading to take over the mainland, and it was predicted to be the "drug plague of the 1990s" that will "supplant crack" (*New York Times* News Service, Sept. 18, 1989; *Time*, Sept. 18, 1989:28; *Los Angeles Times*, Oct. 9, 1989; *Newsweek*, Nov. 27, 1989:37–39). Seizures of labs making ice (by allowing methamphetamine to stand in water or alcohol until it crystallizes) increased, and the drug began to be defined as worse than crack. It was said to be longer-lasting, more potent, more dangerous, and by now was judged to be even more addicting than crack. And again, as was claimed for crack and other scary drugs of the year, ice was described as instantly addicting. Supposedly, ice produces exactly the same effects as cocaine on the reuptake of dopamine and the receptor sites in the nerve cells but with a stronger and more lasting punch (Miller 1989; Wilson 1989; *Newsweek*, Nov. 27, 1989:37).

Lessons of the Scary Drug of the Year

Perhaps ice will be next in line as the most scary drug ever known. But if it does, it will not be based on any firm evidence at this time that its use is anywhere near or about to become epidemic even in southern California, where it is believed to be concentrated (Pennell 1990). For the first time in the 1990 NIDA survey of high school seniors, a question was asked about use of ice (3 percent reported having ever used it), and we have no way of measuring trends at this time. Another scary drug of the year may come along to take its place. Even LSD, the pride of the hippie subculture and the focus of official horror in the 1960s, is making something of a new appearance (*Gainesville Sun*, June 19, 1989). We can expect that new episodes or epidemics will occur, either a rediscovery of an old drug or a new substance. The bizarre practice of ingesting bufotenine by "toad licking" is the latest hallucinogenic fad to periodically get reported (Uzelac, Feb. 1, 1990).

Which of these substances, or others we have not yet heard about, will turn out to become widely used and the focus of law enforcement, education, and treatment programs remains to be seen. As the new threats appear, we need to learn from the past history of the scary drugs of the year. Those lessons are twofold: First, the more hysterical alarms should be greeted with skepticism. The old dictum of "don't believe everything you read" certainly holds for the mass media coverage, statements by drug-policy officials, local law enforcement, and others on the contemporary drug scene. We have seen drug scares come and go; epidemics develop, peak, and decline with few of the horrors predicted coming true. Second, the potential dangers of each drug should be taken seriously. Often there is real, substantive basis for the alarm, even though it may get exaggerated or distorted. No form of cocaine use has proven to be as instantly addicting, harmful, irresistible, and expanding to all segments of the population as was once believed; yet who can deny the enormous damage to American society that cocaine use and abuse has caused. As Erich Goode (1989b) reminds us concerning the drug scares of the 1980s, public concern about drugs as instigated by and reflected in popular media coverage is based not only on an entirely subjective "social construction" of the problem but also on objective indices of a real drug problem. The assumption that the public perception is always wrong or simply media hype is not warranted. Blasé assurances about harmlessness and safety of drugs by those attempting to debunk the beliefs of a gullible public are also not justified by the history of the scary drug of the year.

SOCIAL PATTERNS AND TRENDS IN DRUG USE

Prevalence and Trends

One of the most important ways that we can separate myth from reality in American drug problems is to take a careful look at what the actual level of drug use is and how it has changed over time. Because of the media attention to scary drugs, we have become accustomed to nearly daily headline news reporting on drugs. Television and other media regularly make special presentations on drugs. Drugs and related crime have been at the top of the list of public concerns for some time. Fighting drugs has been given priority at both the federal and local levels of government. Some illicit drugs can be found in all regions of the country and in all social classes. The illegal drug business is thriving, drug deaths are very high, and drugs are devastating many urban ghetto neighborhoods. It is unusual for someone to arrive at college without some knowledge about drugs and without some opinion on the problem. This easy familiarity with, coupled with tremendous concern about, drug use contrasts sharply with the relatively drug-free state of society three decades ago. But given the common public perception of a current societywide drug crisis, it might also come as a surprise to many that we are a more drug-free society than we were just a decade ago.

Marijuana was practically unknown in the United States before the 1930s when smoking marijuana began to spread into the slums of the big cities and became part of the drug subculture along with heroin, cocaine, and other drugs. After World War II, marijuana use spread rapidly among the youth of lower-class areas and black neighborhoods of the cities, reaching a peak about 1949–1950, continuing at a higher rate until the mid-1950s, and declining somewhat toward the end of that decade. LSD and other hallucinogens were, in essence, unknown to all except a small group of experimenters before the mid-1960s. To all intents and purposes, until the mid-1960s illicit drugs were absent from campuses and from almost all other sectors of society. The problem was essentially restricted to drug subcultures confined largely to minority and lower-class communities.

Marijuana first, and then other drugs, broke out of these confines and began to spread to other parts of society that had been virtually isolated from drugs. The increase was most dramatic for young adults, principally college and university students. Although pot smoking was virtually absent from campuses in 1960, by 1970 42 percent of college students had smoked marijuana and 21 percent were current users (within the past month). The proportion of college students who had some experience with marijuana doubled from 1969 to 1970. The trend continued throughout the 1970s so that by the end of the decade two-thirds of young adults (both in and out of college) had some experience with marijuana and 35 percent were current users. Those of this same age group in the military also took up drug use, reflecting the level and types of drugs used in the civilian population.

Significant increases also occurred among adolescents, as the college drug scene swiftly moved down into the high schools, and the age at first use of marijuana and other drugs dropped. By the mid-1970s, two-fifths of teenagers (age 12 to 17) had tried marijuana. By the end of the decade, about one-third had used marijuana and 17 percent had smoked it in the past month. By the end of the 1970s, when drug use had peaked in the United States, 60 percent of male and female high school seniors had used marijuana and 36 percent were current smokers.

The spread was not confined to the young, however. Illicit drugs of all kinds became known among the general adult population. Drug use among the older adult population (age 26 +), while involving lower percentages than among the younger population, followed the same pattern. In the wake of the spread of marijuana, there were increases in illicit use of LSD, other hallucinogens, amphetamines, barbiturates, and other drugs for all age groups. (See the reviews by Radosevich et al. 1979 and Akers 1984 of research and surveys conducted during these periods.)

Figure 3.1 and Tables 3.1 to 3.6 show these earlier trends in drug use and also show clearly the remarkable turnaround in overall drug use that occurred in the 1980s after the peak years of use about 1979–1980. The tables show that the biggest jumps in rates of use occurred up to the mid-1970s whereas increases in the latter years of that decade were more modest.

From Table 3.1 we see the increases in marijuana use throughout the 1970s among both the general adolescent population (age 12 to 17) and the high school seniors on three measures. In the latter part of that decade the rate of increase had leveled off, and after 1979 marijuana use began declining. The dropoff was slow at the beginning of the 1980s, but in the latter

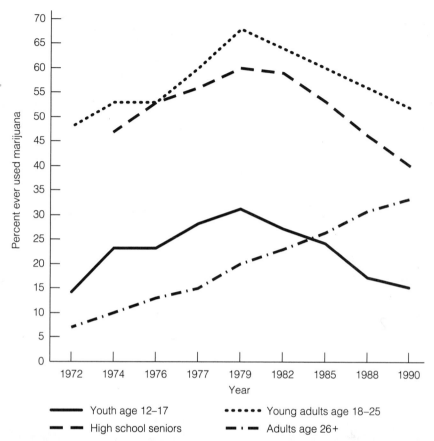

F I G U R E   3 . 1   *Trends in lifetime prevalence of marijuana use*
Sources: Johnston, O'Malley, and Bachman 1988; Johnston 1989; University of Michigan 1991;
NIDA 1986, 1989a, 1989b, 1990a.
Note: Data given for 1974 for high school seniors is from 1975.

part of the decade there were sharper decreases. For the first time since 1975,
less than a majority of graduating high school seniors reported experience
with marijuana in the 1988 University of Michigan survey. By 1990, 14 percent of the seniors and 5 percent of the general adolescent population were
current users of marijuana. Moreover, the percent of seniors reporting daily
marijuana use (not shown in Table 3.1) declined to 7 percent by 1981 and
by 1990 had dipped below 3 percent. Proportions of adolescents who have
used marijuana as low as these had not been seen since the early 1970s.

Sedatives were used by lower proportions of the seniors in the last
half of the decade, but in the early 1980s use began to creep upward again.

The High School Senior Survey and the NIDA Household Survey

The trends in drug use in American society are observed primarily from two continuing national surveys of representative samples of respondents who self-report behavior, attitudes, and opinions regarding drugs and alcohol. The first of these is the annual survey of high school seniors that Lloyd Johnston and his associates at the University of Michigan (Institute for Social Research) have conducted for the National Institute on Drug Abuse (NIDA). NIDA has also sponsored periodic national surveys of households in the United States that sample the whole population 12 years of age and older. Prior to the beginning of these surveys in the early 1970s, we had to rely on regional, local, and campus studies which, while often of high quality for purposes of testing theories of drug use, presented problems of representativeness. These studies were unable to provide an accurate picture of the prevalence and epidemiology of drug use at any given time and offered little basis for mapping trends. The two national surveys give firm bases for both current prevalence and changes through time.

There are four measures of drug use prevalence commonly used in the University of Michigan and NIDA surveys:

1. *Lifetime prevalence*: the percent who have reported having ever used a drug.

2. *Annual prevalence*: the percent who have used sometime during the past year.

3. *Current prevalence*: the percent who have used sometime during the past month.

4. *Daily prevalence*: the percent who have used at least twenty days out of the past thirty days.

Methaqualone use, which had remained at about 8 percent of seniors in the 1970s, climbed above 10 percent by 1982. Other drugs which had been taken up by ever-increasing numbers of young people in the 1970s, however, had their growth stopped. Nevertheless, the proportion reporting use of any illicit drug besides marijuana continued to increase, albeit at a slow rate. Although at this time overall drug use apparently was not declining, anyone knowledgeable about the leading role that marijuana had played in previous increases should have been able to see what was coming.

T A B L E   3 . 1   *Trends in marijuana use among adolescents*

	Percent Have Ever Used	Percent Used in Past Year	Percent Used in Past Month
		Age 12–17	
1974	23	18	12
1979	31	24	17
1985	24	20	12
1988	17	13	6
1990	15	11	5
		Graduating High School Seniors	
1975	47	40	27
1979	60	51	36
1985	54	41	26
1988	47	33	18
1990	41	27	14

Sources: NIDA 1986, 1988a, 1990a; Johnston 1989; University of Michigan 1991.
Note: Except for figures of less than 1 percent, percentages are rounded to whole numbers in this and all tables in this chapter.

T A B L E   3 . 2   *Trends in use of any illicit drugs among high school seniors*

Year	Percent Have Ever Used	Percent Used in Past Year	Percent Used in Past Month
1975	55	45	31
1979	65	54	39
1985	61	46	30
1988	54	38	21
1990	48	32	17

Sources: Johnston 1989; University of Michigan 1991.

While use of any illicit drug continued to increase for a time after marijuana use peaked in 1979, Table 3.2 shows that by 1985 the decline of all illicit drug use was quite evident and by 1988 was back down below 1975 levels. Whereas in 1979, two-fifths of the seniors had used drugs in the past month, by 1990 less than one-fifth had current experience with any illicit drug.

T A B L E   3 . 3   Trends in marijuana use among college and adult populations

Year	Percent Used in Past Year	Percent Used in Past Month
Young Adults Age 18–25		
1974	34	25
1979	47	35
1985	37	22
1988	28	16
1990	25	13
College Students 1–4 Years Beyond High School		
1980	51	34
1985	42	24
1988	35	17
1990	29	14
Adults Age 26+		
1974	4	2
1979	9	6
1985	9	6
1988	7	4
1990	7	4

Sources: NIDA 1986, 1989a, 1990a; Johnston, O'Malley, and Bachman 1988; University of Michigan 1991.

The pattern of change in adolescent drug use has been fairly well matched by change in drug use in the college and adult populations (see Table 3.3). As noted previously, illicit substance use by young adults, both in and out of college, remains at somewhat higher levels than teenagers' use but also reached a peak in 1979. By 1985 lifetime and annual prevalence of marijuana use among young adults was back to mid-1970s levels, and current use dropped to its lowest level since 1970 and continued to decline through 1990. Similarly, marijuana smoking by college students decreased throughout the 1980s back to the level of use at the beginning of the 1970s.

Drug use among adults older than 25, while still much lower than young adult and college populations, did not peak in 1979. Indeed, the percentages continued upward in the 1980s, and by 1985 lifetime prevalence among older adults surpassed that among teenagers for the first time since the beginning of the surveys in the early 1970s. This trend is primarily due to a "cohort effect" in which the generation who were teenagers and young adults with high levels of illicit drug use in the 1970s enter into their late 20s or early 30s. Even if they stopped taking drugs as they got older, the lifetime prevalence measure still continues to count their former use when they were teenagers

T A B L E   3 . 4   Substance use among adolescents

	Percent Ever Used					
	Seniors			Age 12–17		
Substance	1979	1985	1990	1979	1985	1990
Alcohol	93	92	89	70	56	48
Cigarettes	74	69	64	54	45	40
Smokeless tobacco	NA	NA	NA	NA	14	12
Marijuana	60	54	41	31	24	15
Hallucinogens	18	12	9	7	3	3
LSD	9	7	9	NA	NA	NA
PCP	13	5	3	4	NA	NA
Stimulants	24	26	17	3	5	4
Ice	NA	NA	3	NA	NA	NA
Cocaine	15	17	9	5	5	3
Crack	NA	6[a]	3	NA	NA	1
Sedatives	15	12	5	3	4	3
Barbiturates	12	9	7	NA	NA	NA
Tranquilizers	16	12	7	4	4	3
Methaqualone	8	7	2	NA	NA	NA
Inhalants	NA	NA	NA	10	9	8
Heroin	1	1	1	1	<0.5	1
Other Opiates[b]	10	10	9	3	NA	7

Sources: NIDA 1986, 1990a; Johnston 1989; University of Michigan 1991.
Note: All percentages exclude legitimate use by prescription.
[a]Not available for 1985; percent shown is for 1987; use in the past year was 4 percent in 1986.
[b]Reported in the NIDA survey as "analgesics."

and younger adults. This would raise the overall proportion of adults using drugs even though lifetime prevalence among those who are older than thirty-something has not changed. There is a tendency to stop drug use as one gets older, however. Therefore, as the annual prevalence and current prevalence of marijuana use by persons age 26 or older indicate, drug use in this age group is also moderating. On these measures, the older adult population (4 percent current users in 1990) is currently less involved in drug use than adolescents are. As the cohort of 1980s teenagers who have been considerably less involved with drugs than were those from a decade earlier enter into this older age group, the overall proportion of adult drug users should decrease.

As Tables 3.4 to 3.6 show, the more socially disapproved the substance, the less it is consumed. The legal substances (for adults) of alcohol and tobacco

T A B L E 3 . 5 *Substance use among adults*

	Percent Ever Used					
	Young Adults (age 18–25)			Older Adults (age 26 +)		
Substance	1979	1985	1990	1979	1985	1990
Alcohol	95	93	88	92	89	87
Cigarettes	83	76	70	83	80	78
Smokeless tobacco	NA	17	22	NA	10	13
Marijuana	68	60	52	20	27	32
Cocaine	28	25	19	4	9	11
Crack	NA	NA	3	NA	NA	<0.5
Hallucinogens	25	12	12	5	6	7
Stimulants	18	17	9	6	8	7
Sedatives	17	11	4	4	5	4
Tranquilizers	16	12	6	3	7	4
Inhalants	17	NA	10	4	NA	4
Heroin	4	1	1	1	1	1

Sources: NIDA 1986, 1988a, 1990a.
Note: All percentages exclude legitimate use by prescription.

are still more often consumed than any of the illicit substances, and this will remain true for some time. However, if the tendency toward stronger social disapproval of tobacco smoking continues, then we can expect the prevalence of marijuana use to become closer to that of tobacco use. If disapproval of marijuana moderates or if it is made legal, then marijuana use may come to exceed cigarette smoking. Although marijuana is socially and legally disapproved, it is less condemned and considered less harmful than other illicit substances. As Tables 3.4 and 3.5 show, higher percentages of both teenagers and adults have ever used marijuana than have ever used stimulants, opiates, or any other illicit substance. Table 3.6 shows that marijuana is clearly more likely than any other illegal drug to have been used in the past month among all age categories. This pattern, too, will very likely remain. Comparatively small percentages of adolescents have ever used any of the other illicit substances. No illegal substance besides marijuana is used on any kind of regular basis by more than 2 percent in any age group (Table 3.6). Daily use of any of the illegal substances (not shown in the tables), including marijuana (2.5 percent of seniors), is a fairly rare event (Johnston, O'Malley, and Bachman 1988; University of Michigan 1991).

All of the trends in drug use in the general population of the United States, therefore, are very encouraging. However, there have been recent

T A B L E   3 . 6   *Current substance use in 1990*

	Percent Used in Past Month		
Substance	Youth (age 12–17)	Young Adults (age 18–25)	Older Adults (age 26 +)
Alcohol	25	63	52
Cigarettes	12	32	28
Smokeless tobacco	4	6	3
Marijuana	5	13	4
Cocaine	1	2	1
Crack	< 0.5	1	< 0.5
Stimulants	1	1	< 0.5
Sedatives	1	1	< 0.5
Tranquilizers	1	1	< 0.5
Heroin	< 0.5	< 0.5	< 0.5

Source: NIDA 1990a.
Note: All percentages exclude legitimate use by prescription.

periods with discouraging increases in the intensification of use and abuse of hard drugs among those who do use drugs frequently, even while overall use was decreasing. Throughout the 1980s the amount of drugs seized in state and federal actions against smugglers continued upward, drug traffic–related deaths increased, and the overall drug trade grew. In the 1988 NIDA National Household Survey, the 37 percent decrease since 1985 in the number of current users of any illicit drug (from over 20 million to less than 15 million) occurred at the same time as a 33 percent increase in weekly use and a 19 percent increase in daily use of cocaine (NIDA 1989b). The number of deaths and hospital emergency room admissions attributed to heroin and other narcotics jumped, and there were five times as many cocaine-related deaths reported in 1986 as in 1981 (Goode 1989a:106–107). By 1987 more emergency room episodes involved cocaine than any other drug (NIDA 1988b). The number of these episodes have since declined, however (see Chapter 7).

S O C I A L   C H A R A C T E R I S T I C S
O F   U S E R S

The social characteristics of users and abusers vary somewhat by type of drug. These variations will be described in greater detail in later chapters. At this point, only a brief overview will be given. As the tables in this chapter make clear, there is a relationship between age and drug use with the peak years of drug involvement coming in young adulthood. Not shown in the tables is the fact that males are more likely than females to be taking drugs, but the difference (especially among young adults and adolescents) has narrowed in recent years. For some categories of substances, such as amphetamines, female users slightly outnumber males. Blacks are more likely than whites to use heroin and cocaine. Whites are more likely than blacks to use marijuana, hallucinogens, amphetamines, and all other categories of drugs except heroin and cocaine. Except for heroin and narcotic addiction and, more recently, cocaine abuse, drug use does not vary much by social class. Usage rates of all kinds of drugs are higher in larger cities and suburban areas than in rural areas and communities (although some rural, nonfarm communities have higher rates than suburbs do). The South has the lowest level of drug use in this country; fundamentalist religious affiliation and strong religious beliefs inhibit substance use of all kinds. (See Fishburne, Abelson, and Cisin 1980; Radosevich et al. 1980; Clayton and Voss 1981; Cochran and Akers 1989; Goode 1989a; Johnston, O'Malley, and Bachman 1988.)

Drug Use and Abuse in American Society: Work, Sports, and Crime

D R U G S   A N D   A L C O H O L
I N   T H E   W O R K P L A C E

Alcohol and drug problems in the workplace appear among blue-collar workers, laborers, skilled craftsmen, white-collar workers, executives, professionals, entertainers and celebrities, government workers, and military personnel. They are evident in public- and private-sector jobs, in high-tech and low-tech industries, in sensitive and nonsensitive jobs, in high-finance on Wall Street and low-finance in the factory (*Newsweek*, Aug. 22, 1983:52–60; *Time*, Mar. 17, 1986:52–61; *Time*, Apr. 27, 1987:54).

The damage that substance use on the job can do has been brought dramatically to public attention with reports of great injury and loss of life, one such incident being the collision of an Amtrak train operated by a crew under the influence of marijuana. The most widely publicized incident was the June 1989 *Exxon Valdez* oil spill in Alaska that polluted thousands of miles of shoreline, cost over a billion dollars to clean up, and resulted in billions of dollars of lawsuits against Exxon. The captain of this ship had a history of heavy drinking and had been drinking (but was not present on the bridge) at the time of the mishap. Although he was later acquitted of charges of intoxication while operating a sea vessel, he had substantial levels of alcohol in his blood even hours after the accident. The officer on the bridge at the time of the collision was not intoxicated, and the collision cannot be directly attributed to operating the ship under the influence of alcohol. However, the officer was inexperienced and unfamiliar with the passageway, and the absence of the captain from the bridge, who could have piloted the ship safely had he been present and sober, was an important factor in the disaster (*Time*, July 24, 1989; *Newsweek*, Sept. 18, 1989; *Gainesville Sun*, July 26, 1990).

It has been estimated that workers who use drugs or alcohol on the job or who work under the influence are one-third less productive and three times more likely to be injured than nonusing co-workers. They are more likely to have job instability and unemployment (Kandel and Yamaguchi 1987), to be absent from work, to steal cash, products, and equipment, and to engage in other workplace deviance (Hollinger 1988). Some experts contend that as many as one-fourth of all U.S. workers use alcohol or dangerous substances on the job or arrive at work high on drugs at least some of the time. The dollar cost of drug- or alcohol-related loss of productivity has been estimated at $16–$17 billion dollars annually, or about $4,200 for each U.S. worker (Scanlon 1986:1). The National Institute on Drug Abuse estimates that 66 percent of newly hired workers have used illicit drugs at some time in their lives and that 44 percent have used such drugs in the past year. The National Institute on Alcohol Abuse and Alcoholism estimates that the U.S. economy loses $66 billion annually to lowered worker productivity (NIAAA 1987). Heien and Pittman (1989) criticize the way that these governmental estimates of drug-related lost productivity are made, however, which tends to overestimate the economic costs.

In one unrepresentative California study, 16 percent of young adults had used marijuana and 12 percent had used hard drugs "in an inappropriate setting" on the job or in school in the past six months (Newcomb 1988). These figures probably overestimate the amount of substance use on the job. In a more representative study of forty-seven corporations in three metropolitan areas, Hollinger (1988) found that 3.2 percent of the hospital employees, 7.6 percent of those in retail businesses, and 12.8 percent of manufacturing employees reported having arrived on the job under the influence of alcohol or drugs in the past year. Even if the true figures are in the lower range of these number and dollar estimates, the national consequences are daunting. The effect of active drug and alcohol use on worker and managerial productivity is so evident that it must be considered as a significant factor, on top of whatever other trade and political factors are involved, in the shrinking industrial leadership and competitiveness of the United States in the world in the past two decades (*Newsweek*, Aug. 22, 1983:52–60). Beyond economic losses, drugs, and alcohol on the job have resulted in injuries and deaths, including train and airplane accidents in which engineers or pilots were under the influence of drugs (*Time*, Mar. 17, 1986:52–61). Drug abuse among physicians, nurses, and other health-care professionals places the well-being and lives of their patients in jeopardy (Moore and Lewis 1989).

Industry, government, business, the professions, the military, and all major sectors of our economy have become increasingly aware of the problem of drugs and alcohol in the workplace. This has led to a number of different programs to control or treat drug and alcohol problems. These include screening and testing for drugs as a prerequisite for hiring and as a way of discovering who is abusing drugs on the job as well as a range of hiring–firing policies, treatment programs, and prevention tactics.

Drug Testing and Employee Assistance Programs (EAPs)

Increasingly, the first line of defense against drug use on the job is the requirement that applicants for a job, in addition to providing self-reported information, also submit to a polygraph test and perhaps even urinalysis for the presence of drugs, some traces of which can be detected for many days after use. Many employers are also having employees already working submit to periodic drug tests. The military has done this for some time now, and more government agencies and private employers are doing it. About one-half of the largest companies in the country have drug-screening programs (*Time*, Mar. 17, 1986:52–61). According to data from the U.S. Department of Labor, 3,941,000 job applicants were tested for drugs in 1988. Of these, 24 percent of the job seekers in the retail trades tested positive for at least one drug and 17 percent of those looking for work in wholesale commerce tested positive. On the low end, only 5 percent of the job applicants in communications and public utilities industries and 7 percent in the financial and insurance sector tested positive. Therefore, in some areas of the economy significant proportions of prospective employees have been found to be drug users (*U.S. News & World Report*, Oct. 30, 1989:82).

Drug testing raises some serious constitutional questions of rights to privacy. San Francisco has an ordinance forbidding employers from requiring such tests (except for firefighters, police officers, and rescue unit workers) unless it is first shown that the employee's drug use would endanger others. Several challenges to drug tests have been heard in court, and many more court cases are pending. However, so far no court has stopped the practice of testing employees for drug use completely, but restrictions based on the nature of risk to others and the sensitivity of the job have been imposed on drug testing. The U.S. Supreme Court has upheld the constitutionality of drug testing of federal employees. Since the 1988 Drug-Free Workplace Act, the government has required all federal contractors to submit plans for a drug-free workplace. Constitutional right to privacy relates to government action specifically and is less an issue with private employers. But even in private industry, workers resist testing, and problems of unreliability, cheating, and error in drug tests continue to raise the spector of "false positives" being unfairly denied or losing employment (*Newsweek*, Aug. 22, 1983:52–60; *Time*, Mar. 17, 1986:52–61; *Newsweek*, Sept. 29, 1986:18–21; *Newsweek*, Nov. 14, 1988:66).

Reacting to the absenteeism and productivity losses due to alcohol abuse, private industry and public-sector employees have turned increasingly to at-work programs for identification and referral of executives and employees with alcohol problems. These programs often allow for persons discovered to be abusing alcohol to continue working while undergoing treatment or return to the job after treatment—rather than being fired. By 1980 there were over 4,000 such programs in this country, and by the late 1980s there were over 8,000. They have been implemented in a growing number of businesses and companies, especially in large firms (over half of the largest firms in the country) and have received strong support from unions. Most began as alcohol-specific programs (occupational alcoholism programs, OAPs), but have come increasingly to be merged into or started as part of *employee assistance programs* (EAPs), which attempt to identify and deal with a variety of employee problems, including alcohol and drugs (NIAAA 1981; Roman 1981; Califano 1982; Sonnenstuhl 1982; Trice and Beyer 1982; Scanlon 1986; Steele 1988).

The technique, pioneered in the 1960s by Harrison Trice, that has proved to be most effective in getting employees into job-related alcoholism programs is "constructive confrontation" (Trice and Roman 1978; Trice and Beyer 1982, 1984; Trice 1984). In constructive confrontation, a supervisor confronts an employee with his or her poor job performance (without necessarily relating it to an alcohol problem). In the process, the supervisor makes it clear that if the employee has some problem interfering with his work, help is available. The decision to take advantage of the help is the employee's, but he or she learns that, if alcohol is causing problems, treatment and support without negative labels is provided. After initial nonthreatening efforts fail, then the supervisor makes it clear to the employee that his or her job is in jeopardy if the reduced efficiency and productivity continues and help is refused. There is strong motivation, then, to face up to the problem and take advantage of the treatment offered. This constructive confrontation has been incorporated into most of the EAPs, but other, less successful, strategies have also been used in them. Trice recognizes the saliency of social learning in this confrontational process:

> Since the social learning paradigm is also a prominent orientation for explaining alcoholism, it would logically follow that it might also be a useful approach to its management and control. . . . The strategy fits, conceptually . . . the social behaviorism framework. . . . The strategy tries to use the same group forces of reward, reinforcement, and punishment

that operate in drinking groups to encourage the development of alcoholism to reverse its course. . . . That is, it acts . . . as a socializing force whereby the problem-drinking employee, in effect, learns new forms of behavior. . . . In the process, it is likely that problem drinking will subside or disappear. (Trice and Beyer 1982; see also Trice 1984:118)

Neither drug testing nor EAPs provide final answers to the problem of drugs and alcohol in the workplace, and other approaches such as "health promotion programs" (HPPs) and "quality of work life programs" (QWLs) have been developed (Sonnenstuhl 1988). Many of the programs are established in name only, and the growth of these programs is based on very sketchy evidence about their effectiveness. The movement toward instituting EAPs, and their rapid diffusion, is driven in large measure by the interests and marketing activities of the burgeoning industry of consultants, counselors, and entrepreneurs in various "purveyor organizations" who sell EAP services to companies (Blum and Roman 1988). The assumption is that it is more cost-effective to salvage trained workers by helping them overcome alcohol or drug problems than it is to hire and train new employees. The next assumption is that the EAPs effectively do this. Neither of these assumptions rests on firm empirical evidence. Also, the workers who are most apt to have alcohol or drug problems—young and new employees—are the least likely to be detected, to be offered treatment and assistance, and to be willing to participate in employee assistance programs (Hollinger 1988).

Some occupational contexts have seemed to provide a more fertile context for alcohol and drug abuse than others have (Newcomb 1988:10–12). Two of these, the military and health-care professions, have been the focus of special studies and programs that have achieved some success.

Special Occupational Contexts

Drugs in the Military.   Drugs began to be a noticeable problem in the military during the Vietnam War and continued to escalate (along with the general increase in the prevalence of drug use in society as a whole) during the 1970s. In 1982 the U.S. Department of Defense instituted a large-scale testing, education, and treatment program in all branches of the armed services. Any commander can order a suspected drug user to undergo a drug test, and unannounced and random testing can be ordered at any time for individuals or whole military units. Those who test positive may be dismissed or committed to a mandatory drug program. In the navy, the programs are organized into three levels: a counseling and education program at the local command site, an outpatient program, and a six-week inpatient program at the Naval Alcohol Rehabilitation Center.

In 1985, 16,500 service personnel were discharged for drug use and an additional 55,900 were assigned to counseling and rehabilitation programs.

According to the 1985 Worldwide Survey of Alcohol and Non-Medical Drug Use Among Military Personnel, there have been dramatic drops in the levels of alcohol and drug use in the military, not only in the navy but in the other services as well. Illicit drug use in the military dropped 10 percent from 1982 to 1985, and marijuana smoking decreased by 75 percent from 1980 to 1985 (*Newsweek*, Nov. 10, 1986:26; Halloran 1987; Newcomb 1988:8–10; Benson 1989).

Drugs in Health-Care Professions.   Every state medical association now has an "impaired" physician program, and many states also have similar programs for psychiatrists, nurses, dentists, and other health-care professionals. These programs represent a growing recognition of the problem of drug addiction and impairment in these professions. It has been estimated that 4 to 6 percent of physicians and nurses experience serious drug problems, believed to be several times the rate of dependence in the general population (*Newsweek*, Aug. 22, 1983; Moore and Lewis 1989). It is not clear exactly what these figures mean for drug use by medical and health-care practitioners because they include drugs, alcohol, and "mental illness." In one careful study, however, among practicing physicians and medical students in Massachusetts, 59 percent of those in practice and 78 percent of the students reported having used some psychoactive substance (other than alcohol) at least once in the past (mainly marijuana and cocaine). A little over 3 percent of the physicians and 5 percent of the students admitted that they had become drug dependent. While these figures indicate a serious level of drug use among physicians, they are not out of line with those of other professional groups (McAuliffe et al. 1986).

DRUGS AND SPORTS

Even as overall rates of drug use and drugs in the military and in the larger society were coming down in the 1980s, the problem of drug use by professional, Olympic, collegiate, and high school athletes grew. The headlines and newscasts have been filled with reports of rampant drug abuse in sports.

Conceptually, this is simply one aspect of the larger problem of drugs in the workplace, and sports may be seen as a special occupational context for drugs. But drugs and alcohol in sports are not confined to sports as an occupation; they have been found at nearly all levels of amateur athletics. The intrusion of drugs into any endeavor undermines its legitimacy and positive contributions to social welfare. However, the special place that sports and sports stars have in our society and the impact they have on children and teenagers who look up to sports figures as heroes and role models make the revelations of drugs in sports especially poignant.

In 1986 Len Bias stood on the edge of a great career in the National Basketball Association. He had just completed his last year of eligibility at the University of Maryland, having led the UM basketball team as one of the top teams in the Atlantic Coast Conference. He was an All-American player whom experts called the best college player in the country. He was drafted No. 1 by the Boston Celtics one day in June for a multi-million-dollar salary. The next day he signed another multi-million-dollar deal with Reebok shoes. He had it all: an outstanding high school career, a stellar college basketball career, and a future full of prosperity and promise. The next day he died of cocaine intoxication. He had been using cocaine for some time but had managed to avoid or pass the infrequently scheduled urinalyses for drugs. What he had taken that day was not a large amount, but it was enough to induce cardiac arrest (*Newsweek*, July 7, 1986:26; Aug. 4, 1986:16–17; *Time*, June 30, 1989:73). Eight days after Bias died, Don Rogers, the star safety for the Cleveland Browns, also died of a heart attack from cocaine overdose. He was only twenty-three and had been a top draft pick just two years earlier. In 1984 he was on the All-Rookie team. He had already made enormous amounts of money and stood to have a brilliant and profitable NFL career. He died the night before his wedding (*Time*, Aug. 25, 1986:53).

Tragically, these were just two of the more publicized of the many cases of top athletes abusing drugs and paying a high price, sometimes the supreme price, during the 1980s. The headlines were filled and continue to be filled with stories of established or promising collegiate and professional sports stars who died from overdose, lost their careers, or were imprisoned for drug use and/or drug dealing. The main drug involved has been cocaine, and the main sports are football, basketball, and baseball. But virtually all drugs and sports have been involved (see, for example, *U.S. News & World Report*, Sept. 12, 1983:64–65; *Newsweek*, Sept. 16, 1985:64–65; *Time*, Aug. 25, 1986:52–55; *Time*, Apr. 13, 1987:67–68; Gildea 1988; Associated Press, June 28, 1989).

Ben Johnson was a native of Jamaica who emigrated to Canada and became a Canadian citizen. It was his adopted homeland, and Canadians came to cherish and honor him. They had every reason to do so, because Johnson became the fastest runner in history, setting a world record in the 100-meter dash. He represented Canada in the 1988 Olympics at Seoul and triumphed again, beating out the American Carl Lewis for the gold medal. In the drug tests that are done on Olympic winners, Johnson's urine showed definite traces of anabolic steroids. The use of steroids is forbidden by the Olympic Committee and is a ground for forteiture of medals and suspension from future competition. His medal was taken away and awarded to Lewis. The Canadian government banned him from ever representing their country again in sports. Large contracts for product endorsements were canceled by embarrassed companies. Johnson went from the top to the bottom fast. He spent the remainder of that year and part of 1989 denying that he had ever knowingly used such drugs. He claimed that someone had secretly spiked a drink of his with steroids just before he ran the final heat. Later, he claimed that his trainers and physicians may have given him steroids without his knowledge. Finally, in May 1989, after weeks of testimony by his coaches and physicians before an investigating committee, Johnson admitted taking steroids. He took them not only to maintain and improve his Olympic runs, but he had been systematically and knowingly taking them for years. Nearly all of his accomplishments were tarnished. He was suspended for life from sports (but later this penalty was softened to allow him to return to competition), and his world record (achieved during the time he was taking steroids) was withdrawn (*Newsweek*, Oct. 10, 1988:54–57; *Maclean's*, Mar. 13, 1989:36–42; *Time*, Sept. 18, 1989:104).

Ben Johnson was not alone. Use of anabolic steroids has become widespread in both amateur and professional sports. Estimates of use have ranged from 50 to 90 percent of top Olympic and professional athletes, and use apparently has increased since 1985 among college athletes (*Newsweek*, July 25, 1988:62–63; Oct. 10, 1988:54–57; Rowan and Mazie 1988; Holyfield 1989; Martin and Thrasher 1989; *USA Today*, July 5, 1989).

The stories of Len Bias and Ben Johnson and similar stories illustrate the two major, somewhat overlapping, dimensions of the drug problem in sports: (1) use and abuse of alcohol, marijuana, cocaine, tobacco, and other "recreational" drugs by athletes and (2) use of "performance-enhancing" drugs.

The first of these, of course, is neither unique nor apparently especially high among athletes. Amphetamines and cocaine fall into both categories, and have been used by some in the belief that they increase athletic performance. Other substances (beta blockers and growth hormones) and techniques (blood doping) are used to increase performance. Also, various kinds of analgesics, cortisone, procaine (local anesthetic), and Butazolidin (a muscle relaxant), which are legitimately used for injuries, may be abused in the hope of improving performance. Nevertheless, the main problem of substance use to increase prowess in sports centers around *anabolic steroids*. The abuse of steroids appears to be nearly unique to sports. There are reports of use outside of organized sports, but these tend to be in the context of health and body-building clubs or use by individuals wanting to "bulk up." Steroids are not used recreationally and at this time constitute only a very small part of the drug problem in society outside of sports.

Anabolic (tissue building and development) steroids are synthetic derivatives of the male hormone testosterone. Steroids are legally prescribed to treat men who through disease or testicular injury cannot naturally produce enough testosterone or to aid the physical and sexual development of boys who are hormonally deficient (androgenic steroids). When used in these therapeutic dosages, the steroids serve only to maintain normal levels of testosterone. When used by males with naturally occurring normal amounts of testosterone (or by women), the anabolic steroids add more than is needed for normal functioning, resulting in increased body mass and lean muscle. Anabolic steroids are also believed to increase strength and endurance, although the scientific evidence is not clear on this point. They also produce mood changes that increase aggressive tendencies. It is these features of greater bulk, strength, and aggressiveness that make steroids attractive to athletes. When combined with the kind of rigorous training programs that all top athletes maintain, steroids can give (or at least are believed by the users to give) the edge that makes the difference between a good and a winning performance.

When taken in the megadosages (up to twenty times the therapeutic dosage) that many athletes take them, anabolic steroids have a number of harmful side effects. In males there is an increased aggressiveness, and other behavioral changes, that sometimes erupts in episodic violence toward others. The artificially elevated level of steroids leads to atrophy of testicles and a decreased ability to produce hormones naturally; impotence is a common result, and sterility sometimes occurs. The breasts may become enlarged, the face and body puff up, acne and boils may break out, blood pressure is elevated, and jaundice turns the whites of the eyes yellow. Steroids induce "masculinization" in women with secondary male characteristics becoming noticeable. The female steroid user's voice lowers, facial hair grows, breasts shrink, and the menstrual cycle becomes erratic. Effects of prolonged and heavy use of steroids for both men and women are life-threatening. They include increased risk of cardiovascular disease, liver and kidney damage (including cancer), and strokes. (See Rowan and Mazie 1988; *Newsweek*, July 25, 1988:62–63; Oct. 10, 1988:54–57; Martin and Thrasher 1989.)

While the problem of drug use in sports seemed to worsen and certainly was more highlighted in the 1980s, it did not start at that time. Major sports figures, such as Mercury Morris of the Miami Dolphins, ruined their careers with cocaine in the 1970s. As early as the 1950s, some athletes were taking amphetamines and steroids. They were first used by weight lifters, body builders, and football linemen, but later spread into running and track events, used by both men and women. The big impetus came when the Soviet, East German, and Bulgarian athletes, widely known to be systematically taking steroids with the approval and support of their coaches, began to dominate the weight-lifting and high-strength events. By the time of the 1968 Olympics, both steroids and stimulants were being taken by a number of athletes from many countries, and by the time of the 1984 and 1988 Olympics, almost all winners with exceptional times or distances were suspected of using steroids (*Time*, Aug. 25, 1986:52–55; *Newsweek*, Oct. 10, 1988:54–57).

Use of both recreational and performance-enhancing drugs is now widely recognized as undercutting the respected position of athletics in our country for players, owners, coaches, fans, and society. All sports leagues and federations from the local school leagues, to the National Collegiate Athletic Association, to the Olympics, to Major League Baseball, to the National Football League, to the National Basketball Association now outlaw the use of both categories of drugs. All of these organizations participate in the U.S. Drug Enforcement Administration's "Sports Drug Awareness Program" (*International Drug Report*, Nov. 1985:7–8). Drug testing is now regularly done in sports, and detection of a drug or alcohol problem or use of steroids will lead to suspension (sometimes with the condition of entering a treatment program), expulsion, or other sanctions, as well as stripping of records and medals.

Following general trends in society, cocaine use by college athletes declined from 17 to 5 percent from 1985 to 1988 and marijuana use dropped from 36 to 28 percent, while use of smokeless tobacco (chewing tobacco and moist snuff) increased from 20 to 28 percent. In spite of the encouraging declines in cocaine and marijuana use, recreational drugs continue to be used by athletes and steriod use has increased (Holyfield 1989). Ways are devised of getting around the drug tests, and athletes continue to perform under the influence (Martin and Thrasher 1989). The "big money" sports—football, basketball, and baseball—are more likely to experience recreational-drug problems, while steroid use is more of a problem in the "high-performance" sports of track and field.

D R U G S ,   A L C O H O L ,   A N D   C R I M E

The question of the link between drugs and crime is of longer-standing interest and has been the subject of much more careful research than the issues of drugs on the job and in sports. There has long been a concern in the criminal and juvenile justice systems at both the federal and state levels with drug use contributing disproportionately to theft, prostitution, robbery, and other crimes. Beyond the question of the individual abuser committing income-producing crimes to pay for drugs, there is the violence and murder that are a routine part of the illegal drug trade. In addition to the traditional Mafia-controlled organized crime killings in connection with the drug trade, the 1980s saw an influx of nontraditional organized criminal gangs into the drug trade. These range from the "Colombian cowboys" and Haitian gangs in southern Florida to the Jamaican "posses" in Washington, D.C., to outlaw motorcycle gangs in California. Youth gangs in Los Angeles, Detroit, Washington, D.C., and other large cities have become increasingly involved in the crack and other drug trade. These newer drug gangs seem even more ruthless and ready to kill. It is these drug-related killings that are believed to be primarily responsible for significant increases in homicides in the late

1980s in the nation's largest cities after many years of declining homicide rates (*Newsweek*, Feb. 9, 1987:30).

But are the assumptions of law enforcement and policy makers about the direct causal linkage between drugs and crime accurate? What really is the connection between substance use and criminal and delinquent behavior?

Clarifying the Issues

To consider the question properly, one must first clarify what is meant by the question. Drug use by adolescents *is* delinquent behavior, by definition. Purchase and possession of alcohol by a minor is a status offense, that is, prohibited only for underage juveniles, and therefore in many places no longer under juvenile court jurisdiction. Possession and sale of drugs are criminal law violations for both juveniles and adults (except for the jurisdictions where possession of small amounts of marijuana for personal use has been reduced to less than a misdemeanor).

Involvement in illegal drug use means that one is by definition involved in criminal acts. The question could be phrased, therefore, Is criminal and delinquent behavior related to criminal and delinquent behavior? Stated this way, an affirmative answer to the question is self-evidently true. Nevertheless, it is not this self-evident connection that is usually meant when the question of the relationship between drugs and crime is raised. Rather, the question is usually stated as, Does drug use or abuse induce the person to engage in theft, burglary, robbery, homicide, and other forms of criminal behavior beyond the specific crimes of violating drug laws?

There are several different types of behavior included under the label of crime and delinquency. Measures of illegal drug acts and measures of illegal acts of theft are, in one sense, simply different ways of gauging crime and delinquency. The same adolescents may burglarize homes and get into street fights. The same person may commit fraud and armed robbery. May we say that fighting causes the breaking and entering, or is it the other way around? We are faced with a similar issue with regard to the consumption and abuse of drugs as related to criminal behavior. But there is a difference: We know that ingestion of some substances produces mood and behavioral change. Do these effects provide the immediate motivation to commit other criminal or deviant behavior? We also know that drugs and alcohol, unlike burglaries, are consumer items which must be purchased. Does this consumption lead to other crimes by inducing people to engage in dealing in drugs, stealing drugs, or stealing money to pay for their own drugs? It is possible that drug use "causes" crime in this sense. Although there is little about other criminal or delinquent acts that could directly provoke drug behavior, it is possible that involvement in them could lead indirectly to substance abuse

T A B L E 4 . 1 Correlation (gamma) of different types of delinquent behavior and sanctions with use of different kinds of substances

	Substances			
Delinquent Behavior	Tobacco	Alcohol	Marijuana	Narcotics
Truancy	.57	.68	.68	.70
Sexual delinquency	.52	.56	.64	.70
Vandalism	.38	.51	.46	.49
Auto theft	.46	.71	.66	.69
Assault with weapon	.42	.43	.48	.50
Theft ($50 +)	.52	.77	.79	.83
Caught and Punished for Misconduct or Delinquency				
School expulsion	.61	.56	.69	.66
Police arrest	.52	.66	.63	.75
Juvenile court	.58	.62	.60	.60

Source: Adapted from Akers 1984.

through placing the adolescent in a setting where drugs are available and acceptable. Or it is quite possible that drugs and delinquency are related because they both flow from another, common set of causes.

L I N K I N G D R U G S A N D A L C O H O L T O C R I M E A N D D E L I N Q U E N C Y

Juvenile Delinquency and Adolescent Substance Use

Table 4.1 shows the correlation of different types of substance use with various forms of delinquent behavior included in a study that I and associates conducted on over 3,000 adolescents in the Midwest (usually referred to as the Boys Town Study). The table also reports the correlations of drug use with experience with school, police, or court sanctions. A look at this table leaves no doubt that substance use is intimately related to delinquent behavior. The adolescents in the Boys Town Study who reported use of drugs were more frequently involved in all of the other delinquent acts, and more frequently expelled from school, arrested by the police, and referred to juvenile court, than were those who did not report use of drugs.

The nature of the interrelationships among drugs and delinquency is shown more graphically in Table 4.2, which presents the differences in degree of delinquent involvement between users and nonusers. For each substance, the vast majority of abstainers have no delinquent involvement, and of those

T A B L E   4 . 2   Percentages of delinquent behavior among users and nonusers of various substances

| Substances | Delinquent Behavior | | | |
	None	Minor Only	Serious	N =
Alcohol				
Nonusers	91%	8%	1%	1,218
Users	57	34	9	1,541
Marijuana				
Nonusers	84	14	2	1,983
Users	39	46	15	778
Stimulants				
Nonusers	80	17	3	2,330
Users	28	53	18	424
Narcotics				
Nonusers	74	22	4	2,644
Users	17	50	33	118

Source: Adapted from Akers 1984.
Note: N is the number of respondents reporting use or nonuse of each substance.

who do, almost all have committed only minor offenses. The majority of users, on the other hand—except for drinkers—have some delinquent experience, and of those a sizable minority have committed serious delinquency. Drinkers and marijuana users are about twice as likely as nonusers to commit delinquent behavior. The differences are even greater for narcotic drug use. More than eight out of ten of the adolescents who have used narcotics admit to some delinquent behavior, and a third to serious delinquent behavior.

Among the users, the greater the level of drug use the greater the level of delinquency. There is also a strong relationship between multiple-drug use and delinquency. Only about 1 percent of the juveniles in the Boys Town Study who use no substance (do not smoke, drink, or use any drug) were involved in delinquency of any kind. The odds change considerably with even one substance, and as multidrug use develops more serious delinquency develops so that 22 percent of the youngsters who have had experience with four or more drugs have also committed both minor and serious delinquent offenses.

The findings and conclusions from other research on drugs and delinquency in adolescent populations agree with those of the Boys Town Study. The trends in both official arrests and juvenile court have moved and are moving in the same direction as adolescent substance use and abuse reported in national surveys. Both increased in the late 1960s, continued upward through most of the 1970s, and headed downward in the 1980s (Akers 1984). In the 1987 Survey of Youth in Custody (Beck, Kline, and Greenfield 1988), 60 percent of the youth in state-run institutions had used drugs regularly (principally marijuana and cocaine) and 40 percent reported being under the influence of drugs at the time of committing their offense. Three-fourths had drunk alcohol and about one-third were under the influence of alcohol at the time of the offense for which they were currently in custody.

One of the earliest studies of drugs and juvenile delinquency utilized police, juvenile court, and other records from 1947–1953 (Kobrin and Finestone 1968). Of those with official records as drug users, 90 percent were heroin users and resided in the same areas with the highest rate of juvenile court cases. Kobrin and Finestone found that delinquency involvement both preceded and followed heroin use. Inciardi (1974) later found the same strong relationship between opiate use and delinquency in a population of street addicts. Inciardi (1980) also studied drugs and delinquent behavior in both a campus sample and a street sample of young people. In the college sample, self-reported law violations were highest among those who were regular drug users (mainly marijuana and alcohol), especially those who were also involved in drug selling. In the sample of active street and institutionalized (age 21 and younger) drug abusers, almost all had official criminal records. For the heroin users, the median age at first drug use (of any kind) was younger than age at first crime and first arrest. For the nonheroin users, the median age at first criminal offense was lower than the age at first drug use, although drug use preceded first arrest. In a national survey of young men, a clear association was established between drug use and crime. The more he used drugs and the more he was involved in selling drugs the more likely he was to have committed nondrug offenses (O'Donnell et al. 1976; Clayton and Voss 1981).

The best data on the sequence of drug use and delinquent behavior over time in an adolescent population come from two national longitudinal surveys. The first is by Lloyd Johnston and his associates at the University of Michigan, and the second is by Delbert Elliott and his associates at the University of Colorado. The Johnston study comes from the annual survey of high school seniors supported by the National Institute on Drug Abuse (NIDA) on which many of the tables in this book are based. The Elliott research, supported by the National Institute of Mental Health (NIMH), is a panel study in which a cohort was first interviewed in 1976 and interviewed each year thereafter for five years. Since both of these studies are longitudinal, they are able to trace the sequence of drugs and delinquent behavior over time. It is with these kinds of data that the question of causal ordering can best be addressed. Unfortunately, even they have not produced a definitive answer.

Johnston found in the first year of the survey a strong relationship between marijuana, alcohol, cigarettes, heroin, and amphetamine use and delinquent behavior. For instance, of the high-delinquency group, 42 percent smoked marijuana and 88 percent drank alcohol, whereas in the low-delinquency group only 6 percent smoked marijuana and 39 percent were drinkers (Johnston 1973). Later, Johnston analyzed data for males over a period of years (Johnston, O'Malley, and Eveland 1978). The cross-sectional relationships for each year of the study were clear: the higher the level of drug use the higher the level of delinquency. The relationship was stronger for a scale of theft/vandalism than for a scale of aggression, for minor than for serious offenses. However, the differences in delinquent conduct existed *before* drug use began. Nevertheless, *after* the drug-using group started on drugs, the difference between their delinquent behavior and that of the group who remained abstinent increased.

In the research by Elliott and his associates, the youngsters who used alcohol and marijuana plus other drugs were found to be twice as likely to be involved in other delinquent activities and four times as likely to be committing serious offenses as were those who abstained (Huizinga and Elliott 1981; Elliott and Huizinga 1983). This strong tie between drug use and delinquency continued in each year of the panel study for all types of drugs and for minor and serious delinquent offenses. For most categories of drug users, initiation of drug use in any given year was accompanied by increased delinquent involvement that year. The research did not permit examining the sequence of events within the same year but was able to trace the temporal ordering of drugs and delinquency from one year to the next. The most common pattern was for the adolescents to continue with neither drugs nor delinquency (46 percent), but the next most common sequence was for drug use to begin in a given year with no subsequent delinquent involvement (26 percent). All other patterns were followed by relatively small percentages of the sample, but the next most common ordering was for delinquent behavior to begin one year followed by the beginning of drug use the next year. However, there was very little difference in the percentage following this pattern and the percentages who began drug use first or began drugs and delinquency in the same year (Huizinga and Elliott 1981).

Neither the Johnson nor the Elliott study found strong support for drugs "causing" delinquency or vice versa. Compared to the abstaining teenager, the drinking, smoking, and drug-taking teen is much more likely to be getting into fights, stealing, assaulting other people, and committing other delinquencies. But the variations in the order in which they take up these activities leaves little basis for proposing causation of one by the other.

Crime, Alcohol, and Addiction in Adults

The connection between narcotic addiction and crime in adult populations has been demonstrated by research findings for a long time. For instance, O'Donnell (1966) studied the criminal histories of federal narcotics cases and found that while addicts did not uniformly commit crimes to pay for heroin, they did dramatically increase criminal activities following addiction. Similarly, Stephens and Ellis (1975) found that in four cohorts of addicts under treatment, about one-third had been involved in serious enough criminal activity to have been arrested prior to becoming addicted. However, there was a threefold increase in the number of arrests following drug abuse—mostly property crimes. Weissman and associates (1976) located a 225 percent increase among a sample of jail inmates in criminal activity (larceny, burglary, robbery, and assault) from the preaddiction stage of drug use to the period following onset of addiction. McGlothin and colleagues (1978) reported similar findings.

More recent research has confirmed these conclusions. For example, the 1986 State Prison Inmate Survey found that 80 percent of the prisoners had used drugs some time in the past and that 52 percent had used a "major drug" (heroin, PCP, methadone, cocaine, LSD). A third of the inmates reported being under the influence of some drug at the time of their offense; 52 percent had used in the month prior to the offense; 25 percent had used a major drug during that time; and 43 percent had used a drug daily in the month prior to the offense. Almost half of the daily major-drug users had illegal sources of income in the year before incarceration, whereas only 10 percent of the nonusers had illegal sources of income during that time (Innes 1988; U.S. Dept. of Justice 1988). Similar findings are reported for heavy use of alcohol among state prisoners (U.S. Dept. of Justice 1983). The Justice Department started a voluntary, confidential drug-testing program among male arrestees in 1987 in twenty-one cities with new samples taken each quarter. The urinalysis results for the third quarter of 1989 showed 54 to 90 percent positive use of any drug—PCP, heroin, marijuana, or amphetamines. Positive tests for cocaine ranged in the last quarter of 1988 from a low of 15 percent of arrestees in Indianapolis to a high of 83 percent in New York (NIJ, Mar./Apr. 1989; NIJ, Mar. 1990). In another study, among defendants released while awaiting trial, 42 percent of drug users were rearrested before their trial came up whereas only 18 percent of the nonusers were rearrested (NIJ 1984).

In a study of New York street addicts, Johnson and associates (1985) found that the addicts committed a large number of both drug-selling offenses and a range of other income-producing offenses (robbery, burglary, theft, fraud, etc.). The regular and daily heroin abusers committed twice as many crimes as irregular users committed. Faupel and Klockars (1987) interviewed thirty-two hardcore addicts (both incarcerated and still on the streets) and found that crime is connected to heroin addiction both through the financial burden of securing drugs which cannot be met through legal income and through the facilitation and encouragement of using crime as a solution to financing the habit. However, this was true only for certain periods (the stabilized and street junkie phases) of the addict's career. During the early or occasional phases, there was no connection between the drug use and crime. Similarly,

Anglin and Speckart (1988) found that half of all property crimes committed by a sample of patients in a methadone program were perpetrated *before* addiction. However, after addiction, the rate of crime greatly increased. Thus, narcotics use does not initiate criminal activity but does act as a "multiplier" of existing criminal behavior. Essentially the same patterns are found for both men and women (Anglin and Hser 1987). In the State Prison Inmate Survey, half of the inmates reported experience with some drugs before first arrest, but only 11 percent reported use of a major drug before the first arrest. Among those reporting major-drug use, half had begun such use only *after* their first arrest (Innes 1988).

Most of the research on drugs and adult crime over the past three decades has focused on heroin addiction or alcohol abuse, but more recently it has come to include cocaine (especially crack) and other drugs. These studies have consistently found a strong relationship between substance abuse and crime. The relationships are clearest for alcohol and hard drugs and are strongest with income-producing crimes but also are related to nonincome violent offenses. Criminal behavior and arrests frequently precede the onset of abuse or addiction, but nearly all of the studies have found an increase in arrests after the onset (for nondrug charges as well as for the expected drug-law charges).

There is the hypothesis in these studies that income-producing crimes are associated with heroin addiction because addicts need to resort to crime to pay for their habits. It is also proposed that alcohol (and sometimes other substances) has a direct pharmacological effect that either reduces inhibitions toward or induces violent behavior. However, there is little to support this causal process, and the research is characterized by disagreement over what causes what and lack of data to answer the question adequately. A specifically drug-produced motivation to commit crime that was not present prior to using drugs has not been established. (See the research reviews and studies in McGlothin 1979; Gandossy et al. 1980; Collins 1981; Gropper 1985; Inciardi 1986; Anglin and Speckart 1988.)

DRUG ABUSE AND CRIME AS THE RESULT OF SOCIAL FACTORS AND PROCESSES COMMON TO BOTH

The reasonably clear conclusion then is that drugs/alcohol and crime/delinquency are highly related but cannot be said to cause one another. Depending on the substance, setting, and group, first commission of illegal acts will sometimes precede and sometimes follow first drug use. The best answer, therefore, to the question with which we began appears to be that the *two are related through the association they hold in common with another set of social factors and processes.* This hypothesis is supported by the fact that, on the whole, drug and alcohol abuse is related to the same social correlates and in the same direction as are delinquency and crime—age, sex, race, socioeconomic status, and residence as well as religion, family, and peer groups. It is also supported by more direct evidence of drugs and delinquency flowing from a common process.

Helene Raskin White and colleagues (White, Johnson, and Garrison 1985; White, Pandina, and LaGrange 1987) have conducted longitudinal research to test the nexus between delinquency and drugs and the extent to which they are the result of a common set of factors. These factors are taken primarily from social bonding and social learning theory (see Chapter 1). Social bonding theory (Hirschi 1969) emphasizes the strength of the ties (through attachment, commitment, and involvement) to parents, schoolteachers, religion, and peers and adherence to conforming beliefs and values. Social learning theory (Akers 1985) emphasizes differential association with conforming or deviant friends and adults, imitation, social reinforcement, and attitudes. These researchers found a clear connection between the commission of a delinquent act and the use of alcohol and drugs for both boys and girls. The best predictor for both is friends' drug use and friends' delinquency. Other social learning and social bonding variables also are strong predictors of both serious delinquency and serious substance abuse by youngsters. Thus, White and colleagues find support for the common-cause explanation of the link between drugs and delinquency.

Both drug use and delinquent behavior are negatively related to strong, intact families with good parental supervision and relationships with children, to strong religious ties and commitments, and to good school performance and experiences. Parental behavior, models, attitudes, and discipline are related to drug use and delinquent behavior. By far the strongest correlate of both drug use and delinquency is the behavior of peer groups, especially friendship groups. Indeed, the single best predictor of adolescent behavior, conforming or deviant, is the behavior of close friends. Both drug use and delinquency are primarily group behavior. Peer groups provide the setting for first involvement and for progression into more serious behavior. The most significant models, favorable attitudes, and social reinforcement for conforming and deviant adolescent behavior are provided by peer friendship groups. This relationship is not just a simple matter of "birds of a feather flock together." Rather, the association with delinquency-prone or drug-prone friends tends to precede the onset of heavy drug use and serious delinquent behavior. However, birds of a feather do flock together, and some of the relationship is based on the attraction to one another of peers who have previously developed drug or delinquency patterns. Once these associations are made, the adolescents influence each other's future drug behavior.

Illegal Drugs

Marijuana

L O N G - T E R M   E F F E C T S : I S   M A R I J U A N A   H A R M L E S S ?

Is marijuana a relatively safe, harmless substance that can be smoked fairly frequently and in sizable amounts over a long period of time with no more untoward personal and health consequences than moderate social drinking has? Is it, in fact, a very beneficial drug that improves health and prolongs life? Many users and pro-marijuana groups supporting legalization of marijuana claim that it is (Smith 1990). Or is marijuana a very dangerous and potent drug that carries acute effects which are dangerous to oneself and others? Does its use carry severe health hazards in chronic, long-term use? Many of those opposed to marijuana have charged that it does.

In the early days of public attention and reaction to marijuana use in this country, many stories of marijuana-induced psychosis, violence, and crime became popular. Marijuana had a reputation in the media and law enforcement as the "killer weed." By the late 1960s, most of these stories had successfully been debunked as having no scientific evidence supporting them. Partly based on this, there developed among marijuana users and proponents a sense that *all* of the horror stories about the harmful consequences of smoking marijuana were hoaxes dreamed up by the establishment to scare people away from using marijuana. Since some of the worst stories were untrue, none of the dangers attributed to marijuana was considered true.

The counter story circulated by pro-marijuana groups was that, far from presenting much risk of harm, marijuana was really quite harmless. I served on a panel discussion of the problems of using marijuana on a university campus in 1969 in which a professor of English on the panel presented a ten-point argument for the benefits of smoking marijuana ranging from improved mental health, to enhanced creative ability, to a happier marriage. To him, not only was marijuana harmless, it had nothing but positive effects. While most supporters of decriminalization did not go as far as he did in defense of marijuana, pro-marijuana groups regularly dismissed any and all claims of damage from marijuana use. Indeed, the old argument that marijuana is very good for you is alive and well today. In 1990 almost exactly the same position taken by the panelist in 1969 was taken by a representative of a marijuana-law-reform organization on another panel at the university where I am on the faculty now.

Research on Effects of Marijuana

However, scientific evidence showing severe damage to health from smoking marijuana continued to be reported that could not easily be dismissed. In 1970 the U.S. Congress passed the Marijuana and Health Reporting Act, which required the Secretary of Health, Education, and Welfare (now Health and Human Services) to submit a yearly report on the state of knowledge about the short- and long-term health risks of marijuana use. These reports examined the claims that chronic marijuana use irreversibly damages the brain, lowers bodily resistance to cancer and infection, raises the risk of genetic defects and hereditary diseases, leads to sterility and impotence in men, causes lung cancer, and has several other deleterious effects on health. Other issues such as whether pot use produces an "amotivational syndrome" that reduces the desire to work and achieve were also studied. While the reports concluded that lung damage is clearly associated with frequent deep inhalation of marijuana smoke, as of the mid-1970s virtually none of the other allegations of long-term health impairment from marijuana use had been upheld by careful research (see U.S. Department of Health, Education, and Welfare 1975).

Nonetheless, research throughout the 1970s with animals and humans continued to produce some disturbing findings about the harmful consequences of marijuana smoking. Some medical scientists became leading opponents of marijuana, warning to "keep off the grass" (Nahas 1980). These newer, and some of the older, reports on marijuana were picked up in the media, and the dangers of marijuana were given a new look in a series of news-magazine and newspaper reports in the late 1970s and early 1980s. One journalist in particular, Peggy Mann, produced several articles (based mainly on Nahas's work) in the *Reader's Digest* as a new "marijuana alert" (Mann 1979, 1980a) and in the *Saturday Evening Post* (Mann 1980b, 1981). She continued to warn of the dangers of marijuana use into the late 1980s (Mann 1985, 1988). She attacked what she termed the "myth of harmlessness" of marijuana and wrote strident warnings of the risk to health from marijuana smoking. These were reported to include temporary and permanent damage of several types: psychological and brain impairment; loss of motivation; memory impairment; sperm and hormonal abnormalities in males; ovum deformation in females; genetic and chromosomal injury; negative effects on the immune system by destruction of white blood cells; other cellular damage; hampering of skill, coordination, and judgment causing driving accidents; more serious lung cancer risk than tobacco has; and physiological addiction.

What is the evidence on these health hazards of marijuana? There is little doubt of individual cases of serious temporary and long-term negative physical and behavioral effects of marijuana use. However, most of the more extreme indictments of marijuana still have not been supported as common occurrences, or they have been considerably qualified by research findings.

Tolerance to marijuana is well documented in heavy use, although there is also some evidence of "reverse tolerance" wherein experienced smokers can experience intoxication even on placebo cigarettes without any THC in them (Ray and Ksir 1987:310–311). The evidence is that physiological dependence with the characteristic withdrawal symptoms does not occur. There is some evidence of temporary impairment of short-term memory and a slowing of learning and intellectual skills, but the evidence is mixed regarding performance of manual skills and tasks. The findings on sperm counts are inconsistent, and in any case the levels affected are within the normal range. The impact of marijuana consumption on reproductive functions would have relevance only for those already marginally infertile. The findings have yet to establish a clear threat of marijuana to the immune system (white blood cells), chromosomes, hormones, brain cells, or the central nervous system. There is sometimes an "acute panic reaction" when an individual first smokes marijuana or when a regular smoker encounters some unexpectedly potent marijuana, but serious psychiatric problems have not been typical. Poor school performance and low motivation are related to heavy marijuana use in some studies, but the research does not make it clear whether these behavioral tendencies preceded or were consequences of marijuana use (Austin, Macari, and Lettieri 1979; Petersen 1980; National Academy of Sciences 1982; Gallagher 1989a). It is most likely the case that both the low school achievement and the marijuana use flow from a common set of problems and causes (Goode 1989a:152–155). There have been controlled studies of chronic (long-term) marijuana smoking in Jamaica, Costa Rica, and Greece. None of these found strong evidence of physical (brain, blood, hormone, chromosome) or psychological (amotivational syndrome, psychosis) damage from marijuana or that marijuana produced physical dependence (Rubin and Comitas 1976; Stefanis, Dornbush, and Fink 1977).

Marijuana contains twice as much tar and other carcinogens as tobacco contains, and marijuana smokers tend to inhale the smoke more deeply and hold it in the lungs longer than do tobacco smokers. It is not surprising, then, that later research has confirmed early reports of serious respiratory tract and lung damage from chronic, heavy marijuana smoking. The link between pot smoking and lung cancer has not been established, but cancer-producing chemicals are found in marijuana smokers, and precancerous changes in the tissues of the respiratory tract have been found in heavy marijuana smokers (Petersen 1980; National Academy of Sciences 1982; Gallagher 1989a; Goode 1989a).

Goode (1989a:151–152) claims that this lung damage is the only finding of adverse effects of marijuana use that has proven to be "robust" and not seriously challenged by research. He states that all other findings have been contradictory. Further, Goode points out that marijuana's effects on body organs seem to be "weak," and he believes that for this reason some studies will find evidence of long-term dysfunction and others will not. Goode is correct if the reference is only to direct physiological effects of marijuana. However, there is another set of "robust" findings pointing to the indirect harm from marijuana in traffic injuries. The evidence is strong that marijuana smoking presents risks to oneself and others if driving while under the influence; marijuana is implicated in many traffic accidents and fatalities. Early research had failed to discover significant effects on muscular coordination or other skills relevant to automobile driving or on the actual driving itself (Weil 1968; Grinspoon 1969). These turned out to be faulty conclusions (perhaps because very low dosages were used in the tests), for later research did show that psychomotor skills, perception and attention to detail, vision, and reaction time are all adversely affected by smoking marijuana. More important, both simulated and actual driving tests indicated that marijuana (alone as well as when taken with alcohol) impairs driving ability and increases the risk of accidents (Austin, Macari, and Lettieri 1979; Petersen 1980; National Academy of Sciences 1982).

National data show that the risks of encountering various psychological and social problems in using marijuana are small, but they are comparable to the risks associated with alcohol and cocaine use. Of those who had used marijuana in the past year, 6 percent attributed problems of depression to smoking marijuana during that time. A number of other problems associated with marijuana were reported by some users during the past year: 6 percent reported problems of anxiety, 4 percent felt suspicious and mistrustful, 4 percent had fights with family or friends, 6 percent achieved less on the job or in school, and 11 percent reported difficulty in thinking clearly. Among those who had ever used marijuana, about one-fifth reported problems of cutting down, control, and dependence, about the same proportion reporting such problems among alcohol users (NIDA 1988a:103–107).

The best description of marijuana effects at this time is that, although most of the severely adverse consequences of marijuana have not been substantiated, it is certainly not a harmless, safe drug. We do not have the generations-long data on marijuana that we have on tobacco smoking and alcohol use, and many of the questions about the harmful effects of marijuana will not be answered until such data are collected.

Possible Medical Applications of Marijuana

Marijuana does not do wonderful things for one's mental capacity or health. However, some medicinal uses of cannabis have been known or suspected for centuries in China and India and since the 1800s in Europe (Taylor 1966; Ray and Ksir 1987). Since 1972, medical research in this country has shown that marijuana may have some beneficial therapeutic effects for certain individuals. The evidence is strongest with regard to the use of marijuana in treating nausea and vomiting as side effects of chemotherapy in cancer patients. It has also shown to be beneficial in treating open-angle glaucoma (narrowing or tunnel vision). However, marijuana has been successful in reducing intraocular pressure only in *some* people. Similarly, smoking marijuana does give some relief in asthma cases by dilating bronchial tissues, but it simultaneously irritates and inflames those same tissues (Petersen 1980).

There are other, more effective medications for each of the conditions that marijuana has helped, and for most patients it is not the medication of choice. "Its action is neither potent nor focused enough to produce the predictable, clear, isolated effects of first-class drugs" (Gallagher 1989a:312). Nonetheless, the potential medicinal benefits of marijuana for chemotherapy patients experiencing nausea were sufficiently established by the early 1980s (National Academy of Sciences 1982) that THC (the active ingredient in marijuana) became approved by the federal Food and Drug Administration for that purpose. Beginning in 1985, the FDA approved the production by one pharmaceutical company of a capsule (Marinol) with THC in it for chemotherapy patients experiencing nausea (Ray and Ksir 1987; Gallagher 1989a).

SOCIAL PATTERNS AND TRENDS

As we saw in Chapter 3, marijuana is the most frequently used of the illegal substances. "It is possible that the total number of times that marijuana is used approaches, and may even exceed, the total for all other illicit drugs combined" (Goode 1989a:138). Marijuana is the bellwether substance;

as it goes, so go other illicit drugs. Marijuana led the increase during the 1960s and 1970s and led the decrease in use of most drugs in the 1980s. These behavioral changes were accompanied and preceded by cultural changes in attitudes toward and public perceptions of marijuana. Negative public opinion toward marijuana softened in the 1960s but became more conservative by the late 1970s. Since then, the trend has been toward harsher judgments of marijuana as a consensus began to build about its harmfulness and as support diminished for its decriminalization and legalization.

Was Pot the Drug of a Whole Generation?

The rapid increase in drug use led by marijuana from the mid-1960s to the late 1970s, and the hang-loose ethic of the hippie subculture that fueled much of it, has been well documented by researchers. It also was headline news at the time and has left a lasting impression on journalists, novelists, and other chroniclers of pop culture. The image was created of a hippie, drug-influenced era that caught up almost all of the youth of a generation in which the badge of membership was smoking marijuana.

This popular image of the drug generation was highlighted in 1987 in a highly unusual way—the nomination for a seat on the U.S. Supreme Court. After having a conservative nominee (Robert Bork) turned down by the U.S. Senate, President Ronald Reagan quickly nominated Harvard University law professor Douglas Ginsberg. The White House staff believed that he represented all that was desired in a Reagan court: legal brilliance, strong credentials, and an impeccable record of private morals and behavior. As the Senate hearings proceeded, however, it was learned that Ginsberg's credentials as a legal scholar, teacher, and practitioner were weak. Worse, Ginsberg (who was 41 years old at the time of his nomination) admitted to having smoked marijuana on numerous occasions while an undergraduate and law student; indeed, he had even smoked it several times after becoming a member of the law faculty. The accumulation of negative news resulted in withdrawal of the nomination.

Most of the mass media stories on the failure of the nomination paid the closest attention to the pot-smoking incidents as the undoing of Ginsberg's chances to become a Supreme Court justice. The tenor of these stories was: Hold on now. What did you expect? Ginsberg comes from the pot-smoking generation. It would not be surprising if he had not only used it but used it with some frequency. Surely, experimenting with pot as a youth should not prevent holding office in one's mature years. If the test for high public office is to have been a marijuana teetotaler, then a whole generation would be lost as public leaders.

As if to underscore this, two Democratic candidates for the upcoming 1988 presidential nomination (Albert Gore and Bruce Babbit) who were of the same generation as Ginsberg, came forward with an admission that they, too, had tried pot in their younger days. It was speculated that the vast majority of members of the U.S. Congress under age 50 who had attended college had used marijuana. (See *Newsweek*, Nov. 16, 1987:47–52; *U.S. News & World Report*, Nov. 16, 1987:24–26.) Public opinion strongly supported this image. In a *Newsweek* poll taken in November 1987, 69 percent of adults believed that half or more persons under age 50 in public office had used marijuana "at least several times" in the past; 68 percent believed that the level of marijuana use among the general population of the United States was holding steady or increasing (*Newsweek*, Nov. 16, 1987:52).

How accurate is this image? Only partly. There is little doubt that use was widespread enough and received enough official and public attention to create a social and cultural tone of drug tolerance and involvement. Compared to generations before and the next generation to follow, the cohort of youth from the 1960s and 1970s was much more drug prone. Among drug users, marijuana was the most frequent choice. As we have seen, by 1979 the majority of high school seniors and over two-thirds of young adults of college age had tried marijuana sometime in their lifetime. Sizable minorities of respondents had admitted to having tried marijuana during most of the years of the decade of the 1970s. As noted in the section below on social learning and drug use, marijuana (and to some extent other drugs) moved from being a strictly subcultural phenomenon to become more mainstream and conventional.

This is very different, however, from the popular image that most of those in Ginsberg's generation had used pot several times and many were regular users or that virtually anyone from that generation had used marijuana. It is not true that using pot was a normally expected activity among the majority of youth. Even in the peak years of use, only about one-third of those age 18 to 25 had used pot in the past month, and at no time did more than a small minority become daily users. Moreover, these peak years did not come until the end of the 1970s; they did not come in the 1960s. Of those in Ginsberg's specific age cohort (40 to 44 at the time of his nomination), only 26 percent had ever used marijuana. If he had used at all as a college student (which would have been in the mid-1960s), Ginsberg was distinctly in the minority. If he had used with any frequency at the time, and especially if he was still using as a law faculty when he was past 25, he was even less representative of his generation (NIDA 1988a).

Among young adults today, high school dropouts are more likely than college graduates to be regular users. But in Ginsberg's over-35 generation, college graduates are much more likely to have tried marijuana and to have been regular users than are high school dropouts or high school graduates (NIDA 1988a). It is stretching, however, to conclude from this that the brightest and best from that generation who became public leaders in the 1980s were somehow especially likely to have been part of the drug scene. The levels of pot smoking, and the other drug use that was a concomitant of involvement in marijuana, during those years when Ginsberg and his contemporaries

T A B L E 5 . 1   *Sociodemographic characteristics of marijuana users*

| | Percent Ever Used | | | | |
| | Age Groups | | | | |
	12–17	18–25	26–34	35 +	Total
Sex					
Male	16.8	56.4	68.1	23.8	36.9
Female	17.9	56.4	56.2	16.0	29.7
Race/Ethnicity					
White	18.2	56.4	65.6	19.3	33.7
Black	13.5	45.3	56.0	24.4	33.3
Hispanic	16.9	42.0	46.5	14.3	27.9
Size of City of Residence					
Large urban	18.5	57.3	64.6	24.7	36.8
Smaller urban	17.7	57.1	66.2	16.5	32.4
Nonurban	15.3	53.7	56.7	14.9	27.9
Region of Residence					
Northeast	17.3	54.5	65.9	21.2	33.4
North central	14.7	65.9	66.8	18.4	34.2
South	17.2	49.2	54.8	17.1	29.5
West	22.3	61.2	66.4	24.2	38.6
Education					
Less than HS	NA	63.3	60.3	12.4	25.8
HS graduate	NA	53.3	61.5	15.1	34.3
Some college	NA	54.9	62.9	29.2	41.5
College grad	NA	60.5	64.0	29.9	42.5
Current Employment					
Full-time	NA	61.7	63.9	28.0	43.9
Part-time	NA	51.6	62.4	26.4	40.2
Unemployed	NA	58.8	67.1	20.0	44.6
Other	NA	43.5	51.7	7.9	16.2

Source: NIDA 1990b (1988 survey).

were young were serious enough when accurately described. They do not need to be embellished. The image revealed in the stories on Ginsberg simultaneously served inaccurately to condemn a whole generation as druggies and to justify those of that generation who did indulge.

Social Characteristics of Users

Table 5.1 presents national figures on marijuana use by sex, race/ethnicity, residence, education, and employment. From this table we learn that if one has ever smoked marijuana sometime in his life, he is most likely to be a young adult white male, residing in a large city in the West or Northeast, with a college education. This description of the social characteristics of marijuana users changes somewhat when we move from examining lifetime prevalence to considering those who have smoked marijuana in the past year or the past month. According to data not shown in the table, the marijuana smoker today who is a regular user is an unemployed, high school dropout, young white or black male, living in a large urban area (NIDA 1990b).

Age. As we saw in Chapter 3, the peak years of marijuana use come during young adulthood. Table 5.1 shows that adolescents and those 35 and older have the lowest lifetime prevalence regardless of sex, race, or place of residence. Whereas young adults and high school seniors previously experienced the highest levels of lifetime use, many of them are now in the 26–34-year-old group and have raised the lifetime prevalence in that group. However, young adults 18 to 25 years of age are most likely, and high school seniors are the next most likely, to have used in the past month or past year (figures not shown in the table). Current usage is highest in the 18–25-year-old group, but thereafter current usage (used in the past month) falls sharply and essentially falls to zero (less than 0.5 percent) after age 50 (NIDA 1988a, 1990b; Johnston, O'Malley, and Bachman 1988).

Sex and Race. As Table 5.1 shows, smoking marijuana is more characteristic of men than women. Difference in proportions of male and female users are minimal among adolescents (where teenage girls are slightly more likely than boys to have used marijuana) and young adults, but men are considerably more likely than women to smoke marijuana in the later years. For each age group, the greater the frequency of use the greater the gap between men and women. From the 1985 and 1988 surveys (findings not shown in the table), we know that twice as many men (12 percent in 1985 and 8 percent in 1988) as women (7 percent in 1985 and 4 percent in 1988) are current marijuana users (in the past month) (NIDA 1988a, 1990b). And for both high school seniors and young adults, about three times as many men as women use marijuana daily—6 percent versus 2 percent. For both high school and young adult respondents, however, both the absolute and the relative difference in marijuana smoking between men and women narrowed in the 1980s (Johnston, O'Malley, and Bachman 1988; NIDA 1990b).

Until the 1960s marijuana users were overwhelmingly black, but by the 1970s whites were more likley to be past and current smokers. Today the racial differences have narrowed. As shown in Table 5.1, there is no overall difference between black and white respondents. This is primarily because of the somewhat higher percentage of users among blacks than among whites in the older age group, 35 and over. White adolescents and young adults have considerably higher lifetime prevalence and slightly higher annual and current prevalence than do their black peers. Among older adults, however, blacks are somewhat more likely to have ever smoked marijuana and to report using

Multiple-Drug Use:
Marijuana as a Gateway Drug

There is nothing inherent in the pharmacological properties of marijuana that induces the user to seek out and use heroin or other drugs. The evidence we have shows that marijuana use is neither a necessary nor a sufficient condition for heroin use (Goode 1969; Clayton and Voss 1981). This does not mean, as it is sometimes interpreted to mean, that the chances of becoming involved with other drugs is no greater among marijuana smokers than among abstainers. Instead, those who have used marijuana are at a much higher risk of becoming involved with other illicit substances than are those who abstain.

Indeed, there is a high intercorrelation of use among the different types of drugs. The use of any one drug (including the legal drugs of tobacco and alcohol) increases the probability that a person will also use some other drug. Use of any illicit drug increases the chances of using other illicit drugs. Among those who use illicit substances, the pattern is apt to be multidrug use, although one drug may be or may have been used more frequently than others. Various substances are mixed (heroin and cocaine, for instance), and alcohol and marijuana are often consumed during the same drug-taking episode. This does not mean that drugs are typically mixed or simultaneously consumed. Although taking up a new drug usually does not mean that the person entirely gives up previously taken drugs, multiple-drug use develops progressively or hierarchically with use of harder drugs. It builds on a broader base of alcohol and tobacco use, followed by marijuana use, but with successively fewer users at each level until the top is reached with a small number of cocaine or heroin users (Kandel 1975, 1978, 1980; Adler and Kandel 1982; Yamaguchi and Kandel 1984a, 1984b). This same sequence of drug use is also found in other countries (Kandel 1984).

The probability of a person's using hard drugs increases with each additional drug used. The stronger the drug the more likely that other drugs have preceded its use. Although heroin users are almost certain to have used other drugs, the reverse is not true; most marijuana or amphetamine users, for instance, have not used heroin. In one study (O'Donnell et al. 1976; Clayton and Voss 1981), *all* of those using any type of illicit drug had also used alcohol; *90 percent* of those who got to the point of using heroin and cocaine previously had indulged in practically all other legal and illegal substances—tobacco, alcohol, marijuana, barbiturates, amphetamines, and hallucinogens.

Thus, although it is true that almost all heroin users have previously smoked marijuana, it is equally true that almost all heroin and cocaine users have used many other substances, including alcohol and tobacco.

Some drug use nearly always precedes heroin use, so in this sense all drugs could be said to lead to hard-drug use for some. However, in the O'Donnell et al. study (1976), only 6 percent of the alcohol drinkers, 7 percent of the tobacco smokers, and 11 percent of the users of psychedelics also used heroin. Kandel and Faust (1975) reported that of those adolescents in their longitudinal study who had begun using alcohol 32 percent went on to use hard liquor and of that group 27 percent became marijuana users; of those who reached the point of smoking marijuana, 26 percent wound up trying other drugs such as heroin, cocaine, and amphetamines.

These percentages are not high enough to say that once a person starts drinking alcohol or smoking marijuana there is very high risk of his or her moving on to opiates or other stronger drugs. Nonetheless, the percentages are high enough to show that there is a clear and present risk for marijuana smokers getting involved with other drugs. Those who move beyond alcohol and tobacco to marijuana run a higher risk of coming to use other drugs than do those who abstain from all three or stop short of marijuana. Moreover, it is clearly the case that the odds of moving on to other drugs, including opiates, increase the more frequently one uses marijuana. Those who have used marijuana in the past month are ten to fifteen times more likely than abstainers to use other illicit substances and as much as thirty times more likely to use cocaine. Among young adults, 27 percent of the current marijuana smokers use cocaine and 22 percent use other drugs, whereas only 2 percent of the abstainers use any of these drugs (NIDA 1988a:42).

The correlation between the use of marijuana and the use of all other drugs is an extremely robust one. Every researcher who has investigated the issue systematically and empirically, myself included, has found a strong positive relationship. There is no question about its existence: Marijuana users are more likely to use any and all illegal dangerous drugs than are nonusers; and the more that one uses, the greater the probability that one will try and use a wide range of illegal drugs, including cocaine, heroin, and the hallucinogens. In addition, the more that one uses marijuana, and the earlier in life one first does so, the greater the likelihood of becoming *seriously* involved with other illegal dangerous drugs. The evidence supporting these relationships is overwhelming, persuasive, and incontrovertible. (Goode 1989a:156)

Thus, while marijuana may not "cause" the use of other illicit drugs in a direct sense that it is both a necessary and sufficient condition for use of other drugs, there is little doubt that marijuana is a "gateway" drug to multiple-illicit-drug use. But it is a gateway in the sense of statistical probability and progression determined by many factors in the social setting and not a gate that once opened inevitably leads to harsher drugs.

in the past year, and among those 35 and over, blacks are twice as likely (2 percent versus 1 percent) to be current users (findings not shown in the table).

In the younger years, the greater tendency for whites than blacks to smoke marijuana holds for both males and females, but the higher probability of use by blacks in the later years is primarily because of the difference between black and white men. The lifetime, annual, and current usages by persons 35 and older are very similar for black and white women. Hispanics* are less likely than either black or non-Hispanic whites to use marijuana (NIDA 1990b).

Socioeconomic Status. The historic shift in marijuana use out of the lower socioeconomic status into the middle-class young-adult population during the years of increasing drug use in the United States has already been noted. This shift is reflected in Table 5.1, which shows a positive relationship between education and lifetime prevalence of marijuana smoking. Except in the young-adult age group, college graduates are the most likely to have smoked marijuana at some time in their lives. For most age categories, full-time employees have a higher probability of using at some time in the past than do the unemployed.

Nonetheless, in the 1980s there was a shift of marijuana use back toward individuals at the lower end of the socioeconomic scale. For instance, 1988 survey findings, not reported in the table, show that among young adults, 34 percent of high school dropouts have smoked marijuana in the past year whereas 24 percent of college graduates have used in the past year. Similarly, unemployed persons today are the most likely to be past-year and current marijuana users (NIDA 1990b).

S O C I A L   L E A R N I N G   I N   U S E   O F
M A R I J U A N A   A N D   O T H E R   D R U G S

A "hippie" subculture developed in the 1960s in which drug experiences were defined as desirable, and the term *psychedelic* spread as a favorable adjective for dress, music, and art styles. The hippie groups were usually college-age and college-oriented young people. College students joined the "counter-culture" in large numbers and developed both antiestablishment attitudes and drug-using patterns. By the middle of the 1970s, this subculture had

---

*The term *Hispanic* refers to both white and black Americans with Spanish surnames or whose origins of nationality are Spanish, Latin American, Central American, or Caribbean. The term *white* refers to non-Hispanic white Americans. Use of other terms to refer to racial or ethnic categories will be apparent from the context of use.

essentially dissipated. Smoking marijuana became a fairly routine part of college and military life and was no longer confined to subcultural settings. Marijuana was smoked in a casual way that would shock the old-time pothead. Before, during, or after sports events, dates, public gatherings, parties, music festivals, class, or work would do; there was no special place, time, or occasion for marijuana smoking. The acceptable places and occasions became as varied as those for drinking alcohol. Even many of those who did not smoke marijuana shared the casual, tolerant attitudes toward marijuana.

This avenue to drugs cannot be described as subcultural in the same sense as the hippie subculture or earlier subcultural context of use. Rather, an essentially conventional path to drugs, which bears all the earmarks of conventional socialization into alcohol use, appears to have emerged. In part, it opened the door to cocaine and other drugs among otherwise conventional groups. As predicted (Akers 1970), many adult users became those who simply continued drug behavior begun in their high school or college years and provided socialization for drug use in the family without participation in a subculture. There are confirmed reports of some parents who participated in the subculture as youth providing direct experiences and parental models for using marijuana and other drugs to their children similar to the routine exposure to alcohol in the home experienced by a great many youngsters (Adler and Adler 1978). Whether through subcultural, deviant, or conventional socialization, initiation of drug use and drug behavior beyond first experiences proceed through a social learning process.

The Social Learning Process in Drug Use

In the following paragraphs, social learning theory is applied to drug use spelling out a typical process of coming to use or remain abstinent, continue, or cease use. Since it is in the teenage years when first opportunities to use drugs typically occur and since the test of the theory presented below is on adolescent substance use, the narrative emphasizes adolescent use. But the process applies to any age group, although the exact nature of the relevant social groups and settings for use may differ. Similarly, the emphasis in this chapter is on marijuana use. But the social learning process is hypothesized to be essentially the same regardless of the substance and will be applied to other drugs in later chapters. Social learning theory was introduced in Chapter 1.

Differential association (interaction) with peers, parents, and others provides the adolescent with the social environment for exposure to definitions (attitudes favorable or unfavorable to drug use), imitation of models, and differential reinforcement (balance of rewarding and negative consequences for use or abstinence). The family usually socializes against drug use but may, in a few cases, foster use of drugs, either indirectly or directly. The most important group in the abstinence, initiation, and continuation of substance use is peers, particularly close friends. Differential association with peer users and nonusers is the best predictor of whether the individual will use or not. More frequent, longer-term, and closer association with peers who do not support drug use is strongly correlated with abstinence from drugs, whereas greater association on balance with drug-using and approving peers is predictive of drug use. Frequency and quantity of use are related to the number and type of current users one has as friends. Other family members, neighbors, church and religious groups, schoolteachers, physicians, the law and authority figures, and other individuals and groups in the community as well as mass media and other more remote sources of attitudes and models have varying degrees of effect on use and abstinence.

Most of the time these groups influences act in harmony to move the youngster in the direction toward abstinence and away from drug use. In those cases where they harmonize in the drug-using direction, the chances of behaving that way are maximized. When they are in conflict, the adolescent will most often behave similarly to close peers, those who are his or her best friends. It is in peer groups that drugs typically are first made available and opportunities for use provided. The process is one of peer influence, however, and does not usually involve peer "pressure," as we shall see shortly.

Definitions, which are the positive (desirable), neutralizing (justifying or excusing), or negative (undesirable) attitudes toward drugs, are learned through imitation and social reinforcement of them by these groups. Once learned they serve as discriminative or cue stimuli (along with such stimuli as physical setting, occasion, place, and others) for using or abstaining. The definitions, combined with *imitation* of admired or valued behavioral models and the anticipated balance of reinforcement, produce the initial use or sustain continued abstinence.

It is at this point that the actual consequences of use (social and nonsocial) first come into play in *differential reinforcement* (balance of reinforcers and punishers). After use has begun beyond the initial attempts and experimentation, imitation becomes less important while the effects of definitions and consequences of use, themselves affected by the experience of having used drugs, continue. These consequences include the actual or perceived physiological effects of the drugs, which may be affected by what the person has previously learned to expect. If the drug effects are intrinsically rewarding to the person or become reinforcing through conditioning, the chances of continuing to use are greater than for stopping. One must learn to take the drug for optimal effect, and for some substances this means certain techniques of ingestion not previously known by the person must be learned in the context of using and observing others using. Reinforcing and punishing consequences also include actual and anticipated reactions of others and other known or expected outcomes of using. That is, positive or negative effects of the drugs are themselves subject to previously learned expectations, and through association with social reinforcement from others, one learns to interpret the effects as pleasurable and enjoyable or as frightening and negative (Becker 1963, 1967). Using and the consequences of using now may begin to have an effect on choice of friends and social settings and, therefore, have some feedback effects on differential association.

Those who want to become more regular or heavy users of illegal drugs cannot depend entirely on the network of close friends for a supply and must develop connections for purchase beyond a small group of known and trusted friends. This gets them involved with others who control availability and provides additional opportunities and associations in support of drug use of various kinds. They may begin to deal in drugs and supply others. Indeed, more extensive involvement in most drug patterns is accompanied by buying and reselling, and perhaps production, on an informal or a mainly money-making basis. This presents a great risk of police action and legal penalties, discovery by nonusers, and disclosure to the authorities by associates and customers. These and other possible negative consequences mean that only some of those who continue use beyond the initial stages will go on to more frequent, habitual drug use.

Thus, the probability of beginning and continuing to use a substance increases when: (1) there is greater exposure to using than to abstaining persons who serve as behavioral models, (2) there is more association with using than with abstaining peers and others, (3) use is differentially reinforced over abstinence, and (4) the individual has come to define use favorably. Among users the probability of developing abusive drug patterns (rather than quitting or developing light or moderate patterns) increases significantly with: (1) more association with high-frequency users, (2) differential reinforcement of abusive patterns over more moderate use, (3) continued adherence to positive or neutralizing rather than negative definitions, and (4) to some extent, with more exposure to rewarding and rewarded abusive models.

A great deal of research testing part or all of the social learning model offers findings that support the theory. (See for instance Kandel 1974; Jessor and Jessor 1977; Dull 1983; Winfree and Griffiths 1983; Dembo et al. 1986; Marcos, Bahr, and Johnson 1986; Burkett and Warren 1987; Orcutt 1987; White, Pandina, and LaGrange 1987; Sellers and Winfree 1990. See also the reviews in Jessor 1979; Kandel 1980; and Radosevich et al. 1980.) Research findings are also consistent with the typical social learning history of coming to use drugs in which the youngster associates differentially with peers (and family members and others) who are users or tolerant of use, learns definitions favorable to use, and then uses (Jessor, Jessor, and Finney 1973; Krohn 1974; Andrews and Kandel 1979; Sellers and Winfree 1990). In addition to this support from other research, the theory has been given strong support by my own research designed to test it.

The Boys Town Study

I, along with colleagues Marvin D. Krohn, Lonn Lanza-Kaduce, and Marcia J. Radosevich, conducted a large-scale self-report questionnaire survey of adolescent substance use and abuse involving 3,065 students in grades 7 through 12 in eight midwestern communities. The study was supported by the Boys Town Center for the Study of Youth Development and therefore is often referred to as the Boys Town Study (see Chapter 4). The adolescents in this survey were asked about their experiences with the full range of substances: alcohol, tobacco, marijuana, stimulants, depressants, psychedelics, and narcotics. The respondents also answered questions designed to measure the major elements of social learning theory.

Imitation was measured by asking the youngsters whom of the persons they admired (friends, parents, etc.) they had observed smoking, drinking, or using the various substances. *Definitions* were measured by questions on the adolescents' own positive, negative, or neutralizing attitudes toward use of the various substances and their law-abiding or violating attitudes toward the law in general and the drug laws in particular. *Differential association* included measures of how many of the respondents' close friends smoked marijuana, drank beer, wine, or liquor, or used any of the other drugs in the study. Differential association also included perceptions of the approving or disapproving attitudes of parents, peers, and others whose opinions were valued.

Differential reinforcement was divided into two categories. The first category, social reinforcement, included the actual or anticipated positive or negative sanctions and reaction for use or abstinence from parents and friends. It also included fear of legal sanctions for use and beliefs about how much drug use would interfere with other valued activities such as athletics. The second category, social/nonsocial reinforcement, included the overall balance of negative and positive consequences attached to using or abstaining, whether consequences were from the reactions of others or from the drug effects themselves.

The results of the study showed strong support for the social learning theory. As shown in Table 5.2, all of the major social learning variables are significantly related to marijuana use and abuse (correlations range from .10 to .79). The combined effects of the social learning variables on use and abuse are very strong ($R = .83$ and $.62$). The strength of these correlations is better understood in light of the fact that in social research reports, correlations of .10 are often considered worthy of noting, correlations of .20 or .30 are often described as moderate, and correlations of .50 or higher are generally considered to be very strong (Akers et al. 1979).

The findings of the study also support social learning theory in explaining use of a range of other substances: alcohol, stimulants, depressants, hallucinogens, and narcotics. The theory is also supported for each stage of

T A B L E 5 . 2 Correlation of marijuana use and abuse with social learning

	Multiple Correlation (R) for:	
Social Learning Variables	Marijuana Use	Marijuana Abuse
ALL VARIABLES	.83	.62
Differential association	.79	.56
Definitions	.73	.44
Differential social/nonsocial reinforcement	.62	.39
Differential social reinforcement	.58	.38
Imitation	.38	.10
N =	2,395	948[a]

Source: Adapted from Akers et al. 1979.
[a]Users only.

initiation, use, abuse, and cessation (Lanza-Kaduce et al. 1984). Further, the social learning model accounts for marijuana use in this sample better than does either a model based on social bonding theory or one based on anomie theory (Akers and Cochran 1985).

Community Context and Marijuana Use

As we have seen, there is variation in rates of marijuana use by size of community and place of residence. These and other group differences indicate that there are social structural contexts which have an effect on the level of marijuana and other drug use. The demographic composition, cultural traditions, and social control systems varying across communities can be expected to produce variations in substance use and abuse. Social learning theory hypothesizes that the process by which these structural contexts have such an effect is that they affect differential association, differential reinforcement, imitation, definitions, and other social learning variables, which in turn affect individuals' behavior. (See the diagram on page 14.)

This hypothesis was supported in further analysis of the Boys Town data. Differences in levels of marijuana (and alcohol) use among the adolescents in four types of communities (farm, rural nonfarm, suburban, and urban) were found to be mediated by the social learning process. Different levels of peer associations, definitions favorable or unfavorable to use, and reinforcement balances across the four community contexts explained the differences in community rates of marijuana and alcohol (Krohn, Lanza-Kaduce, and Akers 1984).

The Myth of Peer "Pressure" in Adolescent Substance Use

I did my best in the interview with the newpaper reporter. I briefly related this social learning process to her. Although I emphasized the importance of peers in this process, I made a point of explicitly disavowing the term *peer pressure*. I said that it was peer influence, not pressure. Peers strongly influence one another, but the idea that all or a majority of teenagers face strong peer pressure to use drugs is not supported by my research findings. Nonetheless, when the news article appeared the heading was "Peer Pressure the Major Cause of Teenage Drug Abuse, Says Sociologist." The "peer pressure" explanation for teenage drug use and other types of adolescent misbehavior has become so commonplace and so ingrained in popular commentary that it is attributed to expert opinion even when denied. It is the favorite of popular-press commentators:

> Parents should realize that even the "straight" kids (non–drug users)— who represent 50 percent of most surveys of junior high and high school classes—are under *constant peer pressure* to "Try it; it's great." (Mann 1980b:38; emphasis in original)

This picture of all adolescents under unrelenting and coercive pressure from their peers to try drugs can be expected to surface in almost any popular magazine or TV talk show when the topic is the problems of young people. This simplistic portrayal of the process of peer influence was not accurate even at the height of adolescent drug use in this country. It nevertheless enjoys such widespread credibility and differs enough from the actual process of coming to use drugs, that it is fair to describe it as a popular "myth." The actual process is more correctly called peer *influence* rather than peer *pressure*.

This is more than a semantic distinction. "Pressure" conjures up images of overt challenge, of forceful peers exhorting the naive and fearful good kid with "Come on, I dare you," and backing up the challenge with threats of ridicule or ostracism. As with all cultural myths, there is some truth to it; teenagers do on occasion face this kind of pressure. And it is true that peers strongly affect one another's behavior; there is nothing mythical about this. *The myth is that this is the main way in which peer influence operates, that it is ubiquitous, constant, and irresistible.* Further, the myth holds that peer pressure always moves the youth's behavior in a deviant direction. For the great majority of cases where peer influence has been felt, it is not pressure of this type; it is pressure only in the subtle sense. It is not blatantly exercised. Its significance is often not recognized by the youngsters themselves, and whenever pressure is recognized it is usually not perceived as something that cannot be resisted. Furthermore, the influence is interactive and works both ways; it does not just reinforce deviant behavior. For the majority of teenagers, peers are more likely to reinforce conforming behavior.

T A B L E 5 . 3 Perception of peer pressure to use drugs

	Tobacco	Alcohol	Marijuana	Stronger Drugs
No	74.0%	58.9%	67.2%	94.1%
Once/twice	18.6	24.6	20.1	3.7
Occasionally/sometimes	5.0	13.4	8.9	1.2
Often/frequently	2.4	3.2	3.7	1.0
N =	2,146	3,016	3,018	3,015

Sources: Original data from Boys Town Study for alcohol, marijuana, and stronger drugs (see Akers et al. 1979); from the Iowa study for smoking tobacco (see Akers et al. 1983).

T A B L E 5 . 4 Perceived importance of parents, peers, and friends in deciding to use or not to use drugs

	Alcohol	Marijuana	Stronger Drugs
Parents	42.7%	53.7%	62.9%
Friends	24.3	31.4	42.9
Peers	11.9	19.1	27.5

Source: Original data from Boys Town Study.

Findings from the Boys Town research on drugs and alcohol use among adolescents underscore this conclusion. Table 5.3 shows that the vast majority of the teenagers report *no* pressure from peers to smoke, drink, or use drugs. A tiny fraction report frequently being pressured by others to try drugs. Pressure to use strong drugs, especially, is a rare event in the lives of these junior high and high school students. Teens are important to one another, and we know that peer variables are more strongly related to drug use than are parental variables. However, as shown in Table 5.4, in the adolescents' own perceptions, the opinions and influence of friends and peers are less frequently important to their substance-use decisions than is the influence of parents.

In Table 5.5, we see that only a small minority of teens associate with friends from whom they anticipate positive reactions for their own use. The most likely response for alcohol and marijuana is neutrality. For any of the substances, the anticipated reaction is more likely to be *critical toward use*. Nevertheless, it is those youngsters who do start using drugs that are more likely to report friends' approval and support for use. The influence is there, but it is not felt as oppressive, unavoidable, or irresistible. Very few adolescents face direct dares or challenges to try drugs. Only a small minority feel directly

T A B L E 5 . 5 *Anticipated reactions of friends to one's use of drugs*

	Alcohol	Marijuana	Stronger Drugs
Becoming closer friends	5.5%	5.3%	1.8%
Encourage use	9.1	7.9	1.6
Do nothing	66.3	40.7	15.9
Criticize me	12.3	28.5	41.5
Tell my parents	2.3	4.9	9.7
Stop being my friend	4.5	12.5	27.7
N =	3,001	2,990	2,968

Source: Original data from Boys Town Study.

pressured by friends either for or against drugs, but when pressure from peers was reported it was more likely to be *pressure to abstain* than to use.

Adolescent peer influence works to support behavior that both conforms to and runs counter to norms related to drinking, drug use, and smoking. It is real, strong, and effective. But it is not readily recognized by the teenagers themselves and seldom fits the popular image of peer pressure. The image of the typical adolescent caught up in a drug-oriented youth culture in which there is irresistible peer pressure to violate adult norms simply does not apply to most teenagers. Social learning presents a picture of a more subtle and complex behavioral process which more accurately captures the real situation faced by teenagers for both their conforming and deviant drug behavior.

Heroin

TRENDS IN PREVALENCE OF HEROIN USE AND ADDICTION

The rate of opiate use and addiction before the Harrison Act of 1914 initiated national legal restrictions was apparently greater than it has been since then. Before that time, one could purchase opiates at moderate prices directly from suppliers, pharmacies, and physicians. Doctors prescribed opiates for many illlnesses, and many patent medicines contained a high percentage of opiates. Society was more tolerant of opiates. Opiate addiction was considered unfortunate, but it was not until the beginning of the twentieth century that it began to be seen as deviant. Neither use nor addiction was considered a serious evil or cause for social ostracism or criminal sanctions. The proportion of the population using opiates was nearly twice what it became at any time in the twentieth century. Some estimates place the total of opiate addicts before 1914 at more than 1 million (Ausubel 1958:62; Eldridge 1962:7). Other estimates range from 100,000 to over 250,000 (Lindesmith 1967:110–111).

After heroin was outlawed and other opiates became more controlled, opiate use and addiction declined steadily to a low point during World War II. There was a marked increase in heroin and other opiate addiction after the war that peaked in the early 1950s, but it dropped again to another low point in the early 1960s (Ball and Cottrell 1965:471–472). The upsurge in marijuana and other hallucinogenic drug use was accompanied in the 1970s by another heroin "epidemic" reminiscent of that of the early 1950s. By the mid-1970s, the estimates of the number of addicts were in the 300,000 to 400,000 range, and the number who had used heroin or other opiates in the past year was estimated at 3 million (Abelson and Fishburne 1976; Hunt and Chambers 1976).

The proportion of the total population involved in heroin use remained very small, and by the end of the decade the epidemic had petered out and heroin and opiate addiction declined. In 1975 the percentage of high school seniors who had ever used heroin was 2 percent, and 1 percent had used in the past year. By 1982 both of these figures had been cut in half. By 1982 daily use (the most accurate indicator of addiction) had virtually disappeared among high school seniors (Johnston, Bachman, and O'Malley 1982). Similar declines occurred among adults. In 1972, 4.6 percent of the young-adult population had used heroin at some time. By 1982 this figure was down to 1.2 percent (Miller et al. 1983).

Accompanying the general decline in drug use of all kinds that was documented in Chapter 3, use of opiates continued to decline or stabilize at a low level throughout the 1980s. By 1985 the annual prevalence of opiate use in the total U.S. population was down to 340,000 and use in the past month was 160,000. In the 1990 survey, current users of heroin were reported to be 48,000, although this number may be inaccurate because of unreliability of estimates in the over-25-year-old age group. In 1990, 1 percent of the surveyed high school seniors reported having ever used heroin and 8 percent reported some experience with other opiates. Of these heroin and opiate users, however, over two-thirds had used only one or two times. There was almost no current use of heroin, and only a tiny fraction of 1 percent of the seniors reported use frequent enough to sustain an addiction on heroin or other opiates. In the adolescent population age 12 to 17, the lifetime prevalence has remained less than 1 percent since 1979. There was a slight uptick in reported heroin use by adolescents in the 1990 survey, from less than 0.5 percent to 0.6 percent ever used, and a slight downturn to less than 0.5 percent for young adults, the first time that heroin use by adolescents has exceeded that by the young-adult group. Current and daily use of opiates among adults is a fraction of 1 percent (Johnston 1989; NIDA 1988a, 1990a).

Social Characteristics of Users and Addicts

Age and Sex.   Studies of opiate users in the latter part of the nineteenth century and the early part of the twentieth century found about two-thirds to be female and the average age of addicts to be between 40 and 50. In the

T A B L E   6 . 1   *Sociodemographic characteristics of heroin users*

| | Percent Ever Used | | | | |
| | Age Groups | | | | |
	12–17	18–25	26–34	35 +	Total
Sex					
Male	<0.5	1.6	3.6	1.0	1.6
Female	<0.5	0.7	1.5	<0.5	0.5
Race/Ethnicity					
White	<0.5	1.1	2.8	<0.5	1.0
Black	<0.5	1.5	1.6	1.6	1.4
Hispanic	<0.5	1.4	2.1	<0.5	0.8
Size of City of Residence					
Large urban	<0.5	2.2	2.4	<0.5	1.2
Smaller urban	<0.5	0.6	2.7	1.0	1.1
Nonurban	<0.5	1.3	2.4	<0.5	0.8
Region of Residence					
Northeast	<0.5	1.1	2.3	0.8	1.1
North central	<0.5	0.7	2.4	0.7	1.0
South	0.7	1.8	2.9	<0.5	1.1
West	<0.5	.8	2.6	<0.5	0.8
Education					
Less than HS	NA	3.8	3.1	<0.5	1.1
HS graduate	NA	0.9	2.1	<0.5	0.9
Some college	NA	<0.5	4.4	<0.5	1.4
College grad	NA	<0.5	1.3	1.2	1.1
Current Employment					
Full-time	NA	0.7	2.2	1.0	1.2
Part-time	NA	1.5	3.9	<0.5	1.0
Unemployed	NA	1.6	1.6	<0.5	2.3
Other	NA	1.6	1.6	<0.5	0.5

Source: NIDA 1988a. (Because of unreliability of estimates for young adults in the 1988 survey, figures in the table are from the 1985 survey. See Chapter 3 for overall estimates from 1988 and 1990.)

decades since, sex ratio among addicts has reversed (about 85 percent of addicts are now men), and the average age of addicts has dropped down to the mid-20s. Rates of opiate use and addiction remain highest in the young-adult group (particularly men), although the difference between younger and older adults narrowed to the point in the late 1980s that the rates were virtually indistinguishable (NIDA 1989a). Table 6.1 shows that the male lifetime prevalence of heroin use is about twice the female prevalence rate.

Residence, Class, and Race.   Although Table 6.1 shows that lifetime prevalences do not differ much by size of city or region of the country, opiate addicts are concentrated in large cities (it is estimated that about half of all addicts in the United States live in New York City).

The proportion of blacks in the known population of addicts admitted for treatment reached about 30 percent, and by the 1970s about 40 percent of those admitted to hospitals or other drug-treatment programs were black. It was estimated that an even higher portion of the untreated cases were black. Addiction was concentrated in the slums among Hispanics and blacks and among those on the bottom of the socioeconomic scales of education, employment, and income. But a combination of some increase among whites and declines among minorities in the 1970s reduced the difference in opiate addiction by race (Chambers 1974; Inciardi 1974; Boyle and Brunswick 1980).

Heroin addicts in treatment and methadone maintenance programs continue to be disproportionately male and black or Hispanic (Johnson et al. 1985; Covington 1986). However, as shown in Table 6.1, the overall rate of use among whites was only slightly less than the rate for blacks and was slightly higher than the rate for Hispanics; by 1988 the Hispanic rate was slightly higher than the white rate (NIDA 1990b; table not shown). The connection between college and drugs established in the 1970s is still reflected in the lifetime prevalence for older adults. But among young adults, heroin use is inversely related to educational and employment status.

SOCIAL LEARNING IN HEROIN USE, ADDICTION, AND RELAPSE

Heroin use and addiction are now at the lowest levels in decades. The heroin drug problem has been overshadowed in the headlines of the 1980s by cocaine, crack, ice, and other drugs. Synthetic opiates have been designed that are more potent than heroin. Heroin has not received the research attention that it previously commanded, and cocaine is widely viewed as a more serious threat for abuse. The size of the illegal cocaine trade is larger than the heroin black market. Yet, heroin remains the paradigm drug against which all other drugs are compared. It is the quintessential addictive drug and the first choice of opiate addicts. Understanding the process whereby one begins heroin use, becomes addicted, gets off the drug, and relapses to use will be instructive for understanding use of other drugs.

In Chapter 5, marijuana use was analyzed from a social learning perspective to portray a general process of substance use and habituation that is applicable to all drugs. That process includes mainly differential associations, modeling, definition, and differential reinforcement. But other mechanisms of learning or conditioning are involved beyond the operant conditioning of differential reinforcement. Specifically, respondent (or classical) conditioning, discriminative stimuli, and schedules of reinforcement may be seen in the process of drug use.

Heroin use fits into this general social psychological process, especially preaddictive use of heroin. But since heroin habituation involves physical dependence, additional processes of physiological withdrawal and negative reinforcement are present that are not involved with marijuana and other drugs for which physical dependence does not develop. The use of drugs that produce physical dependence have a much sharper demarcation between initial, addictive, and relapse phases of drug behavior. In this chapter, the social learning model is extended to heroin use, addiction, and relapse.

Initial and Preaddictive Use

Peers and Social Reinforcement of Use.   In the initiation of drug use, exposure to definitions favorable to drugs and differential association with other users who provide models and social reinforcement for use are critical. The slum areas of big cities in the United States are the principal locales for a distinct drug subculture, although it stretches beyond these areas. The drug subculture is a characteristic way of life revolving around drugs, with special attitudes and definitions of use addiction and a drug-oriented jargon sustained by a concentration of drug addicts, users, dealers, suppliers, and others involved in drug-related business and crimes (Finestone 1964; Sutter 1970; Johnson et al. 1985; Mieczkowski 1986). This does not mean that a majority of people in these areas will become addicts, users, or even tolerant of drugs. Even in neighborhoods with a high density of users, addicts, and dealers, only a minority are heavily involved in the drug subculture (Johnson et al. 1985). But there are enough that the adolescent growing up in such an environment is likely to be directly exposed to hard drugs. It is in proximity to this subculture that there is heightened exposure to heroin use (as well as to cocaine and other serious drug use). Addicts are visible on the streets, drugs are traded and dealt openly on the streets, and it takes little to know where drugs can be obtained. These neighborhoods provide a receptive climate for initiation of drug use and sustain a specifically drug-oriented subculture that is tolerant of drugs and provides social reinforcers such as approval, recognition, and prestige for experimentation. Of course, as we saw in the previous chapter, one does not have to be familiar with this drug subculture to be exposed to drugs. There are other "social worlds" of a more conventional nature in which youth are introduced to drugs (Glassner and Loughlin 1987).

Just as is true for other drugs, first use of heroin is not usually pushed aggressively on a person by proselytizing friends or pushers giving away free samples to recruit more customers. Rather, introduction most often occurs in intimate group settings with friends and acquaintances who support experimentation with drugs, offer legitimizing definitions of use, and make drugs available, but who seldom apply direct pressure to try them. It nearly always takes place in the company of peers on the street, a rooftop, at a dance or party, in a car, or at school. This first experience is typically not planned, and the presence in the group was not only for the sake of trying the drug. Rather, the opportunity arises in this context and there is the chance to try something new and the anticipation of social rewards of gaining acceptance, identification, or status in the group.

> Heroin use started in an unsupervised street setting, while the subjects were still teenagers. The youthful initiate usually had smoked marijuana with neighbourhood friends before using opiates. In the case of both marijuana smoking and heroin use the adolescent peer-group exercised a dominant influence. (Ball 1967:412)
>
> In all, 90 percent say the event [first drug use] was neither planned nor expected. . . . Rather than being sources of pressure, peers were far more often described as legitimators of the activity and suppliers. . . . Experienced users were usually present when the subjects first tried marijuana, and . . . they provide both marijuana and approval. . . . There is no single type of gathering within which first drug use occurs—such as a party, clandestine meeting, or initiation rite. . . . The reports taken together suggest the importance of the right mix of curiosity, availability of the substance, and friends who are engaging in the same activity. . . . These same elements are present as well in reports of the first time subjects use "harder" drugs. Most such events are unplanned and viewed as ordinary with about three-quarters occurring with friends and most of the remaining with family. The drugs are available as part of a social context. First use of these drugs is seldom for instrumental reasons like self-medication or escape, but instead is recreational. The heavy users typically try these drugs, when the substances are offered during a gathering in which their use seems appropriate and natural. (Glassner and Loughlin 1987:160–163)

Thus, these peer and friendship groups make drugs available and provide social reinforcement for learning the techniques and definitions of drug taking, first marijuana and other drugs, and then later for initial and subsequent use of heroin. Preaddiction use of opiates and other drugs, then, tends to be recreational and supported primarily by positive social reinforcement.

> We was sitting around with friends of ours. We all grew up together and they were into it [heroin] before we were. We wanted to know what kind of feeling that was, the way we watched them high. And they looked like they felt so good. So I stayed for a while and tried it.
>
> Using heroin in those days was a fad. You wasn't cool unless you used it and, you know, you want to be like your big brother, gang fightin'.

You want to be hip, and you wasn't in the crowd unless you were getting high. (in Beschner and Bovelle 1985:77–78)

Definitions Favorable to Use.   The probability that the person will try heroin (or other opiates) and continue to use it is also increased by definitions favorable to drug use. Many who are exposed to deviant subcultures define drugs in positive terms from the beginning or are exposed to drug-tolerant attitudes. In these cases, there are few moral obstacles to overcome, just as most people encounter few negative attitudes in trying soft drinks or alcohol the first time. These activities may have been defined as desirable themselves or as ways of gaining acceptance from others. Most, however, are aware of negative connotations of drug use.

Even in the drug subculture, initiates learn both positive and negative definitions of drugs. They may initially be morally neutral, may be ignorant of the probable consequences of drug use, or may give it little thought, but they are likely to be familiar with favorable definitions of recreational drug use and notions that one can get good feelings from drugs. However, even in a tolerant subculture, persons are also familiar with definitions of drug use as illegal, dangerous, or stupid. They may have firsthand acquaintance in their families or neighborhoods of the tyranny the drug can have over the addict and the negative consequences of use. Family, clergy, and neighbors warned them of the dangers. They believe that drugs are bad for one's health, are costly, and force one to do immoral or illegal acts. Those who define drugs in this way and do not neutralize the definitions are unlikely to begin using heroin. Those who are relatively isolated from these definitions are more likely to initiate drug use (Chein et al. 1964; Hanson et al. 1985).

Perhaps the most prevalent negative definition of this type is that although controlled drug use is all right, it is bad to get a habit or become "strung out" on drugs. Even in a subculture receptive to experimentation with drugs, addiction is frowned upon. Fear of addiction is one of the most potent deterrents to trying some drugs (Glassner and Loughlin 1987). Although certain categories of heavy heroin use and addiction may have prestige in the slum street world and experimentation with a range of drugs may be supported, addiction itself is seen as a sign of weakness. This type of prohibitive definition can be neutralized by rationalizing that one can control drug intake at the occasional, recreational stage without getting hooked. No one begins heroin use with the specific intent of becoming an addict. But the common rationalization among beginning users is that "it won't happen to me," and many are surprised when they become addicted.

Not all opiate addicts begin with exposure to a drug subculture or in interaction with other users as youths, exposed to positive definitions and social reinforcement for initiation. Some are first exposed to opiates as medical patients. Availability, administration, and definition of the drug ingestion as acceptable are all taken care of in this medical context. Some patients move from this nondeviant use to securing opiates after the medical purposes are no longer present. Some are administered opiates long enough to develop tolerance and dependence but few go on to become addicted. Those who do may later become participants in the addict subculture, but initially they become users without contact with the urban drug subculture or with a youth subculture.

Another nonsubcultural path to opiates is taken by physicians. The problem of opiate and other drug use among physicians and others in the health profession was discussed in Chapter 4. Contrasted with the average street addict, who is a young, unmarried slum dweller addicted to heroin who started drug use at a young age, the typical physician addict is older, started the habit later, and uses Demerol, Dolophine, or morphine (Modlin and Montes 1964; Winick 1964; Moore and Lewis 1989). They know only indirectly of the addict subculture and are not introduced to drugs through early association with heroin addicts. Availability for health practitioners is provided through the occupation. They may not freely expropriate opiates for their own use, but there are fairly safe ways of getting drugs. Congruent with availability, physicians do not become addicted to heroin to which they have no legal access but to morphine, Demerol, or other prescription narcotics. Physicians learn about the analgesic effects of opiates and how properly to administer them as part of their professional education. Similarly, nurses, pharmacists, dentists, and other professionals who prescribe or dispense drugs are at risk of addiction.

Physicians also know from their training that opiates are addicting, and they share the public view of the addict as a deviant. They have moral objections to illicit drug use and negatively define nonmedical use of opiates. Therefore, in the process of coming to use drugs physicians must apply a set of neutralizing definitions—verbalizations consonant with drug use. Each does not dream up a new definition; rather, they apply a set they have learned from the conventional culture and from their specialized training: Drug use is all right if it is for medication. They come to view their drug use as self-medication. The usual justification given by physician addicts for beginning to use drugs is the need to take drugs to enable them to continue providing medical care under the handicap of overwork, chronic fatigue, various kinds of ailments, personal, and professional problems (Modlin and Montes 1964; Winick 1964). Also, physicians who start taking opiates, like the subcultural initiate, believe that they will not become addicted. Physicians' beliefs are based on their confidence in their knowledge of drugs and their ability to take drugs in a controlled way.

> Their professional familiarity with the effect of drugs appears to have provided a rationale for their semi-magical belief that the drugs would somehow have a different effect on them than they had on nonphysi-

cians. . . . The majority of these physicians believed that they were too smart to become "hooked." (Winick 1964:270)

Addicted physicians . . . [use] rationalization and justification of using the drugs or alcohol to allow them to continue functioning as professionals. This is generally said to be due to fatigue, chronic pain, or a variety of other somatic concerns. In actuality, this is a method they employ to prevent them from having to admit to themselves that they are addicted. (Moore and Lewis 1989:137)

The relief of the various complaints in a negative sense and whatever pleasure the drugs provide in a positive sense provide the anticipated and actual reinforcement for use; accompanied by these kinds of justifications, drugs provide the motivation for first and subsequent use long enough to develop tolerance and dependence. The self-medicating physician may then go on to become the self-fixing physician addict.

Reinforcing Effects of the Opiates.   Whether or not the first use and occasional use thereafter are defined as nonaddictive, the discriminative stimuli provided by the positive or neutralizing definitions and the social reinforcement from friends operate alone in determining whether one will try drugs the first time. After that first time, another important element enters the picture: *the reinforcing effects of the drug.* If initial drug effects are pleasant or desirable, it is likely that drug use will be positively reinforced. If the initial experience is aversive, it is not likely that the person will continue using the drug unless the effects can be reinterpreted or conditioned to become positive.

Not all drugs act as unconditioned reinforcers in animal studies, but opiates are one type of drug that easily act as reinforcers to establish and maintain a pattern of responses in most animals tested (Young and Herling 1986). In humans, heroin and other opiates are often reported to have a euphoric effect, producing a "high" or a "kick" on first administration, and the reinforcing effect of the "flash" should not be underestimated in establishing and maintaining heroin use. We have known since the earliest studies that experiencing a pleasurable sensation from opiates induces further use (Chein et al. 1964:154). However, Lindesmith (1968), among others, notes that first ingestion of opiates, far from creating anything that can be called euphoric, may produce very unpleasant effects such as nausea, anxiety, and dizziness. The addict learns to enjoy these effects, but the uninitiated may not enjoy them at all. In one study, only about 10 percent of subjects naive to opiates liked what they felt when given morphine (Blum 1967:42). Two-thirds of the addicts in another study reported positive effects on first using heroin, but these positive effects were typically reported to be occurring after nausea and vomiting that also usually accompanied first use (Waldorf 1973:34–35). In another study, 84 percent of the heroin users reported feeling euphoric with the first use, even though 32 percent of them became nauseated with the first use (Beschner and Bovelle 1985).

The effects do not depend entirely on the intrinsic pharmacological properties of opiates; they also depend on the social setting in which the drugs are taken. Even with animals, the extent to which opiates are ingested in free-choice situations, differs depending on characteristics of the environment. Rats caged in more natural settings (dubbed the "rat park" by the researchers) are much less likely to take and increase consumption of opiates than are rats placed in the more traditional isolated, constrained-movement cages (Peele 1985). Other research on animals has shown that

> the statement that a drug serves as a reinforcer says at least as much about the conditions of its availability as about its pharmacological nature. This is not to argue that different drugs do not vary in their potential to act as reinforcers or punishers under various conditions. Rather, the ability to serve as reinforcer or punisher is not an inherent property of a drug but the result of the drug's interactions with the environmental and physiological conditions under which an organism encounters it. (Young and Herling 1986:43–44)

The probability that one will experience uplift, euphoria, kick, buoyancy, or other positively reinforcing outcomes is increased if he or she has learned to expect such results. The first few times, the drugs are usually used in the company of supportive others who encourage the users and enhance the pleasure. Even if the intrinsic drug effects are aversive, one can be conditioned to enjoy them. We have long known that when an unpleasant consequence is presented as necessary for reinforcement, it may become a discriminative stimulus, signaling that reinforcement is just ahead, or become a conditioned reinforcer itself (Ayllon and Azrin 1966). The initially unpleasant or neutral effects can become redefined as desirable attributes of the drug by pairing them with the social approval, attention, and recognition of significant others. If this conditioning does not take place, taking the drug will continue to be punishing and use will cease. Both respondent and operant conditioning are involved (Goudie and Demellweek 1986).

In initial and preaddiction use, the rewards of new experience and the social rewards from other users combine with the reinforcing effects of the opiate itself. This offsets the punishing consequences associated with opiate use. Whatever the source of reinforcement, initial and continued use in this early stage is sustained largely by *positive reinforcement*. People use drugs to gain recognition, approval, and acceptance into a peer group. They learn by imitation and direct tutelage the proper method of taking drugs and how to recognize the desirable effects. They come to enjoy the effects of the drug itself. They may continue this usage pattern for some time, using only occasionally. The odds are against such an outcome, however. The positive reinforcement of this stage will probably sustain use long enough for the individual to develop physical tolerance and dependence. Once this happens, the stage is set for addiction, in which negative reinforcement is more important.

Of course, both positive and negative reinforcement are involved at all stages. People may initially use heroin to avoid the disapproval of their peers as well as to gain their approval, or they may use drugs as a nonadaptive avoidance of personal problems. As they become addicted, they become more and more incorporated into the hard-core addict subculture; eventually almost all of their associates are other addicts, dealers, and suppliers. The mutually reinforcing reactions of associating with other addicts and the positive effects the drugs continue to have are combined with the negative contingencies in the maintenance of the habit. But in general, trying drugs initially and the early stages of use are more a function of the positive consequences of such behavior, whereas addiction is sustained more through negative reinforcement.

Opiate Addiction

Conditioning and Negative Reinforcement. Some opiate users have developed regular patterns of taking heroin or other opiates over a long period while managing to control consumption enough to remain free from physical dependence (Zinberg 1979; Blackwell 1983). This is difficult to do, however, and no one knows how many have actually accomplished it. Ingesting opiates long enough (sometimes within one month) will produce physiological dependence, and the person will suffer withdrawal pains without the drug. These withdrawal symptoms are intrinsic to the effects of withholding opiates and conditioned responses.

> Most of what are traditionally regarded as signs of opioid withdrawal are unconditional respondent behaviors that can be said to be elicited by the discontinuation of agonist administration. . . . However, many interesting behavioral aspects of drug addiction involve conditional respondent and operant behavior. (Katz and Valentino 1986)

Although physical dependence, with the characteristic withdrawal sickness, is necessary, it is not sufficient for one to begin and sustain addictive use—habitual, daily (or nearly daily) ingestion over time. In the late 1930s, Alfred Lindesmith proposed the classic theory of opiate addiction. One must first undergo a withdrawal experience, learn to associate the distress with abstinence from the drug, and then take an *active* part in the alleviation of the distress by taking more opiates. Thereafter, habitual use is sustained by taking the drug to avoid the distress of withdrawal. Anyone who gets to this point is hooked, will crave the drug, and will continue regular use of opiates (Lindesmith 1938, 1968, 1980).

Addiction occurs only when opiates are used to alleviate withdrawal distress, after this distress has been properly understood or interpreted. . . . If the individual fails to conceive of his distress as withdrawal distress brought about by the absence of opiates, he does not become addicted, but if he does [form this conception] addiction is quickly and permanently established through further use of the drug. (Lindesmith 1968:191)

Patients can be given doses long enough to cause dependency, but they can experience withdrawal without connecting it to lack of the drug. Therefore, they do not take more opiates to alleviate the distress and do not become addicted. The physiological dependence is the same whether a person is the passive recipient of drugs as a patient or takes drugs on his or her own. But the distinction between *passive* and *active* participation in alleviation of withdrawal once dependence has developed is crucial for addiction. This central notion in Lindesmith's theory is consistent with learning principles. If a person does nothing—is the passive recipient of distress-alleviating drugs— then the outcome, reduction of an aversive condition, is not contingent on his or her behavior and the behavior will not be reinforced. On the other hand, if the person engages in the voluntary behavior of self-ingestion, he or she has done something that is capable of being reinforced by the outcome it brings about. And each time the person's actions have this outcome, the response is strengthened further. Laboratory studies of experimental addiction of rats, monkeys, and other animals confirm Lindesmith's central contention based on interviewing addicts.

In the classic series of animal experiments, John Nichols produced physiological dependence to morphine in rats by injecting them with the drug. He then split the rats into experimental and control groups, and the drugs were stopped to allow withdrawal to set in. Withdrawal in the control group was alleviated by further injections, whereas the rats in the experimental group were allowed to drink a morphine–water solution to alleviate their own withdrawal symptoms. The amount of morphine was the same, but the control group passively received relief, and the animals in the experimental group actively effected their own relief of withdrawal distress. When the drugs were stopped again and withdrawal set in, both groups were given the opportunity to drink either plain water or the morphine–water solution. The rats that had been taking morphine themselves chose the morphine–water solution and voluntarily increased intake. Those that had been injected all along chose the plain water even though they were undergoing the same withdrawal symptoms as the other rats were (Nichols and Davis 1959; Nichols 1965).

These experiments demonstrated that addiction is behavior learned through a process of *negative reinforcement* wherein behavior is sustained by removal or reduction of some aversive stimulus. Other early studies by

James Weeks (1964) lent further clarification. Weeks set up a voluntary self-injection routine for rats in which he had produced dependence on opiates. Then he manipulated amounts and schedules of reinforcement. When he increased the number of responses (bar pressing) needed for one injection, the animals compensated with higher response rates. The animals rapidly pressed the bar the required number of times until the injection of morphine was delivered, and then they stopped responding "until time for another shot."

Since these pioneering studies, research on drug addiction with animal models has continued. Apparatus which allow the experimental animals to inject themselves have been improved, a greater variety of drugs have been tested, and sophisticated procedures have been developed. Further ways in which addiction can be explained by learning principles have been demonstrated, but the basic findings from the first studies have been confirmed (Goldberg and Stolerman 1986).

The pattern found in the animal studies of opiate addiction in which there is a high level of response followed by a period of quietude after the injections is analogous to the behavior of subcultural addicts who are daily "taking care of business" (Johnson et al. 1985). They often have to do quite a lot to obtain drugs—secure money, perhaps through stealing; locate their connection or supply for the day; get their equipment; prepare their heroin by cooking it with water in a spoon or bottle cap; get the heroin properly strained into the syringe; and so on. All of this may be done just before or while they are sick. Subcultural addicts sometimes appear to be engaged in a continuous, almost frantic, search for a fix; they will do whatever is necessary as many times as needed to get their drugs, after which their activity levels are reduced until the approach of the time for the next shot. Street addicts have been conditioned on this kind of low-probability intermittent schedule of reinforcement. The addict with a reliable supply, such as the physician addict, is on a high-probability schedule and does not evince the frantic response pattern of the street addict.

One way addiction in humans differs from that in animals is that animal addiction appears to be more strictly *escape* behavior (removing an already aversive condition), whereas humans are capable of *avoidance* (anticipating and therefore avoiding or delaying the onset of aversive conditions). The extent to which human addicts can plan ahead for their drug needs is, of course, subject to the reliability of their supply, but if possible they do secure drugs ahead of time and take shots before the withdrawal sickness begins.

Combination of Positive and Negative Reinforcement. McAuliffe and Gordon (1974, 1980) question this explanation of the general process of addiction, which gives more weight to the negative reinforcement of avoiding or escaping withdrawal symptoms than to positive effects of the opiate and the social rewards of use. McAuliffe and Gordon's survey of sixty male and four female addicts in Baltimore led them to conclude that even for chronic addicts, "desire for euphoria appears to be a major factor in the explanation of their behavior" (McAuliffe and Gordon 1974:797). They include in the concept of euphoria both the initial "impact effect" of the flash or rush when the opiates are injected and the "continuing impact" of the prolonged sense of contentment as the drug spreads through the addict's system. "Weekenders" experience the euphoria less frequently than do the hard-core addicts who seek opiate euphoria every day.

McAuliffe and Gordon report that almost all addicts report getting high some of the time, and four out of ten do so at least once a day. Moreover, the frequency with which euphoric effects are reported increased with larger dosages when the amount of opiate was more than needed to make the addict feel normal. Nine out of ten of the addicts expressed a desire to get high at least once a day. All used more drugs than needed to avoid withdrawal sickness. The average "deluxe ratio" used was two and one-half times as much opiate as needed to avoid withdrawal sickness. For both weekenders and hard-core addicts, getting high was given as a more important reason for taking drugs than was security from the pains of withdrawal.

> Addicts *need* a drug that prevents withdrawal sickness, but they *crave* a drug that makes them high . . . . A combination-of-effects explanation appears to summarize the data better than one based on withdrawal alone. . . . According to our theory, . . . addiction starts to gain strength at the very beginning of opiate use and continues to grow incrementally with each of the many positive reinforcements experienced during the "honeymoon" period. With the onset of physical dependence, euphoria and withdrawal sickness combine in various proportions to yield a complex schedule of reinforcement for the typical long-term addict. (McAuliffe and Gordon 1974:811, 812, 829; emphasis in original)

McAuliffe and Gordon incorrectly include social learning theory as an approach that is based on "withdrawal alone." In fact, it is a little difficult to see how this "combination-of-effects" and complex schedule of reinforcement theory presented by McAuliffe and Gordon differs much from the learning theory just presented here. Learning theory does not rely only on withdrawal sickness as the explanation of heroin addiction; it hypothesizes a combination of effects. Both theories claim that both positive and negative reinforcement are important in addiction; both recognize euphoria and withdrawal sickness, propose the primacy of positive reinforcement in the early stages, share a behavioral emphasis, and have other features in common. But McAuliffe and Gordon seem to place more emphasis on intermittent positive reinforcement from the pleasurable effects of the drug as the basic process sustaining addiction even after physical dependence has been established, with negative reinforcement from withdrawal playing no role or a decidedly secondary role. Their findings seem to support that position. The levels of dosage taken above that needed to alleviate or avoid the pain of withdrawal are high enough to argue that euphoria is prominent in continuing addiction. But do their findings show that the positive euphoric effects are more important than the avoidance of withdrawal distress in sustaining addiction? In my judgment, the answer is no. There are findings in McAuliffe and Gordon's own research that cast doubt on the proposition that euphoric effects are the main reason addicts continue to take opiates.

Questions remain to be answered before the relative importance of positive and negative reinforcement processes in addiction can be more accurately determined. First, even among participants in a subculture that extols the heroin high, as studied in the McAuliffe, and Gordon research, when given a choice, less than half of their subjects would choose a drug *for euphoria only*, rather than one which would keep them from being sick all day. Second, only one of the addicts in their study reported getting high each time he injected heroin, and over half the addicts in the study reported getting high less than fifteen out of the past thirty days. Third, the researchers did not ask the addicts how often they used opiates to feel better or keep from getting sick compared to how often they took them just to get high. Fourth, the question of whether euphoria is experienced relatively more or less frequently after addiction than during the preaddiction phase is not addressed in the McAuliffe and Gordon research. Fifth, they did not ask the question, Would use of drugs continue even if there were no pleasure from them but if their discontinuance were to cause sickness? One would need to have answers to these questions in order to sort out better the relative importance of alleviating withdrawal and producing euphoria in the motivation to continue taking opiates.

More recent research suggests that addicts do, indeed, continue to take opiates to alleviate withdrawal pains even when no euphoria is present and that euphoria is experienced less frequently after addiction than it was in the preaddiction phase of use. Addicts do attempt to recapture the first-time high. Continuing to take heroin may produce positive sensations for addicts. But the first-time high is seldom achieved, and the main effect of heroin on addicts seems to be one of producing a normal state of feeling and relaxation (Beschner and Bovelle 1985). According to O'Brien and colleagues (1986), positive and negative reinforcement are involved in a different mix at different stages of drug use. In the initial phase, "incentive motivation" (positive reinforcement) is the more important. In the early stages of addiction, daily use may alternate with self-detoxification and incentive motivation is still important. In later stages of addiction, the addict becomes more and more concerned about withdrawal, and there is a corresponding lessening of the importance of incentive motivation. If the addict enters a methadone maintenance program so that the fear of withdrawal is reduced, seeking out heroin is motivated by the desire to regain euphoria.

As the addictive phase progresses, the patients report fewer highs and they report becoming more concerned with avoiding "sickness." . . . They report planning their whole day around the acquisition of heroin, beginning with that first shot in the morning. When they are short of money or unable to obtain drugs, they resort to diazepam or other sedatives to diminish opioid withdrawal symptoms. If they are asked why they use heroin, they often still say, "to get high." But if they are asked *when was the last time they actually became high after an injection, it may have been months or years in the past.* (O'Brien, Ehrman, and Ternes 1986:333; emphasis added)

Relapse to Opiates

An outstanding feature of opiate addiction is the frequency with which those who successfully withdraw from dependence on the drug start all over and become readdicted. The rate of relapse to opiates should not be exaggerated, however. The belief that addicts are almost never really "cured" is erroneous; addicts are not inevitably consigned to a lifetime of dependence on the drug. Most addicts do manage to get off and stay off the drug for periods of time and eventually accomplish complete abstinence for the rest of their lives, even after a long period of addiction (Winick 1965). Many addicts stop using and recover from addiction entirely on their own without relapsing (Waldorf 1983; Biernacki 1986), and self-management techniques can be taught as an effective way of preventing relapse (Marlatt and Gordon 1985).

The research on relapse to opiates presents a mixed picture, with varying rates of relapse found, from a low of 8 percent to a high of nearly 90 percent relapse, depending on the population studied. The extent to which one finds a high rate of relapse also depends on the criterion by which the addict is judged to relapse. If the criterion is any relapse of any duration after withdrawal, the rate is higher; if the criterion is the total amount of time addicted compared with the amount of time abstinent during some follow-up period, the rate is lower. For instance, one of the earliest studies of relapse found that although 73 percent of the men and 62 percent of the women relapsed to opiate use at least once after release from treatment, 38 percent and 79 percent, respectively, were completely abstinent some of the time during the same period (O'Donnell 1964:954).

A study of returning Vietnam War veterans found that 20 percent considered themselves addicted (almost all smoked or sniffed opium rather than injected heroin), and 11 percent had used opiates in the twenty-four hours prior to their discharge. After return to civilian life in the United States, less than 10 percent continued to use narcotics of some kind, and only one in three of those using drugs at the time of discharge continued to be addicted to opiates (Robins 1973). Even among those who continued to use in the first ten months after returning, only 7 percent were addicted after two to three years (although 62 percent were still using drugs). Among the veterans in the study, only 0.1 percent were addicted prior to their Vietnam service; 19.5 percent became addicted while in Vietnam, but two to three years after discharge the proportion still addicted was only 1.8 percent. The number of men in this cohort who were addicted after Vietnam was eighteen times greater than before Vietnam service, but this much greater number represented only one-tenth of those who had been addicted in Vietnam (Helzer 1985).

Nevertheless, the evidence is clear that the risk of returning to opiates after withdrawal is high, especially for the street addict. The drug user may fall into a cycle of addiction, abstinence, relapse, and readdiction. Addicts may be forced to undergo withdrawal in a jail or gradual withdrawal under treatment, and the same day they are released they will go back to mainlining; in fact, they may have had a supply of drugs cached for that very purpose. Some voluntarily commit themselves to a treatment program to "dry up" or "get resistance down" only in order to have a brief return to the high enjoyed before they became addicted or to reduce their habit back down to a level they can financially support.

This problem of relapse is perhaps the most difficult part of opiate-taking behavior to explain. Why, after they no longer need to avoid withdrawal distress and after they have experienced firsthand the problems of being addicts, do they relapse? One can understand how people who have never been addicted can proceed into it; they have not yet learned what addiction can mean. One can also understand that addiction can be sustained because addicts, however much they want to stop, are kept going on the drug by the need to avoid the pain of withdrawal. But why, after they no longer need the drug to get away from this and after they have experienced what addiction can do, do they so often go back to it?

Former addicts may go back to the same or similar circumstances in which they started using opiates in the first place, and they may simply repeat the process in relapse that they underwent in initial use. But this is not all; it is clear that the experience of addiction itself conditions individuals to be even more receptive to opiates than they were before that experience. Just what it is about the experience that produces the increased receptivity is not entirely clear. However, there seems to be some agreement in the literature that aspects of the environment and behavior while addicted become conditioned stimuli in connection with both the euphoric drug effects and the withdrawal symptoms and that these can trigger relapse even after physiological dependence is gone (Biernacki 1986; O'Brien 1986; Siegel, Krank, and Hinson 1988). Experimental, clinical, and epidemiological evidence show that environmental cues can elicit withdrawal behavior and craving for the drug long after detoxification. Relapse is most pronounced when the "environment of readdiction is most similar to the environment of original addiction"

(Siegel, Krank, and Hinson 1988:94). "Repeated pairings can bestow motivational properties on the environmental stimuli via instrumental and classical conditioning. This conditioning can then increase the probability of return to drug use" (O'Brien 1986:335).

The surrounding environment, situations, and circumstances when addicts experience symptoms of withdrawal until relieved by further injections can become discriminative stimuli that elicit feelings of withdrawal, even though these feelings have no physiological basis. Nonetheless, they induce addicts to take a shot. Similarly, environmental stimuli can be associated with the experience of a drug high and later induce the ex-addict to crave a recapturing of that euphoria. "Urges to use could be evoked in certain social settings or by stimuli—the sight of cotton, the smell of a kitchen match, or the rustle of a glassine bag" (Waldorf 1983:270).

About half of the methadone patients in one study (O'Brien 1986) reported feeling withdrawal symptoms for no apparent reason in response to items on a list of drug-related stimuli (e.g., seeing a bag of heroin, a person shooting heroin, or a movie about a junkie or being in the old neighborhood). One patient remained drug-free without withdrawal symptoms for three weeks while visiting in California, but when he arrived back in his old neighborhood in Philadelphia, he experienced withdrawal feelings. A range of conditioned environmental stimuli can elicit craving or withdrawal-like feelings, but

> most involve seeing people using drugs, seeing drugs, and possessing the money to buy drugs. . . . Most stimuli are found in the patient's neighborhood. However, some patients report that they felt illness or drug craving when watching movies or experiencing fantasies about drug use. Some of our patients even reported craving or illness when they viewed an antidrug poster in the hospital because it showed a person "shooting up." (O'Brien 1986:341)

As they avoid the pain of withdrawal by using drugs, addicts come to cope with other pains and deprivations by taking opiates. Hence, taking drugs becomes a general response to a range of problems; they can escape the unpleasantness of a disliked job, interpersonal problems, the negative reactions of others, failure to live up to expectations of achievement, and other difficulties. Drug taking can become conditioned as an escape adaptation to life's difficulties. Complete withdrawal from the drug cures addicts of the problem of withdrawal symptoms, but it does not cure whatever other problems they may have had while addicted. When they encounter such problems again, they are likely to respond in the manner to which they have become accustomed— taking a fix. Also, opiates not only relieve pain; ingesting an opiate drug can partially substitute for food and sex. Drug taking then may develop as the addict's main response to pain, hunger, or sexual deprivation. After withdrawal, ex-addicts still feel pain, get hungry, and feel sexual deprivation, and they may revert to their old habits of responding by taking opiates.

One of the most important elements added by the experience of addiction is an effect emphasized in labeling theory, namely the changed reactions of others to former addicts and the application of changed labels of their actions. One thing street addicts learn is "once a junkie, always a junkie." They return to their old associates and encounter the same labels. Other addicts continue to treat them as fellow addicts and expect them to take up drug use again. They are likely labeled addicts and criminals by the police. Their preaddiction friends and families have seen former attempts to abstain fail; they remain suspicious and do not accept the ex-addicts back as nonaddicts. They continue to react toward them as they acted when they were addicted, and they fail to reward attempts to remain drug-free, thus playing out a self-fulfilling prophecy (Ray 1964). Physician or middle-class addicts, on the other hand, in addition to having undergone withdrawal under more favorable conditions, probably return to a very different set of circumstances. They are more likely to be received by family and associates as having undergone a period of sickness and needing help in recuperation. Family and associates have been accustomed to interacting with the ex-addicts in terms other than their addiction, and they receive them back in much the same light.

That the probability of relapse is associated with differences in the social environment to which former addicts return is shown in one study in which all ex-addicts who were more involved in a subculture of criminal activities, occupationally unstable, and less educated relapsed within three years, whereas only about one-third of the steadily employed, better educated, and noncriminal did so (DeFleur, Ball, and Snarr 1969). In another study, 69 percent of those who managed to stay off drugs for at least three months "did not associate with other addicts or users" and 70 percent "were not treated like addicts by others" (Waldorf 1970:233).

Time is salient for relapse for two reasons. First, as we have seen, human addicts are likely to avoid rather than merely escape withdrawal symptoms. While addicted they often anticipate their need of another shot and take the drug regularly enough that they do not experience withdrawal for a long time. They become conditioned to respond in anticipation of the withdrawal distress, not actual drug absence. And even after they have withdrawn, when failure to take the drug will not result in an aversive outcome, they continue to behave as addicts. If they continue long enough to behave as addicts even after it is no longer necessary, it will, of course, become necessary again. Second, it should be remembered that initial drug use is in part a function of the positively reinforcing effects of the drug itself. The euphoric high comes in the beginning. It is not until later that the negative aspects become predominant. This period of time between initial drug use and the disruption of life concomitant with addiction is a fairly long one. Addicts who have taken the cure are essentially in the same position with regard to drug effects as novices are. They want to recapture the euphoria; if anything, they are more likely to enjoy initial drug effects, and these are right now, immediate. The problems, even though they are now familiar to them, lie in the more distant future. The longer the time lapse between a response and its consequence, the less control those consequences exert over behavior. The immediate, more pleasant outcomes of drug taking have greater impact on taking up use again than do the more distant, unpleasant outcomes, even if they are vividly remembered.

Cocaine

ARE COCAINE AND CRACK ADDICTIVE?

The answer to this question depends on the definition of addiction. If we accept the definition in Chapter 2 which requires that there be clear-cut evidence of physiological dependence on cocaine then the answer is no. If the definition requires only that the effects of cocaine positively reinforce "compulsive" or abusive use of cocaine, without physical withdrawal symptoms, then the answer is yes. At the overt behavioral level, it is difficult to distinguish cocaine abuse from heroin abuse or abuse of any other drug. For all practical purposes, it makes little difference to the person who uses cocaine in an abusive way, with psychological, personal, and social functioning grossly impaired, whether his "addiction" is physical, psychological, or both. He feels addicted and out of control regardless of the basis for that feeling. But by this definition all drugs are addictive, although not necessarily equally so, and qualitatively the term is meaningless.

In Chapter 2, we reviewed the general concept of addiction and how controversial it has become in labeling drug use. Recall that the traditional concept of addiction, based on physical dependence, has been largely moved aside for the newer uses of the term that have broadened it to include habitual use of any drug and a whole range of nondrug behavior. The newer concepts of addiction may be partly based on dissatisfaction with the precision of the traditional concept or the belief that it is too narrowly restricted to pharmacological properties. I believe that they have developed mainly because of unease about calling obviously destructive use of drugs nonaddictive and thereby seeming to be soft on drugs. Goode (1989a) argues that the concept of psychological dependence on drugs that do not produce physical dependence was developed by such organizations as the World Health Organization mainly for ideological purposes. He contends that the concept was introduced in order to broaden the range of drugs that could be brought under social control. This characterization may also apply to the newer definitions of addiction. No one wants to be seen as condoning drug abuse or downplaying the seriousness of the problem. To say a drug is not addictive is seemingly to say that it is all right to take it, it can be controlled, and one does not have to worry about going beyond recreational use. To call a drug addictive is to place oneself squarely in the camp of those condemning, rather than tolerating, drug use because it clearly labels the drug as powerful and harmful. It is a clear warning to the potential user. If it cannot be shown that a drug is addictive in the traditional sense, one can still show that the drug should be condemned as addictive simply by changing the meaning of the term.

The clearest example of this tendency to change the meaning of addiction is what happened in the 1980s in the redefinition of cocaine addiction. Although there were arguments by some federal authorities in the 1930s that cocaine was addictive just as heroin was, as recently as the mid-1980s few texts, authorities, researchers, or treatment agencies listed cocaine as addictive. It was believed to produce little tolerance and no physical dependence, and was viewed as primarily a recreational drug. As the public perception of cocaine (first cocaine hydrochloride and later crack cocaine) as "the" drug problem of the 1980s became solidified, however, the language of addiction became inextricably attached to cocaine use. Cocaine researchers, the popular media, governmental and law enforcement leaders, and others came increasingly to use the language of addiction when describing cocaine problems.

It quickly became, and remains in the 1990s, the conventional wisdom that cocaine is extremely addictive. Crack cocaine was defined as the most highly addictive form of all drugs. In fact, it is seldom simply called crack anymore. As noted in Chapter 2, in print and speech, it is nearly always "highly-addictive-crack" as if this were one word. Heroin, which at one time was considered the most addictive drug, became redefined as only mildly addictive compared to crack, and it was reported that "kicking crack is almost impossible" (Kolata 1988). The Partnership for a Drug-Free America and other anti-drug groups sponsored print and electronic media ads that described crack as the worst and most addictive drug ever known to humankind, and news stories reported that it could take up to nine months to get over the withdrawal from cocaine (Associated Press, Feb. 21, 1986). Television and news magazines ran public service ads which stated that "if anyone tells you cocaine is not addictive, they lie!" After that, who has the nerve to say it is not addictive?

The public, media, drug education and treatment programs, and others quickly incorporated, and still retain, in their thinking that cocaine in any form is highly physically addictive. It is taken for granted, as unequivocally demonstrated fact, that people who use cocaine will very quickly, if not instantaneously, become physically hooked on it. For instance, in its "Educational Newsletter on Addictions," the Florida Alcohol and Drug Abuse Association Clearinghouse (1989) unequivocally states:

COCAINE.
Dependence Potential: psychologically and *physically* addictive.

Crack is very addictive. Because it is smoked, high doses of cocaine reach the brain almost instantly causing a dramatic high. This rapid "high" is followed by a profound "low" that leaves the user craving more. As a result, *physical* and psychological addiction can occur in as little as two weeks.

Withdrawal Symptoms: People who stop using cocaine often experience irritability, nausea, agitation, sleep disorders, severe depression, muscle aches and an intense craving for the drug. (emphasis added)

Thus, for many public action groups, government agencies, and media reporters, the designation of cocaine as highly addictive is based on the belief that cocaine is physically addicting and produces severe physiological withdrawal sickness. But for many in the research community, the addictive terminology is used even though they find no evidence that physical dependence develops with cocaine use. This means that they must redefine addiction so that a drug can be called addictive even in the absence of physical dependence.

Animal Studies

A clear illustration of the unwillingness to designate cocaine as nonaddictive by leading researchers in the field is found in a volume by Spitz and Rosecan (1987) reporting the latest findings on cocaine treatment and research. Although they begin by saying that addiction is a complicated process of interaction between the individual, environment, and the drug, they "reconceptualize cocaine as a uniquely addicting drug, based on its neurochemical actions" (Spitz and Rosecan 1987:2). The chapter on animal research in the volume reports the by now well-known finding that rodents, primates, and other carnivores will continue to self-administer cocaine (as well as other drugs) at high frequency when freely available, even to the point of death (Geary 1987; see also Goldberg and Stolerman 1986). Nevertheless, it is clear from these same animal studies that research has yet to show that cocaine does produce physical dependence.

> Similarly, there is no evidence that self-administration was maintained by negative reinforcement. That is, animals do not appear to respond for cocaine administration in order to avoid some aversive consequence of cocaine abstinence. . . . Cocaine did not produce signs of physical dependence. . . . Drug-naive animals learned to self-administer at high rates before any dependence would have had time to develop. . . .
> Periods of abstinence, for example, usually began when the monkeys suffered states of exhaustion or seizures. Despite this degree of toxicity, monkeys did not become physically dependent on cocaine. If cocaine availability was withdrawn, they quickly returned to a normal healthy state. (Geary 1987:33–34)

In spite of these findings of no physical dependence or withdrawal syndrome, Geary labels the behavior of the monkeys as addiction to cocaine. Under the traditional concept, these findings show that cocaine is not addictive. It can be labeled as addictive only if one means something different by the term. But neither Spitz and Rosecan nor Geary say anything about the concept of addiction as physical dependence or how their concept of cocaine as uniquely addictive relates to the traditional concept of addiction. Rather, they simply assert that cocaine is addictive because of its "unparalleled rewarding potency" which renders cocaine even "less controllable than opiates" (Geary 1987:33–34). This is, of course, entirely different from what we have traditionally meant by addiction. The urge to describe cocaine as highly addictive, even though the evidence in the volume is that it is not addictive in the same way that opiates are, shows up elsewhere. For instance, the following statements can be found one page apart in the same chapter:

> Based on our early clinical experience, crack is the *most addicting form of our most addicting drug*, cocaine.
> Crack use per se is not an indication for inpatient treatment, since the cocaine withdrawal syndrome (lethargy, depression, overeating, cocaine craving) *does not require the medical interventions needed with alcohol or heroin withdrawal.* (Rosecan, Spitz, and Gross 1987:301–302; emphasis added)

In other words, crack will not cause withdrawal sickness, but it is still highly addictive. Similarly, Nunes and Klein (1987) find little evidence of permanent toxic effects of chronic use of cocaine and report research showing that half of those who use cocaine remain recreational users, 40 percent become mild habitual users, and 10 percent become heavy abusers smoking freebase. Nevertheless, they believe that cocaine is highly addictive because it is a "uniquely powerful reinforcer" (Nunes and Klein 1987:281). Washton

(1989) makes similar assertions about the addictive power of cocaine even in the absence of physical withdrawal symptoms. He takes the stand that since cocaine has physical effects on the brain, it is a physically addictive drug. Recognizing that all drugs have physical effects, he concludes that "all mood-altering drugs are physically addictive, even if abrupt discontinuation of use causes no physical withdrawal symptoms" (Washton 1989:37). Thus, cocaine is addictive because all drugs are addictive; all drugs become addictive simply by changing the definition of addiction.

Studies of Cocaine Use on the Streets

Ethnographic studies of crack use on the streets also report the intensity of the pleasurable effect from smoking crack. Strong positive reinforcement from the physical and psychological effects of the drug and feelings of craving and compulsion are consistently reported, but there are few reports of physical withdrawal sickness. Compulsive or obsessive behavior characterizes cocaine hydrochloride and crack use during drug-taking episodes, but most users manage to control use at least some of the time even during periods of heaviest use (Reinarman, Waldorf, and Murphy 1989).

> Treatment clinicians routinely claim, and the media routinely echo them, that crack is instantly addicting, and that once users get that first good hit they will stop at nothing to get another and another until their very lives are destroyed. Most of our crack cases suggest that this view is overly simple. Many of our freebasers and crack users experimented with this mode of ingestion for months without getting into a pattern that could be called seriously abusive or addictive. A few even continued to freebase or smoke crack on an occasional basis without letting the drug overtake their lives. Others quickly recognized the powerful lure of this mode of ingestion and simply walked away from it—*without experiencing physical withdrawal.* (Reinarman, Waldorf, and Murphy 1989:17; emphasis added)
>
> And, perhaps most telling, the majority described their obsession as *episodic* rather than chronic. Very few sat smoking their pipes all day, day after day; most used in a clearly compulsive manner *during a session,* but did not remold their lives into one long session. (Reinarman, Waldorf, and Murphy 1989:42; emphasis in original)

Many users who have gotten high on cocaine report experiencing "crashing" after the drug effects wear off and report craving more during these crashes. They may feel addicted. They may also show symptoms of coming down from a state of high stimulation, such as depression and anxiety, as well as other symptoms that accompany long-term use. But they are not the physical symptoms associated with withdrawal of such central nervous system depressants as barbiturates and heroin. In one study of 345 crack users in New York (Fagan and Chin 1989a), the vast majority of the users believed crack and cocaine were harmful and addictive; 40 percent reported being unable to stop taking crack. However, only 8 percent reported getting sick when they did stop. Similarly, while almost a third of cocaine HCL (powdered cocaine) users felt they could not stop, only 9 percent reported getting sick during the times when they did cease using for a while. There was no evidence in this study of instant addiction to crack; the lapse of time between first and second use was about the same for crack as for cocaine and heroin (about 17 to 19 days). Waldorf and associates (1988) found in a study of cessation of cocaine use that many ex-users had simply stopped taking cocaine on their own, without treatment, and with only minor discomfort. In a later study of ex-dealers in the San Francisco Bay Area, these same researchers found that many quit selling in order to stop or reduce their own cocaine use.

> For a small number this meant going to treatment for their cocaine abuse. By far the majority simply stopped or cut down on their usage without formal assistance. . . . In most instances sellers who quit using cocaine on their own suffered only minor withdrawal symptoms and if they experienced craving it was manageable. . . . Many in the sample were very heavy users of cocaine . . . but this heavy use did not seem to impede their ability to stop or control their usage. (Waldorf, Murphy, and Lauderback 1989:24)

Similarly, Shaffer and Jones (1989) report "natural recoverers" from heavy cocaine abuse who quit entirely on their own by tapering down or quitting cold turkey and managed to remain abstinent by taking steps to prevent or overcome relapses.

The replication of findings, from both animal and human studies, that cocaine does not produce physical dependence presents cocaine researchers with a dilemma. If the traditional technical concept of addiction is adhered to, one must conclude from the evidence that cocaine is nonaddicting. But to do so would appear somehow to be insufficiently alarmed about a drug as bad and as powerfully motivating as cocaine. The resolution many have come to is to declare that cocaine, especially crack, has to be addictive, even if one must renominate it as "uniquely" addictive or to broaden the concept of addiction so that cocaine abuse may be included. To say otherwise is to get on the wrong side of the issue.

Must Cocaine Be Addictive to Condemn It?

Opiate use also produces strong positive reinforcement (both physical and psychological) for repeating use, and there are psychological withdrawal symptoms. But in addition, it produces physical dependence so that when the drug is absent, clear-cut characteristic signs of physical sickness sets in. To call both opiate and cocaine habits addiction without distinction misses a key difference. Based on the preponderance of evidence thus far, I conclude that cocaine is not addictive in the traditional sense that its use produces physical dependence and its discontinuance causes withdrawal sickness. Future research may discover strong evidence of physical dependence with cocaine use (see the box "Effects of Cocaine on Neurons and Neurotransmitters"), but at this time, it can be described as addictive only if a new definition of addiction is adopted.

If cocaine is not physically addictive, does this mean that it is a safe drug, easier to quit than heroin? Of course not. It is not uniquely so, but cocaine is a powerful, for some users a lethal, drug. One may legitimately condemn cocaine on its own merits without being forced to label it addictive. It has a high potential for abuse. Users have been known to go to great lengths— give up friends, family, and fortune and do some despicable things—to get the drug. It is an awful, destructive drug for many who start using it. Concluding that it is not physically addictive is not the same as condoning it. There is a high risk of behavioral dependence, and one can become as absorbed in cocaine use as in heroin use. For the person deeply involved in cocaine abuse, finding it extremely difficult to quit using, the distinction may be irrelevant. For careful research, theory, and treatment it is not irrelevant.

SOCIAL PATTERNS AND TRENDS IN COCAINE USE

Historical Trends

Cocaine comes from the South American (Peruvian and Bolivian mainly) coca plant, the leaves of which traditionally have been chewed by Andean Mountain natives. Cocaine is leeched from coca leaves by soaking them in kerosene or other solvents. The resins are skimmed and dried into a cocaine paste. The final step is to refine the product into a white powder. Cocaine was introduced to European and American societies in the nineteenth century where its effects both as a local anesthetic in medical practice and as a mood-altering drug became well established. For a time it enjoyed a favorable reputation in medical and psychiatric circles (Sigmund Freud's advocacy of it was well known) as a beneficial drug for combating opiate addiction and as having other uses without adverse side effects. As mentioned in Chapter 2, until just after the turn of the century, cocaine was the stimulant ingredient in (and source of the trade name for) Coca-Cola and in over-the-counter medicines, preparations, and other drinks. Its virtues as a stimulant, "restorative," and medication for a wide range of illnesses and maladies were widely touted.

Effects of Cocaine on Neurons and Neurotransmitters

New evidence may change the conclusion that cocaine is not physiologically addictive by demonstrating that cocaine does induce physical dependence. We know from the current research that cocaine has dramatic neurochemical effects which we must assume play a significant role in strong habituation. Both animal studies and studies of human users show unequivocally that cocaine effects, especially when those effects can be produced very quickly by smoking crack, produce very intense pleasurable reactions which are strong reinforcers for continuing use. The evidence is clear that the subjectively experienced effects have a physical base. All drugs have physical effects (see Chapter 2) by directly producing changes in the neurons and neurotransmitters in the central nervous system. It may be that future research will reveal that these positive reinforcing effects sustain use over time such that cellular adaptation takes place establishing physical dependence and producing physical withdrawal symptoms.

At this point, the exact neurobiological actions of cocaine are not fully understood. There are a number of hypotheses related to effects on such neurohormones as norepinephrine and serotonin. According to Nunes and Rosecan (1987), however, the evidence most strongly supports the hypothesis that the effects come from changes in dopamine (DA) levels indued by cocaine.

Cocaine use began spreading in the United States in the late 1880s, a trend that did not peak until 1907. During that time, increased public and political concern about the dangers of cocaine, especially fear of "dope fiend" and "cocaine-crazed" black laborers in the South and criminals in the big cities, led to more and more legal regulation. Many states enacted anticocaine legislation, and cocaine was included as a narcotic along with heroin in the 1914 Harrison Act. The criminalization of cocaine possession for nonmedical purposes added to the trend of declining use that was already under way. Use continued to decline until the 1920s when cocaine spread as an illicit drug among the ghetto and lower-class drug subcultures, but by the 1930s use again was waning (Austin 1978).

Its use in black and lower-class urban neighborhoods following World War II was overshadowed by marijuana and heroin use. Marijuana, LSD, amphetamines, and other drugs were also of greater concern than cocaine in

According to this formulation, cocaine acutely enhances DA neurotransmission by blocking DA reuptake and increasing DA synthesis. This stimulatory effect on mesocortical and mesolimbic DA tracts results in the highly pleasant and rewarding cocaine euphoria. Repeated use rapidly leads to presynaptic DA depletion and postsynaptic DA receptor supersensitivity which results in tolerance, dysphoria, and craving. (Nunes and Rosecan 1987:86)

Nunes and Rosecan do not suggest that these actions result in physical dependence. It is possible, however, that in long-term use the increased number of DA receptors on the receiving end of the neurons and the depletion of neurotransmitters or similar neurological adaptations to cocaine are the kind that can produce physical dependence. As of now, however, no such evidence exists. The withdrawal from cocaine consists of lethargy, oversleeping, overeating, and craving for more cocaine. The stimulation, the high, is missed and dysphoria sets in. These appear to be psychological symptoms rather than the physical signs accompanying withdrawal from central nervous system depressants such as heroin (Rosecan and Spitz 1987). If it is found that cocaine use produces physiological dependence on cocaine, then cocaine habits would fit into the traditional concept of addiction. The point is that cocaine researchers have not declared cocaine to be highly addictive because they have discovered new evidence of physical dependence. Rather, it has been declared addictive *before* such evidence has been produced, by changing the definition of addiction to fit cocaine.

the drug epidemic of the 1960s and 1970s, which spread to all segments of the population.

Recent Trends: Images and Realities

Until the advent of crack in the 1980s, cocaine was the most expensive street drug per ounce, and effective use of powdered cocaine and its freebase required purchases of expensive quantities. Although its use continued in the black ghettos, its great cost restrained use in lower classes, and the locus of its consumption shifted out of the ghettos. Cocaine came into wider use in the 1970s among affluent groups, including middle-class youth and young adults, but especially among wealthy urbanites, professionals, executives, actors, entertainers, and professional athletes. Partly because it was expensive, its use and possession (as well as owning of scales, spoons, straws, and other paraphernalia) became status symbols in some of these groups. The severe problems that could accompany cocaine use and the fact that it had high potential for abuse were well known to researchers. Those problems began to be reported to the public in the 1970s. Nevertheless, cocaine acquired a reputation as a drug that could be used recreationally without much danger of abuse or addiction. Indeed, it was felt to be an energizer that boosted productivity and creativity (Block 1979; Grinspoon and Bakalar 1979; *Newsweek*, July 6, 1981; *Time*, Apr. 11, 1983).

By the mid-1980s, cocaine had publicly undergone a redefinition to become regarded as a very harmful drug. Freebasing—using volatile chemicals such as ether or ammonia and heat to reduce the cocaine to its base of concentrated active ingredients (without salts, solids, and impurities) that can be vaporized and inhaled—came along in the 1970s. This produces a stronger high than snorting powder does. As we saw in Chapter 3, cocaine became the most scary drug in the 1980s. Television, magazines, and newspapers were filled with horror stories of cocaine madness. The devastation of cocaine became a common, almost daily story in the media: deaths among athletes and celebrities (sometimes from even very small amounts); highly successful cocaine users who had lost family, homes, and jobs; lives and relationships destroyed by cocaine abuse; and impaired babies born to cocaine-using mothers. A national 1-800-Cocaine hot line was established in 1983 (operated by a for-profit drug abuse treatment hospital), and in 1986 the federal government, through the National Institute on Drug Abuse, established another hot line (1-800-662-HELP) to offer some help to cocaine abusers (Dequine 1985; Maranto 1985; *Los Angeles Times*, July 11, 1986; *Newsweek*, July 28, 1986; *Reader's Digest*, Jan. 1987:31–38).

The most dramatic change in the image of cocaine was produced by the explosion of crack cocaine on the scene in 1985–86. In the first reports, it was referred to as "rock" cocaine, but the term *crack* quickly became the accepted label (*Newsweek*, Feb. 11, 1985; Mar. 17, 1986; June 16, 1986; *Time*, June 2, 1986). Crack is produced by a newer and simpler technique of reducing the powdered cocaine down to a more easily smokable form. This system uses bicarbonate of soda and water and low heat to produce a freebase type of cocaine that is less pure but cheaper than the earlier method and is just as easily smoked. By the mid-1980s, crack had come largely to replace the ether method of freebase, and the distinction between the two types of smokable cocaine virtually disappeared (Reinarman, Waldorf, and Murphy 1989:5–6).

Crack has two major features that distinguish it from powdered cocaine. First, it can be sliced into tiny units that can be sold in small quantities at very cheap prices. This means that one is able to purchase enough to get high, at least for a short time, with $10 or less, and one can become a crack dealer with very little capital outlay. Youth and children can both better afford to use and become more involved in the trade—and they have done both. Second, because it is smoked, crack acts on the brain within seconds, much faster than does snorting powder, which must first be absorbed through the mucous membranes before getting into the bloodstream. The crack high, therefore, is experienced as much more intense, and since the effects do not last long, the euphoria is fleeting and there is motivation to smoke some more right away. Thus, there is a ready-made market for frequent purchases.

By the late 1980s, crack use was said to be so widespread throughout the population and so enslaving that it had produced a divided nation—one made up of normal humans with normal appetites and the other the "crack nation" made up of those with insatiable crack appetites (*Newsweek*, Nov. 28, 1988). Its use was reported as epidemic and devastating in the black community and among the poor, but also in middle America, in every segment of society and in every section of the country. Crack came to be viewed as much worse than powdered cocaine, more implicated in crime and murder, and more productive of all the problems of cocaine use. As mentioned in Chapter 3, it was reported to be the most highly addictive, most dangerous, most destructive drug ever known to humankind. By the end of the 1980s, there was little doubt that crack had become ensconced as *the* drug problem in America (*Newsweek*, Mar. 13, 1989; Apr. 3, 1989; Sept. 11, 1989; *Time*, Nov. 6, 1989).

> In 1986, American news media and politicians began an extraordinary anti-drug frenzy. . . . In 1987, the media and politicians focused much less attention on drugs. But in 1988, drugs returned to national attention as stories about "drug lords" and "crack epidemic" again regularly appeared on front pages and TV screens. . . .
>
> By mid-1986, *Newsweek* claimed that crack was the biggest story since Vietnam and Watergate. The words "plague," "epidemic," and "crisis" had become routine. In April 1988, an ABC News "Special Report" again termed crack "a plague" that was "eating away at the fabric of America." . . . In a scant 48 minutes of airtime, millions of viewers were told drugs, especially crack, were destroying virtually every institution in American life—jobs, schools, families, national sovereignty, community, law enforcement, and business. In 1988, just as in 1986, crack cocaine was defined as supremely evil—the most important cause of America's troubles. (Reinarman and Levine 1989:115–118)

There were conflicting stories in the popular press, however, about crack's status as the most addictive substance ever known, as news stories began to appear about crystalline methamphetamine, nominating it as even more potent and addictive than crack. Supposedly, "ice" or "crank" produces exactly the same effects as cocaine on the reuptake of dopamine and the receptor sites in the nerve cells, but with a stronger and more lasting punch (Miller 1989; Wilson 1989; *Newsweek*, Nov. 27, 1989; *Time*, Sept. 18, 1989).

T A B L E   7. 1   Trends in cocaine and crack use among high school seniors: 1981–1990

	1981	1985	1988	1990
Cocaine				
Ever used	16.5%	17.3%	12.1%	9.4%
Past year	12.4	13.1	7.9	5.3
Past month	5.8	6.7	3.4	1.9
Daily use	0.3	0.4	0.2	0.1
	1986[a]	1987	1988	1990
Crack				
Ever used	NA	5.6%	4.8%	3.5%
Past year	4.0%	4.1	3.1	1.9
Past month	NA	1.5	1.6	0.7
Daily use	NA	0.2	0.1	0.1

Sources: Johnston 1989; University of Michigan 1991.
[a]Estimated percentage; respondents who reported any cocaine use in past year were asked which technique of ingestion was used (smoking, snorting, oral ingestion, or injection); this is the percentage reporting smoking, assumed to be either freebase or crack.

In previous drug scares, the amount of public and political concern with the threat and spread of a particular drug typically has not coincided with actual behavioral trends, and the same has held true for the crack scare (Reinarman and Levine 1989). As we saw in Chapter 3, according to both the high school senior and national household surveys, cocaine use in the general population peaked in 1981–82. At the time of the greatest media attention to cocaine in the mid-1980s, it had been on a downward curve for some years and continued downward in the late 1980s.

Table 7.1 shows trends in cocaine and crack use in the annual surveys of high school seniors from 1981 to 1990. The real increases in cocaine use among high school seniors came in the last half of the 1970s when both lifetime and annual prevalence doubled. At the beginning of the 1980s, fewer seniors reported experimenting with cocaine. After a slight increase in 1985, cocaine use among seniors leveled off and dropped each year in the latter half of the 1980s. By 1990 lifetime (9.4 percent) and annual (5.3 percent) prevalence of cocaine use by seniors had dropped to about half of what it had been in 1985. Current and daily use declined to less than a third of what they had been in 1985. This occurred at the time the 1980s were being widely portrayed in the popular media as the decade of cocaine. Although there was an uptick in use in the mid-1980s, public perception at the time that overall cocaine use was dramatically increasing obviously was way off the mark.

T A B L E 7.2 *Trends in cocaine use by age group: 1979–1990*

	1979	1985	1988	1990
12–17				
Ever used	5.4%	4.9%	3.4%	2.6%
Past year	4.2	4.0	2.9	2.2
Past month	1.4	1.5	1.1	0.6
18–25				
Ever used	27.5	25.2	19.7	19.4
Past year	19.6	16.3	12.1	7.5
Past month	9.3	7.6	4.5	2.2
26 +				
Ever used	4.3	9.5	9.9	10.9
Past year	2.0	4.2	2.0	2.4
Past month	0.9	1.2	0.9	0.6

Sources: NIDA 1989a; 1990a.

There were also some signs in the mid-1980s that increasing proportions of users had begun to smoke cocaine rather than snort it. Crack cocaine was introduced at about this time, and the change can be taken as a sign of increased crack use. The media predictions that crack would sweep across the nation devouring our youth, however, were off by a long shot. No question regarding crack was specifically asked in the survey until 1987 when lifetime prevalence among high school seniors was reported as 5.6 percent, current use as 1.5 percent, and daily use as a fraction of 1 percent. By the next year, all indicators of use were down. They continued to decline so that by 1990 current (1.9 percent) and daily (0.1 percent) use of crack had essentially disappeared in this group of seniors.

The picture of moderating and declining consumption of cocaine among high school seniors is duplicated in the general population surveys shown in Table 7.2. Annual prevalence (used in the past year) and current use (used in the past month) among older adults, many of whom were adolescents and young adults in the high-use years of the late 1970s, increased through 1985, but since then they have declined. Youth and young adults were less likely to use cocaine in 1988 and 1990 than were the same age groups in 1985 and 1979. In 1985 it was estimated that 5.8 million persons 12 years of age (3 percent of the population) had illegally taken cocaine in the past month; by 1990 that figure had been cut to 1.6 million (0.7 percent). In 1990, 494,000, less than 0.2 percent of the 12-and-older population had used crack in the past month (NIDA 1990a).

Cocaine Abuse Continued to Increase for a While

The media scare was way off when depicting the scourge of cocaine and crack in the general population. But it would be a mistake to move too far in the other direction, concluding that the problem was never serious and has been largely solved. Even though the percentages presented in the tables are low, the numbers of people still snorting, injecting, and smoking cocaine in 1990 are daunting, if not staggering. Moreover, the image of a cocaine epidemic portrayed in the print and electronic media was close to the mark for some cities, in some areas of the country, and for some segments of the population. The overall favorable trends have masked enormous difficulties, increases, and problems in cocaine and crack abuse for significant portions of Americans.

The former Director of National Drug Control Policy, William Bennett, described the war on drugs as two-tiered in that great inroads have been made on casual or recreational drug use while battles are not being won against heavy abuse and the illegal drug traffic. This description was wrong for most drugs (both recreational and heavy/abusive use had declined), but it was chillingly accurate for cocaine. Even as the total numbers and percentages of cocaine users decreased in the middle of the decade, a higher proportion of the remaining users were frequent or heavy users. In 1985, 5 percent of the past-year cocaine users used on a weekly basis and 2 percent were daily users; by 1988 the percentages had doubled to 11 percent weekly and 2 percent daily users. Among high school seniors, the percentage that reported smoking cocaine (assumed to be freebase or crack) doubled from 1983 to 1986; daily use doubled from 0.2 to 0.4 percent, and twice as many (from 0.4 to 0.8 percent) felt they were addicted to cocaine, unable to stop. In 1985 there were an estimated 647,000 weekly cocaine users and 246,000 daily users; three years later there were 862,000 weekly and 292,000 daily users. Hard-core cocaine abusers did not go away; they multiplied.

There are other indications that these hard-core users continued to pose a serious problem at the same time that cocaine use in the general population was becoming less of a problem. They became more prone to use cocaine in ways that enhance its potency and effects, by smoking crack and injecting cocaine. Partly because of the greater frequency and potency, evidence has accumulated of the health and life-threatening dangers of cocaine use. Sharing of infected needles by intravenous drug users has become one of the leading routes of spreading AIDS. People who are sensitive to cocaine react strongly even to small dosages of the drug. Among both novice and long-term users, cocaine can produce fatal cardiac arrest and toxic shock.

Part of the public perception of a cocaine problem out of control came from reports of these deaths. In Miami in 1970 there were two cocaine-related deaths; in 1984 there were twenty-four. In Washington, D.C., there were three cocaine deaths in 1981; in 1984 there were eighty-eight (*Reader's Digest*, Mar. 1985). In ten of the largest cities reporting in the DAWN (Drug Abuse Warning Network) system, the total number of mentions of cocaine in emergency room admissions increased from 8,831 in 1984 to 46,020 in 1988 (a 520 percent increase!). The proportion of these admissions attributed to smoking crack or freebase jumped dramatically from 1985 to 1986, and by 1988 one-third of the admissions were reported to be due to smoking cocaine. In those same cities, the number of mentions by medical examiners of cocaine overdose as a factor in deaths increased from 628 in 1984 to 1,724 in 1987 (NIDA 1989a).

By the mid-1980s, drug-treatment programs in the large cities of the United States were reporting increasing numbers of admissions for cocaine abuse, usually in combination with other drugs (NIDA 1985). In some cities, 80 percent or more of the beds in residential treatment programs were occupied by admissions for cocaine abuse as the primary presenting problem (NIDA 1985). Not only did cocaine abusers fill the drug-treatment agencies, they disproportionately filled our jails and prisons as well. In 1989 one-fourth to three-fourths of the male and female arrestees tested for drugs (urinalysis) in thirteen large cities tested positive for cocaine; in ten of these cities, the percentage testing positive was higher for cocaine than for any other drug (including marijuana). In 1984, 50 percent of arrestees tested positive for some drug; by 1989 it was 70 percent (Wish and O'Neil 1989). There can be little doubt that heavy abusers of cocaine did not share in the general decline of drug use in American society.

Is Cocaine Abuse Even Worse Than We Think?

All of this is bad enough, but can it be that the problem was and still is even worse than we think it is? "It is important to note that crack use may be disproportionately located in the out-of-school population relative to most other drugs" (Johnston 1989:63). Statements such as this have been included in the reports on the annual high school seniors surveys from the beginning. Self-reports of deviant behavior generally must contend with problems of underreporting, but by and large they have been found to be reliable and valid measures of deviant behavior (Akers et al. 1983). Undercounting probably occurs to some extent in all categories, but it has long been recognized that the NIDA household surveys more frequently undercount heavy drug users because many are in jail or prison, under treatment, homeless, or otherwise less available to be surveyed.

But is this undercounting so severe that we have been totally misled by the surveys as to the true magnitude and trends of drug use in the United States? Is there a secret horde of drug addicts, and unknown thousands of crack users, so large that we can place no confidence in the findings from surveys? Is it true that there is massive undercounting of cocaine and crack users so serious that "the streets are filled with coke," as one headline claims (*U.S. News & World Report*, Mar. 5, 1990)? These media reports are based in part on research by Eric D. Wish (1990), who used the findings from the drug testing of arrestees in 21 large cities (Drug Use Forecasting—DUF) to conclude that there are as many as 1.3 million frequent drug users just in the 61 largest cities, compared to the estimate of 862,000 in the whole population from the 1988 NIDA household survey.

However, do Wish's findings drastically alter what we know about cocaine use and abuse from the national household surveys? Wish has no way of knowing what proportion of the arrestees is represented in the national surveys or what proportion of the prevalence in the surveys is accounted for by frequent users who show up in arrested populations. Making reasonable estimates from DUF and adding those to the total of weekly users estimated from the NIDA surveys may mean a revision in the estimated number of cocaine users. They do not make a large difference in the percentage of the general population estimated to be frequent cocaine users. By my calculation, in 1988, it would have raised the percentage from 0.4 to 0.8 percent.

Further, such estimates make no difference in the description of trends in cocaine abuse. Since there is little reason to believe that the surveys have gotten worse about undercounting, the trends would have been exactly the same using only the NIDA survey findings or adding Wish's estimates. Both would have shown an increase in weekly cocaine use from 1985 to 1988 of about the same magnitude. The national surveys may undersample the most frequent and criminal cocaine users, but they still capture changes that occur in this population without including special counts of arrested populations. Similar conclusions are reached about the effects of not including absentees and school dropouts in the annual survey of seniors on estimates and trends in cocaine use (Johnston 1989: 338–339).

Moreover, after 1988, there were clear signs of an abatement in cocaine abuse, following the same trend as general use as measured in the national surveys. DAWN reports show that in the last part of 1989 there was about a 20 percent drop in the number of cocaine mentions in emergency room cases, a significant decrease in cocaine-related deaths, and a reduction in the percentage of arrestees testing positive for cocaine and another 20 percent drop in emergency room mentions in the first part of 1990 (NIDA 1990a; Treaster 1990). Abuse of cocaine in both its powdered and crack form remains a serious problem for law enforcement and treatment in the midst of the overall moderation of drug use in American society. The severity of the cocaine problem should not be underestimated, but it is not worse than we thought, and in fact, the situation is improving. This is, of course, no guarantee that the improvement will continue.

T A B L E   7 . 3   *Sociodemographic characteristics of cocaine use:*
lifetime prevalence

	Age Groups				
	12–17	*18–25*	*26–34*	*35 +*	*Total*
Sex					
Male	3.3%	22.2%	32.3%	5.3%	13.1%
Female	3.4	17.4	21.0	2.8	8.5
Race/Ethnicity					
White	3.6	21.2	28.6	3.7	10.8
Black	2.1	10.4	19.8	6.4	9.3
Hispanic	4.6	18.7	21.5	3.4	10.9
Size of City of Residence					
Large urban	4.4	22.0	32.5	6.2	13.6
Smaller urban	3.0	22.3	25.0	3.1	10.4
Nonurban	2.4	13.3	17.7	NA	6.2
Region of Residence					
Northeast	3.9	23.8	29.7	4.8	11.8
North central	3.9	23.0	28.6	2.9	10.9
South	1.5	13.1	16.9	2.8	7.1
West	6.5	24.9	39.1	6.6	16.2
Education					
Less than HS	NA	21.5	20.6	2.7	7.6
HS graduate	NA	18.8	25.3	2.1	11.2
Some college	NA	17.4	30.6	5.2	13.1
College grad	NA	26.6	29.3	8.4	16.1
Current Employment					
Full-time	NA	22.6	27.8	5.9	14.9
Part-time	NA	15.4	25.3	4.9	11.8
Unemployed	NA	23.3	38.1	NA	19.3

Source: NIDA 1990a (1988 survey).

A R E   W E   E X P E R I E N C I N G A   R E - G H E T T O I Z A T I O N   O F C O C A I N E   A B U S E?

What is more likely to result from undercounting heavy users in the national surveys is distortion in the recorded racial and socioeconomic characteristics of cocaine users. Table 7.3 presents the social distribution of lifetime prevalance of cocaine use from the 1988 NIDA household survey. The table shows that the spread of overall cocaine use to the white, middle-class, and more affluent segments of the population in the 1970s continued in the 1980s. The 1988 survey, however, shows that a significant increase of cocaine use did occur among Hispanics (categorized by Hispanic lineage and surnames and includes both black and white Hispanics). Lifetime prevalence of cocaine use (ever used) remained stable for blacks and declined among whites. Thus, by 1988 cocaine use among Hispanics exceeded use among blacks and equaled that among whites. Indeed, among adolescents, cocaine use by Hispanics is higher than that by whites, and among older adults use by blacks is higher than use by whites. Note also from Table 7.3 that, while college graduates remain the most likely users, highest rates of cocaine use are found among the unemployed (NIDA 1989a, 1989b, 1990b).

In addition to these trends in overall use, there is some indication, then, that heavy abuse of cocaine may again be concentrating in lower-class, black, and other minority populations along with an increase in the illegal cocaine traffic in those neighborhoods. Recall that, as overall substance use in the general American population has declined, cocaine abuse has increased in some groups in society. Recall also that there are signs of heroin use again becoming concentrated at the lower end of the socioeconomic scale. Both cocaine and heroin use are becoming more characteristic of those who are arrested and incarcerated at the local, state, and federal levels, and these individuals are disproportionately of lower socioeconomic status, unemployed, and black (Wish 1990).

Although white and middle-class abusers are included, the "crack nation" is reported in the popular media to be concentrated among the poor and black in Detroit, New York, Los Angeles, San Francisco, Houston, and Washington, D.C. (*Newsweek*, Nov. 28, 1988). The enormous increase in homicide in our nation's capital, with its predominantly black population, has been attributed to the crack trade (*Newsweek*, Mar. 13, 1989), and youth and children have been reported to be increasingly involved in selling crack in urban black neighborhoods and housing projects (*Time*, May 9, 1988; *Newsweek*, Sept. 11, 1989). Even the reports of the spread of the crack trade to small, rural towns indicate that these tend to be predominantly black communities (*Newsweek*, Apr. 3, 1989; *Gainesville Sun*, July 30, 1989). As we have seen, the media image of the drug problem can be mistaken, and it may be that the picture of the re-ghettoization of crack is simply wrong. There are some grounds for believing, however, that the picture may reflect reality.

The DUF data show that the NIDA household surveys are most likely to miss populations under control of the criminal justice system and that these individuals are much more likely to be heavy drug users than is the general population. Arrestees and prison populations are also disproportionately black and Hispanic. If the disproportionately black and lower-class users among the large number of abusers that Wish (1990) says are not counted are added, there is reason to suggest that heavy cocaine users are disproportionately black. Wish believes that the DUF data show an increase in drug use in the "underclass."

The 1990 survey of high school seniors found that the highest levels of cocaine use in the past year were reported by Hispanic and American Indian seniors and that the highest proportion of users of other stimulants was reported by Asian seniors. A high school survey by PRIDE in 1988–89 in thirty-eight states, including inner-city schools in Atlanta, Chicago, Dallas, Houston, New York, and Washington, D.C., found that black seniors reported crack and cocaine were more available than did white seniors. White seniors were more likely to report use in the past year, but black students were more likely to use weekly. Thus, while the findings on casual and recreational use reflect what has been found in the general population surveys, this study also shows that crack is more endemic in the black neighborhoods and that black students are more likely to be using cocaine frequently. It must be remembered, however, that for both black and white students the proportion of users is very small.

Table 7.4 shows that, according to the 1988 NIDA national household survey, crack use (considered a sign of more abusive use than snorting powdered cocaine) is more prevalent in black and Hispanic populations than in the white population; moreover, Hispanics are twice as likely and blacks are four times as likely as whites to have used crack in the past month. We should not make too much of these data, however. In no group, white or minority, male or female, is the percentage of lifetime prevalence of crack use much more than 2 percent. But it is reasonable to hypothesize that the numbers making up these small overall national percentages are concentrated in lower-class minority neighborhoods in the large cities where they constitute a much higher proportion of the local community population.

Field studies of crack use in urban areas report a disproportionate concentration in the inner-city, poor, black, and Puerto Rican neighborhoods.

> At first, crack was mass marketed in inner city neighborhoods in or near cocaine importation points such as Miami, Los Angeles, and New York. . . . Reports from users in treatment, popular press, and criminal justice agencies also confirmed that . . . within two years, crack use and trafficking were widespread and highly visible throughout New York City, especially in its most socially and economically deprived neighborhoods. . . . Crack appeared in inner city neighborhoods that had experienced intensification of poverty, weakening of social institutions, and declining legitimate economic activities in the decade preceding its appearance. (Fagan and Chin 1989a)

The nonrandom sample of users and dealers in this study, drawn mainly from treatment and criminal justice agencies, were predominantly male,

T A B L E   7 . 4   Sociodemographic characteristics of crack use: lifetime prevalence

	Age Groups				
	12–17	*18–25*	*26–34*	*35+*	*Total*
Sex					
Male	0.9%	3.0%	4.5%	<0.5%	1.6%
Female	1.0	3.7	1.3	<0.5	1.0
Race/Ethnicity					
White	0.9	3.3	2.5	<0.5	1.0
Black	0.9	2.8	6.0	<0.5	2.4
Hispanic	1.3	5.4	2.6	<0.5	2.2
Region of Residence					
Northeast	<0.5	7.4	<0.5	<0.5	1.6
North central	1.4	<0.5	<0.5	<0.5	0.5
South	0.4	2.4	3.5	<0.5	1.2
West	1.8	4.3	4.5	<0.5	1.9
Education					
Less than HS	NA	5.3	4.2	NA	1.6
HS graduate	NA	3.9	2.9	NA	1.0
Some college	NA	NA	3.7	NA	1.0
College grad	NA	NA	NA	NA	0.7
Current Employment					
Full-time	NA	3.8	3.5	NA	1.7
Part-time	NA	3.0	NA	NA	1.0
Unemployed	NA	5.4	3.7	NA	3.4

Source: NIDA 1990a (1988 survey).

lower-class, and black or Hispanic. Nearly 70 percent were black and two-thirds were male, half were high school dropouts, and 84 percent were not employed in legitimate occupations (Fagan and Chin 1989b). A study of cocaine freebase and crack users in the San Francisco area (also using a non-random sampling) found users to be "significantly more often Black or Latino" (Reinarman, Waldorf, and Murphy 1989:10), similar to the sample of another San Francisco area study (Waldorf, Murphy, and Lauderback 1989). Nationally, nearly half of clients in drug-treatment programs are black or Hispanic or belong to another minority group (NIDA/NIAAA 1990).

We may be heading for a drug situation similar to that of the 1950s in which drug use, especially heavy drug use, was rare outside of the lower-class, black ghetto and minority areas and criminal/drug subcultures of the big cities. The drug surge of the late 1960s and the 1970s moved the drug scene out of these contexts into the larger society. Since then, drugs of all kinds have become much less prevalent overall in society. Unfortunately, the lower-class ghetto drug subculture (which has never disappeared) may have been re-invigorated. Crack has added to the social problems already extant in these areas.

The trend is not yet clear. My view that we may be returning to 1950s patterns of drug abuse is more in the nature of a prediction than established fact. If we are indeed heading in that direction, it would be a grave mistake for the public and policy makers to become complacent about the brightening overall drug picture or to use the re-ghettoization of drugs as an excuse to ease off of drug control since it is "their" problem. There is a danger that a more narrowly confined (even if disproportionately severe) drug problem would be more easily "forgotten" and taken off the national agenda. This would not only be an injustice to the residents of the high-drug-use areas, but, it would also set the stage for a recurrence of what happened with drugs after the 1950s—they could explode again into the larger society.

Social Control and Public Policy on Drugs: Law Enforcement

COMPONENTS OF SOCIAL CONTROL AND PUBLIC POLICY

Public policy on drugs is expressed in legislation, executive directives, and drug-agency actions. This policy both reflects and influences public opinion on the drug problem and what to do about it. The nature of this mutual influence is unclear, however. Law enforcement and treatment approaches that are seriously out of line with what the public wants and will support are likely to be ineffective, at least in the short run. But policy will always reflect to some extent what is publicly and politically acceptable, and over time the "educative effects" of law itself along with public-education campaigns may bring the two closer together.

In the final analysis, however, the nature of and solution to the problems of drugs and alcohol in society rests on the informal control system and the operative set of norms setting the limits of what society will tolerate. Strong values and socialization into self-control and drug-incompatible behavior in the family, religion, and primary groups and other components of informal social control are the most effective mechanisms of drug control. Public policy may hinder or complement these basic social processes but cannot replace them. That may sound platitudinous. It is also true.

Public policy on drugs has varied both through time and by type of drug. The aims of public policy, and private efforts coordinated with it, have been and continue to be to control deviant drug use and to lessen its consequences. The strategies devised for accomplishing these goals have long included various combinations of tolerance, harshly punitive legal enforcement, treatment of drug users and abusers, and prevention. Sometimes the policy has focused on stopping or containing the *supply* of drugs, and other times it has focused on stopping usage or getting users to decrease their *demand* for drugs. Whatever the variation in attention given in stated public policy, most of the money attached to actions taken to carry out the policy has been spent on law enforcement, primarily to attack drug trafficking to control supply. Most arrests, convictions, and imprisonments for possession, however, are of users, who are likely also to be involved in the drug trade. Therefore, most of the street-level law enforcement, in effect, is directed toward users, controlling to some extent the street demand.

Law enforcement has always been and remains the predominant approach in public policy, at the federal, state, and local levels. Even in the current "war on drugs" begun in the mid-1980s, where greater attention has been paid to prevention and treatment, the major part of drug-policy budgets continues to go to law enforcement. Prevention, education, and treatment programs get almost universal endorsement, but relatively little funding. Of course, research into the causes of drug use and the effectiveness of drug policy of any kind runs a very distant last in funding. There was strong sentiment in the 1970s for decriminalization. Under decriminalization drugs would remain illegal, but the penalties for violations would be lowered to misdemeanors. Also beginning in the 1970s was the movement for legalization in which some or all of the presently illegal drugs would become legally produced and purchased without criminal penalties. The legalization movement has been revived in recent years with a blend of liberal and conservative scholars, newspaper and magazine columnists, special-interest groups, and judges calling for legalizing drugs. Thus far, legalization has not been adopted as public policy.

LAW ENFORCEMENT

Law enforcement is directed against the growing and processing of marijuana (domestic and foreign), coca (cocaine), and poppy (opium, heroin) as well as the illegal production of amphetamines, barbiturates, LSD, opiates, and other dangerous substances. It is intended to control the illegal importation of illicit substances and their wholesale distribution after they are smuggled into this country. Finally, law enforcement attempts to control the illicit retail trade by targeting both consumers (arrested for possession of a controlled substance) and dealers/sellers (possession of quantities sufficient to show intent to sell). Drug-law enforcement by the federal government is addressed to production, smuggling, and high-level wholesale distribution. Control of midlevel wholesale and retail trade on the streets is primarily a function of local police departments and sheriffs' offices (see Polich et al. 1984; Hayeslip 1989; Moore and Kleiman 1989).

History and Changes in Law Enforcement

As an outgrowth of an international agreement to control the opium trade and other drug traffic, to which it was a signatory, the United States passed the 1914 Harrison Act. Because it was intended to be a regulatory law, little publicity about a drug problem and apparently little political maneuvering by organized interest groups accompanied its passage. Even though it was a regulatory law, it represented the first major federal legislation to foster the criminalization of drug use and addiction (although a number of states had already enacted controlling legislation). The theory behind it was that the federal government could control drugs because it had constitutional authority to tax but not to control criminal behavior in general. This was the underpinning for all subsequent federal legislation until 1970 when statutes began to lean more on the constitutional right of the national government to regulate interstate commerce and to control influx of illegal goods across our national borders. In fact, the effect of federal law-enforcement policy (as well as state and local efforts to control drugs) has been to impose criminal penalties on violations and to treat the drug trade and drug dealers as a criminal matter, not a revenue or commercial matter.

Enforcement Agencies and Their Role in Influencing As Well As Enforcing the Law.   Responsibility for enforcing the provisions of the Harrison Act was subsequently lodged in the same federal bureau that was set up to enforce the nationwide liquor prohibition beginning in 1918. The law was stiffened with stronger penalties in 1922. By 1930 a separate narcotics law-enforcement agency, the Federal Bureau of Narcotics (FBN), was formed within the Department of the Treasury to enforce federal drug laws. In 1968 the FBN was moved to the Department of Justice as part of the Bureau of Narcotics and Dangerous Drugs (BNDD). Later the Office of Drug Abuse Law Enforcement was created and was merged in 1973 with the BNDD to form the Drug Enforcement Administration (DEA), which remains as the principal federal narcotics-control agency. Since 1982, however, it has shared responsibility for enforcing U.S.

drug laws with the Federal Bureau of Investigation (FBI). In addition, there have been various drug task forces run from the office of the President, and since 1989 there has been a presidentially appointed drug "czar" (Director of the Office of National Drug Control Policy).

The FBN and its successor agency not only have vigorously enforced drug laws but have functioned as political pressure groups that promote antidrug legislation and punitive enforcement policies at both the federal and state levels. Partly as the result of agencies' efforts, major federal legislation was enacted in each decade from the 1930s to the 1960s. Each decade saw the expansion of law enforcement jurisdiction over drugs, a harsher stand toward users and dealers, and lengthened prison terms for drug-law violators. By 1956 selling drugs to a minor under 18 was punishable by death. The prevailing pattern of law enforcement throughout the United States became harassment of street addicts, frequent arrests of low-level sellers and dealers, and infrequent arrests of high-level dope smugglers and wholesalers. The federal and other narcotics enforcement agencies fostered the emerging public definition of the addict as a dope fiend and criminal. As other drugs like marijuana came into use, the criminalized conception of the opiate and cocaine user extended to them as well (Lindesmith 1968).

The bill that eventually became the Marihuana Tax Act of 1937 was originally drafted by the FBN, and its lobbyists testified during the hearings. The popular press picked up stories, released by the FBN, of atrocities and heinous crimes committed by people supposedly under the influence of marijuana. The interests of medical, pharmaceutical, industrial, and other groups were accommodated, and there was no organized opposition to the act. Although ostensibly a revenue act, in effect it banned possession of marijuana. Subsequently, marijuana became classified with opiates and narcotics and carried similar penalties for possession (Becker 1963; Dickson 1968; Grinspoon and Bakalar 1969). There remains disagreement about the various influences and the role they played in the passage of the act (Galliher and Walker 1977), but the case does illustrate the way in which organized interest groups, including an enforcement agency, have shaped public policy.

Another illustration comes from the control of "head shops," retail outlets where drug paraphernalia is sold. The "gear" sold in these shops is designed and manufactured explicitly (and for the most part exclusively) for the growth, production, preparation, or ingestion of illegal drugs. The most common products are those for use with marijuana and cocaine (both powdered and crack). In addition to the hardware and materials in the shop, there are likely to be books, magazines (one of which, *High Times*, is found in many magazine racks outside of head shops), and manuals that praise drug use and provide detailed instruction in how to grow, obtain, prepare, and take drugs.

Head shops operated legally and openly in spite of the efforts of local law enforcement, citizens, and government to close or regulate them. For many years, little could be done about the shops. Appellate courts overturned convictions of head-shop owners and questioned the constitutionality of the state and local laws regulating or banning the sale of the drug products. Then in 1979, the DEA prepared a Model Drug Paraphernalia Act and distributed it to state and local governments. The model act defined precisely and exactly what constitutes drug paraphernalia and described in detail the pieces of equipment that fall within the definition. The provisions called for a complete ban on most of the head-shop products and for criminal penalties, fines, and incarceration for violation. By 1982 over thirty states and many county and city governments had enacted laws based on the DEA model. They have been upheld as constitutional (Vawrinek 1982). In spite of these court rulings, head shops continue to operate in many cities. They also continue to be closed down by law enforcement, and their owners prosecuted.

Public Opinion, Interest Groups, and Drug Laws: Punishment and Treatment. A small band of sociologists and medical researchers objected to the unsubstantiated claims about the horrors of marijuana, but did not form as a political-interest group and were largely ignored for two decades. In the 1950s and early 1960s, social scientists and lawyers began to point out some of the negative consequences for society that are fostered by a strict law-enforcement policy toward drugs (Lindesmith 1967). These voices were gradually heeded, and by the mid-1960s there were notable changes in law enforcement. The balance of political power and public sentiment began to shift somewhat in the direction of less punishment and more treatment. Federal and state policy became less restrictive of medical practice in the area of addiction and more relaxed about unofficial attempts to treat addicts.

Although concern over the emergence of the illicit use of LSD and other drugs such as amphetamines was high enough to produce the 1965 Drug Abuse Control Act, these drugs were defined in the law as "dangerous drugs," not "narcotics" as they would have been defined earlier. In 1966 the first federal drug legislation containing the term *rehabilitation* in its title was enacted—the Narcotic Addict Rehabilitation Act (NARA). Although the act did retain law enforcement concerns and provided for compulsory treatment (civil commitment) of addicts, it did represent a modification of the policy of almost total reliance on law enforcement in federal policy. The liberalizing trend continued through federal legislation that shifted greater attention to dealers and drug smuggling and de-emphasized control of the user.

The 1970 Comprehensive Drug Abuse Prevention and Control Act authorized greater treatment and prevention efforts by federal agencies and set up drug information and funding institutes and offices in the National Institute of Mental Health. The law also allowed for stepped-up law enforcement. Drugs were now referred to as "controlled substances" and classified into five "schedules" (under the Controlled Substances Act, which is Title II

■

Drug Enforcement Administration
Schedules of Controlled Substances

The legal basis for the schedules enforced by the United States Drug Enforcement Administration (DEA) is the Controlled Substances Act (CSA), Title II of the 1970 Comprehensive Drug Abuse Prevention and Control Act with subsequent amendments from such acts as the Narcotics Penalties and Enforcement Act of 1986. These laws define five schedules, with Schedule I drugs having the most severe and Schedule V drugs having the least severe legal penalties for violation.

The administrator of DEA determines the classification of drugs for the schedules according to the following standards:

Schedule I: The substance has a high potential for abuse, has no accepted medical use, and has no accepted standards of safety for use under medical supervision.

Schedule II: The substance has a high potential for abuse and severe dependence (psychological and/or physical) but does have an accepted medical use with restrictions.

Schedule III: The substance has less potential for abuse than do Schedule I and II drugs, a moderate level of risk of physical dependence or high risk of psychological dependence, and has accepted medical uses.

Schedule IV: The substance has a lower potential for abuse and dependence than do those in the preceding schedules and has accepted medical uses.

Schedule V: The substance has a low potential for abuse and dependence and has accepted medical uses.

---

of the CDAPC Act) based on medical use, potential for abuse, safety, and dependence liability. Penalties are provided for first and second offenses of possession and trafficking of various quantities with the stiffest penalties attached to Schedules I (e.g., heroin, methaqualone, and most hallucinogens) and II (e.g., cocaine and PCP). Marijuana is also classified as Schedule I. There have been changes and reclassification and amendment legislation through the years, but this remains the basic federal law governing drugs (DEA 1988a).

Table 8.1 shows the current schedule and classification for the major types of drugs. Tables 8.2 and 8.3 summarizes the penalties for first and second offenses of trafficking in various drugs. (See the discussion of the bases for the schedules and classification of drugs in the box "Drug Enforcement Administration Schedules of Controlled Substances.")

T A B L E   8 . 1   Schedules and classification of drugs under the Controlled Substance Act (CSA)

Drugs/CSA Schedules	Trade or Other Names
Narcotics	
Opium/II, III, V	Dover's Powder, Paregoric, Parepectolin
Morphine/II, III	Morphine, MS-Contin, Roxanol, Roxanol-SR
Codeine/II, III, V	Tylenol w/Codeine, Empirin w/Codeine, Robitussin A-C, Fiorinal w/Codeine
Heroin/I	Diacetylmorphine, Horse, Smack
Hydromorphone/II	Dilaudid
Meperidine (Pethidine)/II	Demerol, Mepergan
Methadone/II	Dolophine, Methadone, Methadose
Other narcotics/I, II, III, IV, V	Numorphan, Percodan, Percocet, Tylox, Tussionex, Fentanyl, Darvon, Lomotil, Talwin[a]
Depressants	
Chloral Hydrate/IV	Noctec
Barbiturates/II, III, IV	Amytal, Butisol, Fiorinal, Lotusate, Nembutal, Seconal, Tuinal, Phenobarbital
Benzodiazepines/IV	Ativan, Dalmane, Diazepam, Librium, Xanax, Serax, Valium, Tranxene, Verstran, Versed, Halcion, Paxipam, Restoril
Methaqualone/I	Quaalude
Glutethimide/III	Doriden
Other depressants/III, IV	Equanil, Miltown, Noludar, Placidyl, Valmid
Stimulants	
Cocaine[b]/II	Coke, Flake, Snow, Crack
Amphetamines/II	Biphetamine, Delcobese, Desoxyn, Dexedrine, Obetrol
Phenmetrazine/II	Preludin
Methylphenidate/II	Ritalin
Other stimulants/III, IV	Adipex, Cylert, Didrex, Ionamin, Melfiat, Plegine, Sanorex, Tenuate, Tepanil, Prelu-2
Hallucinogens	
LSD/I	Acid, Microdot
Mescaline and peyote/I	Mesc, Buttons, Cactus

T A B L E   8 . 1   (continued)

Drugs/CSA Schedules	Trade or Other Names
Hallucinogens, continued	
Amphetamine variants/I	2, 5-DMA, PMA, STP, MDA, MDMA, TMA, DOM, DOB
Phencyclidine/II	PCP, Angel Dust, Hog
Phencyclidine analogs/I	PCE, PCP, TCP
Other hallucinogens/I	Bufotenine, Ibogaine, DMT, DET, Psilocybin, Psilocyn
Cannabis	
Marijuana/I	Pot, Acapulco Gold, Grass, Reefer, Sinsemilla, Thai Sticks
Tetrahydrocannabinol/I, II	THC, Marinol
Hashish/I	Hash
Hashish Oil/I	Hash oil

Source: Drug Enforcement Administration 1988.
[a]Not designated a narcotic under CSA.
[b]Designated a narcotic under CSA.

The most dramatic liberalization of drug policy and opinion occurred with marijuana. Opposition to marijuana laws grew in the 1960s and accelerated in the 1970s as groups such as LEMAR (Legalize Marijuana) and NORML (National Organization to Reform Marijuana Laws) pressured to change the law, to decriminalize and eventually to legalize marijuana (Goode 1970; Kaplan 1971). Powerful official and unofficial voices, including a national commission, the Consumers Union, and the American Bar Association spoke for liberalization of the laws to remove criminal penalties for possession of marijuana for personal use.

Public opinion came to favor liberalization of marijuana laws. By the mid-1970s, a majority of adults under 35 supported making possession of small amounts of marijuana legal or subject only to a civil fine. Several states lowered marijuana violations from felony to misdemeanor. The decriminalization movement was in full swing, and by 1978 eleven states, incorporating about a third of the population in the United States, had removed all criminal penalties from possession of a small amount (in all but one state, one ounce or less) of marijuana for personal use. An additional seventeen states had significantly reduced penalties to the level of a minor misdemeanor. Less than half of the states retained statutory provision for high fines or stiff jail sentences for possession of small amounts of marijuana. Regardless of what the statutes provide, in all parts of the country, having an ounce or less of marijuana in one's possession even if it is not solely for personal use, became and remains

T A B L E 8 . 2 Federal trafficking penalties according to Narcotics Penalties and Enforcement Act of 1986

CSA	PENALTY		Quantity	DRUG	Quantity	PENALTY	
	2nd Offense	1st Offense				1st Offense	2nd Offense
I	Not less than 10 years. Not more than life. — If death or serious injury, not less than life. — Fine of not more than $4 million individual, $10 million other than individual.	Not less than 5 years. Not more than 40 years. — If death or serious injury, not less than 20 years. Not more than life. — Fine of not more than $2 million individual, $5 million other than individual.	100–999 gm mixture	**Heroin**	1 kg or more mixture	Not less than 10 years. Not more than life. — If death or serious injury, not less than 20 years. Not more than life. — Fine of not more than $4 million individual, $10 million other than individual.	Not less than 20 years. Not more than life. — If death or serious injury, not less than life. — Fine of not more than $8 million individual, $20 million other than individual.
			500–4,999 gm mixture	**Cocaine**	5 kg or more mixture		
			5–49 gm mixture	**Cocaine base**	5 gm or more mixture		
and			10–99 gm or 100–999 gm mixture	**PCP**	100 gm or more or 1 kg or more mixture		
II			1–10 gm mixture	**LSD**	10 gm or more mixture		
			40–399 gm mixture	**Fentanyl**	400 gm or more mixture		
			10–99 gm mixture	**Fentanyl analog**	100 gm or more mixture		

CSA	Drug	Quantity	First Offense	Second Offense
	Others[a]	Any	Not more than 20 years. If death or serious injury, not less than 20 years, not more than life. Fine $1 million individual, $5 million not individual.	Not more than 30 years. If death or serious injury, life. Fine $2 million individual, $10 million not individual.
III	All	Any	Not more than 5 years. Fine of not more than $250,000 individual, $1 million not individual.	Not more than 10 years. Fine of not more than $500,000 individual, $2 million not individual.
IV	All	Any	Not more than 3 years. Fine of not more than $250,000 individual, $1 million not individual.	Not more than 6 years. Fine of not more than $500,000 individual, $2 million not individual.
V	All	Any	Not more than 1 year. Fine of not more than $100,000 individual, $250,000 not individual.	Not more than 2 years. Fine of not more than $200,000 individual, $500,000 not individual.

Source: Drug Enforcement Administration 1988.
[a]Does not include marijuana, hashish, or hashish oils; see Table 8.3.

T A B L E 8 . 3 *Federal trafficking penalties for marijuana according to Narcotic Penalties and Enforcement Act of 1986*

Quantity	Description	First Offense	Second Offense
1,000 kg or more	**Marijuana** Mixture containing detectable quantity[a]	Not less than 10 years, not more than life. If death or serious injury, not less than 20 years, not more than life. Fine not more than $1 million individual, $10 million other than individual.	Not less than 20 years, not more than life. If death or serious injury, not less than life. Fine not more than $8 million individual, $20 million other than individual.
100 kg to 1,000 kg	**Marijuana** Mixture containing detectable quantity[a]	Not less than 5 years, not more than 40 years. If death or serious injury, not less than 20 years, not more than life. Fine not more than $2 million individual, $5 million other than individual.	Not less than 10 years, not more than life. If death or serious injury, not less than life. Fine not more than $4 million individual, $10 million other than individual.
50 to 100 kg	**Marijuana**	Not more than 20 years. If death or serious injury, not less than 20 years, not more than life. Fine $1 million individual, $5 million other than individual.	Not more than 30 years. If death or serious injury, life. Fine $2 million individual, $10 million other than individual.
10 to 100 kg	**Hashish**		
1 to 100 kg	**Hashish Oil**		
100 or more plants	**Marijuana**		
Less than 50 kg	**Marijuana**	Not more than 5 years. Fine not more than $250,000, $1 million other than individual.	Not more than 10 years. Fine $500,000 individual, $2 million other than individual.
Less than 10 kg	**Hashish**		
Less than 1 kg	**Hashish Oil**		

Source: Drug Enforcement Administration 1988.
Note: Marijuana is a Schedule 1 controlled substance.
[a]Includes hashish and hash oil.

in actual practice very unlikely to result in arrest. It almost certainly will not result in a prosecution or conviction. To all intents and purposes, possession of small quantities of marijuana was decriminalized by the end of the 1970s. That further liberalization and outright legalization of marijuana has not developed is due to the fact that a backlash and reassertion of a more conservative perspective developed in public opinion and policy. Although some very influential academicians, judges, and opinion leaders, both liberal and conservative, have argued for legalization of marijuana, cocaine, and other drugs, the dominant position today remains antilegalization.

Opinion drew back somewhat from the view of marijuana as a fairly harmless substance and toward support for stricter control. This shift toward more restrictions on drugs is evident even among young people who typically have held the most liberal attitudes toward marijuana. In the annual surveys of high school seniors, since 1977 there has been an increase in the disapproval of marijuana use and since 1979 an increase in the proportion of seniors who see marijuana as a harmful drug and personally disapprove of its use. In 1977, 22 percent of the seniors agreed that marijuana possession should be a criminal offense, whereas 31 percent believed that it should be treated as a minor civil violation. By 1988, 49 percent agreed that possession of marijuana for use should be a crime, and the proportion supporting the treatment of marijuana violations as equivalent to parking tickets was down to 22 percent. Disapproval of the recreational use of cocaine, crack, heroin, barbiturates, and other drugs has also increased among both high school seniors and adults. Regular use or abuse of almost all drugs has long been disapproved by strong majorities, and there has been little change in that attitude (Johnston 1989). The opinions of the general public are similar to those of the high school seniors (Colasanto 1990).

The influence of political-interest groups such as NORML has declined as they have moved to strong support of outright legalization of marijuana and to defend growers, dealers, and smugglers as simply courageous farmers and businessmen only trying to supply a demand for a harmless pleasure. NORML unsuccessfully attempted to block Florida from spraying the illegal fields of marijuana with the herbicide paraquat. Some of the researchers, academicians, and policy makers who supported liberalization of marijuana laws and even legalization of marijuana in the early 1970s have since had second thoughts and do not now support legalization. I count myself in this group. As with the others, my change of mind has come about for the reasons against legalization discussed on pages 158–161. A National Academy of Sciences report whose authors had considered recommending legalization of marijuana sale and possession stopped short of that and instead proposed federal decriminalization of marijuana possession. Even this milder stance was rejected, however, by the president of the National Academy of Sciences and the National Institute on Drug Abuse, the federal agency that funded the report.

There remains strong public sentiment supporting a strict law-enforcement approach regarding drugs, especially regarding dealers, sellers, and smugglers. Legislative reaction to a new drug around which problems have developed is still likely to be to make it illegal or increase penalties for trafficking in it. For instance, in 1982 a new Florida statute totally prohibiting all sales of methaqualone, even through prescription, went into effect. The law was upheld as constitutional. By 1984 all legal manufacture of methaqualone had ceased in the United States. There has been a resurgence of harsh, punitive legislation on crime in general as well as drug violations with many states having enacted mandated and determinate sentencing (imprisonment for a definite period without chance of parole) and increased penalties for both property and violent crimes. In spite of the political consensus on the need to get tough with drug traders and users alike, there has been a growing recognition in public opinion and public policy that law enforcement strategies should be used alongside of prevention and treatment strategies. Although still receiving less funding than law enforcement, the increased emphasis on these strategies is reflected most notably in the "war on drugs."

The War on Drugs.   In 1986 President Ronald Reagan declared a war on drugs. The cornerstone of the war was passage of the Anti-Drug Abuse Act along with administrative changes in law enforcement and appointment of a special drug-interdiction task force headed by the vice-president. The stated goal of the new law and policy changes was to reduce drug demand as well as staunch the supply flow of drugs. Most of the money appropriated, however, went for prisons, radar, aircraft, and support to other nations in the interdiction efforts. Drug testing of employees was provided for on a large scale, including high-level government workers. Prevention and treatment programs received some boost, but the major non–law enforcement effort in Reagan's war was the support of his wife for the "Just Say No" campaign (*Newsweek*, Aug. 11, 1986:14–20).

When George Bush (who was vice-president under Reagan) was elected president, he declared his own war on drugs and pushed for the passage of the 1989 Omnibus Anti-Drug Abuse Act. By this time, the federal budget for the drug war had grown considerably and Congress actually appropriated more money (over $8 billion) than Bush had requested. Only one-eighth of this was "new" money. A higher proportion was targeted for prevention and treatment programs than in past years, but again the bulk of the appropriations was earmarked for other strategies in the war on drugs, including such actions as assisting state and local criminal justice agencies enforce drug laws. They also included instituting drug-free workplace requirements and drug testing for employees, arrestees, and prisoners. The appropriations were also for implementing stiffer penalties for convicted drug users, interdiction of air drug smuggling, and tracking down laundered drug money. Some appropriations were designated to assist the governments of the Andean Mountain countries, which are the sources of cocaine, in various ways, as we will discuss in the next section. President Bush also appointed William Bennett (later succeeded by Robert Martinez) as Director of the Office of National Drug Control Policy, popularly referred to as the drug "czar," to implement and coordinate federal antidrug policies (*Los Angeles Times* News Service, Jack Nelson, Sept. 6, 1989; *Time*, Sept. 11, 1989:12–17).

GOALS, TYPES, AND RESULTS OF DRUG-LAW ENFORCEMENT

Throughout the changes in drug policy, passages of laws, and various declarations of war, the goals of law enforcement have remained to cut off or curtail supply and distribution and to lower demand by controlling users/abusers. Seizures, forfeitures, arrests, convictions, and imposition of legal penalties in the form of fines and prison sentences are meant to punish violators and deter further drug crimes by increasing the certainty and severity of punishment. These goals are pursued in three interrelated areas or types of law enforcement strategies: (1) attacking drugs at the *source*, the growing of plants from which drugs are derived and the processing or production of drugs for consumption, both foreign and domestic; (2) disrupting and interdicting the flow of drugs *smuggled* into the United States; and (3) interrupting the supply, distribution, and sales at both the wholesale and retail (street) level of *drug trafficking* in the United States.

Foreign and Domestic Sources of Drugs*

The demand for illicit drugs in the United States has created a drug production and distribution system that is virtually worldwide. This system is well known and documented. The specific sources of the major drugs abused in the United States (as well as increasingly in other countries) are known, mapped, and targeted. All cocaine and heroin, and most marijuana, is imported; illicit amphetamines, barbiturates, and designer drugs are primarily domestically produced. The DEA and other federal agencies have agents

---

*The information in this section on sources of drugs is based on Thomas 1985; Inciardi 1986; Abadinsky 1989; James 1989; Weisheit 1990a; Associated Press, Jan. 11, 1986, Sept. 17, 1989; *Newsweek*, Oct. 25, 1982, April 25, 1988:25, Sept. 11, 1989:12–13, 30–31, May 15, 1989:42–43; *Time*, Feb. 16, 1987:37, Mar. 7, 1988, Aug. 28, 1989:11–12, Sept. 4, 1989:13–14, Sept. 18, 1989:28; *U.S. News & World Report*, Nov. 5, 1989:27–30, Feb. 19, 1990:18–20.

working with law enforcement in the source countries; military and law enforcement aid is granted to the governments of the source countries to engage in eradicating drug crops, destroying processing laboratories, and battling the drug "lords" who run the illegal drug system in these countries. Often, these are leaders of rebel and guerrilla armies, and fighting drugs means warring against political insurgencies (e.g., the Shining Path rebels in Peru). The fight has always been extremely violent. Thousands of people on both sides have been killed in the source countries.

Cocaine.   The Andean Mountain countries of South America are the sources of cocaine (see the map on page 150). The largest quantities of coca leaves are grown by peasant farmers in Peru (110,000 metric tons in 1989), followed by Bolivia and Colombia. The leaves are processed into coca paste and cocaine for sale and smuggling into the United States; this is done mainly (75 to 80 percent) in Colombia. These are sizable operations in which the partially processed paste is turned into refined cocaine hydrochloride. Crack is processed from this powdered cocaine, but this is typically done in crack houses and kitchen labs in the United States.

Cocaine (and other drug) trafficking in Colombia is controlled by various cocaine cartels, the largest of which is the Medellin Cartel. The Colombian government has declared war on these cartels, and the cartels have declared war on the government. One of the consequences of cocaine habits in the United States is the death of thousands of Colombians. The Colombian drug lords have killed government officials (including the justice minister), politicians (including several candidates for president of Colombia), judges, and citizens who happened to be present when a public building was bombed. Many of the cartel leaders have been killed, by other cartels and by Colombian law enforcement. Some have been captured and extradited to the United States for trial on drug charges here. The most notorious of these is Carlos Lehder Rivas, reputed to be the "kingpin" responsible for 80 percent of Colombian cocaine shipped into the United States. Some cartel leaders have surrendered to the Colombian government in exchange for the promise that they would not be extradited. Also, Manuel Noriega, the former dictator of Panama and a major link in cocaine trafficking, was on the payroll of the U.S. Central Intelligence Agency for many years, in spite of his known drug activity. In 1989 he was indicted, captured after the U.S. invasion of Panama, and brought to this country for trial. This pressure has had some effect, because by 1990 it had become more difficult for coca leaves to be delivered into Colombia, processed, and shipped out. There are reports that the backed-up supplies have dragged down the price of coca leaves below the cost to produce them.

Heroin.   There are two major sources of poppy crops from which natural opiates are refined. The "Golden Triangle" area of Southeast Asia, Burma

(1,300 metric tons of opium in 1989), Laos, and Thailand is now the biggest producer. About half of the heroin sold in the United States comes from opium grown in this region. This production is closely followed by the quantities of opium from Iran (750 metric tons), Afghanistan, Pakistan, and other countries in the Middle East and southwestern Asia. Opium is also produced in Mexico, and about one-third of the heroin smuggled into the United States is refined in Mexico (see the map on page 151).

Just as in Colombia, the drug lords in these countries are extremely violent and have assembled armies, not only to wage a rebellion but also to control the growing of opium poppy and the opium/heroin traffic. With U.S. assistance, Thailand and Laos have eradication and interdiction programs in place, but they are not extensive, and Burma essentially has made no law enforcement effort against the opium trade. Heroin is processed from the opium in laboratories located in Mexico, France (at one time the major source of smuggled heroin), and elsewhere. There is some evidence of domestic processing operations.

Marijuana.   The biggest single source of smuggled marijuana is Mexico (about 4,700 metric tons in 1989) with most of the rest (about 7,000 metric tons) coming from Colombia (until the mid-1980s the source of over half of the illegally imported marijuana) and the Caribbean area. The United States and the governments of the source countries are cooperating in eradication, extradition, and other law enforcement actions, with limited success.

But that has been more than offset by the burgeoning U.S.-grown marijuana, which is now estimated to account for 25 to 50 percent of the total marijuana supply in this country. At one time, the only marijuana grown in this country was low-grade "window box" pot cultivated in very small quantities for personal use or harvested wild ("ditchweed") from the remnants of the large hemp fields grown in the Midwest and South during World War II as a secure source of rope material. In the late 1970s, it became apparent that growing the hemp plant for harvest and commercial sale of marijuana had moved into the stage of big agribusiness with extensive cultivation in northern California, the Pacific Northwest, and the South and with sizable cultivation in the Midwest. The marijuana grown in this country is of higher quality and potency than is cannabis from Mexico and Colombia, because much of it is cultivated from improved strains and is produced as *sinsemilla*, which contains higher levels of THC (up to 16 percent compared to 3 to 6 percent for foreign-grown marijuana). Sinsemilla is "seedless" cannabis produced by killing the male plants and harvesting the flowering tops of the female plants, which have excreted extra, concentrated amounts of cannabis resin on the flower buds (Weisheit 1990a).

Attempts to control this domestically grown marijuana have been partially successful through aerial surveillance over rural areas and ground-level destruction and spraying with the herbicide paraquat. In spite of this, it has been estimated by NORML that marijuana is America's largest single cash crop; others estimate its cash value to place it third to fifth, behind corn, soybeans, and wheat (Weisheit 1990a). Much of this increase is due to the development and cultivation of higher-yielding strains and to the utilization of high-tech agricultural equipment and techniques to grow marijuana indoors where it is more difficult to detect (openly advertised in *High Times* magazine with instructions in such books as *The Marijuana Growers Guide*).

Other Drugs.   The influx of drugs from outside of the country is supplemented by increased domestic manufacture of illicit drugs and diversion of legally produced drugs. Some unknown portion of illicit drugs sold in this country comes from the diversion into the black market from legal production by pharmaceutical companies. This is augmented by production of the same drugs, as well as others that are never manufactured for the legal prescription market, in clandestine laboratories, most of which are located in the United States. Barbiturates, amphetamines, PCP, methadone, synthetic heroin such as fentanyl, LSD, mescaline, and other hallucinogens, methaqualone, and other substances come from these labs for distribution all over the country. Most of these are small operations in garages, houses, campers, and even boats, so there is no way to know how many there are, but in 1987 647 illegal drug laboratories were raided by law enforcement agencies, a 250 percent increase in the number discovered in 1981. The most lucative of these operations produce "ice"—crystal methamphetamine. Some ice comes from labs in Korea and the Philippines, but most of it is produced in domestic labs.

Drug Smuggling

Smuggling of illicit drugs into the United States, sale on the internal black market, and international laundering of drug profits is a huge, multibillion-dollar enterprise. Supplying and dealing in the drug black market is the most profitable enterprise of organized crime and has attracted many unorganized, amateur, and new criminal groups. The vast amount of money that smugglers, dealers, and suppliers make in the illicit market offsets the risks of apprehension (which are not very great), and some of it is used to corrupt law enforcement officials. Narcotics and law enforcement agents sometimes get directly involved in the smuggling business themselves. Bankers, accountants, and lawyers are involved in the laundering of drug money.

Florida is the focal point for the smuggling trade. About 70 percent of imported illegal drugs and as much as 90 percent of the illegal cocaine come through Florida. The drugs are brought in by private aircraft and by sea mainly through the Miami area and in the rugged, rural gulf coastal counties of the Florida peninsula. Drugs also come through virtually every international

Drug Smuggling Routes

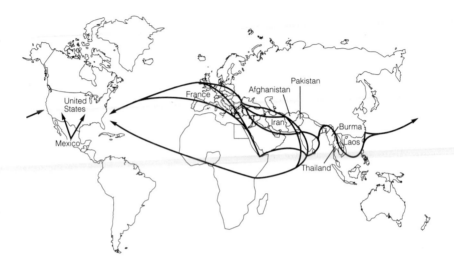

Major heroin smuggling routes into the United States.
Source: *DEA Quarterly Intelligence Trends.*

seaport and airport in the country and across the Mexican border. Drug interdiction makes use of the Coast Guard, and local, state, and federal (DEA) law enforcement, and sometimes the U.S. military. As the smugglers become increasingly sophisticated, law enforcement has become more and more high-tech with laser radar, drug sensors, and electronic detectors. The money and property of drug traffickers are seized and may be declared forfeited where they are used by law enforcement to continue to fight drug traffic.

Efforts to stem this tide of drug smuggling have produced many arrests and seizure of enormous quantities of drugs but thus far have been successful in slowing down only a small portion of the business. When serious inroads are made into the amount of drugs smuggled through one entry point, the trade simply is diverted to other points. Estimates are that interdiction seizures represent only about 10 percent of the total volume of smuggled drugs. No

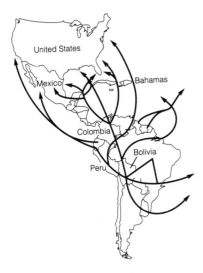

Major cocaine smuggling routes into the United States.
Source: *DEA Quarterly Intelligence Trends.*

one knows what the exact proportion is, however, and the quantities seized could go up or down independently of how much smuggling is attempted. (See *Newsweek*, Oct. 25, 1982, Nov. 23, 1987:29, Sept. 4, 1989; *USA Today*, July 18, 1986; *Time*, Dec. 18, 1989:50–56; *U.S. News & World Report*, Feb. 19, 1990).

The Wholesale and Retail Drug Traffic

The organized cartels and armies controlling drug crops and production in source countries link up with organized criminal gangs that control the importation and internal distribution and sale of illegal drugs in the United States. In addition to traditional organized crime (the Mafia), there are four major groupings of gangs involved in the wholesale and retail drug trade. These are Jamaican "posses" (in various parts of the country but concentrated in the Washington, D.C., area, Texas, and the Midwest); Haitian, Colombian, and other gangs of immigrants (legal and illegal) from the Caribbean and Latin America, who operate in Florida and the Southeast; Dominican gangs in the Northeast; and black street gangs. While they deal in all types of drugs, these groups are especially active in the crack trade, which is the biggest money maker in drug traffic and accounts for the majority of street-level drug arrests. The street gangs bear longstanding names and colors of juvenile delinquent gangs. There are the Bloods and Crips in Los Angeles, El Rukn (first known as the Blackstone Nation) and the Vice Lords in Chicago, the Miami Boys in Miami, and many other gangs in Washington, D.C., Detroit, and other cities. These drug gangs are ruthlessly violent and armed with assault rifles and weapons of war (DEA 1988b; *Newsweek*, Mar. 28, 1988:20–28).

In Detroit, and presumably elsewhere, heroin is still sold at the retail level in "dope pads" where customers come for supplies and sometimes shoot up on site. But this style of selling heroin has largely been replaced by a street distribution system with a "big man," lieutenant, crew boss, and runners. The street contact of the customer is the runner. These are typically young black males (usually beginning in the business at about age 14 to 16). The runner is "fronted" by a crew boss with a quantity of heroin to sell on the street. He returns the money to the crew boss, who pays him a percentage of the take. The crew boss, who is usually a former runner who has moved up, is the intermediate seller between the wholesale supplier and runners. He recruits and supervises runners in "his" crew and is responsible for the drugs and money. The crew boss works for a "lieutenant," who in turn works for the "big man," who is the wholesaler. Some crime organizations control several hundred runners, organized into many crews, but they still do not totally monopolize the heroin trade, some of which is handled by freelance operators and less organized gangs (Mieczkowski 1986).

The cocaine (as well as other drug) trade is organized similarly. Crack deals are made openly on the streets, to customers driving by in cars, and in crack houses (often heavily fortified). "Kingpins" sell to midlevel distributors, who supply lower-level dealers, who control street sellers. The street-level "boss" may get a kilo of cocaine from the wholesaler and have his workers cut it with lidocaine (a synthetic cocaine) and cook it up into crack (producing about three times as much drug as he started with). His crew packs various quantities of crack into vials (from one rock to as many as six) and sells them on the street for $3 to $20 a vial. The street crew consists of the dealer, a lookout, a steerer, a stasher, a muscle or guard, and runners who make the actual delivery to the street user. The runner collects the money and returns it to the boss. In addition to street distribution through the crews, there are crack houses where users come to buy the drug and often consume it on the premises. Crack houses are concentrated in lower-class black neighborhoods and are most often abandoned houses and apartments, frequently in publicly subsidized low-income housing projects (Hayeslip 1989; *Newsweek*, May 29, 1989:37).

Federal policy provides funding and technical assistance, and federal agents are involved in controlling drug trafficking at all levels. However, federal law-enforcement efforts are mainly crop eradication, disruption at the drug source, interdiction of imported and interstate shipments, investigation of organized crime, and the tracing of money laundering. High-level smugglers and organized-crime bosses are arrested by the DEA and FBI, indicted by federal prosecutors, and tried in federal courts. Local police and sheriffs are primarily responsible for enforcing drug laws at the street level; their arrests are indicted by states' attorneys and their cases tried in state courts. A number of traditional and new strategies are in use by local law enforcement against this level of the drug black market.

The police respond to citizen calls regarding drug violations, patrol the streets, arrest drug users and dealers, conduct undercover investigation, and carry out "buy/bust" operations against dealers. They also conduct reverse sting operations in which they clear an area of drug dealers and then establish undercover agents as dealers and arrest the drug customers who buy the drugs. In some areas, there are intensive drug crackdowns with saturation of patrols, shutting down of dope houses, and disruption of street trading, as in the Operation Pressure Point program in New York City. In many communities, individual citizens and neighborhood organizations have taken aggressive actions on their own: patrolling the streets for drug deals, directly interrupting sales, confronting drug dealers and users, declaring drug-free zones, tearing down vacant houses known to be used as crack houses, and suing owners of buildings where drug dealing is done. The police have come increasingly to utilize, aid, and promote these community resources and to establish innovative programs such as working the schools in drug-education programs. Although some communities and police departments report great success, it is not clear how effective these strategies are in affecting either supply of or demand for drugs. They appear to have clear deterrent effects in the short run with reports of reduction in the drug traffic and fewer drug-related crimes in the targeted areas, but these effects tend to decay in the long term (Brown 1988; Dickson 1988; *Newsweek*, Mar. 28, 1988:29; Hayeslip 1989; Moore and Kleiman 1989; *Time*, Sept. 11, 1989:15–18; Sherman 1990).

Results of Law Enforcement

Not only is it difficult to show direct and sustained success of these special tactics, but it has not been established that the intended results of any of the law enforcement policy regarding eradication, interdiction, reduction of the drug trade, and arrest of drug-law violators have been accomplished to a substantial degree. Crop production has been stopped or severely curtailed in some countries, such as Turkey, which once were major producers of opium. Marijuana, coca, and poppy farms have been eliminated and processing labs closed down in many places. But production is not down; it seems simply to shift elsewhere. Seizures of shipments, both in quantity and value, have increased, but the shifting of smuggling away from the crackdown sites and the importation of drugs do not seem to have been reduced.

Street prices for cocaine and other drugs have been declining for some time, and some interpret this as a clear indication that the quantities grown and smuggled in are increasing so much that prices are being discounted to move the merchandise. However, other, equally plausible, arguments exist regarding the street value of drugs. One is that prices may be declining because even as the supplies are being reduced by law enforcement strategies, there has been an even greater reduction in overall drug use in the last decade. Thus, the demand for illegal drugs has dropped. A lowered demand will reduce prices as surely as a surplus supply will. A second argument is that street prices undergo temporary fluctuation in ways which are not always tied to supply and demand so that there is a lag between reduction of supply and street value. Indeed, there are some recent indications that the price of cocaine on the streets has gone back up and its purity has gone down (*Newsweek*, July 2, 1990:24). One reason might be that for the first time in more than a decade there is evidence that the production of cocaine is down in the producing countries, as the prices and the wholesale supplies on the U.S. market have been significantly reduced (Jehl 1990). Whether reduction has resulted from the lowered production and disrupted supply or other factors is not known.

It has not been established that tough laws and criminal justice practices have increased deterrence of drug-law violations. The effects of only one such law have been adequately studied. In 1973 the state of New York enacted the Emergency Dangerous Drug Act in which prison terms for all drug violations and mandatory sentences were imposed for possession of certain quantities of drugs, even for first offenders. The evaluation of the effectiveness of this "nation's toughest law" in 1976 showed that the narcotics trade was as brisk as it had been. There was some evidence of a temporary effect on heroin use, but reduction was not sustained. The risk of punishment for drug offenders was not significantly increased, and drug offenses and serious drug-related crimes were not deterred through imprisonment (Joint Committee 1977). Rather than significantly increase deterrence, the main result of tough laws and harsh sentences has been the explosion of the jail and prison populations.

Drug-law enforcement at all levels has produced other negative consequences. Many have argued that the main effect of drug laws has been to set up a "crime tariff" (Packer 1968) and other conditions promoting a profitable black market for drugs, which in turn supports criminal organizations and violence. The illegality inflates the prices and profits for organized crime and others willing to run the risks of smuggling and dealing in an illegal product. One of the major arguments of drug-legalization proponents is that legalization would undermine the criminal groups in the drug trade. This outcome is uncertain, however; legalization probably would not be any more successful in producing its intended consequences than drug prohibition laws and policies have been in producing their intended consequences, as discussed on pages 156–161. But there is little doubt that one of the unintended consequences of prohibitive drug laws is the development of the enormously profitable illegal drug trade. Enforcement of drug laws and the war on drugs have also been implicated in questionable police practices and infringement of individual rights.

While enforcement of laws prohibiting injury to persons and property is aided by the willingness of victims and witnesses to testify, enforcement of laws against "victimless" offenses such as the sale or possession of drugs cannot rely on these sources of information and help in prosecution. Because the parties involved either are willing partners in a commercial transaction or are mainly victimizing themselves or others, such as their unborn babies and their children who are unable to do anything about it, there are no complaining victims. Few people in the drug subculture or involved in the drug trade are motivated to call the police or act as voluntary witnesses. Therefore, enforcement must rely heavily on undercover agents who secure evidence and testify in court as witnesses against dealers and on evidence supplied by drug-using informers.

This means that police may slip over the edge of legal surveillance and investigation into entrapping users or illegally inducing someone to commit drug crimes in buy/bust and reverse sting operations. Police informers are most often themselves addicts and dealers in known violation of the law. Yet in order to gain enough evidence to make an arrest, narcotics agents must ignore those violations and even maintain informants' addictions by paying them off with drugs or money. Because buyer, seller, and user are all motivated to dispose of drug evidence to avoid conviction, police are pushed to making surprise raids and illegal searches and seizures. Tactics of nighttime raids, forced entries, and raids on the wrong houses are not confined to the distant past.

The war on drugs has produced other questions of violations of constitutional and civil rights. Privacy issues have been raised regarding drug-testing programs for private employees, government workers, and school students; stop-and-frisk actions by police; and the use of drug-courier profiles to stop and question people at airports, train stations, and bus stations. Also, innocent second parties, who have leased or rented property unwittingly to drug dealers, have sometimes suffered as the result of their property being seized. The seizures and forfeitures of money and property under the Continuing Criminal Enterprise Act and the Racketeer Influenced Corrupt Organization Act have been challenged as unconstitutional. At this time, all of these practices, under certain conditions, have been upheld by the Supreme Court as constitutional and not illegally infringing on civil rights (Abadinsky 1989; *Time*, Sept. 18, 1989:28; *Journal of Criminal Law and Criminology*, 1990:996–1085; *Newsweek*, Apr. 23, 1990:17–20).

Is Legalization the Solution?

In my opinion, the answer is no. There are influential proponents of complete legalization of all currently illegal drugs. The shortcomings and failures of law enforcement, and the range of unintended costly consequences that we have just reviewed, form the primary basis for these proponents to argue for legalization. As noted earlier, there was a strong marijuana-legalization movement in the early 1970s that spilled over into support of legalization of other drugs. Indeed, at that time, I supported decriminalization and eventual legalization of marijuana and other drugs. I have since changed my mind on the issue for the reasons given later in this section in opposition to legalization. Others, such as the conservative economist Milton Friedman, who argued for legalization then, continue to do so. They have been joined by a strange mixture of conservative (e.g., columnist William Buckley), liberal (including the ACLU, political scientist Ethan Nadelman, lawyer Rufus King), and radical voices (sociologists William Chambliss and Craig Reinarman, among others). The mixture also includes some prominent judges, mayors, and prosecutors (*U.S. News & World Report*, Apr. 9, 1990:26–27).

In 1987 Arnold Trebach of American University founded the Drug Policy Foundation with over a $2 million endowment to sponsor conferences for and give monetary awards to public figures and academicians who favor alternatives to maintaining drug prohibitions. All of the awards have gone to proponents of legalization, and the conferences have largely revolved around papers favoring repeal of drug laws. (See Reinarman and Levine 1990.)

Thus, some powerful and well-financed groups are pushing for legalization of cocaine, heroin, marijuana, and other drugs. But many academicians, politicians, government officials, and organizations (such as National Families in Action) are just as opposed to legalization. Thus far, public opinion and the political consensus in Congress and state legislatures are opposed to repeal of drug laws. The proponents of legalization have had little success in repeal of current laws or in passage of new laws. They have been attacked by William Bennett, the former Director of the National Office of Drug Control Policy (Bennett 1990; *Newsweek*, Aug. 21, 1989:16–18, Dec. 25, 1989:46–48), rejected by the U.S. Conference of Mayors (*USA Today*, June 14, 1988), and roundly criticized by academicians (Kaplan 1988; Inciardi and McBride 1990; Jacobs 1990).

Arguments in Favor of Legalization.   The case for legalization made by the proponents focuses on the failures of the present system of drug control. They maintain that virtually any other system would work better and that almost all of the problems associated with drug use would be remedied by legalization. They argue that we have failed to solve the drug problem with current policy and that we are losing the war on drugs. Indeed, some proponents of legalization maintain that it is a hopeless fight that can never be won and probably has already been lost. Far from reducing drug use and controlling problems associated with drug use and abuse, outlawing drugs has simply made the drug problem worse. If drugs were legalized, the crime tariff would be removed and the lucrative profits of the black-market drug trade, with its attendant corruption of the system and violence, would disappear. There also would be fewer deaths, violence, and crime because addicts would have no motivation to commit crimes to support their habits. Proponents of legalization believe that legalizing drugs would make them no more available than they are right now and neither drug use nor abuse would be likely to increase. Or, even if there were an increase, it would be minimal, manageable, and well worth the gain from legalization. According to proponents, the drug trade could be taxed, and even after tremendous increases in funding for treatment, there would be net increases in revenues. The costly expenditures on law enforcement fighting the drug war would be saved. Thus, there would be something of a peace dividend, and the money could be spent on other, more worthy causes.

The proponents of legalization are specific about what they see as the problems of the present system and what problems would be solved with legalization. But they are vague in showing what the new policy would be and how it would work to solve the drug problem.

> The lack of a fleshed-out legalization proposal makes it extremely difficult to assess or to criticize the legalization position. Skeptics vainly try to fix their sights on a moving target. . . . Those attuned to the debate are asked to endorse drug legalization "in principle" and to think about implementation later. (Jacobs 1990:28)

The most frequent references to alternative systems in the pro-legalization literature are to either: (1) a physician-controlled, prescription-based system patterned after the early British system or (2) a legalized regulatory system something like that in place now for alcohol and tobacco. Under the physician-controlled or public-health system, addicts would be supplied with whatever drug they were addicted to by physicians in the course of treating their addiction. Just as methadone maintenance programs now maintain heroin addicts, physicians would maintain heroin and other habits through prescriptions in the course of treatment. This would both treat the problem and remove the drug supply from criminal organizations. Under the regulatory system, drugs that are currently illegal would be treated as legal substances but subject to advertising, content, purchase, age, and other restrictions on their production, distribution, and sale. The enforcement of the regulations would control the problems associated with drugs and drive out criminal traffickers. (See Chambliss 1988; Benoit 1989; Buckley 1989; Nadelman 1989; Postrel 1989; Reinarman and Levine 1990; Weisheit 1990b).

Arguments Against Legalization. Some critics of legalization tend to attack it as an immoral policy that is essentially a declaration of unconditional surrender to criminals. One does not have to react this extremely, however, to see that there are serious problems with the legalization proposals. Ultimately, the issue is a moral one, and legalization does imply moral approval. But there are issues other than the moral objections that undermine the case for legalization. The case for legalization rests almost entirely on failures of the present social policy and the promised successes and benefits of a new system of legalization. The failures of the present system are neither so great nor so intractable, and the benefits of legalization are neither so certain nor as risk-free, as proponents of legalization claim. On balance, there are insufficient grounds for legalization at this time.

The basic argument that the battle against drugs is being or has already been lost cannot withstand empirical scrutiny. As we have seen in Chapter 3, by virtually any measure one wants to use, the drug problem in this country is less widespread now than it was a decade ago. There is little room for complacency; the successes are often modest, and we do not have good knowledge as to what has worked to produce the improvements. But there can be no doubt that we have been doing something right. In spite of all the failures and the need for reform in the present system, the headway that was made in the 1980s leaves little grounds for arguing that something totally opposite is needed.

There is no way to know what the achievements and failures of legalization would be, but we can get some idea by examining what has happened with the major drugs of abuse that are currently legal, alcohol and tobacco, and the earlier British prescription system. That examination leaves little room for hope that the legalization models will solve our nation's drug problems.

The prescription system in Great Britain has not contained the spread of drug use and addiction. The legal supply leaked to nonaddicts and recreational users, which led to a large number of new addicts being formed. The failures of the prescription system have been known at least since the early 1970s, and it has essentially been abandoned in Great Britain. In the United States, barbiturates, amphetamines, and various opiates are already available on a presciption basis. This legal route is sufficiently restricted for addicts, abusers, and recreational users that it has essentially no effect on the illegal traffic. Indeed, diversion from this legal market is a major source of supply for the illegal market. How would a new prescription system, even one in which some addicts would have access through prescription, be sufficiently different to guarantee that there would be no diversion to nonauthorized consumption?

There is also little doubt that drug prohibition has had serious, unintended consequences, the most notable of which are the violence and crime associated with the illegal drug trade. By definition, legalization would eliminate violations of laws prohibiting manufacture, distribution, and possession of certain drugs. Legalization would undoubtedly have some effect in reducing organized crime and most likely would reduce the violence that drug gangs, smugglers, and dealers now commit. There is also some chance that legalization would lessen the corruption which goes with using huge drug profits to buy protection and the threats to civil rights that drug-law enforcement sometimes makes. It is highly doubtful, however, that legalization through a regulatory system would wipe out organized crime or significantly reduce its overall criminal activity. We have seen in Chapter 4 that the argument that the use or abuse of drugs causes crime cannot be sustained by the evidence. The correlation of crime with the currently legal drug alcohol is stronger than it is for any of the currently illegal drugs.

Any monetary peace dividend that would come from ceasing the costly war on drugs is likely to be as evanescent as the peace dividend from the end of the cold war. Legal drugs cause more deaths and present more health problems and higher treatment costs to society than do all of the illegal drugs combined. It is unlikely that enough savings from lowered law-enforcement costs could be shifted to handle the greater treatment and other costs. Judging from what has happened in states that have legalized and taxed gambling, great expectations about enhanced state revenues used for socially useful purposes would be disappointed. There is little ground for believing that the costs of constructing and running a regulatory system for legalized marijuana, cocaine, and heroin would be much less than current law enforcement costs. Why should we believe that a strict regulatory system would be any more effectively enforced or have any more success in preventing the construction of an illegal system to get around the regulatory restrictions than the present system has?

> [A] cynical disdain for drug enforcement is replaced by a naive faith in the effectiveness of government regulation. . . . While the specifics of regulation have yet to emerge, all of the legalization proposals actually involve *increased* regulation. . . . The point is that there is a real naiveté to the belief that drug *laws* are unenforceable but drug *regulations* are. (Inciardi and McBride 1990:3; emphasis in original)

Judging from the present regulatory system on tobacco and alcohol, legalization would also produce its own set of costly unintended negative consequences. Undoubtedly, legalization would increase the general level of use of marijuana, cocaine, heroin, and other drugs. References to marijuana

use declining in states (such as Oregon) that decriminalized it are unconvincing. Prohibition was not removed in those states; only the sanctions for
violation were decriminalized (and in fact Oregon has since increased the
penalties for marijuana-law violations). More important, equal or greater
reductions in marijuana use were experienced in states that maintained
criminal sanctions. Also unconvincing are examples from the Netherlands and
other European countries that have instituted policies approaching (but not
completely achieving) legalization of certain drugs and which have less of a
drug problem than they did before legalization, and much less than the drug
problem in the United States. The drug problem in the United States has
abated even more rapidly than it has in other countries, and some European
cities are experiencing increased cocaine and opiate use. The differences in
the amount of drug use and abuse between the United States and European
countries is less now than it has ever been.

Although there are periods when not much of a connection exists between availability and frequency of use, in the long run, the more freely
available a substance is the more likely it is to be used. The more regulated
and controlled it is the less it is used; it is least likely to be used when it
is totally banned and the ban is enforced. Control of use is especially likely
when the substance is disapproved in the informal social control system and
legal prohibition has strong support in public opinion—a description that fits
the current state of affairs in our country. Legal prohibition not only reflects
that public opinion but over time helps to shape and undergird it as well.
Removal of legal prohibition over time can be expected to undermine informal social disapproval.

Of course, social and legal approval or disapproval are not the only
variables involved in how frequently a drug is used. The real and perceived
harm balanced against the pleasures of taking the substance also play a role.
Therefore, marijuana use has the potential to grow to the same level as tobacco
and alcohol use with basically the same magnitude of threat to health and
life. Legalized recreational use of amphetamines and hallucinogens also could
be expected to rise to exceed any historical levels of use. Use of cocaine and
heroin probably would not increase as much as that of these other substances,
but it makes little sense to argue that their use would remain steady or decline.

If the level of use of presently prohibited drugs even comes close to
creating the problems for individuals and society now created by alcohol and
tobacco, financial and human costs would not be reduced by legalization. They
would increase. Fewer deaths would result from drug smugglers killing one
another or from other drug-related killings; more deaths would result from
more people taking hazardous drugs. There is some hope that if drugs were
legalized, intravenous drug users would be less motivated to share needles
and that the spread of AIDS by drug taking would be reduced. It is difficult
to see how this would result, however. Needles are inexpensive now, and even

giving away free needles to drug addicts as some communities have begun doing has had no appreciable effect on reducing the spread of AIDS. While there might be some reduction in the proportion of intravenous drug users sharing needles with legalized heroin, the increase in number of addicts could offset that. The people dying from drug overdoses and AIDS contracted through IV drug use would be just as dead as the people killed in illegal drug trafficking, and there might be more of them. Fetuses would be just as harmed by their mothers taking legal cocaine as they are by their mothers using the drug illegally. If cocaine were legalized, a larger number of fetuses might be damaged.

The greater the extent to which legal regulations attempt to control these problems (through control of advertising, sales to minors, restrictions on retail and wholesale distribution, etc.) the more such regulations move back toward prohibition, much as has happened with increased restrictions on tobacco. The higher the taxes imposed on drugs in a system of legalization, the closer they come to effectively criminalizing use in the way that the Marihuana Tax Act criminalized that drug's use. There is little basis for believing that tough controls through strong regulation of a legal drug would be any more enforceable and avoid any of the problems of tough legal controls over a drug that is illegal. The crime-tariff effects and support for a black market in drugs would be essentially the same. (See Kaplan 1988; Inciardi and McBride 1990; Jacobs 1990.)

The drug problems in this country are awful. Nevertheless, they are less so today than a decade or two decades ago. The benefits of legalization of drugs are no more certain than are the harmful consequences of legalization. Eight out of ten Americans believe that legalization is a bad idea which would make the problem worse than it is now (Colasanto 1990). This is not the time to legalize drugs.

Social Control and Public Policy on Drugs: Treatment and Prevention

D R U G   T R E A T M E N T

The most commonly promoted alternatives to the law enforcement approach in the control of deviant drug use are treatment and rehabilitation of drug abusers and programs aimed at prevention of drug use (see the discussion on pages 177–182). Most treatment programs are based on the idea that drug abusers are sick—more victims than criminal offenders—and in need of treatment to help them get off drugs or control their use of them. This disease concept (see Chapter 2) is most frequently applied to opiate, cocaine, and alcohol abusers, but it has at one time or another been applied to abusers of all types of drugs. It has also expanded to include less and less seriously abusing cases (Peele 1989).

This approach toward drug abuse is meant to inspire a more sympathetic and less punitive treatment. The central approach is to help people lead drug-free lives or to cope with their addiction. The aim is not to punish drug users for legal transgressions, although most public treatment programs are populated mainly by law violators who are ordered by the court to enroll in them. If enough drug abusers can be cured of their disease, then the level of use will be reduced, the demand will diminish, black markets will dry up, and crime and other drug-related social problems will be alleviated. Therefore, treatment programs of one kind or another have been in operation since the beginning of public control of drugs. They have received new emphasis as the idea of combating the drug trade by working to reduce the demand side has been revived in current national drug policy.

The Drug Treatment Industry

Drug (and alcohol) treatment and rehabilitation is a large and growing industry. In 1982 approximately 170,000 persons were under treatment for drug abuse in one or another of over 3,000 of these programs in the United States. This was down from over 200,000 drug treatment clients in 1977. But by 1989 there were over 344,000 clients in 6,100 programs (NIDA/NIAAA 1990). From 1978 to 1984, for-profit residential programs increased 350 percent and the number of clients increased 400 percent. Private programs generate over $1 billion a year in revenue. However, two-thirds of all clients are in nonprofit rehabilitation programs, operated or funded by federal, state, or local governments. Nine out of ten of these treatment facilities are for adult drug abusers. Federal funding for drug rehabilitation programs has increased every year since 1981. For fiscal 1989 the federal budget was about $2 billion for prevention and treatment programs. For fiscal 1990 President Bush requested about $8 billion for federal antidrug programs and personnel, of which about $3 billion was for drug rehabilitation and prevention programs. In addition, private funding for nonprofit programs grew from about $4 million in 1983 to over $32 million in 1989 (Polich et al. 1984; Cox News Service, July 9, 1989; *Los Angeles Times*, Sept. 6, 1989; *New York Times* News Service, Oct. 3, 1989; Peele 1989; NIDA/NIAAA 1990).

In spite of this increased effort in money, programs, and personnel, treatment facilities in many places do not have enough beds and funds to meet the demand. Crack, cocaine, and opiate abusers often find it difficult to get treatment. The private facilities are too expensive for all but the affluent and well insured, and they tend to be less utilized (about 60 percent of capacity). Many public and nonprofit private facilities are too crowded, underfinanced, and inundated by court-referred and criminal cases. The available programs in some areas are able to handle the treatment demand, but those in other areas are well over capacity. For the nation as a whole, treatment programs are filled to more than 80 percent of capacity (NIDA/NIAAA 1990).

Why should this be so? As we have noted in all previous chapters, the total number of users and the rate of drug use have declined noticeably in the past decade. Why do we have the increased expenditures and expanding number of patients, programs, and persons seeking help during this same time? Why has membership of Alcoholics Anonymous, Narcotics Anonymous, and similar alcohol and drug abuse groups grown? One answer is that the number of serious abusers has increased even while the overall level of use has gone down. As we have seen, this is not true. Addiction and abuse have abated. A plausible answer is that because there is such a large, unmet treatment need for all types of severe addiction and drug problems, the number of programs has grown and will need to continue to grow just to try to catch up with the untreated army of drug abusers. Thus, there could be tremendous increases in the number of persons under treatment without any change or even a decline in the total number of drug abusers.

Net-Widening in Drug Treatment.   Another plausible answer is that the growth in programs and patients has come about as a result of extensive "net-widening" in the treatment industry. Public opinion and political interests have converged on a consensus that drug abuse is a top social problem in this country. There has been enormous support for combating the problem in both law enforcement and treatment, but little public or political consensus on just what it is that constitutes serious drug abuse. The concept of what constitutes deviant drug use serious enough to require treatment has expanded so that many cases which professionals previously would not have considered to be in need of treatment now become defined as necessitating treatment. Public attitudes are more likely to see drug abusers as in need of treatment rather than prison. The criminal and moral stigma attached to being an addict or a drug abuser has been reduced. As drug addiction comes increasingly to be seen as a disease and the addict as the victim rather than perpetrator of morally disgraceful actions, seeking treatment for drug problems is becoming more acceptable. Public admission that one has a drug problem and that one has sought or will seek treatment to overcome the problem is as likely to be seen as a courageous facing of a personal difficulty as it is an admission of deviant motives and behavior.

In fact, checking into a drug or alcohol clinic for treatment has become almost chic in some circles as one celebrity and public figure after another admits to having had a drug or drinking problem. They dramatically enter the clinic and emerge a month later, something of a hero for having recognized and conquered their problem. They then have a time on the lecture and talk-show circuit as a spokesperson for drug treatment programs, encouraging people to recognize their problem early and to enter a rehabilitation program. An increasing number of people are motivated to define themselves as drug abusers and attempt to get treatment. In many of these cases, the actual level of abuse is low and would have been viewed in earlier years as recreational or moderate use. The ability of the affluent self-referrals to pay for their treatment, the increase in federal and state budgets for drug treatment, and the insurance coverage of drug treatment motivates providers of treatment programs to expand the category of users certified as in need of treatment.

Peele (1989) argues that the drug treatment industry has worked hard to cast a widening net, to increase the number defined as having a problem, to promote the idea that treatment is needed at the earliest stages even before serious problems develop, and to open up new categories of persons defined as needing treatment, such as co-dependents and members of addicts' families. Some research has confirmed this tendency on the part of treatment providers. Moberg (1986) reports that when adolescent drug-treatment programs find themselves in a situation of ample services but a stable flow of clientele, they widen the referral sources and take in youngsters with less serious drug problems. For instance, under conditions of service overload, only adolescents defined as clearly drug "dependent" are admitted. Any adolescent believed to fit the broader category of "harmfully involved" with drugs is admitted when the number of referrals slackens.

Types of Drug Treatment Programs

The specific treatment techniques used singly or in combination in these programs have included abrupt, or "cold turkey," withdrawal, gradual withdrawal, drug-assisted detoxification, individual counseling, group therapy, self-help groups, and simply maintenance of addiction. These techniques have been incorporated into a great variety of programs and treatment settings, each of which has enjoyed some moment in history as the best hope for solving drug problems for individuals and society.

The major programs can be categorized into four general types: compulsory treatment, drug-free residential, drug-free nonresidential, and methadone maintenance.

1. *Compulsory treatment* refers to the legally mandated or coerced participation by drug abusers. The earliest compulsory treatment was incarceration of federal-drug-law violators in two narcotics hospitals. Later, civil commitment to institutions for drug treatment was used by a few states and the federal government. Today compulsory treatment takes the form of enrollment of incarcerated criminal offenders who are drug abusers in in-prison drug programs or the court-ordered requirement that drug offenders enroll in treatment programs as a condition of their probation or community control (house arrest). The nonprison programs in which offenders are required to enroll are typically the other three types of programs.

2. *Residential* or semiresidential *therapeutic communities,* hospitals, and clinics have live-in clients who undergo detoxification and a program of individual and group counseling.

3. *Nonresidential, outpatient* clinics and *self-help* or support programs (most of which are based on the Alcoholics Anonymous model, such as

as Narcotics Anonymous), which also use individual and group treatment approaches, approximate therapeutic-community programs without the closed environment of live-in facilities.

4. *Methadone maintenance programs* differ significantly from all of these other approaches. Methadone maintenance programs do not aim primarily to end drug habits. Although some programs attempt to get some clients to withdraw from drugs, methadone programs are designed simply to provide addicts with an inexpensive and ensured supply to maintain their addiction with one form of legal opiate (methadone) as a substitute for illegal opiates (heroin). These programs are exclusively for heroin and other opiate addicts. There are no cocaine or crack maintenance programs.

Multidrug use is the typical pattern for those in rehabilitation programs. The largest number of persons under treatment for drug abuse of all kinds—crack, barbiturates, amphetamines—is found in nonresidential, outpatient programs that attempt to get them off drugs and then keep them drug-free (Statistical Abstracts 1983). The federal prison system has a program for treatment of inmates with drug problems, and many state and local correctional facilities have a drug treatment unit or program. But these are for inmates imprisoned for other criminal offenses who also have drug problems, not for persons specifically incarcerated for drug treatment. There are few people now under compulsory confinement specifically for treatment of drug problems, although most of the people in the various public residential and nonresidential programs are there, to some degree, involuntarily. They either have been placed there by court order as a condition of probation or have taken up the treatment because they have been pressured by law enforcement, employers, or others. Heroin addicts under treatment are most apt to be in some type of methadone maintenance program.

Compulsory Treatment and Civil Commitments.   Since the 1920s efforts have been directed at forcing addicts and other drug abusers to undergo treatment in prisons, in hospitals, and in the community. The procedures in these compulsory programs have moved from abrupt and gradual withdrawal to group therapy, individual counseling, ex-addict counseling, and whatever else is popular at the time. Whatever the treatment procedure and whether institutional or community, compulsory treatment is closely tied to criminal justice actions. Although more recent analyses report that for some offenders involuntary treatment works better than voluntary commitment, compulsory treatment has a history of failure, and the newer reports do not report much of a change (Anglin 1988; Leukefeld and Tims 1988).

In 1935 the first federal narcotics hospital was opened in Lexington, Kentucky, as a U.S. Public Health Service hospital, and three years later one was opened in Ft. Worth, Texas. Both were closed as narcotics treatment hospitals and placed under the jurisdiction of the federal prison system in 1974. In fact, all along they resembled medium-security prisons more than hospitals. The "patients" had been convicted of federal drug charges and sentenced to the facility instead of to time in prison. However, it was possible for addicts to commit themselves to the narcotics hospitals, and eventually these "voluntary" patients (given a choice by the court of self-commitment in the hospital or incarceration in prison) outnumbered those directly committed by a federal judge. The technique in the narcotics hospitals was initial maintenance on morphine, methadone, or meperidine and then gradual detoxification and withdrawal to remove the physiological dependence on opiates. The relapse was extremely high for both types of inmates (O'Donnell 1965).

In the 1960s, state prisons began to incorporate counseling, support groups, and other drug rehabilitation programs for inmates judged to have serious drug problems and detoxification programs were introduced in some local jails. Under the NARA (Narcotic Addict Rehabilitation Act, 1968), drug treatment programs were instituted in federal prisons. By 1979, 4 percent of the inmates in state prisons and correctional facilities were enrolled in drug treatment programs. The increasing percentage of prison commitments for drug offenses and of inmates who were drug abusers prior to incarceration meant that participation in these prison drug programs nearly tripled to 11 percent by 1987. Very few of these programs offer comprehensive treatment with vocational, individual, group, and family counseling. Surprisingly, drug education (see pages 177–182), rather than drug rehabilitation, is the most common program (Chaiken 1989).

Only a handful of programs in prisons have been evaluated. Only five programs have reported lower recidivism of program participants compared to recidivism of drug offenders who were not program participants. Even among the best in-prison programs, none has been shown to be highly effective in reducing drug behavior either in the institution or after release (Chaiken 1989).

California and New York began institutional "civil commitments" in the 1960s as alternatives to imprisonment. These were meant to be hospitals in which addicts and others with severe drug problems would be committed by a process resembling the civil commitment of persons to mental hospitals. The commitment was for a minimum of six months in the institution followed by three years under community supervision. During that time the person was to submit to periodic and unannounced urinalysis drug tests. The programs also allowed voluntary admission. The standard treatment procedure was detoxification followed by group counseling sessions. The relapse rates from these state, and also federal, civil commitments were about as high as those among individuals who had been committed to the federal narcotics hospitals.

Although eventually twenty-five states came to have some type of legislation permitting compulsory drug rehabilitation through civil-commitment proceedings, federal and state programs were in full operation only from 1965 to 1975. Civil commitments are still in operation, but commitment to institutions has largely been replaced by court-ordered compulsory participation in community-based drug treatment programs or residential therapeutic communities (De Leon 1988a; Leukefeld and Tims 1988). The civil-commitment proceedings were established to rehabilitate drug addicts, but they recently have been examined as one way to control the spread of AIDS by intravenous drug users. The major source of the spread of AIDS to the heterosexual population is the transmission of the human immunodeficiency virus (HIV), which causes AIDS, through the sharing of contaminated needles, prostitution by HIV-infected IV drug users, and sexual relationships between infected drug users and uninfected partners. Involuntary incarceration of IV drug users at risk of AIDs who will not voluntarily enter treatment may work to contain their role as AIDS transmitters, even if it does little to end their drug use (Leukefeld and Tims 1988).

Residential and Nonresidential Programs: Therapeutic Communities, Hospitals, and Self-Help Groups. Both residential and nonresidential programs share with in-prison programs the primary goal of stopping drug abuse and producing a drug-free life. These programs may be either publicly or privately operated and financed through some combination of public and private support. The approval of drug and alcohol treatment for coverage by health insurance has produced a proliferation of private hospitals and clinics. Some of these are part of national hospital or health-care corporations, and some are very expensive programs that cater primarily to wealthy and celebrity clients. In addition to court referrals, the residential and nonresidential programs receive voluntary referrals and referrals from employee assistance programs (see Chapter 4).

The best-known residential programs are those that attempt to provide a "therapeutic-community" environment run mainly by ex-addicts promoting an entirely drug-free life-style. The idea is to provide an antidrug normative climate and to counteract addicts' self-deception and rationalizations for drug use. The programs offer social support for a positive, non–drug dependent image of oneself, and help individuals who have reached bottom regain control of their lives without recourse to drugs.

All of the current therapeutic communities in operation today can be traced to Synanon. Synanon was established in California in the late 1950s by a small group of addicts led by an ex-alcoholic who was convinced that the self-help, admission of defeat by alcohol, and group-support techniques used by Alcoholics Anonymous would work with drug addicts. The chief technique used by Synanon to provoke and maintain abstinence from drugs was regular, intensive group confrontation sessions in which members attacked each others' rationalizations and excuses for using drugs in the first place. Synanon was scornful of the addict who blamed society or other people for becoming a junkie and belittled the addict's complaints about how bad the addiction was. The attempt was to promote disparaging stories about drug experiences and to make the addicts feel worthless and without hope until they got off drugs. There was no detoxification, and there were no professional counselors or court referrals—only junkies voluntarily entering Synanon and confronting other junkies (Yablonsky 1965).

The Synanon approach appeared at a time when there was little else available but the official, compulsory facilities described earlier. It promised an end to the dismal failure record of attempts to treat drug addicts. It received favorable press coverage and expanded to other locations. Other therapeutic communities modeled after Synanon were started. This approach gained momentum throughout the 1960s and into the 1970s as the whole idea of confrontation and sensitivity-training groups gained faddish currency. Daytop Lodge and Daytop Village, Phoenix House, Reality House, Odyssey House, and other names were attached to the programs modeling the Synanon approach in one way or another. Although Synanon has disappeared (after a bizarre period of converting to a violent cult), many of these other houses are still in operation and expanding. Although the reliance on ex-addicts and self-help has been retained, federal and state support is sought, professional staff are hired, and involuntary residents are accepted.

The therapeutic-community movement also inspired a whole array of nonresidential programs, drop-in centers, hot lines, and "rap" centers in the 1970s, designed especially for adolescents and offering peer-group talk and counseling on drug problems whether or not the youngster had serious drug abuse problems. These continue in modified form today for both adults and teenagers in most communities, often as part of the sort of overall community drug prevention and education programs described later in this chapter. State and county mental-health clinics as well as nonprofit and for-profit organizations offer nonresidential drug treatment relying heavily on group sessions.

In spite of its claims to almost complete success with addicts, there is no objective evidence that Synanon was ever able to do any better than any other approach in treating drug problems. Since Synanon deliberately kept no records and released no information on what happened to addicts when they left the program, it was protected from having the claims tested. The programs fashioned after Synanon have kept records, and follow-up studies have been done on several of them. The conclusions from these studies agree that the programs do have some success, but they have not demonstrated effective treatment for most addicts or other drug abusers who were enrolled in them (Waldorf 1973; Lukoff 1974).

The studies show that the overall success rate of those who finish the program is better than the success rate of those coming out of the prison and civil-commitment programs. However, all of the programs exercise strict screening of referrals and tend to admit only those who appear most committed to change or most amenable to treatment. Therefore, they have a better risk group from the start. A very high proportion (75 to 80 percent) of this select group drop out quickly from the program but do not get counted as failures, leaving a tiny residue of people who have a pretty good chance of success in any program. The successful cases tend to be those who stay within the program as staff or obtain employment in some other drug treatment facility as counselors (Waldorf 1973).

The traditional therapeutic communities have been joined by a variety of other hospitals, residential clinics, halfway houses, group homes, and other residentially based programs. They have broadened the methods used. Almost all have retained the group sessions (often in the form of group-therapy sessions run by professional counselors), and many have tried to maintain the intensive family feeling and antidrug community found in therapeutic communities. Most programs, however, cannot be described as therapeutic communities. There are about 500 drug-free residential treatment programs, but less than one-third incorporate the main features of the traditional therapeutic community. The therapeutic-community approach is oriented primarily toward voluntary clients, and in many programs only self-admissions are taken. But from 1965 to 1975 drug abusers remanded by courts as an alternative to state institutionalization under civil-commitment laws, were accepted by some therapeutic communities. Since then coercion to treatment has been primarily through legal referrals by court or other criminal justice agencies. Other residential programs have been quite ready to accept involuntary referrals, and some serve criminal justice clients almost exclusively (De Leon 1988a).

Clients from the whole range of residential programs have been followed up as part of evaluation studies using the Drug Abuse Reporting Program (DARP), Treatment Outcome Prospective Study (TOPS), and Client Oriented Data Acquisition Process (CODAP). These studies report both short-term and long-term improvement over pretreatment status for about half of the clients in such areas as reduction of criminal behavior and increase in employment, but not specifically reduction in drug behavior. These studies also show little difference between legal referrals and voluntary commitments in the residential programs. In short, the more recent evaluations have found what the earlier studies found. For certain drug addicts and under certain conditions, therapeutic communities offer some help and hope, but evaluations have not established that these communities are effective for most addicts (De Leon and Rosenthal 1979; Brook and Whitehead 1980).

Certain aspects of therapeutic communities and some institution and nonresidential programs are compatible with the treatment implications of a social learning perspective. For instance, the stress on involvement in groups, which has become very common in these programs, is an approach that can be and has been derived from differential association and learning principles. To the extent that these groups influence their members to take on antidrug attitudes and to counter pro-drug rationalizations and neutralizations, they are promoting change in previously held definitions favorable to drug use. Also, these programs may provide, at least for a while, a change in the pattern of differential association with drug using and abusing friends, models of drug-free living, and both rewards for remaining drug-free and negative sanctions for relapsing.

The social learning dimensions of these programs, however, have been, for the most part, inadvertent; they were not predicated explicitly on learning principles. In the 1980s, an increasing number of residential and non-residential programs and clinics added several behaviorally oriented therapies based directly on learning principles. These techniques are designed to change drug behavior by changing aspects of the environment and one's control of that environment so that desired abstinent behavior is reinforced. These include behavior modification, behavior therapy, contingency contracting, contingency management, and token economy. The behavioral therapies take into account both pharmacological and environmental factors. Used both by themselves and in combination with other approaches, the behavioral techniques have shown good results in some programs, but they are not the final answer for treating drug abuse (Grabowski, Stitzer, and Henningfield 1984; Childress, McLellan, and O'Brien 1985).

Methadone Maintenance Programs. For over two decades, the most common public program to which heroin addicts are referred has been some type of methadone maintenance program. The basic goal of such programs differs dramatically from that of the other programs described so far. Although some now combine methadone maintenance with other forms of treatment and other goals have been added, the main emphasis in methadone maintenance is not to end the addict's habit. Rather, it is to provide a stable and inexpensive supply so that the habit can be reasonably maintained; the assumption is that criminal behavior to obtain money to buy expensive drugs will be curtailed and legitimate employment can be held. This was hailed as a rational, humane, and enlightened alternative in the 1960s when maintenance using methadone was introduced and is still seen by some public officials and journalists as a radical new approach. In fact, some version of the idea has been with us since the beginning of federal law enforcement against the use of heroin and other drugs.

After the passage of the Harrison Act of 1914, several clinics operated and staffed by private physicians were set up in various parts of the country to treat those who had become addicted prior to the outlawing of opium and heroin use. Gradual withdrawal and detoxification from heroin was a major aim of these clinics; if necessary, though, opiates would be prescribed for an indefinite period to maintain the patient's habit. But this approach, prescribing morphine or some other legal opiate merely to keep patients comfortable at their customary habit, was declared illegal by federal enforcement agents just prior to 1922. A few physicians were arrested and convicted of criminal charges, and the clinics were all closed down by 1922.

Later court decisions upheld the right of physicians to prescribe opiates for addiction, so long as they did not become involved in the illegal drug trade. However, few physicians wanted to risk trouble with the law just for addicts, whom many considered to be criminals anyway, and law enforcement agents pursued a policy which, in fact, made almost any medical practice with addicts illegal, whether for purposes of maintenance or withdrawal (Lindesmith 1967). In Great Britain, even though the statutes were essentially the same as American law, addiction was considered basically a medical problem to be handled by physicians at their discretion. If this meant prescribing heroin or some other opiates merely to maintain a habit at the customary level, so be it. Eventually, addicts were required to register themselves as addicts with the British government, but private physicians could prescribe heroin and pursue whatever treatment they thought best.

By the mid-1950s, several American drug experts (Schur 1965; Lindesmith 1967) were pointing to the British system as a good model for the United States. The extremely small numbers of addicts in all of Great Britain; the absence of a black market, deviant drug subculture; drug arrests; and the lack of a relationship between addiction and crime were listed as results of the enlightened British system. That system was held up as an example of how much better addiction can be handled if it is treated as a medical rather than a criminal problem. Law enforcement personnel strenuously objected to adopting the heroin maintenance system here. Moreover, some social scientists observed that the differences between the American and British drug problems existed before, during, and after the differences in policies of the respective countries developed (Ausubel 1960).

Neither the benign policy nor the small number of British addicts lasted much longer. The addiction rate in Great Britain began to increase dramatically in the 1960s; within a decade, the number of registered addicts increased fourfold. Although the strong organized criminal drug traffic such as we have in the United States has never developed in Great Britain, by the 1970s there was a noticeable illegal market in drugs and an addict subculture became visible. British policy changed, to enact tougher law enforcement and to restrict physicians' freedom to prescribe opiates. Government-controlled addiction treatment centers were established as the only ones legally mandated to treat and prescribe for addiction, and most heroin-addicted patients were switched to methadone maintenance (Brantingham 1973; Judson 1974). But by the

1980s, it was clear that the system had not worked very well; most addicts were not registering for treatment, and a thriving illegal drug market and subculture had become well established. At a time during the 1980s when the number of addicts in the United States had stabilized and the rate of addiction had declined, the rate of addiction in Great Britain took another jump up by nearly 300 percent (Inciardi 1986). In spite of this dismal outcome, the British approach, in which even heroin may be prescribed as a maintenance drug (although now very few British addicts are in fact maintained on legal heroin), continues to have great appeal to some drug experts in the United States. Calls for legalizing heroin for maintenance purposes (along with other legalization proposals) continue to be made by prominent, well-financed, and visible drug experts (Trebach 1982, 1987).

Heroin maintenance has not yet been adopted, but the first modern application of the maintenance approach in this country came in 1965 when a program to maintain addicts on methadone was started in New York. Similar programs began to be established all over the country. By the mid-1970s, over 300 such programs were in operation, ministering to about 75,000 addictions. This phenomenal growth is attributable less to demonstrated success through the years than to other features of methadone maintenance.

The maintenance approach came into its own at a time when there was dissatisfaction with law enforcement and the drug-free programs had failed to live up to their early promises. The first methadone programs were based on the theory that addiction is not a social disease but rather a metabolic disease which must be treated by periodic ingestion of opiates, just as diabetes must be controlled by regular injections of insulin. It was claimed that methadone "blockaded" the effects of heroin and produced no euphoric effects itself. The notion that addicts are sick, then, was carried beyond the implication that they should not be punished; they are sick in the strict medical sense and therefore should be treated with a drug. Methadone maintenance seemed to offer a quick, inexpensive, politically acceptable medical solution to the addiction problem. Unfortunately, neither the metabolic-disease theory nor the blockade theory were correct (Epstein 1974). Methadone, itself a synthetic opiate, serves the same physiological function as heroin in alleviating withdrawal distress and if injected produces much the same effects. There is nothing about the pharmacology of methadone that would allow it to counter the effects of heroin. Not only methadone but other maintenance drugs such as LAAM (levo-alpha-acetylmethadol) function the same as heroin in alleviating withdrawal distress. These drugs do not block heroin effects; they merely substitute for heroin in the maintenance of addiction.

The positive features of an addiction maintenance program, however, do not depend on the validity of the blockade theory. Even as a substitute, rather than a block, for heroin, methadone does provide addicts with enough opiate at nominal or no cost to maintain their customary habits without getting sick. This characteristic is at the heart of the major claim of methadone programs—namely, that they attack the problems for society that result from the high cost and attendant problems of maintaining a drug habit on illegal drugs. Because these drugs are available only through illegal channels, ensurance of connections is one reason addicts get involved in deviant subcultures. The high cost of the drugs implicates many addicts in income-producing crimes. Stable employment at regular jobs characterizes only a small minority of addicts. In addition to whatever strain the addiction itself puts on relations with family and friends, the need to hustle to get the drug further jeopardizes normal relationships (family and friends are often the victims of the addict's thefts) and erodes the ability to hold down a steady job. Methadone maintenance programs promise to break the connection between addiction and these social problems. A legal opiate is supplied that is easily affordable or which can be dispensed free of charge. Assured of a safe and steady supply at low cost, addicts are then able to hold regular jobs, seek whatever other help they need, restore social relationships, and in general become contributing members of society. If individuals are thereby enabled to reduce or quit their habits, so much the better. But the goal would be accomplished if they simply maintained their habits indefinitely without creating problems for society.

Unfortunately, methadone maintenance programs have not delivered very well on this promise either. The first programs were widely acclaimed and reported unqualified success, but subsequent re-evaluations of the early programs showed that these claims were unfounded. Evaluations of later programs have shown that methadone maintenance, at best, works in the intended way for only some clients. Many of the programs did not sufficiently control the supply and distribution of the methadone to patients; consequently, methadone leaked considerably into the drug black market where it became second only to heroin in street use (Inciardi 1986). There is some evidence in some programs of reduced heroin use, decreased arrests, and decreased self-reported criminal behavior. But the findings are based on counting the behavior only of retained cases, and of course, illicit use of drugs and crime are prime reasons for people being dropped from the maintenance programs. There has been mixed success in improving the employment status of addicts who do remain in the program.

The attrition (dropout) rate is very high for all maintenance programs, and older, longer-term addicts are most apt to stay in the program and benefit from the ensured maintenance of their habit on methadone. There is reason to believe that at least for some of these addicts, however, staying on methadone means that they are kept on a drug habit which they might otherwise quit on their own. Younger addicts still caught up in the drug subculture are more apt to drop out of the program; or if they stay in, they are more likely to continue using heroin and taking extra doses of methadone bought on the street and are more likely to continue criminal behavior. The more selective the program can be in taking only those with the best prognosis for stable family life, employment, and conforming life-style, the better it is able to claim successful outcomes. The less selective programs are less successful.

It may be that methadone is simply a step that many addicts take who are moving out of the heroin street subculture anyway. Similarly, much of the evidence that crime has been reduced by participation in methadone maintenance is suspect. The reduction appears to be primarily in arrests and incarceration for drug-law violation rather than in drug-related, income-producing, predatory crimes. In short, it seems that maintenance assists addicts who are motivated to leave the illicit drug world and try to live a more conventional, noncriminal life. Methadone maintenance has proven to be neither the panacea for the addiction problem as many of its supporters once believed nor substantially successful in achieving more limited goals (Epstein 1974; Lukoff 1974; Tims and Ludford 1984; Hargreaves 1986).

How Effective Is Drug Treatment?

The outcome of the old narcotics-hospital treatment, civil commitments, therapeutic communities, hospitals, clinics, and methadone maintenance is by and large quite discouraging. A high relapse rate is a frustrating characteristic of all treatment facilities, regardless of the approach used. The very question of how successful treatment of any kind has been may not be answerable in any clear way, because recovery may be a long drawn-out process whereas relapse is observed immediately. Moreover, the typical career of the habitual abuser of virtually any substance includes multidrug abuse and periods of use, abstinence, reduction, and relapse. What, then, constitutes relapse or failure? Is it relapse only to the primary drug of abuse, or is it relapse to any drug? Some subgroups of drug abusers, such as physicians, have better success than others almost without regard to type of treatment (Tims and Leukefeld 1986).

In examining the success of drug treatment and rehabilitation, it must be remembered that many people quit drugs on their own without treatment (Waldorf 1983; Biernacki 1986; Peele 1989). There is no way of knowing how many who enter and complete a treatment program would have done just as well without treatment. At the same time, those who undergo treatment voluntarily or under compulsion are likely to include a great many who have tried to quit drugs without formal treatment. Although motivated to change, the clients and patients under treatment may well be the most difficult cases.

All treatment programs can show some improvement (though not all programs have the same level of improvement) by clients during the time they are under treatment. The problem is that usually only a small part of this improvement lasts after release from treatment. Although the overall success rates appear to have improved since the 1950s and 1960s, only about a third of those persons who have undergone some kind of rehabilitation remain abstinent during the follow-up periods from the primary drug for which they had been treated. And even among those who abstain from the primary drug many will use other drugs. Criminal behavior is reduced during treatment and for a time after treatment, but the direct effect of treatment on employment is not clear (Tims and Ludford 1984).

Comparison of success of the different programs is difficult, because they have different goals, assumptions, and populations. Also, random assignment to different programs is not possible, and selection of clients with different chances of success prevents attribution of different relapse rates to the kind of treatment given. However, evaluations have been done comparing different types of treatment programs. The best known of these are studies evaluating all types of programs (therapeutic communities, methadone maintenance, clinics, and hospitals) using a unified and common system of measurement based on the Drug Abuse Reporting Program (DARP). In one analysis of these data done in the 1970s, it was found that the patients in all programs tended to undergo some favorable change in drug behavior while still in treatment. However, none of the programs had success rates after treatment of more than about one-third. This rate was better than the rate for clients who entered the programs but dropped out before treatment was completed. However, this no-treatment group was the highest risk group anyway and would be expected to have the lowest success rate. When the differences in background, social characteristics, and other risk factors among the different programs were taken into account, those completing methadone maintenance programs and residential therapeutic communities did somewhat better than expected. Those from the nonresidential treatment programs did worse than expected, although this type of program was more effective than the others for persons 19 and younger (Sells 1979).

A later study by Simpson and Marsh (1986) followed a large number of DARP clients who were in various types of treatment for opiate addiction from 1969 to 1972 in 52 federally funded agencies for outcome evaluation at 6 years and 12 years. In the first year after release, 53 percent had no relapse to daily opiate use, but relapse had increased to 66 percent the next year; by year 3 it was up to 72 percent. By year 6 the relapse rate was up to 75 percent and remained at that level at year 12. Two-thirds of the ex-patients who quit heroin use at some time in the 12-year period had relapsed by year 12. A somewhat more encouraging finding was that two-thirds of the sample had managed to abstain from daily use (and were assumed therefore not to be addicted) for a period of 3 years or more sometime during the 12-year follow-up period. Also there was some improvement in the clients' ability to stay out of prison and hold employment. These were modest gains, however. During the last year of the study, only 11 percent of the sample used no drugs, were fully employed, and had served no time in jail.

TOPS (Treatment Outcome Prospective Study) is another large-scale evaluation project meant to assess the treatment process and its relationship to client behavior, characteristics, and environment. TOPS measures rehabilitation by recurrence of drug use, alcohol use, and criminal behavior, and by the patient's mental health and economic productivity through legitimate employment. TOPS data show that outpatient programs have low retention; over a third of those who enter drop out after only four weeks. Half of the methadone patients are unemployed when they start the program, and the same percentage remain unemployed during the time in the maintenance program. Therapeutic communities produce improvement in drug use and criminality, and pro-social behavior is demonstrated, depending on time in treatment. McAuliffe and colleagues (1986) estimate that relapse rates for addicts who have stopped opiate use are around 50 percent among graduates of methadone maintenance, 10 percent of therapeutic-community graduates, and 50 to 90 percent for discharges from the Public Health Service narcotics hospitals. Tims and Ludford (1984), however, conclude from DARP, TOPS, and other sources of data that there is not much difference in outcome between methadone maintenance programs, therapeutic communities, and outpatient treatment.

PREVENTION AND EDUCATION

Treatment is intended to reduce or eliminate use by those who are already abusing drugs. Prevention programs, on the other hand, have the goal of reducing the rate, delaying or preventing altogether the onset of use. *Primary prevention* is directed toward nonusers or to experimenters who are in the earliest stages of use. *Secondary prevention* is directed to those who have developed a pattern of regular or irregular use to prevent their moving to the next stage of heavy/abusive use. Sometimes prevention programs are addressed to schools or neighborhoods where drug use is already high or to youth who have already become involved in delinquency (Hawkins, Lishner, and Catalano 1987). But in both primary and secondary prevention, the messages are broadcast to, and the program involves, the general population or some subpart of the population, such as adolescents, without knowledge or identification of the actual or probable use by individuals in that population (Dupont 1989).

Alcohol education/prevention programs have been around for decades. These were fairly limited in scope and number until the 1960s when prevention of drug use was added. Since the 1970s we have seen an explosion in the number and variety of these programs. The groups and organizations now involved in treatment and prevention provide us with an avalanche of acronyms.

A sizable portion of the drug prevention efforts in this country are supported by privately funded and voluntary organizations that sponsor public-service messages for television, magazines, and billboards aimed at the general public. Many of these groups also have an ongoing antidrug program of disseminating information, influencing legislation and governmental actions, providing curriculum material for schools, holding meetings and conferences of citizens and agency personnel, and coordinating prevention and treatment efforts locally, statewide, or nationally. For instance, in my community of Gainesville (Alachua County), Florida, there is a Community Council on Alcohol and Drug Abuse (CCADA). This is a private coordinating group holding monthly meetings of citizens, professionals in various public and private treatment and prevention programs, and university faculty to discuss issues of common interest, share information, and attempt to detect trends and developing problems of drugs and alcohol in the community. It also sponsors an annual conference on some aspect of community involvement in drug/alcohol treatment and prevention, such as the role of religion and the churches in drug and alcohol prevention in the community. The Council distributes information pamphlets, public announcements, and a drug and alcohol abuse resource guide for the county. One of the principal organizations represented on the Council is Corner Drug Store, Inc., which has a number of ongoing, including after-school, programs and an annual sponsorship of a communitywide substance-free high school graduation party. The Council members and the organizations represented by them are dedicated to helping solve drug problems in the community and bring a high degree of citizen concern and professional competence to the task. Although perhaps not as active or comprehensive as this Council, there are similar organizations and groups in most communities in the United States. Every state has several drug prevention/education organizations, such as the Florida Alcohol and Drug Abuse Association. At the national level, there are such organizations as the American Council on Drug Education (ACDE), the National Federation of Parents for Drug Free Youth (NFP), Parents' Resource Institute for Drug Education (PRIDE), and Partnership for a Drug-Free America (PDFA).

Often these efforts are in cooperation with (and sometimes underwritten by) federal, state, and local government agencies or officials. Sometimes the assistance of a prominent public figure such as the President's wife is enlisted. The best known of these efforts is the "Just Say No" campaign. Thus, even when not a part of an official program, the private organizations reflect general public policy. Governmental policy on drug prevention is more directly reflected, of course, in legislatively and administratively created agencies. The two major federal agencies are the National Institute on Drug Abuse (NIDA) and the National Institute on Alcohol Abuse and Alcoholism (NIAAA), both under the Alcohol, Drug Abuse, and Mental Health Administration of the Department of Health and Human Services (DHHS). These agencies are best known in the academic community for funding research. But they also are the major federal agencies for information services, telephone hot lines, and publications, and they provide technical assistance and funding for demonstration treatment and prevention programs. The National Clearinghouse for Alcohol and Drug Information of the Office of Substance Abuse Prevention (OSAP, created in 1986) is a resource for printed and audiovisual materials on prevention programs, operates a RADAR (Regional Alcohol and Drug Awareness Resource) Network in nearly every state, publishes a newsletter ("Prevention Pipeline"), and provides technical services for education and prevention programs. OSAP also funds demonstration prevention projects and supports community-based prevention programs and a national training system for persons interested in drug prevention. Virtually every state has some office, bureau, or division with the responsibility of drug treatment and prevention. For instance, in Florida there are state offices of the Alcohol and Drug Abuse Program, the State Coordinator for Drug-Free Schools, and the Governor's Drug Policy Task Force.

The designation of "prevention/education" is frequently used because prevention efforts are almost always tied to "education," that is, to provide knowledge or information that will warn people away from drugs and teach them to make the right decisions about drug and alcohol use. Thus, public-service advertising and media campaigns, resource materials, and community prevention programs are typically called educational campaigns. An increasing number of these media-based antidrug campaigns have been run by the Advertising Council and the Partnership for a Drug-Free America. Prevention is education in a more direct sense, however; the overwhelming amount of drug/alcohol prevention is carried out in the schools. Almost all of the organizations and programs, whatever else they may do, include a school-based component. Every state has a K–12 drug and alcohol curriculum. Virtually every child in the United States will have been exposed to some kind of in-class alcohol/drug education by the time of high school graduation.

Types of Drug and Alcohol Prevention/Education Programs

There are a wide variety of techniques, programs, and approaches to drug education programs for children and teenagers, but they are commonly classified into three major types or categories: information/knowledge, affective, and social influences (see Polich et al. 1984). Particular programs may be only one of these types or involve some combination of them.

1. *Information/knowledge education.* These programs focus on information-oriented drug education and are the most frequently offered. They are based on the assumption that drug use results from lack of understanding of drugs and their dangers. Therefore, if children and

teenagers are given the correct information about drugs and alcohol, they will decide not to use them at all or decide to use them in a responsible, controlled manner.

2. *Affective education.* The next most frequently encountered program is the type which attempts to inculcate students with the right "affect"—emotional or attitudinal orientation to oneself in general and to drugs in particular. The goal is to teach values, attitudes, and self-esteem. The assumption is that drug use results from personal inadequacies, poor social skills, low self-esteem, and emotional instability. Therefore, if a student's inadequacies can be solved and self-esteem enhanced, he or she will not use drugs.

3. *Social influence/skills education.* These programs are designed to teach students about the various influences that can affect drug-using and abstaining decisions, especially peers, media, and family, and to teach them the social skills needed to interact with and get along with others without using substances. These programs assume that drug use results more from these social influences and deficiencies in social skills than from lack of knowledge or self-esteem. They attempt to teach students to deal with and resist drug-using influences and develop stronger social skills. Sometimes, the programs are peer oriented and involve students in role-playing, socio-drama, and modeling drug-free behavior. This type of program is less likely to be found than either knowledge or affective programs but is becoming more common.

DARE.   Indeed, DARE (Drug Abuse Resistance Education), which has become one of the most frequently used approaches in drug education, incorporates elements of social influences and skills, although information and affective elements are also prominent in it. This program was started jointly by the Los Angeles Police Department and the LA Unified School District for elementary and junior high school children. It has received media attention (see *Newsweek,* June 5, 1989:77) and has been heavily promoted by the National Institute of Justice. DARE programs or variations on it have been adopted by school districts all over the country. As the name implies, DARE is designed mainly to provide students with social skills for resisting peer pressure to use drugs and alcohol.

Specially selected and trained police officers are assigned full-time to the project. They come into school classrooms and present seventeen one-hour lessons that stress the consequences of using drugs and teach students how to say no to drugs and alcohol. The activities in the program include student role-playing to demonstrate strategies for resisting peer pressures and influences to take drugs, group discussion about ways to enhance self-esteem, and alternatives to drugs, decision making, and understanding media influences (DeJong 1986; Bureau of Justice Assistance 1988).

The popularity of the DARE program has come about in spite of the fact that it has yet to be shown to be successful in curtailing or preventing drug behavior. It has seldom been evaluated, and what studies have been done on it tend to be short-term evaluation without random assignment to treatment and control groups. When it has been more rigorously studied, no significant effect by DARE on self-reported drug use, intentions to use drugs, or self-esteem have been found. A longer-term study is under way by Richard Clayton and his associates (Clayton et al. 1990) at the University of Kentucky, testing students in grade 6 and following them up through grade 10, with random assignment in the first year and pre- and posttests. The study is investigating curriculum effect and officer effect on general attitudes, drug-specific attitudes, self-esteem, peer relationships, peer-pressure resistance, and reported drug use. The long-term effects have yet to be studied, but the findings on short-term effects are disappointing. Significant positive effects are found on general and drug-specific attitudes. However, no differences between the students in the program and those in the control group can be shown on peer-pressure resistance or on actual use of cigarettes, alcohol, or marijuana.

Success of Prevention/Education Programs

The vast majority of these prevention/education programs at any level, federal, state, or local, have never been and never will be evaluated to determine the extent to which they have the intended outcomes. However, evaluation research on prevention programs has been done for over thirty years, and there is a significant body of literature on the operation and effectiveness of these programs. The findings of the early studies were almost uniformly dismal. The general conclusion was that drug education programs essentially had no effect on the drug problem. Although studies of the more recently developed programs leave some room for optimism, the findings still do not provide strong evidence of highly effective programs. Typically, the programs produce at best modest effects (see reviews in Braucht et al. 1973; Hanson 1980; Polich et al. 1984; Bell and Battjes 1987; Goodstadt 1988; Dupont 1989). In spite of some promising leads, the truth is that we still have not clearly established whether or not the programs are having the desired effect, no effect, or undesirable effects.

The goal of these programs has been to affect three basic areas: (1) *knowledge*, (2) *attitudes*, and (3) *behavior*. Programs have had some success in increasing knowledge and, to a lesser extent, attitudes toward drugs, at least in the short run. But increased knowledge and changed attitudes do not mean much if the actual drug behavior is not affected. The programs, by and large, appear unable to show effects on drug behavior such that it is significantly reduced or delayed. However, some programs appear to have modest, short-term effects on drug behavior.

According to the review of findings by Polich and colleagues (1984), the programs that concentrate only or primarily on providing drug information are largely unsuccessful; they increase knowledge of drugs to some extent but affect neither attitudes nor behavior. In fact, there is some evidence that such programs, by reducing anxiety and fear of drugs, may increase the likelihood of drug use. The affective education programs have been somewhat more successful in affecting attitudes but cannot show behavioral effects. The social-influence programs show the most promise in reducing or delaying onset of drug use. These conclusions are supported by other reviews of prevention research (Bell and Battjes 1987). Other research has also found "psychological" approaches in which social influences and skills are stressed to be more effective than alternative approaches (Hansen et al. 1988). The effectiveness of media campaigns either alone or in conjunction with school programs in reducing drug use is also uncertain. Often the messages are misunderstood, and the "hard sell" negative approach typical of these campaigns may turn off some of the very audiences they are meant to reach. There is some preliminary evidence that the media campaigns may play a role in declining drug use, but systematic evaluation of them has just begun (*U.S. News & World Report*, June 11, 1990:53).

The differences in approaches are shown most clearly in Tobler's (1986) analysis of 143 of the best studies of secondary-school drug education programs. The studies were selected because they used comparison or control groups and measured before-and-after program effects on knowledge, attitudes and feelings, and drug behavior. Tobler divided the approaches into five modalities and examined the findings on the size of the effect within each. "Knowledge Only" and "Affective Only" approaches (which made no specific reference to drugs) were the least effective of all the modalities; they had essentially zero effect on drug behavior. Even programs that combined these two approaches were found to be ineffective. The most effective programs in influencing both attitudes and behavior were "Peer Programs," which included either or both: (a) refusal skills with more direct emphasis on behavior and (b) social and life skills. "Alternatives" programs, which focused specifically on high-risk youngsters and placed direct emphasis on behavior and peer influences, were also effective with these special groups. But these special programs tended to be very expensive to produce, whereas the general peer programs were low intensity and low cost. It should be noted, however, that even the best programs had small effects on behavior. The type of modality accounted for only 4.2 percent of the variance in drug use; that is, 96 percent of the difference in drug behavior was unaffected by program participation.

What Is Working?

Something appears to have worked. All indicators of general drug use, and almost all of the indicators of drug abuse, showed a significant decrease in the 1980s. But we do not know just what it is that is working. It could be the magazine and television campaigns against drug use. It could be the school-based or community-based prevention programs. It could be the various treatment programs. All of these efforts may be working in combination. There are some promising reports of programs having modest success, but we are hard pressed to locate any program that has unequivocally demonstrated effectiveness in preventing or treating drug abuse. In fact, we cannot establish empirically that the dramatic changes in drug behavior in American society have anything at all to do with any of the treatment and prevention efforts. The general reduction in drug use in American society may be the result of changes in social norms and the informal control system unrelated to conscious and deliberate prevention, treatment, or law enforcement efforts.

Legal Drugs

Alcohol: Physiological, Psychological, and Social Factors in Drinking Behavior and Alcoholism

P H Y S I C A L   A N D   H E A L T H E F F E C T S   O F   A L C O H O L *

Alcohol and *alcoholic beverages* are generic terms that refer to three major forms in which *ethyl alcohol* (ethanol) is consumed: (1) *wine*, made from fermentation of fruits and usually containing up to 14 percent, although some wines are "fortified" up to about 20 percent of ethyl alcohol; (2) *beer*, brewed from grains and hops and usually containing 3 to 6 percent; and (3) *liquor*, whiskey, gin, vodka, and other distilled spirits usually containing 40 percent (80 proof) to 50 percent (100 proof) alcohol. Alcohol's primary physiological effects come from its *depressant* action on the brain and central nervous system. Typically, each full drink of beer consumed is a 12-ounce bottle or can; the typical drink of wine is a 4-ounce glass, and liquor is taken in single "shots" of 1 ounce to 1½ ounces, either straight, with water, or as a cocktail mixed with nonalcoholic beverages. Therefore, each drink contains about the same absolute amount of ethanol (about ½ to ¾ ounce). If consumed in these

---

*This section is based on NIAAA (1981, 1987) and Royce (1989).

typical drinks, it makes no difference in the amount of absolute alcohol contained in each drink, which beverage is drunk, whether it is beer, wine, or whiskey.

Alcohol does not have to be digested; it is absorbed directly from the stomach and somewhat more quickly from the intestines into the bloodstream. The greater the amount of alcohol absorbed the higher the percentage of the total blood supply in the person's body that is composed of ethanol. The higher this *blood alcohol content* or concentration (BAC) or *blood alcohol level* (BAL) the greater the physiological effects of alcohol. The heavier the person is the larger the total volume of blood in the system and therefore the lower the BAC will be with the same amount of alcohol absorbed. Food in the stomach, especially high-protein food, will slow alcohol's passage to the intestines and its absorption into the system. Carbonated water in the stomach tends to speed absorption by facilitating passage to the intestines, but non-carbonated water tends to retard rate of absorption. Because of the water content, the alcohol in beer is absorbed most slowly; it takes less time for wine and the least amount of time for distilled spirits. Once absorbed, alcohol is oxidized, or metabolized, at a fairly uniform rate (drinking coffee, exercise, and deep breathing do not affect the concentration of alcohol in the blood). Some of the alcohol is eliminated from the body in urine, sweat, or breath without being metabolized. Since this elimination is at a fixed ratio to the amount of BAC, the amount of alcohol in the person's breath (measured by the Breathalyzer) is an accurate measure of how much alcohol is in the bloodstream.

The BAC, then, depends on the absolute amount of alcohol a person drinks in a given time period and the person's body weight. There is some evidence that alcohol is more toxic and is more slowly metabolized by elderly than by younger people. Women have a higher proportion of body fat and therefore a slightly lower volume of blood per pound than men do; at the same total body weight, the same amount of alcohol will constitute a slightly higher BAC for women. Some research has shown that there is no gender difference in rate of metabolism of alcohol, but other findings indicate that women may metabolize ethanol somewhat faster than men do (Cole-Harding and Wilson 1987). On the other hand, there is some preliminary evidence that women tend to have a lower production of a stomach enzyme which begins to break down the alcohol even before it is taken into the bloodstream (*Newsweek*, Jan. 22, 1990:53). However, it appears that the significant variables involved in the level of alcohol found in a person's bloodstream are simply time, amount of alcohol consumed, and body size.

An average-size man can consume one alcoholic drink every hour essentially without physiological effect. Drinking at this rate for a man weighing 150 pounds would result in an alcohol concentration of only 0.02 percent, and for one weighing 200 pounds it would be 0.01 percent. The greater the number of drinks within a given time the higher the BAC and the more noticeable the intoxicating effects. Supposedly, the perceptual and coordinating functions of the upper brain are affected first. With a BAC of 0.05 percent, motor-skill impairment begins. If the 150-pound man consumes four drinks in an hour, he will have a blood alcohol content of 0.10 percent, enough to be legally defined as too intoxicated to operate a motor vehicle in almost all states. At this level, the lower motor functions of the brain are dulled, speech is somewhat slurred, and vision becomes blurred. At 0.25 BAC (about ten drinks in an hour), the motor impairment becomes severe; the person is extremely drunk, staggers, and becomes incomprehensible. At 0.35 percent one is anesthetized, and 0.40 percent produces unconsciousness. The effects are not cumulative. When alcohol is gone from the system, the intoxicating effects are gone.

Alcohol is an irritant to tissue lining in the mouth, throat, and stomach and is toxic to body organs. It has no food value other than calories, and the neglect of nutritional foods usually accompanying heavy drinking over a long period of time will produce malnutrition and ill health. Even moderate drinking may cause some degree of damage to vital organs. Excessive drinking of large amounts of alcohol over time is definitely associated with cirrhosis of the liver, hepatitis, heart disease, high blood pressure, brain dysfunction, neurological disorders, sexual and reproductive dysfunction, low blood sugar, cancer, and other medical illnesses and complications.

SOCIOCULTURAL AND PSYCHOLOGICAL FACTORS IN DRINKING AND DRUNKEN BEHAVIOR

The overt behavior of persons who are drinking alcohol is only partly a function of the direct physical effects. How people behave depends also on how they have learned to behave while drinking in the particular social setting and with whom they are drinking at the time. People do not develop immunity to alcohol, but experienced drinkers can learn to give the appearance of sobriety even when they have drunk enough to be intoxicated. Thus, variations in individual experience, group drinking customs, and the social setting combine with the physical effects to produce variations in observable behavior while drinking. The loss of coordination and motor skills is largely determined by the physical assault of alcohol on the body, but the social-learning and psychological factors become paramount in "drunken comportment"—the behavior of those who are "drunk" with alcohol before reaching the stage of impaired muscular coordination (MacAndrew and Edgerton 1969).

The conventional explanation for why people fight, commit sexual indiscretions, and do other things while drunk that they would not ordinarily do is that alcohol affects the brain center responsible for inhibitions; this causes people to lose civilized control over their baser animal instincts, producing a direct alcohol-caused disinhibition. MacAndrew and Edgerton (1969) find no support for this argument. Rather, they find that the outcome of drunkenness may be no change in behavior, greater inhibition, or lowered inhibition, depending on what the person learns to do under given circumstances.

> In and of itself, the presence of alcohol in the body does not necessarily even conduce to disinhibition, much less inevitably produce such an effect. . . . We must conclude that drunken comportment is an essentially learned affair.
>
> Over the course of socialization, people learn about drunkenness what their society "knows" about drunkenness; and, accepting and acting upon the understandings thus imparted to them, they become living confirmation of their society's teachings. (MacAndrew and Edgerton 1969:87–88)

MacAndrew and Edgerton base their conclusions on anthropological reports from various societies and observations in our own society. The conclusions have received support, however, from a survey of 6,000 households in the United States by Kantor and Straus (1987). The research investigated the "drunken bum theory" of wife beating. This is a popular version of disinhibition theory which holds that alcohol is implicated in male violence against spouse and children because alcohol pharmacologically reduces the man's inhibitions against beating up women. He becomes drunk, cannot control himself, and then proceeds to commit physical violence against his wife; he is a drunken bum who would not do such things if he could remain sober. The findings from this study do not support disinhibition theory. Drinking is related to wife abuse, but it is not an immediate antecedent to violence in the majority of the cases and is not the major factor in explaining spouse abuse. Rather, the strongest predictor of wife abuse is the extent to which the man adheres to the cultural norm of approval of violence by men against women. Drunk or not, the more the man endorsed the attitude that there are situations in which he would approve of a husband hitting his wife, the more likely he was to have engaged in wife abuse.

The Think-Drink Effect

MacAndrew and Edgerton are also supported by a famous series of experimental research on the "think-drink" effect by Marlatt and Rohsenow (1981). They report on their own and review a series of other controlled experiments which provide strong evidence that learned expectations have more to do with behavior while drinking than do the purely physiological effects of alcohol.

Marlatt and Rohsenow's experiments were conducted using a balanced-placebo design. In this design, subjects are divided into four groups based on what they are told they will be drinking and what they in fact are given to drink: (1) expect to drink alcohol and in fact get alcohol; (2) expect to drink alcohol but in fact get nothing but plain tonic water (or some other nonalcoholic beverage); (3) expect to get tonic water but in fact get alcohol; (4) expect to get tonic water and in fact get tonic water. This design was carried out as a double-blind study; that is, neither the subjects nor the researchers were aware of who was drinking alcohol and who was drinking tonic water until after the study was over.

This kind of study allows researchers to isolate the physical effects of alcohol on behavior from the tendency to act in ways the person has come to expect from drinking alcohol. The motor skills of subjects are directly tied to the actual amount of alcohol consumed both by those who think they are drinking alcohol and by those who think they are consuming a nonalcoholic drink. However, virtually all other aspects of behavior while drinking were clearly more the result of what the people in the studies thought they were drinking than what they actually were drinking. These other aspects studied included amount consumed, anxiety reactions, aggression, and sexual arousal, all of which have been linked to drinking.

Both alcoholics and social drinkers drink more when they think they are drinking alcohol (even when they are drinking tonic water with no alcohol in it) than when they think they are drinking a nonalcoholic beverage. Many of the physical symptoms that alcoholics have (tremors, craving for alcohol) are alleviated when they think they are drinking alcohol (even when their drinks contain no alcohol) and continue when they think they are drinking tonic water (even when they in fact are consuming alcohol).

The anxiety levels of both men (who become less anxious) and women (whose anxiety levels increase) are tied to what they expect to happen when they drink alcohol, regardless of what they actually drink. Men become more aggressive when they think they are drinking alcohol and less aggressive when they think they are drinking a nonalcoholic beverage. This effect remains whether or not the men are provoked by verbal attacks. Both men and women report feeling more sexually aroused when they think they are drinking alcohol, regardless of what is in their glasses. According to Marlatt and Rohsenow (1981):

> People will act in stereotyped ways when they *think* they're drinking alcohol—even when there's nothing stronger than tonic water in their glasses. Laboratory studies demonstrate how much drinking behavior

is due to high expectations. . . . The cue effects are the same regardless of the pharmacological properties of alcohol, as long as the people involved believe they are really drinking liquor. (p. 61)

It is clear from this research . . . that cognitive processes exert a powerful influence on our drinking behavior—both in the beliefs that we hold about the expected effects of alcohol and the attributions we make about alcohol as an agent that enhances certain behaviors or "disinhibits" the expression of others. More than 25 published studies that use the balanced-placebo design have replicated the expectancy effect with a variety of social and affective responses that were previously thought to be influenced primarily by the physiological or chemical properties of alcohol itself. (p. 69)

Cross-cultural studies, social surveys, and social psychological experiments, then, all lend support to the position that both the response to alcohol and the behavioral outcomes of alcohol use are less a function of the direct physiological effects of alcohol and more a function of the "environmental contingencies operating when people drink and the expectancies people develop from repeated exposure to such associations" (Lang and Michalec 1990:195).

HISTORICAL AND RECENT TRENDS IN DRINKING BEHAVIOR

In the Gallup Polls taken since 1939, the proportion of current drinkers in the adult population declined from about two-thirds in the 1940s to less than 60 percent in the 1950s. This percentage began to increase in the late 1950s, reaching about 70 percent by 1970 where it remained through the 1982 Gallup Poll. These polls also showed a greater increase in drinking among women than among men (Sandmaier 1980). Other surveys taken during this time, however, showed no consistent increase or decrease in the post–World War II period, although some researchers interpreted the findings as indicating an increase (Mulford 1964; Cahalan, Cisin, and Crossley 1967). The NIAAA surveys indicated no significant changes in frequency or quantity of overall drinking or of heavy drinking for either men or women from 1970 to 1980. Another national study reported little change during the 1970s in male drinking behavior but did find an increase of about 10 percent in female drinkers in both youth and young-adult groups (Fishburne, Abelson, and Cisin 1980).

Whether the proportion of drinkers changed much or remained static, the quantity of alcohol consumed by the average drinker clearly did change.

There had been a century-long trend toward a declining per capita consumption of absolute alcohol (Keller 1958). This was produced mainly by the fact that the American drinker in the twentieth century increasingly turned from high-alcohol-content liquor to low-alcohol-content beer and wine. In the late 1960s, however, drinkers began increasing their average intake of beer and wine. From 1970 to 1978, the annual per capita beer consumption in the United States went up by 30 percent and wine consumption increased by 19 percent (per capita consumption refers to the amount of alcohol *sold* divided by the population age 14 and older). The total amount of absolute alcohol consumed by the average drinker in a year grew to a high of 2.76 gallons in 1981, equaling or exceeding that of the hard-drinking years in the early twentieth century before Prohibition (NIAAA 1981, 1987).

By 1982, however, the downward trend began, and Americans have continued on a decade-long reduction in drinking of alcoholic beverages, accompanied by dramatically increased consumption of bottled water and non-alcoholic drinks (including beer with low enough alcohol content to be labeled as "nonalcoholic brew"). The decline abated somewhat with the introduction and popularity in the 1980s of wine coolers (mixtures of wine and fruit-flavored beverages with about 5 percent alcohol), but by the end of the 1980s sales of these drinks also declined. From 1980 to 1987, per capita beer sales were down 7 percent, wine consumption fell 14 percent, and liquor consumption declined 23 percent. By 1989 sales of distilled spirits dropped another 2 percent and wine sales were off an additional 9 percent, with wine cooler sales off 19 percent (NIAAA 1987; *U.S. News & World Report*, Nov. 30, 1987, pp. 56–63; *New York Times* News Service, Mar. 16, 1989; Associated Press, Feb. 3, 1990).

The trend toward less consumption of alcohol is also reflected in the percentages of drinkers in the population reported in the national surveys shown in Table 10.1. Lifetime and annual prevalences of drinkers for all age groups in the population 12 years of age and older were significantly less in 1990 than in 1979. The relative reductions for adults are not great, however, and proportions remain very high. By the time of high school graduation, nine out of ten have used alcohol at least some time. Eight out of ten seniors and young adults and two-thirds of older adults have consumed alcohol in the past year. Most of this is light to moderate consumption; the modal pattern of drinking in the United States has long been and continues to be nondeviant, light-to-moderate social drinking. There are indications of even greater moderation as both current drinking (in the past month) and frequent (daily) drinking also have declined. A further indication is that both high school seniors and young adults (age 19 to 28) reported less likelihood of heavy drinking (consumed five or more drinks in a row sometime during the last two weeks) in 1990 than a decade earlier (not shown in the table). In spite of these clear signs of lower levels of drinking in American society, it appears

T A B L E   1 0 . 1   *Trends in alcohol use by age group, 1979–1988*

	1979	1985	1990
12–17			
Ever used	70.3%	55.5%	48.2%
Past year	53.6	51.7	41.0
Past month	37.2	31.0	24.2
Daily	1.0	1.0	NA
High School Seniors			
Ever used	93.0	92.2	89.5
Past year	88.1	85.6	80.6
Past month	71.8	65.9	60.0
Daily	6.9	5.0	3.7
18–25			
Ever used	95.3	92.6	88.2
Past year	86.6	87.2	80.2
Past month	75.9	71.4	63.3
Daily	10.0	5.6	NA
26 +			
Ever used	91.5	89.4	86.8
Past year	72.4	73.6	66.6
Past month	61.2	60.6	52.3
Daily[a]	12.0	11.2	NA

Sources: Fishburne, Abelson, Cisin 1980; NIDA 1989a; 1990a; Johnston 1989; University of Michigan 1991.
[a]For age 26–34; percent daily drinking for age 35 + = 12.0.

that more people are defining themselves as alcoholic or in need of help with their drinking problems. Alcoholics Anonymous membership, for example, increased from 612,000 in 1977 to 1.6 million in 1987.

P R O B L E M   D R I N K I N G   A N D   A L C O H O L I S M

Estimates of Prevalence of Alcoholism

Cahalan and colleagues (1967) in a 1965 national survey characterized 6 percent of the general adult population and 9 percent of the drinkers as "heavy-escape" drinkers, the same figures reported for a 1967 survey (Cahalan 1970). These figures do not seem to have changed very much in the years since. In the 1979 national survey of adults 18 years of age and older (NIAAA 1981), 9 percent reported consuming an average of one or more ounces (about two or more drinks) of ethyl alcohol per day in the past month, which is the NIAAA definition of heavy drinking (Clark and Midanik 1982). A national survey in 1984 found that 5 percent of the adults (7 percent of the drinkers) reported at least a moderate level of dependence on alcohol and 7 percent of the adults (10 percent of the drinkers) experienced problems of alcohol abuse (NIAAA 1987). In the 1985 national survey (NIDA 1988a), high-quantity drinking characterized 6.5 percent of the drinkers. About 6 percent of the drinkers reported feeling that they were dependent on alcohol, and 12 percent of the high-quantity drinkers reported having experienced withdrawal symptoms.

These figures suggest that 6 percent of the general population are problem drinkers and that about 9 percent of drinkers abuse or do not control their intake of alcohol. These estimates seem to be supported by Royce (1989), who reports National Council on Alcoholism estimates of 12.1 million alcoholic/problem drinkers in 1988 (versus 10.5 million in 1972). This would represent about 6 percent of the general population and 9 percent of those reporting drinking in the past year in 1988 (NIDA 1989a).

Royce (1989) estimates that only 4 percent of the general population in the United States, and 6 percent of an adult population in which three-fourths are drinkers, are "true" alcoholics. Vaillant (1983) also estimates that 4 percent of the general population are alcoholic. Royce does not define general population, but if the 4 percent estimate were applied to the estimated population 12 years of age and older used in the 1988 NIDA survey (NIDA 1989), the total number of alcoholics would be about 8 million (7,933,000)— about 6 percent of those reporting drinking in the past year and 7.5 percent of those drinking in the past month.

THE CONCEPT OF ALCOHOLISM: DISEASE AND BEHAVIOR

The concept of alcoholism (and drug addiction) as a disease was discussed in Chapter 2 and will be discussed further in the next chapter. The definition of alcoholism has long been and remains controversial. The idea of alcoholism as a sickness traces back at least 200 years (Conrad and Schneider 1980). However, the prevailing disease concept of alcoholism today is based directly on the work of E. M. Jellinek (1960) from 1940 to 1960. Jellinek defined alcoholism as a disease identified by the "loss of control" over drinking which progressed through clear-cut "phases." The concept has subsequently been criticized and defended (Trice 1966; Plaut 1967; Keller 1976; Cahalan and Room 1974; Conrad and Schneider 1980; Vaillant 1983; Rudy 1986; NIAAA 1987; Fingarette 1988; Royce 1989).

There are essentially two sides to the concept of alcoholism as a disease. The first has to do with public policy toward alcoholics. To say that alcoholism is a disease has been taken to mean that it should not be punished as a criminal offense but that it should be treated humanely, with sympathy and with genuine effort to help the person. Those with the disease should have the opportunity to receive medical, behavioral, and mental health attention. This is the aspect of the disease concept that Rudy (1986) refers to as its "utility" dimension. There are those who argue cogently that the concept does more harm than good by discouraging most of the problem drinkers from seeking help (Fingarette 1988; Peele 1989). Although I agree that it does not have the usefulness in helping alcoholics which is often claimed, I have no serious disagreement with this aspect of the disease concept.

I, and many other social and behavioral scientists, do have serious disagreement with the other side of the disease concept—the side which reifies alcoholism as a medical entity, like any other disease. That is, it is not treated as a convenient analogy, "as if" alcohol were a disease; it *is* a disease, literally— a primary, self-contained disease that exists independently of other features of one's life. The problems, abuse, and loss of control over drinking by those defined as alcoholic are the result of suffering from this disease. The disease renders the person helpless to control use of alcohol. It is progressive, with definable stages of pathology, and will almost inevitably lead to physical and mental deterioration unless it is treated. The disease is inherent in the person and can never be cured, but it can be treated to the point where the alcoholic can be helped to stop drinking so that he or she is in "remission" or "recovering." But one is always suffering from the disease even when sober; controlled drinking is impossible for the person suffering from the disease. Once an alcoholic, always an alcoholic.

Such a concept is used as a tautological (and therefore untestable) explanation for the behavior of people diagnosed as alcoholic. The diagnosis of the disease is made on the basis of excessive, problematic alcohol-related behavior and then in turn is used to explain the excessive, problematic behavior. This disease concept views alcoholism as something that happens to someone through no personal fault and over which he or she has no control. It robs the person of will, value, and responsibility for his or her own behavior.

> The primary function of most disease explanations is that they release the individuals from personal responsibility for becoming alcoholic. ... Diseases are generally not viewed as the fault of the person affected. Disease explanations lessen personal responsibility [and] allow for excuse accounts of past problematic behaviors by utilizing vocabularies of motive. (Rudy 1986)

Fingarette (1988) labels the disease concept of alcoholism a *myth*. It is a myth because, insofar as it can be tested, the overwhelming weight of scientific evidence is against it. "Almost everything that the American public believes to be the scientific truth about alcoholism is false" (Fingarette 1988:1). Peele (1989) also contends that virtually everything popularly believed to be established scientific fact about alcoholism as a disease is basically folk wisdom that predates any scientific research. Scientific evidence, in fact, "strongly *contradicts* the contentions of the alcoholism movement" (Peele 1989:56; emphasis in original).

Nevertheless, the disease concept reigns supreme in public opinion and discourse on alcohol (according to a 1987 Gallup Poll, 87 percent of the public believe that alcoholism is a disease). It is the principal concept used by the vast majority of the treatment professionals and personnel offering programs for alcoholics. The fact that it continues to be so dominant in face of its scientific and explanatory deficiencies is attributed by Fingarette (1988) and Peele (1989) to the power of the alcohol/addiction treatment industry. Rudy (1986) and Conrad and Schneider (1980) also find little empirical verification of any of the major aspects of the disease concept.

Whether or not the disease concept is adopted, most definitions include some reference to frequent, heavy, or excessive drinking that interferes with or causes problems in personal, health, or social functioning or causes loss of control. Following Jellinek's definition, the loss-of-control criterion is often used to distinguish alcoholism from problem drinking (Vaillant 1983; Royce 1989). However, there is little that can be observed objectively which distinguishes the two. Therefore, I prefer a concept that simply refers to these drinking problems and behavior; the term *alcoholism* then is nothing more than a label attached to a category or configuration of behavior (Mulford and Miller 1960; Conrad and Schneider 1980; Rudy 1986) without assuming that the drinking behavior and its attendant problems are merely manifestations or symptoms of some underlying disease or pathology. When drinking stops, or moderate drinking is resumed and drinking does not cause social and personal problems, a person is no longer alcoholic. Behavior we label as alcoholic is on one extreme end of a continuum of drinking behavior with abstinence at the other end and various other drinking patterns in between. Here such terms as alcoholism, problem drinking, and deviant, excessive, and abusive drinking will be used interchangeably to refer generally to seriously deviant drinking characterized by "heavy" drinking—high frequency/quantity of intake—and to accompanying personal and interpersonal problems.

Heredity and Alcoholism

Is alcoholism inherited? Or as the question is often phrased, Is alcoholism an inherited disease? In fact, the issue of genetic or inherited factors in alcoholism is a separate issue from the question of whether or not alcoholism is a disease. Contrary to what is regularly asserted, evidence that there may be genetic or biological factors in alcohol abuse is evidence neither in favor of nor against the disease concept, any more than evidence that there may be genetic variables in criminal behavior shows that crime is really a disease. A definition can never be empirically tested. One may speak of inherited behavioral tendencies as readily as one may speak of an inherited disease.

Reports appear in the popular media about the dramatic discovery of an "alcoholism gene" (*U.S. News & World Report*, Apr. 30, 1990:15), only to be followed shortly by reports of medical research disputing this finding (Associated Press, Dec. 26, 1990). Few serious researchers claim to have found evidence that a specific disease entity is inherited or that there is a genetically programmed and unalterable craving or desire for alcohol. Similarly, no one has argued seriously that all drinking patterns—abstinence, light, social, moderate, heavy—are biologically preprogrammed. Rather, the notion is that only one type of drinking pattern, defined as alcoholism, has some genetic factors in its etiology. Some people may have a genetic makeup that produces a neurological response to alcohol which puts them at higher risk than others to drink alcohol in a way that creates problems for them and others. That is, it is genetic susceptibility to alcoholism, not genetic determinacy, which is the predominant perspective. What is the evidence for such a genetic component in alcoholism?

The major evidence for the existence of hereditary factors in alcoholism comes from studies that have found greater concordance between the alcoholism of identical twins than between siblings and from studies of adoptees in which offspring of alcoholic fathers were found to have an increased risk of alcoholism even though raised by nonalcoholic adoptive parents (Goodwin 1976; NIAAA 1982, 1987). There are some reports of a "male-limited" inherited tendency toward alcoholism unaffected by environmental factors in contrast to a "milieu-limited" inherited pattern found in both men and women in which environmental factors play a more significant role (NIAAA 1982, 1987).

Serious methodological problems in the studies reporting hereditary factors limit their support for inherited alcoholism, and the conclusions remain basically what they were decades ago (Lester 1987). The conclusion of significant difference in alcoholism between the natural offspring of alcoholics and those without alcoholic parents hinges entirely on what definition of alcoholism is used. If the definition of what constitutes a case of alcoholism is only slightly modified to include persons with serious drinking problems, then the difference in drinking behavior between the children of alcoholics and those of nonalcoholics disappears (Lester 1987; Peele 1989).

Moreover, even the studies finding the strongest evidence for an inherited susceptibility to alcoholism report that only a small minority of those judged to have the inherited traits become alcoholic, regardless of the definition used, and an even smaller portion of all alcoholics have indications of hereditary tendencies (Fingarette 1988; Peele 1989). For instance, among the alcoholic pattern identified as the most strongly inherited (male-limited alcoholism), only 18 percent of the male offspring of men with this type of alcoholism became alcoholic; among daughters of alcoholic parents (mother or father) reared in adoptive homes in which the parents were not alcoholic, only 7 percent developed alcohol problems (NIAAA 1982). Of course, even for these small percentages of offspring, it cannot be established that it was the hereditary factors acting independently, without reference to environmental factors, which produced the alcoholic behavior.

Thus, there is some evidence of genetic variability involved in the development of some cases of extreme alcoholic behavior. However, whatever genetic factors or variables there are come into play in only a small portion of cases of alcoholism. Therefore, depending on the definition of alcoholism, biological inheritance makes no difference or makes a difference for only about one out of ten persons who become diagnosed as alcoholics (Fingarette 1988).

Alcohol: Social Structure and Social Process

SOCIAL CORRELATES OF DRINKING BEHAVIOR

Age: Teenagers and Adults

In surveys up to the mid-1980s, a substantial majority of teenagers reported some experience with alcohol. In the latest national surveys, about half report having drunk alcoholic beverages. Nine out of ten have had some alcohol experience by the time of high school graduation. However, the kind of exposure to alcohol experienced most often involves isolated or infrequent use of low-content beverages, and only a minority of adolescents drink to an extent that would be recognizable as regular drinking if done by an adult. Four out of ten have had alcohol in the past year, but only a fourth have had one or more drinks in the past month. Little of the drinking that teenagers do is high-frequency or high-quantity. Only 1 percent report daily drinking, and only a few of these are alcoholic in the adult sense. But since all of this is under-age drinking, these percentages are still too high. The proportions of teenagers who drink and who are problem drinkers exceed the numbers and proportions of teenage users and abusers of any other

T A B L E   1 1 . 1   Drinking and heavy drinking by age and sex in national surveys

Age	Drinking		Heavy/ Frequent Drinking	
	M	F	M	F
21–29	84%	70%	28%	9%
30–39	86	72	30	9
40–49	79	65	29	12
50–59	73	50	29	3
60 +	65	44	20	2
18–20	95	69	10	4
21–34	85	77	19	5
35–49	74	67	15	8
50–64	70	47	11	3
65 +	60	38	8	2
45 +		77		32
under 65		63		17
65 +		53		7

Sources: Cahalan and Cisin 1968; NIAAA 1981; Borgatta, Montgomery, and Borgatta 1982.

substance. They are clearly high enough to cause serious alarm among officials, the public, the media, and even the alcoholic-beverage industry.

By the time of high school graduation, the percentage of current teenage drinkers (still under the legal age in most states) rivals that of young adult drinkers and exceeds that of older adult drinkers. Table 11.1 (and also Table 11.3 on page 206 and Table 10.1 in the previous chapter) show that the peak years for drinking are the last year of high school (17 to 18 years of age) and the young adult years of age 18 to 25. In this age group, eight out of ten drink, two-thirds are current drinkers (drank in the past month), and one in twenty is a daily drinker. The many young men and women of this age who are in college are even more likely to drink (Berkowitz and Perkins 1986). For both men and women, the probability that one will drink at all stays relatively high up to about age 35. Heavy/frequent drinking peaks out in later years, somewhat sooner for men than for women. After that the probability for both drinking and heavy drinking declines noticeably, particularly among the elderly.

Age: The Elderly

It is evident from Table 11.1 that after age 60 the proportions of both drinkers and heavy drinkers decrease. Studies of older adults who are under treatment or institutionalized for alcohol or medical problems have suggested that there is a lot of unrecognized and underreported abuse of alcohol by the elderly (Zimberg 1974a, 1974b; Petersen and Whittington 1977; NIAAA 1982; Maddox, Robins, and Rosenberg 1984). However, local, regional, and national surveys since the mid-1960s have consistently found that in the general population the elderly are less likely than younger persons to be drinkers, heavy drinkers, and problem drinkers (Cahalan and Cisin 1968; Barnes 1979; Fitzgerald and Mulford 1981; Meyers et al. 1981–82; NIAAA 1981; Borgatta, Montgomery, and Borgatta 1982; Smart and Liban 1982; Holzer et al. 1984; Wilsnak and Cheloha 1987). Relatively few elderly use or abuse alcohol.

There is some evidence pointing to greater toxicity and slower metabolism of alcohol for the elderly so that less drinking is needed to produce the same effects as in younger populations. Less-lean body mass and less body water in older adults combine to compound the effects of ethanol, even at low levels of consumption. Also, alcohol exacerbates health problems associated with aging and interacts harmfully with several types of medication taken by the elderly (Hartford and Samorajski 1982; NIAAA 1982; Vogel-Spratt and Barrett 1984). Thus, it may be that even a low level of drinking among the elderly is enough to cause problems.

Also, the elderly portion of the total population will get larger as the American population ages with increased life expectancy. Currently, 11 percent of the population is 65 years of age and older; that percentage will increase to about 16 percent by early in the next century. Thus, the total number of elderly drinkers and alcoholics will increase even if their proportions among the elderly population do not change. There is some reason to believe, however, that the percentage of the elderly who drink and have problems with alcohol will not stay the same but will become higher in the remainder of this century and in the first part of the next century.

This increase is predicted because the lower levels of drinking among the elderly are not due entirely to aging effects. That is, those who are young or middle-aged now will reduce their level of drinking as they get older, but they will not necessarily drop down to the very low levels typical for those who are elderly now. Some of the difference by age is the result of a cohort effect; that is, the lower prevalence of alcohol use among elderly in the surveys of the last twenty years may result from the sociohistorical context of the cohort of people born in the first two decades of this century. They are of a generation that came of age and spent their young-adult years during Prohibition and the Great Depression. This era reflected a less-substance-oriented and more alcohol-proscriptive culture. Whatever else were its failures, the Prohibition era did produce very low rates of drinking and these continued for at least ten years following its repeal. Persons socialized into the drinking and abstinence patterns of that time, who are the elderly of today, not only currently drink less than younger persons because they are older but they have always had relatively low levels of drinking and were less likely to drink in their young and midlife years than are the young and middle-aged of today.

As the new cohort of elderly ages from the baby boom period after World War II, with a history of higher levels of drinking and sharing a culture that has been more tolerant of alcohol and substance use, we can expect increased prevalence of drinking and alcohol problems for the elderly (Fitzgerald and Mulford 1981; Meyers et al. 1981–82; Glantz 1982; Holzer et al. 1984). Of course, if the present trends toward less drinking at all age levels continue, and those who are young and middle-aged today reduce their consumption levels, the proportion of drinkers among the elderly in the years to come will not increase.

Table 11.2 reports findings from a study of alcohol behavior among the elderly that I conducted with Anthony J. La Greca and others at the University of Florida (see Akers et al. 1989; Akers and La Greca 1991). The percentages of drinkers in this study are generally comparable to those found in national surveys. Four out of ten persons 60 and older in that study were abstainers in the past year and past month. As is true for younger groups, the vast majority of the drinkers (90 percent) imbibe lightly or moderately. About one in five were daily (or nearly daily) drinkers, and the typical quantity consumed placed about 9 percent of the drinkers (6 percent of the total sample) in the heavy-drinking category. Only 1 percent of the drinkers had a frequency/quantity pattern of drinking that would define them as excessive drinkers, and only 5 percent of the drinkers (a total of 44 persons) reported one or more problems of personal or interpersonal functioning and control during the past year.

Nevertheless, the few elderly in our sample who had been engaged in deviant behavior or had been arrested, convicted, or jailed came disproportionately from among this small number of problem drinkers. Only 3 percent of the nondrinkers and 6 percent of the drinkers in our study had any kind of contact with the criminal justice system in the past year, but 15 percent of the problem drinkers had such contact. Similarly, only 5 percent of the abstainers and nonproblem drinkers in the study self-reported illegal behavior in the past year, whereas 20 percent of the problem drinkers reported involvement in illegal behavior. Thus, the elderly problem drinker runs nearly five times the risk of criminal sanction and four times the chance of illegal behavior as does the elderly nondrinker (Akers and La Greca 1988).

Late Onset and Life Events.   A common hypothesis in research on older adults and alcohol use is that the elderly either initiate or increase drinking as a means of coping with the stress of aging and therefore are at risk of becoming alcoholic. This phenomenon of late onset has been supported by research on clinical populations (Schuckit 1977; Glatt, Rosin, and Jauhar 1978; Hubbard, Santos, and Santos 1979), but not by survey research on general populations of older adults (Borgatta, Montgomery, and Borgatta 1982; Meyers et al. 1982). The stress associated with the late-onset hypothesis is typically seen as stemming from upsetting and stressful life events common to older adults, including loss of spouse, illness, retirement, and other negative happenings

TABLE 11.2 *Drinking among the elderly, age 60 and over*

Frequency of Drinking During Past Year

No drinking	38.2%
Monthly drinking (up to 2 or 3 times a month)	19.6
Weekly drinking (up to 3 or 4 times a week)	21.1
Daily drinking	21.1

Frequency of Drinking During Past Month

No drinking	41.3%
1 to 3 times	16.9
1 to 4 times a week	20.6
Daily drinking	21.0

Quantity/Frequency Index of Drinking During Past Year

	Total Sample	Drinkers Only
No drinking	38.2%	—
Light drinking	30.5	49.3%
Moderate drinking	25.0	40.4
Heavy drinking	5.7	9.2
Excessive drinking	0.7	1.1

One or More Alcohol-Related Problems During Past Year

Total sample	3.1%
Drinkers only	5.5

Drinking After Age 60

No drinking	36.7%
No change in drinking	54.6
Decreased drinking	3.9
Increased drinking	2.9
First began drinking	1.1
First began heavy drinking	0.8

Source: Akers and La Greca 1991.
Note: N = 1,410 in four communities in Florida and New Jersey.

that potentially adversely affect the well-being of older adults (Cohen, Teresi, and Holmes 1985; Krause 1986).

The bottom of Table 11.2 shows that there is very little late onset of alcohol use among the elderly in the Akers–La Greca study. The most common pattern is to continue drinking in old age as one did at younger ages; the next most common pattern is to remain or become abstinent after age 60. Among those who continue to drink but change the level of consumption, the change is as likely to be a decrease as it is to be an increase in drinking. Transition from abstainer or moderate drinker to problem drinker accompanying stresses of old age is a rare phenomenon (less than 1 percent). If late-onset problem drinking does occur, it is most likely to occur in those older adults who enter later life having already developed a pattern of heavy drinking. It is not likely to be provoked by stressful life events; the elderly are, by and large, quite capable of dealing with them without recourse to alcohol. They deal with stress in old age the way they learned to deal with it in younger years—by drawing on their own coping skills and leaning on supportive others. There is no association between the occurrence of life events and the frequency, quantity, or problems of drinking behavior among the elderly (La Greca, Akers, and Dwyer 1988).

Other Social Correlates

Sex.   As can be seen from Tables 11.2 and 11.3, drinking of any kind is disproportionately a male activity. Although the difference is not as great as it once was, more men than women drink and more men are problem drinkers in all age, religious, racial, social class, and ethnic categories and in all regions and communities. Teenage boys are more likely than girls to drink and to drink more frequently, but the difference between male and female percentages of current drinkers at this age is less than it is in any older age group. There are also some indications of a decreasing male–female difference in drinking among college students (Engs and Hanson 1987). If they are not abstainers, women are more likely than men to be light drinkers. Men are more likely to be daily drinkers, to have more frequent episodes of high-quantity consumption, and to experience negative personal and social consequences of drinking (NIAAA 1987).

Region and Residence.   All of the national studies over the past three decades have found both drinking and heavy drinking to increase with urbanization and industrialization. There is proportionately more drinking in urban and suburban areas than in small towns and rural areas. Table 11.3 reveals that as the whole country has become more urbanized the regional differences have leveled out so that, while the South continues to have the lowest proportion of drinkers, there is no difference in drinking among the other regions. Although there are fewer drinkers in the South, those who drink tend to drink more per person than drinkers in other regions (NIAAA 1987).

Social Class.   The proportion of men and women who drink at all, and to some extent the proportion of men who drink frequently, tends to be higher in the middle and upper classes than among those in the lower class. In Table 11.3,

T A B L E   1 1 . 3   *Sociodemographic characteristics of current (used in the past month) drinkers, 1985*

	Age Groups				
	12–17	18–25	26–34	35+	Total
Sex					
Male	33%	78%	80%	68%	68%
Female	28	64	61	48	51
Race/Ethnicity					
White	34	76	72	59	62
Black	21	57	66	44	47
Hispanic	22	58	65	50	50
Size of City of Residence					
Large urban	28	67	76	57	59
Smaller urban	32	74	74	60	62
Nonurban	31	70	62	54	55
Region of Residence					
Northeast	33	76	79	65	66
North central	33	78	75	63	65
South	26	64	58	43	47
West	35	69	72	68	65
Education					
Less than HS	NA	61	63	34	41
HS graduate	NA	71	66	61	64
Some college	NA	75	76	71	73
College grad	NA	83	75	76	76
Current Employment					
Full-time	63	76	74	70	72
Part-time	39	66	71	61	58
Unemployed	53	71	63	54	62
Other	23	60	55	41	40

Source: NIDA 1988a.
Note: Percentages are rounded to two digits.

the more highly educated and the fully employed are more likely to be current drinkers than are the less educated and unemployed. Unlike studies of adults, however, no consistent relationship of drinking to social class has been found in the research on adolescents (Radosevich et al. 1980). Drinking by elderly adults increases as education increases, but there are either mixed or inconsistent findings regarding the correlates to drinking of occupational status, employment status, and income level among the elderly (Borgatta, Montgomery, and Borgatta 1982; Holzer 1984; Akers and La Greca 1991).

Race, Ethnicity, and Religion.   Earlier studies found that the rates of excessive drinking and alcoholism were higher among blacks than among whites (Robins, Murphy, and Breckenbridge 1968). More recent national surveys, however, do not report these differences. Rather, as Table 11.3 shows, the later studies have found that among all age groups the percent of drinking is higher among both white males and white females than among black men and women. Drinking among non-Hispanic whites is also higher than among Hispanic whites. The proportion of problem or heavy drinkers is about the same for black and white Americans (Fishburne, Abelson, and Cisin 1980; NIAAA 1981; NIDA 1988a). There may be a tendency for blacks to fall into the two extreme categories, heavy drinkers or abstainers (Brown and Tooley 1989), and black males suffer the highest rate of mortality from cirrhosis of the liver (NIAAA 1987). American Indian and Alaskan natives have rates of alcohol abuse and problems several times the rates in the general population (NIAAA 1987).

The relationship between drinking and race or ethnicity found in recent studies of adult populations is also found in studies of adolescent populations. As shown in Table 11.3, white youth are more likely to drink than either black or Hispanic youth. Although the overall prevalence among Indian adolescents is in this middle range, the quantity of alcohol consumption by drinkers is high, and Indian youth are more likely to report problems with drinking than is the general adolescent population (NIAAA 1987).

Relatively high proportions of drinkers are found among members of the Catholic, Lutheran, and Episcopalian religions. Relatively few fundamentalist Protestants, Baptists, and Mormons drink. Of those who do drink, Jews have low proportions of problem drinkers, and Catholics have relatively high rates of alcoholism. Irish-Americans have high rates of both drinking and alcoholism. Italian-Americans drink frequently and heavily but apparently do not have high rates of alcoholism (see Mulford 1964; Cahalan, Cisin, and Crossley 1967). Catholic and Jewish adolescents are more likely to drink than are their Protestant peers. Strong religious beliefs and commitment, regardless of denominational affiliation, inhibit both teenage drinking and heavy drinking (Cochran and Akers 1989). Similarly, among college students, high religiosity is associated with low probability of drinking and fewer problems with drinking (Berkowitz and Perkins 1986; Perkins 1987).

SOCIAL LEARNING AND ALCOHOL BEHAVIOR

The general social learning process in marijuana and other drug behavior was explained in Chapter 5. The principal dimensions of that process are differential association with peers, parents, and others, definitions favorable and favorable to drinking, imitation of models, and differential reinforcement. The remainder of this chapter outlines social learning as an explanation of drinking and alcoholism and provides some research evidence in support of it.

Social Structure and Process in Alcohol Use and Abuse

The group variations just presented testify to the socially patterned nature of all drinking behavior, from abstinence to alcoholism. Within American society persons are subject to different group and cultural influences, depending on their location in the age, sex, social stratification, religious, racial, ethnic, and other axes of social structure. Whatever genetic or other biological factors and mechanisms may be involved, both conforming and deviant alcohol behavior are products of the general culture and the more immediate groups and social situations with which individuals are confronted. The cross-cultural and societal differences in rates of drinking and alcoholism reflect the varied traditions regarding the functions alcohol serves and the extent to which it is integrated into eating, ceremonial, and other social contexts. The more immediate groups within these sociocultural contexts provide learning environments in which the positive and negative sanctions applied to behavior sustain or discourage drinking.

The most significant groups through which the general cultural, religious, and community orientations toward drinking have an impact on the individual are family, peer, and friendship groups. The normative patterns of acceptance, rejection, or tolerance of drinking to which one is exposed in these groups are usually referred to as "norm qualities" (Krohn et al. 1982; Wister and Avison 1982; Orcutt 1991). These patterns can be classified into at least four types: (1) *Proscriptive* norms prohibit drinking altogether and hold up abstinence as the ideal. (2) *Prescriptive* norms permit drinking and provide definite standards and limits on what is the proper amount and what is acceptable drinking behavior. (3) *Ambivalent* learning environments present one with vague, incomplete definitions that neither clearly prohibit nor adequately prescribe guidelines for acceptable alcohol use. (4) *Permissive* groups positively define and sanction drinking, including frequent and heavy drinking. There are also normative climates in which one is associated with groups and individuals supporting contradictory or conflicting drinking norm qualities. This conflict may occur among members of one's peer groups (Wister and Avison 1982) or among the norm qualities of one's religious, family, and peer groups (Krohn et al. 1982).

The general American cultural orientation to drinking is best described as ambivalent or conflicting. In both everyday life and the media, there are frequent occasions for approved alcohol use and appealing models of drinking behavior. Most phases of drinking behavior are not deviant; there is even acceptance of some underage drinking. Coming to drink is seen as a normal part of learning adult roles. For the majority of people in American society, sociable, moderate drinking is legally and socially acceptable in a variety of situations. Groups fostering strong antidrinking norms do not command enough power to make total abstinence the prevailing morality or law.

At the same time, negative definitions of alcohol are well known. Excessive, abusive, or alcoholic drinking is condemned. The dangers of alcohol on the highway, and the other health, social, and personal problems connected with alcohol, are well known. Moreover, there are variations in religious, ethnic, and other group norms that sometimes conflict. Thus, persons who have received their primary socialization in one type of normative setting become aware of, and at one time or another may be exposed directly to, different groups and conflicting norms. Therefore, even among groups in which the prevailing norms are proscriptive, some still use alcohol, and in those groups in which some drinking behavior is approved there are still some who do not indulge. Nevertheless, one's drinking behavior is by and large congruent with the normative-sanctioning patterns of primary groups of family, friends, and religion.

Generally, groups with prescriptive norms have high rates of drinking, whereas those with proscriptive norms have low rates of drinking. In some religious groups, such as Jewish groups, which have prescriptive norms defining the proper use of alcohol, controlled moderate drinking is common, but rates of heavy drinking and alcoholism are low. Proscriptive religious groups, such as Mormons and Baptists, tend to have the lowest rate of drinking overall and low rates of alcoholism. There is some indication that the permissive and ambivalent normative environments produce high rates of both moderate and excessive drinking.

Also, a tradition in the literature on alcohol norm qualities asserts that if persons who interact in a social context which prohibits drinking of any kind do begin to drink they are at a much higher risk of becoming problem drinkers than are persons who drink within a prescriptive or permissive environment (Mizruchi and Perruci 1962; Larsen and Abu-Laban 1968; Wister and Avison 1982). Orcutt (1991) disputes this view and persuasively argues that, consistent with social learning theory, both adolescents and adults whose peers hold to proscriptive norms not only experience the lowest levels of drinking but also run the lowest risk of becoming problem drinkers. Orcutt (1991) maintains that those who claim to find high rates of problem drinking, or pathology, among those who drink in proscriptive environments do not adequately take into account differential association and the balance of norm qualities. Differential association in which the balance of definitions is unfavorable will effectively control deviant, troublesome drinking. That there appear to be more severe personal consequences for the heavy drinker in a proscriptive environment results simply from the fact that it is in such an environment that deviant drinking is most likely to be punished with negative social consequences.

Those who drink have been differentially associated with those who ap-
ove of drinking and reward drinking behavior. They learn definitions
favorable to drinking. Drinking is the expected behavior in many groups and
situations, and as long as it stays within the acceptable limits, it is accompanied by conviviality, acceptance, and other pleasant social sanctions and
reactions. People may learn to drink in groups in which the social reactions
to drinking are uncertain or neutral at best. But as long as their behavior is
not positively punished, their starting to drink and proceeding to a regular
pattern of alcohol consumption is based on positive social reinforcement. For
some their initial reaction to the effects of alcohol is positive; even when prior
learning has been neutral, they like the taste and what they feel from drinking. But for many, the initial reaction is dislike or at least not noticeable enjoyment. If they do not initially like it, people may acquire the enjoyment
of the taste, smell, and effects of alcohol through association with social
rewards. Those who have been associated with groups in which drinking is
not tolerated, not rewarded, and positively discouraged have a low probability of initiating drinking; if they do experiment with alcohol, they are less
likely to continue its use.

The importance of the individual's definitions favorable to drinking is
seen in the extent to which persons' behavior is associated with their own
approval or disapproval of alcohol use. Those who abstain consistently define
alcohol in negative terms. They see it as morally or religiously wrong or as
bad for one's health and happiness. They disapprove of drinking in general
and see alcohol as harmful to society. Drinkers, on the other hand, tend to
report positive definitions of alcohol. They see it as promoting congenial social
interaction, celebration, relaxation, and pleasure. More personal definitions
of alcohol, such as anxiety reduction, are less frequently reported; these
reasons are associated with heavy drinking. At the same time, even those who
approve of alcohol use are aware of counterdefinitions and recognize potential and actual negative aspects of drinking. However, these are seen chiefly
as accompanying excessive or uncontrolled drinking. Such negative definitions as applied to one's own behavior are neutralized by the acceptability
and positive features of moderate drinking. Thus, those who apply abstinent
definitions to drinking alcohol tend not to drink, and those who do drink tend
to apply positive or tolerant definitions, at least on a conditional or situational
basis. Both the close peer associations and learned alcohol-relevant attitudes
predict later drinking behavior (Downs 1987; Sellers and Winfree 1990).

But the behavioral and normative situation is more complicated than
simply drinking or not drinking. A person learns to make fairly fine distinc-
tions among situations in which particular levels of drinking are or are not
likely to be socially acceptable and rewarded. One's drinking becomes
associated with a whole range of social and physical discriminative stimuli
(in the form of situational norms, physical setting, and others present) which

define what, where, how much, how frequently, and under what conditions certain kinds of drinking will be reinforced. As we saw in Chapter 10, how one is supposed to behave and what is expected when drinking or intoxicated are also learned (Marlatt and Rohsenow 1981).

Social Learning in Alcoholism

The pattern of drinking that one establishes is initiated and sustained in social normative contexts by imitation of models of drinking behavior, positive and justifying definitions favorable toward that pattern, and positive social reinforcement, as well as the enjoyment of the effects of alcohol. Progression into more abusive and problematic patterns of use are part of this same process. However, just as with serious drug habituation, negative reinforcement comes to play a larger role in the development and perpetuation of alcoholism. That is, individuals may drink to escape or avoid unpleasant situations or to forget their problems by drinking (Conger 1956; Kepner 1964). For that small percentage of alcoholic drinkers who develop physiological addiction, the negative reinforcement also comes from drinking to avoid alcohol-withdrawal symptoms.

The negative reinforcement of drinking behavior is combined with positive reinforcement of pleasurable effects and social rewards. At some point, drinking "like virtue, is its own reward and is not likely to stop simply because no other rewards are contingent upon it" (Kepner 1964:282). The social environment can reinforce drinking through the sympathetic actions and reactions of others, which reward the behavior and mitigate the consequences of heavy drinking that would otherwise be punishing.

The Role of Drinking Groups in Alcoholism.   Many years ago Harrison Trice provided a thorough analysis of the way in which other people's reactions to a person's drinking can play an important role in the development of alcoholism. Trice (1984) explicitly placed his explanation within the social learning paradigm when he later "revisited" the scheme, adding new information and insights. In both his earlier and later work, Trice explains a process in which "drinking-centered groups," such as tavern groups, formal and informal party groups, clubs, and skid-row bottle gangs, constitute short-lived "simulated primary groups" that reward heavy and alcoholic drinking (Trice 1966).

More specifically, this social-psychological scheme for explaining alcoholism has the following parts: (1) personality features that set the stage, making one a candidate; (2) qualities of drinking-centered groups that uniquely attract and reward the use of alcohol for such persons, linking "readiness" with alcohol; (3) the uneven, but usually inevitable, shift from reward to rejection within drinking groups; and then (4) the

> seeking out of more tolerant drinking companions, providing continued support and protection for alcoholism to develop. (Trice 1966:43)

Members of these drinking-centered groups provide one another with models for patterns of drinking and rates of alcohol consumption (Garlington and DeRicco 1977; Caudill and Lipscomb 1980). Trice (1966:1984) reveals several other features of many drinking groups that are attractive and rewarding for the drinker. They accept and legitimate the use of alcohol, permit congenial social interaction, relatively free of competitive overtones, and provide the rewarding intimacy of "pseudo-primary" relationships. Some drinking groups hold that heavy consumption and the ability to drink more than others without appearing drunk are signs of virility, and they grant status to the one who can "drink like a man." Drinking groups are also lenient with the heavy drinker and slow to apply negative sanctions to the person who drinks more than others in the group. Even persons who may become concerned about the developing alcoholic's drinking fail to apply social sanctions until it is too late to be effective. Thus, the "negative sanctions that define and penalize undesirable drinking behavior are weak, irregular, and infrequent, contrasting clearly with the abundance of rewarding positive sanctions" (Trice 1966:53).

But at some point (varying from one group to another) a person's drinking begins to be seen as showing a lack of self-control, and sanctions short of rejection begin to give way to more severe reactions; eventually the person may be ostracized. He or she begins to seek out more congenial drinking groups that are tolerant of the level of drinking and kinds of behavior the previous group has come to consider excessive.

> Thus, if a developing alcoholic's drinking violates the norms of a rather conservative group, he can find emotional rewards by affiliating with more lenient sets of drinking companions. In the process his dependence on alcohol increases, but he is not confronted by realistic social controls with clear negative sanctions. (Trice 1966:5)

> Absent from these accounts are indications that drinking groups tried to exert consistent pressures or controls on the undesirable behavior. . . . These descriptions convey the feeling of social exclusion with little, if any, effort at social control. (Trice 1984:114)

One may move to more permissive drinking situations without too much cost, simply by making the rounds of the taverns and bars. But as this shifting from group to group continues and the person's drinking becomes increasingly excessive, he or she becomes isolated from conventional social controls; to find ever more permissive groups, the drinker is propelled toward ever more deviant roles in groups clearly labeled deviant, such as skid-row drinking groups. The person becomes more excluded from avenues returning to sobriety and continues to move toward heavier and more problematic drinking.

Research Evidence on Social Learning in Alcohol Behavior

Evidence in support of this social learning theory of drinking behavior comes from previous research on the importance of peers', parents', and others' social reinforcement for drinking or abstinence (White, Bates, and Johnson 1990). Supportive evidence also comes from the research that I and my associates (Marvin Krohn, Lonn Lanza-Kaduce, and Marcia Radosevich) conducted in the Midwest on adolescent substance use. This is the Boys Town Study described in Chapters 4 and 5. Support also comes from the study of drinking patterns among the elderly, introduced earlier in this chapter.

Social Learning in Teenage Drinking

One part of the Boys Town research investigated specifically the effect of norm qualities (as part of the normative element in differential association) on teenage drinking and drug use. The norm qualities of significant adults, peers, and religious affiliations were studied. The hypothesis was that the teenager's own definitions and alcohol/drug behavior would be related to the norm qualities of these groups. The highest percentages of drinking should be among permissive groups and the lowest percentages among proscriptive groups with percentages of drinkers in prescriptive groups in between these two extremes. The findings supported the hypothesis. The extent to which the individual approved or disapproved of alcohol and marijuana use was related to the perceived norms of all three reference groups, but most strongly to the norms of significant peers. Perkins (1985) found a similar pattern among college students, in which drinking behavior conformed more closely to the peer norms and friendship groups on campus than to parental norms and religious traditions. Also, the levels of use were lowest for teenagers reporting exposure to proscriptive norm qualities and highest for those reporting social climates of permissive norms. Levels of use among those reporting prescriptive and ambivalent environments were high but not as high as the level in permissive groups. There was no evidence of a greater tendency among teenagers who had started to use alcohol in spite of having family, religion, and friends supporting proscriptive norms to become problem drinkers. Among teenagers, proscriptive environments are conducive not only to total abstinence but also to moderation among users.

Another part of the research tested the full social learning model on teenage alcohol behavior. As shown in Table 11.4, the social learning variables are related to drinking behavior among teenagers. The social learning variables combined are highly correlated with whether or not the teenager will drink ($R = .74$). The same social learning process is involved in whether or not those teenagers who do begin drinking will come to drink abusively or have health, personal, or social problems with drinking ($R = .56$). Thus, the whole range of alcohol behavior from abstinence, to light/moderate drinking, to heavy/problem drinking among teenagers can be understood as resulting from

*T A B L E   1 1 . 4   Correlation of teenage drinking and
alcohol abuse with social learning variables*

Social Learning Variables	Multiple Correlation (R) for:	
	Drinking	Abuse
ALL VARIABLES	.74	.56
Differential association	.68	.50
Definitions	.60	.33
Differential social/nonsocial reinforcement	.53	.37
Differential social reinforcement	.48	.26
Imitation	.16	.13
N =	2,414	1,764 (drinkers only)

Source: Akers et al. 1979.

differential association with drinking patterns and norms, imitation of drinking/abstaining models, favorable/unfavorable definitions, and differential social and nonsocial reinforcement.

Differential association is the strongest variable set, and within this peer association is the most important. Also, social reinforcement/punishment from peers is more strongly related to teenage drinking than is reinforcement/ punishment from parents. However, parental influence is more important and comes closer to matching the influence of peers in teenagers' drinking behavior than in their marijuana use. Friends' positive or negative reactions are correlated with one's own drinking and marijuana use. Parents' punishing or reinforcing reactions are correlated with their children's drinking and less strongly with their marijuana smoking. Parental reactions are even more strongly related to their teenager's tobacco smoking.

The impact of other socializing agents on teenage drinking is less than that of either family or friends. The salient influences of parents and peers on adolescent drinking are generally recognized in the literature (Kandel 1980; Radosevich et al. 1980) and appear to hold for adolescent alcohol behavior in other countries as well as the United States (Adler and Kandel 1982). As we saw in Chapter 5, peer influence is paramount but it is not often in the nature of irresistible pressure to drink. Whether or not drinking among peers represents imitation of adult models or a rebellion against adult authority depends on the setting. In communities of families in which adults regularly drink and support prescriptive drinking norms, drinking serves to symbolize adult status. On the other hand, in groups where adults typically neither drink nor approve of alcohol of any kind, it may be that for some youth, drinking is rewarding because it expresses a general alienation from and rejection of conventional adult expectations.

Both the behavior of adolescents in prescriptive environments in which adult drinking models are imitated and the rebellious behavior of drinking adolescents in proscriptive milieux are explainable by the social learning process. In both cases, parents are carriers of, and probably effective socializers into, conventional normative standards where drinking is conventionally acceptable behavior for adults, a sizable portion of the teenage population will use alcohol. Where abstinence is the expected behavior of adults, relatively few teenagers will drink. But in both cases, there will be unsupervised peer-only drinking, and peers will provide the major source of settings, occasions, and reinforcement for drinking and for abstinence.

The impact of family drinking background continues through late adolescence and into adulthood. Those who were abstainers in a proscriptive family context tend to remain abstinent or to drink lightly. Persons from prescriptive drinking families continue to have a higher probability of drinking. Adolescents from heavy-drinking families are more likely to be heavy drinkers as adults. However, direct parental influence lessens as one's drinking behavior comes more and more under the influence of adult peer associates and one's own life circumstances. Drinking in college is sustained or changed under the influence of fellow students in friendship groups, on dates, at parties, and in fraternities and sororities. The peer drinking context in college affects how much one drinks, where one drinks, and one's beverage preferences (Berkowitz and Perkins 1986; Engs and Hanson 1987). It is also the major variable in problem drinking among college students:

> It may be concluded from our review of the relevant literature that, among social context variables, peer influences have outweighed the effects of family and environment and become stronger in adolescence and young adulthood. In addition, young problem drinkers appear to have weaker ties to parents and are more oriented towards peers, who provide influential models for their heavier alcohol use. Thus, in a recent study of a college population, [it was] demonstrated that the influence of peers upon heavy drinking was far greater than that of other environmental and family characteristics. (Berkowitz and Perkins 1986)

Social Learning in Drinking Among Older Adults

Adult drinking remains very much a social activity with spouse, relatives, friends, and work or business associates. Research has shown that among adults, just as among adolescents, the best predictor of a person's drinking behavior is the drinking behavior of those with whom he or she associates (Dull 1983), and controlled experiments have shown that drinkers' rate of consumption, whether a little or very much is drunk at a given time, closely matches that of their drinking companions (DeRicco and Niemann 1980). Drinking continues as a socially patterned behavior into the elderly years.

T A B L E   1 1 . 5   Correlation of drinking variables with social learning variables among the elderly

	Multiple Correlation (R) for:	
Social Learning Variables	Frequency	QF Index
ALL VARIABLES	.77	.72
Definitions	.62	.57
Differential association	.67	.62
Differential reinforcement	.71	.66
Balance of social reinforcement	.51	.50
Balance of physical effects	.61	.58
Balance of rewards/costs	.65	.62

Source: Adapted from Akers et al. 1989.

As shown in Table 11.5 in our study of elderly drinking behavior, we found the same social learning variables (except for imitation, which was not included in the study) which are strongly related to drinking among adolescents also to be strongly related to drinking among elderly adults. The social learning model with all of the variables included shows a very high multiple correlation with both the frequency of drinking ($R = .77$) among the elderly in the past year (from abstinence to daily drinking) and a quantity/frequency index ($R = .72$) of the pattern of drinking adopted (abstinence, light, moderate, heavy, or excessive).

Problem drinking is not shown in Table 11.5, but a separate analysis was done which showed that learning variables make a very substantial difference in the probability of problem drinking among those elderly who drink. Those who are interacting in the strongest anti–heavy drinking social environment (wherein one has a light- or moderate-drinking spouse, family members, and friends as well as differential reinforcement and definitions favoring moderate drinking) have essentially a zero chance (predicted probability = .001) of being a problem drinker. Those at the other extreme, interacting in an environment and holding attitudes most supportive of heavy drinking, have a very high likelihood of being among the problem drinkers (predicted probability = .683). Just as in younger groups, elderly problem drinkers differentially associate with heavy drinkers and the balance of social reinforcement for heavy drinking is positive. Problem drinking is sustained by the support from friends with similar drinking habits and the fact that the problem drinker experiences the inducements and rewards for drinking as considerably outbalancing the costs and aversive consequences of drinking.

Thus, the general social-learning model is supported for both drinking and problem drinking for both adolescents and elderly adults. There are some differences, however, in the findings on elderly drinking as compared to those on adolescent drinking. Among adolescents, both definitions and differential association have a stronger effect than does differential reinforcement. In the study of the elderly, the strongest variable is differential reinforcement. The overall reinforcement balance of social/nonsocial costs and rewards attached to drinking has the most effect, but the more direct "physical" reinforcement of the alcohol effects also has powerful effect, even more than does the social reinforcement from family and friends. Obviously, social reinforcement is very important in both adolescent and elderly drinking, and we should not make too much of the difference. Nevertheless, the findings would suggest that adolescents' use of alcohol is somewhat more socially conditioned and tied to peer contexts and reactions than is that of the elderly, for whom drinking appears to be sustained more by the effects of the alcohol itself.

Community Context, Social Learning, and Alcohol Use.   As we have seen, there is variation in rates of drinking by size of community and place of residence. These and other group differences indicate that structural contexts have an effect on the level of alcohol consumption. Demographic composition, cultural traditions, and social control systems vary across communities, and these contexts can be expected to produce variations in alcohol use and abuse. We saw in Chapter 5 that differences in levels of marijuana use among the adolescents in four types of communities were mediated by the social learning process. The same is true for the level of adolescent drinking in these communities. Different levels of peer associations, definitions favorable or unfavorable to use, and reinforcement balances across the four community contexts explained the differences in community rates of teenage drinking (Krohn, Lanza-Kaduce, and Akers 1984).

There are also noticeable differences in levels of drinking among the elderly in four different communities, from a high of 76.4 percent in a Florida retirement community to a low of 41.5 percent for a medium-size Florida age-integrated community. Moreover, 30 percent of the respondents in the Florida retirement community reported drinking every day (or nearly every day), which is more than twice the level of daily drinking in the other community. Similar to the findings on adolescent drinking, the findings from the study of elderly drinking confirm that these different community contexts very likely affect the drinking behavior of the elderly residents through the operation of the social learning variables.

Living in a community with certain age, sex, racial, and demographic and socioeconomic characteristics does affect how much one is likely to drink alcohol. This community context has an effect on the social learning process (with whom one associates, the behavioral models that one imitates, the normative orientations to which one is exposed and internalizes, and how reinforcing one finds alcohol use to be), which in turn affects one's drinking behavior (Akers and La Greca 1991).

CHAPTER TWELVE

Social Control and Public Policy on Alcohol

Societal control and public policy on alcohol has revolved around basically two strategies: (1) regulation and prevention in the *general population* and (2) law enforcement and treatment programs directed toward *populations of deviant and problem drinkers.*

REGULATION AND PREVENTION IN THE GENERAL POPULATION

Alcohol education and prevention programs sponsored by the brewery and liquor industries and by government and school systems have been in place for a long time. These programs are aimed mainly at teenagers and children, attempting to convince them to wait until they reach the legal drinking age before buying and consuming alcohol. These are now almost always combined with drug education/prevention programs, which were discussed in Chapter 9. However, since alcohol is a legal substance, prevention programs directed to the general adult population and even many of those directed to teenagers, unlike drug prevention messages, do not have the goal of preventing drinking altogether. Rather, the goal is to prevent only deviant or abusive alcohol use. Two different but overlapping approaches in pursuit of this goal have developed: (1) a "cultural" or persuasional approach and (2) a regulatory "control" approach.

The first approach emphasizes educating the public to use alcohol responsibly, to adopt a drinking norm of moderation. Adhering to this responsible-use norm would not necessarily affect the overall level of alcohol consumption; in fact, the proportion of drinkers in the total population and the average per capita consumption could increase. But the goal is to spread out that consumption more among moderate and light drinkers so that abusive drinking will decline. The campaign against drunk driving, encouraging people to have a sober driver in their group, not allowing a friend to drive while intoxicated, and general advice to know when to say when, are all part of this approach. Even the manufacturers of liquor, beer, and wine have joined in this campaign to promote the norm of responsible, nonabusive drinking. They have full-page ads in mass-circulation magazines and television spots that contain basic messages of moderation—advising hosts not to encourage heavy drinking at their parties and teenagers to take it easy if they drink, as well as other ways of expressing the dictum "If you choose to drink, drink responsibly." BACCHUS, a private pro-responsibility organization, has spread this message of sane and sensible use of alcohol on college and university campuses for many years.

The second control approach emphasizes non-normative techniques of lowering overall consumption by: (1) restricting availability through increasing the price of alcohol either directly or through taxation; (2) closing bars earlier and otherwise regulating hours and conditions of sale; (3) lowering the alcohol content of beverages; (4) restricting retail outlets; and (5) raising the legal age for drinking (Whitehead 1975). The idea behind this approach is that there is a more or less consistent relationship between the total level of consumption and the level of abusive drinking regardless of social or cultural contexts. Peele (1987) seriously questions this assumption and other aspects of the control-of-supply approach not only for alcohol but for other drugs as well. He points out that overall consumption and the proportion of that consumption which is abusive vary considerably by sociocultural traditions in the same society and across different societies. Room (1987) argues that pricing and other controls do tend to lower the level of negative physical consequences of alcohol consumption such as cirrhosis, but they have less of an impact on social and psychological indicators of problem drinking. His contention is that such control policies can have a preventive effect on alcohol problems but that they must be combined with the cultural approach.

The typical pattern of public policy is state and local regulation (but not criminalization) of alcohol through control of sales and distribution. Some states are "monopoly states" in which a state liquor-control board is the sole purveyor of bottled liquor. All states and the federal government tax alcohol, primarily for revenue but also to regulate its distribution and consumption. All states have a system of licensing the sale and consumption of alcohol on the premises of trade establishments. All states use the licensing and regulatory laws to control the character of the owners, managers, and patrons of the establishment.

All states also have a minimum age for people to purchase alcohol legally. Changing the legal drinking age is a control strategy that has been somewhat effective in reducing alcohol problems. The legal age was almost universally set at 21 years of age in the United States prior to the 1960s. Drinking levels and problems were relatively high in the age group just below this minimum age. Then, following the lowering of the voting age in the 1960s, many states also lowered to 18 the age at which one could legally purchase alcohol. Subsequently, drinking increased among those just below this age (16–17), there was a dramatic increase in traffic accidents among teenagers involving alcohol, and problems with alcohol increased in the schools. In the late 1970s, states began moving the age of drinking eligibility back up to 19 or 21. By 1987 all states had revised the minimum age for legal purchase of alcohol back up to 21. This was forced by federal legislation, which provided for the cutoff of federal highway funds to states that maintained the 18-year-old legal age.

In each state where the effects have been studied, raising the minimum drinking age was followed by substantial reductions in traffic fatalities and accidents and related problems among adolescents in the state and the age at which the problems were most visible rose again to 19–20, just below the legal age (Whitehead and Wechsler 1980; Califano 1982). Nationally, there was a 34 percent drop in fatal automobile accidents involving underage drinkers following the raising of the drinking age in most states in the 1980s and a 17 percent drop in fatalities involving intoxicated drivers of legal age (Associated Press, Dec. 16, 1988).

However, research has failed to find that the increased drinking age reduced drinking, driving violations, or drinking problems in college populations (Engs and Hanson 1986, 1989; Lanza-Kaduce and Bishop 1986). There has been a noticeable drop in the heavy drinking by college students on spring break at Daytona Beach and other places in Florida, but research has been unable to show that this resulted from the raising of the drinking age; college alcohol-education programs may play a stronger role in the reduction (Gonzalez 1990).

CONTROL AND TREATMENT OF PROBLEM DRINKERS

Legal Policy and Law Enforcement

Legal policy on the direct control of deviant alcohol behavior has been directed toward public drinking offenses, mainly through arrest and conviction of people drunk in public and of people driving an automobile while under the influence of alcohol.

Controlling the Drunk Driver.   One of the most devastating outcomes of the presence of alcohol in society is the high number of traffic accidents and fatalities attributed to drunk driving, estimated by the National Highway Traffic Safety Administration to be about half of all fatal crashes. Lanza-Kaduce and Bishop (1986) have questioned the idea that drunk driving actually "causes" crashes and fatalities on the highway in either the scientific or the legal sense. In fact, the direct connection between level of blood alcohol concentration (BAC) and driving problems has been shown both in laboratory experiments using simulated driving tasks and in studies of BAC in persons who have been involved in traffic accidents. There is clear evidence that the risk of accident increases with increases in BAC; significant effects are observed beginning when the percent of blood volume containing alcohol is 0.05 percent (Ross 1982). Driving while under the influence of alcohol can be said to "cause" highway fatalities under ordinarily accepted meanings of causation.

The effect of alcohol consumption on driving has been known for a long time, and beginning in the 1930s many countries (including Scandinavian and European countries, Canada, and the United States) have enacted laws that make driving while having a certain level of BAC (usually 0.10 percent, but 0.08 percent in three states and 0.12 percent in one state) itself a violation. In the United States, all states have made it illegal to drive while drunk and many have outlawed having an open container of alcohol in the vehicle and/or consuming alcohol while driving or riding in a vehicle. Most states have adopted provision of the Uniform Vehicle Code, which defines driving drunk as a violation (DWI—driving while intoxicated or DUI—driving under the influence). Refusal to take a Breathalyzer test or blood test to determine BAC is cause for suspension of driver's license and admissable as prosecution evidence in most states. The penalties for drunk driving range from imprisonment to fines, community service, license revocation or suspension, and participation in an alcohol treatment/education program depending on the severity of the offense and the person's prior-offense record (Flanagan and McGarrell 1986).

Research shows that adoption of these laws can have a deterrent effect on driving while drinking and reduces accidents, deaths, and injuries on the streets and highways. Such legislation works best when it is accompanied by much publicity to increase public perception of high risk of apprehension for drunk driving. Research also supports the conclusion that highly visible police crackdowns on drunk driving (such as the ASAP, Alcohol Safety Action Projects, in the United States) are effective in deterring driving while under the influence and reducing traffic accidents. Unfortunately, these effects do not last long, apparently because the actual risk of having an accident while drinking is very low (a small fraction of 1 percent) and the chances of getting arrested and convicted for DWI are low, even during law enforcement crackdowns. This state of affairs is quickly learned by persons who have had experience with drinking and driving. If they come to believe that a new law or a law enforcement crackdown significantly increases the odds of getting caught because of publicity, they will reduce their drunk-driving episodes. But this perception of increased certainty of penalty cannot be sustained for long because the odds can be increased only for a short time. The experience of again getting away with drunk driving nullifies fears of getting caught that were initially raised by the publicity surrounding a crackdown (Ross 1982). Moreover, other research makes it clear that the direct deterrent effect of law enforcement in preventing drunk driving is secondary to the inhibiting effects of social influence of friends and family and one's own moral objections to driving while intoxicated (Berger and Snortum 1986; Lanza-Kaduce 1988).

The carnage produced on the highways by drunk drivers and the personal tragedy of the victims and victims' families coupled with the common practice in court of meting out very lenient sentences and penalties even in cases where deaths have been caused by drunken drivers, produced outrage and moral crusades to get such drivers off the road. Organizations such as MADD (Mothers Against Drunk Drivers), SADD (Students Against Drunk Drivers), and RID (Remove Intoxicated Drivers) formed to push for stiffer penalties by judges and tough laws against driving while under the influence. The image of the problem of drunk driving promoted by these groups is that almost all of the traffic deaths are the result of besotted drivers who run down sober, innocent victims while the offender walks away unharmed, facing only a legal slap on the wrist. This image is only partially true. In fact, most of the victims of drunk driving are the drivers themselves (52 percent of the fatalities connected with alcohol) or pedestrians who are themselves drunk and walk into traffic (11 percent of the alcohol-related traffic deaths) (*Cincinnati Enquirer*, Oct. 15, 1990). But enough of the victims are totally innocent of any drinking involvement that these groups' sense of outrage at drunk drivers carries considerable weight.

Partly in response to the campaigns of these groups, many states have legislated more severe and mandatory penalties for drunk-driving offenses (Califano 1982; BJS 1985). To the extent that such laws result only in stiffer penalties without affecting public perception of certainty of arrest, they will not have much effect. Also, programs that offer driver's education, rehabilitation, or treatment as an alternative to the imposition of penalties serve mainly to reduce the deterrent perception of risk and are not effective in curtailing alcohol-related driving offenses and accidents.

Controlling Public Drunkenness.   Until the 1970s, the common practice in controlling public drinking offenses was to arrest, detain, convict, incarcerate for a short time, and release people found drunk in public and presenting a nuisance. Arrests for alcohol or alcohol-related offenses accounted for more than half of all criminal arrests. Thus, a considerable amount of police work and public funds was devoted to dealing with law enforcement problems having to do directly with alcohol (not to mention the role of alcohol in other crimes reviewed in Chapter 3). The crackdown on driving while intoxicated as a legal policy is now popularly supported as a necessary police function that protects the public from drunk drivers. However, the practice of arresting people for being drunk (or disorderly while drunk) in public is not popular with everyone; indeed, it has come under intense criticism from many areas.

The typical pattern of arrests for public drunkenness was concentrated on the winos, bums, and homeless street people of the skid-row and downtown areas of the city. These were a sort of floating population of arrestees who regularly were picked up by the police and held in the drunk tank, appeared in court, received a short sentence, served it in the county jail where they dried out, were released back to the streets, quickly got drunk again, and then were rearrested to begin the cycle again. This revolving door in and out of the courts and jails—punctuated with a round of the skid-row missions and homeless shelters offering meals and a place to sleep—became and remains a way of life for many skid-row inhabitants. It was not uncommon for the "police-case inebriate" to have been arrested over a hundred times in the same city, not to mention an arrest record elsewhere (Pittman and Gordon 1958; Spradley 1970).

The Diversion-to-Treatment Movement in Controlling Public Drunkenness. Dissatisfaction with this revolving-door phenomenon as inhumane, unjust, and ineffective led to an alcohol *diversion* movement, beginning in the 1960s, to get the chronic drunks entirely out of the criminal justice system and into treatment programs. The primary argument of this diversion movement was that alcoholism is a disease and being arrested for public drunkenness is the same as making it a crime to have a disease. This is unconstitutional; disease problems ought to be handled by public health, not criminal justice, officials. In *Powell* v. *Texas*, it was argued before the U.S. Supreme Court that because the Court had earlier ruled that drug addiction is a disease condition which cannot constitutionally be outlawed (*Robinson* v. *California*) it should now declare public-drunkenness laws to be unconstitutional; they, too, made a condition—alcoholism—illegal. The states should be constitutionally compelled to control the public nuisance of drunken comportment without recourse to the police–court system; they would need to do so through a system of detoxification and treatment. However, the Court's majority opinion did not uphold this argument. Instead, it ruled that the state laws made the overt act of being drunk in public—not the condition of alcoholism itself—illegal. The Court noted that there was no consensus on what constitutes the disease of alcoholism. Further, the Court found that adequate treatment facilities did not exist and that involuntary diversion of an offender to a place where no real treatment occurred (whatever that place was called) is the same as sending him or her to jail.

In spite of this negative decision, the diversion movement accelerated. Some facilities for diversion were already in use, and others were constructed. The Court's reference in the decision to the need for real treatment facilities and the objection mainly to the compulsory nature of commitment to them by the courts, along with the dissenting opinion's emphasis on alcoholism as a treatable disease, provided impetus to get the chronic drunks out of jail and into treatment, even if on a more or less voluntary basis. It also seemed to motivate the passage of state and federal legislation to do what the Court did not do—mandate putting into place a widespread alcohol treatment system.

In 1968 the Alcoholic Rehabilitation Act was passed by the U.S. Congress which provided for federal aid for alcohol treatment programs. This act fostered the movement toward incorporating the disease concept of alcohol into official public policy. In 1970 the Comprehensive Alcohol Abuse and Alcoholism Act (known as the Hughes Act) was passed which not only provided for additional federal assistance to state and local alcohol treatment facilities but also established the National Institute on Alcohol Abuse and Alcoholism (NIAAA). The act officially defined alcoholism as a disease and directed that public intoxicants be treated rather than placed in the criminal justice system. In 1971 a national commission proposed the Uniform Alcoholism and Intoxication Act. Many states adopted its provisions, which called for diversion of public drunkenness, driving while under the influence, and other misdemeanor alcohol offenses to detoxification and treatment on a voluntary basis or, under certain circumstances, on an involuntary basis. Federal laws were also amended to provide support for communities to offer programs for diversion of alcohol offenders. In practice, the laws resulted mainly in "padding the revolving door" by placing inebriates in detoxification centers more comfortable than the drunk tanks. But the effects on the numbers of common police-case type of drunks moving in and out of that revolving door were not very apparent (Fagan and Mauss 1978; Dunham and Janik 1985).

Both private and public hospitals, clinics, and other facilities in which alcoholics can be placed have been in existence for some time, and new ones have opened up as the result of new laws and insurance policies. Many of the private facilities are experiencing financial difficulties as the result of efforts by insurance companies to restrict the length of covered treatment for alcoholism. The publicly financed detoxification and treatment centers are usually specifically connected to the court or jail and receive their treatment populations from these sources. There are residential halfway houses and nonresidential clinics or drop-in centers operated or funded by the states and counties.

For the range of problem drinkers who come to the various programs, missions, and centers by self-referral or referral by a social-service agency or from the court, some success is attained in achieving stable sobriety in the short run while in the program (Dunham and Mauss 1982). This effect disappears almost as soon as the person is released; usually the programs fail to have any effect on the drinking behavior or life-styles of the typical police-case inebriate (Wiseman 1970; Fry and Miller 1975; Rooney 1980).

Alcohol Treatment Programs

Just as for drug treatment, the underlying rationale for the typical treatment program for alcohol problems in lieu of or in addition to law enforcement is the concept of alcoholism as a disease. The disease concept is that chronic drunkenness and drinking problems indicate an underlying disease entity which has distinct and characteristic symptoms, phases, and progression just as does any other medically diagnosed disease. As with any disease, alcoholism is seen as something that happens to a person which can be diagnosed and cured through a prescribed treatment regimen. It is confirmed public policy and commonplace to speak of alcoholism as a disease. Virtually any public statement on the problem will make reference to or start with the assumption that alcoholism is a disease.

In spite of the long history and almost universal acceptance of the disease concept, it has not been established that alcoholism is a disease in the usual medical sense, and the concept continues to be severely criticized by many alcohol researchers. The widespread acceptance of the concept does not mean that alcoholism has been scientifically demonstrated to be a disease. It may simply mean that alcoholism has been successfully "medicalized" and socially defined as a health problem. In this sense, it may make no difference that there is no disease entity identified by the label of alcoholism. It is a disease because it has been socially defined as such (Conrad and Schneider 1980). The conception of alcoholism as a disease is the established policy of the National Institute on Alcohol Abuse and Alcoholism and is endorsed by the American Medical Association. It provides the supporting philosophy for the vast majority of alcohol treatment programs, even though they do not really treat alcohol problems as medical disease and use no medical procedures in their teatment.

Alcohol treatment programs cover the same range of program alternatives described in Chapter 9 for drug programs; indeed, they are commonly part of the same program or facility. These range from detoxification units, to hospital wards, to residential and nonresidential programs. There are over 1,400 alcohol treatment programs and nearly 5,000 more facilities that treat both alcohol and drug problems. Nine out of ten of the 374,000 clients in these programs are served on an outpatient or a nonresidential basis. In some states, the programs are crowded beyond their stated capacity, and the utilization rate for the country as a whole is 80 percent (NIDA/NIAAA 1990). The level of success of these programs is about what it is for drug programs—that is not very high.

Alcoholics Anonymous.   The best-known private self-help organization to combat alcohol problems is Alcoholics Anonymous (AA). It is the largest single program for alcoholics in the world, with chapters now even in the Soviet Union (*Time*, Apr. 10, 1989:31–34). AA consists of sober alcoholics helping others become and stay sober. To AA, there is no such thing as an ex-alcoholic. The guiding philosophy is "Once an alcoholic, always an alcoholic." AA is widely known as a strong advocate of the disease model and urges alcoholics not to have even one drink because it will lead inevitably to another binge (Denzin 1987). However, there is nothing in the official AA "big book" even approaching a systematic presentation of a disease concept of alcoholism. The closest to this is the brief "doctor's opinion" dating from 1934 by Dr. William Silkwood stating that alcoholism is "not entirely a problem of mental control." Silkwood also expounded the now discarded theory of alcoholism as an allergic disease (Alcoholics Anonymous 1976:xxiii–xxx).

Whether or not AA or its members really adhere to the disease concept (see Rudy 1986; Denzin 1987), the AA program is in fact primarily a program of spiritual and moral growth in order to gain the power to overcome the craving for alcohol and to live an abstemious life. It relies on the now widely copied self-help model. The mechanism is mutual support and help of others who are also struggling to control their drinking. There is no reliance on professional practitioners or treatment programs. Everything is done through the AA meetings, which are basically sharing and testimony-giving sessions and through reliance on other members to come to one another's help in an alcohol crisis. The AA book gives a brief history of the founding of AA by two alcoholics, based on the philosophy and practice of the Oxford Group, an early religiously based self-improvement group (see also Rudy 1986). Most of the book is dedicated to the stories of individuals who have had success with the AA program. Almost all of these stories have a spiritual basis to them, although one chapter is for agnostics, who are told they can become a part of AA because they do not have to believe in God, only in a "power higher than ourselves."

The heart of the AA program is the "twelve steps" to recovery (Alcoholics Anonymous 1976:59–60). These begin with "We admitted we were powerless over alcohol—that our lives had become unmanageable." Then the step is taken, "We made a decision to turn our will and our lives over to the care of God as we understood him." At the end, the twelfth step is "Having had a spiritual awakening as the result of these steps, we tried to carry this message to alcoholics, and to practice these principles in all our affairs." Nothing in any of the twelve steps refers to alcoholism as a disease. They portray a spiritual recovery process based on faith in God (or a higher power) after a recognition of powerlessness over alcohol.

Nevertheless, at the AA meetings members inculcate one another with "one of the most central tenets in the A.A. ideology—the idea that alcoholism is a progressive disease" (Rudy 1986:45). According to Rudy, the disease explanation is emphasized in the early phases of getting into AA and telling one's story. In the later stages, moral explanations predominate. My interpretation of this is that members of AA believe that alcoholism is a disease, but they may see it as a moral disease with a moral cure.

AA has been highly praised and continues to receive well-deserved accolades as providing the best hope and the only place to turn for many alcoholics (Califano 1982; Denzin 1987). Physicians, courts, and rehabilitative agencies regularly refer clients to AA. The basic model evolved by AA is now the cornerstone of a great many other self-help groups dealing with various compulsions—Narcotics Anonymous, Gamblers Anonymous, and Overeaters Anonymous, for example. AA also has fostered the development of collateral groups such as Al-Anon and Alateen for the members of alcoholics' families. AA has the reputation of being a model, highly successful program for alcoholics, and many other treatment programs incorporate the twelve steps or some other aspects of AA.

But is there hard evidence of AA's effectiveness? Basically the answer is no. Certainly the great many personal testimonies about overcoming alcoholism through AA should not be taken lightly and must be given credence. However, there is no reliable research or systematic data on outcome of participation in AA compared to that of participation in other programs or to no treatment at all. The extent of AA's success is difficult to judge because records are not kept, and scientifically valid research on AA effectiveness is difficult to do. As even its strongest supporters recognize:

> A.A. moves forward, without records, regularly kept statistics, or information on whether or not its methods and assumptions do in fact work. (Denzin 1987:65).

Although some reports show nearly half of AA members have maintained at least one year of sobriety (Emrick 1987), several other studies show that "slipping," or relapsing to drinking, is a very common pattern among active AA members (Rudy 1986; Fingarette 1988). The aura of AA's infallibility persists in spite of the lack of proof that it works any better than other approaches or even better than alcoholics simply left on their own (Peele 1989). My view is that confidence in AA's effectiveness is more a matter of faith than science. Nevertheless, AA has the right philosophy and offers hope to millions struggling to gain or maintain control over their own drinking who otherwise would have none. The faith may not be misplaced.

Can Alcoholics Become Controlled Social Drinkers?

One aspect of the AA philosophy and the disease concept of alcoholism that has been most widely adopted in treatment programs is the emphasis on complete sobriety as the only possible goal of treatment. So important has this become as an unquestioned component of alcohol treatment programs that a storm of controversy is raised whenever anyone suggests that alcoholism is reversible so that many ex-alcoholics have resumed moderate, social, or controlled drinking. Two of the most visible of these instances occurred in the late 1970s with the controversy surrounding them continuing into the 1980s.

The first of these revolved around a comprehensive review of research and evaluation of treatment programs by the Rand Corporation that found many former alcoholics do successfully resume moderate drinking patterns following treatment (Armor, Polich, and Stambul 1976; see also *Newsweek*, June 21, 1976, and Hamburg 1975). The report did not urge programs to abandon sobriety as the treatment goal; it simply reported that many alcoholics were able to end their alcoholism and maintain a pattern of moderate social drinking. In addition to total sobriety, controlled, nonproblem drinking was reported to be a reasonable and achievable goal of treatment for some. But *any* questioning of the notion that one can never be cured of alcoholism and must never take even one drink is apt to meet with as much opposition and incredulity as questioning the disease concept itself. The vehemence of the counterattack underscores the strong ideological component in the disease concept. It is not just a convenient or useful concept, helpful in treatment; it is the heart of an entire belief system and treatment industry.

The second major controversy followed when research on patients from a behavior modification program designed to teach alcoholics to drink moderately showed them to be doing as well or better than a control group who attempted total abstinence after release from a treatment program. It was found that many were able to return to social drinking (Sobell and Sobell 1978). Other researchers who located the same patients later presented findings at variance with the earlier reports and claimed to have found no evidence that the patients had learned how to drink moderately after the treatment program. Indeed, they reported very poor outcome and high mortality for the treatment group (Pendery, Maltzman, and West 1982). Pendery and colleagues not only questioned the Sobells' findings but also severely criticized their procedures and labeled as "dangerous" their attempt to retrain alcoholics to drink socially. The Pendery et al. study, however, followed up only the experimental treatment group; it did not compare it with the control group. Therefore, it does not answer the question of whether or not alcoholics who pursue that goal of total sobriety are any more successful in avoiding relapse than are those who pursue a goal of attempting controlled drinking. Perhaps neither is able to do it very well. But the question addressed by the Sobells' study was this: Can controlled drinking be achieved and is a social behavioral treatment program with that goal more effective than traditional treatment with a goal of total sobriety? Pendery and colleagues cannot answer that question because they followed up only one group.

In a point-by-point response to the critique, the Sobells review many other problems with the Pendery et al. study (Sobell and Sobell 1984). Pendery and colleagues questioned the design of the Sobell's research claiming that comparability of the treatment and control group was not adequately ensured and that at least four of the treatment subjects were not "true" alcoholics. Both the scientific and the personal integrity of the Sobells was called into question. Two independent commissions formed to investigate the procedures and methodology of the Sobells' study answered the question: The procedures were valid and sound, and the research had been carried out with integrity. The Sobells' own response to the critique (Sobell and Sobell 1984) also presented clear evidence that the original study did in fact have random assignment and that there were comparable alcoholics in both the treatment and the control groups.

The Pendery et al. study reported findings at variance with the Sobells during the two-year follow-up period of their study and reported very poor outcomes for the long-term follow-up of the controlled-drinking treatment group up to eleven years afterward. One of the most devastating findings was that after the initial two-year follow-up period, four of the Sobells' treatment subjects died of alcohol-related causes. The claim was that this was the tragic result of the misguided encouragement of the alcoholics to attempt to drink in a controlled manner. Not only had they failed to do this, but the return to drinking caused their deaths. What Pendery and colleagues (1982) did not report was that none of these deaths occurred sooner than six years following the termination of the Sobell study and that more subjects (six) from the traditional treatment program emphasizing total abstinence suffered alcohol-related deaths during the same time period (Sobell and Sobell 1984). A sizable portion of alcoholics will return, following treatment, to heavy, injurious drinking leading to all kinds of problems and perhaps even death regardless of what that treatment was. For this group of ex-patients, including a goal of returning to social drinking apparently carried less risk than having only the goal of total abstinence.

Denzin (1987:40–42), along with other defenders of the disease concept, believes that the Pendery et al. critique is an irrefutable "indictment" of the Sobells' learning theory and behavioral treatment of alcoholism. In so doing, Denzin and others simply ignore the Sobells' response to Pendery and colleagues and the long history of other studies reporting return of alcoholics to a lower, more controlled level of drinking. The Sobells note that they were not the first to suggest that alcoholics can return to controlled drinking:

> The notion that some individuals with alcohol problems may recover fully or improve significantly without abstinence was not novel in the early 1970s when the IBTA [Individualized Behavior Treatment for Alcoholics] study was conducted. In fact, a major foundation of the IBTA study was that there had been repeated reports in the scientific literature

of persons who had recovered and were able to resume drinking without incurring serious problems. Such reports have multiplied considerably in recent years. (Sobell and Sobell 1984:414)

An example of these more recent reports is Nordstrom and Berglund (1987), who also note that there is a body of research evidence dating back to the 1950s showing that at least some alcoholics get over their drinking problems and resume social drinking. Their research followed up sixty male alcoholics two decades after they had been released from a hospital alcoholic-treatment unit. About half of the group at the time of follow-up had relapsed to alcohol abuse. But of the thirty-two who had not relapsed, twenty-one had resumed moderate, controlled drinking, while only eleven had resisted relapsing to alcoholism by total abstention.

Sobell and Sobell (1984) report that there were explicit attempts by those in the alcohol treatment establishment to suppress, forestall, and discredit both the Rand report and their own studies. They argue that the issue of reversibility of alcoholism to moderate drinking is at the heart of the increasingly strong challenge to the dominant disease paradigm by behavioral research and treatment. They believe supporters of this dominant disease paradigm react so strongly because they realize how crucial the challenge is to maintaining the hegemony of the disease concept in alcohol treatment and research.

I do not quite understand how it is that the goal of not returning to alcohol at all is so central to the disease concept of alcoholism. I know that it is defended against all challengers by supporters of the disease concept. But the identification of the goal of total sobriety with the concept of alcoholism as a disease may be more of a historical accident than a crucial link. From its very beginning, before the disease concept became so entrenched, Alcoholics Anonymous took a strong stand on total abstinence as the only possible state for an alcoholic to avoid problems. All of the subjects in the study on which Jellinek based his original formulation of the disease concept came from AA (see Rudy 1986), and it may be that Jellinek was influenced as much by the AA philosophy of total abstinence as he was by the necessity of including a nonreversibility element in his disease concept.

Is the nonreversibility component essential to the disease concept? As we have seen, the evidence is clear and longstanding that some (perhaps a great many) of those diagnosed and treated as alcoholic have resumed a social-drinking pattern sustained over many years without returning to the type of drinking that would be classified as alcoholic. In addition, an unknown number of persons are alcoholics for a while but on their own, without entering a treatment program or joining AA, cut back their drinking to manageable levels. A hypothesis that *no* alcoholic, or even that only a very small portion of a population of alcoholics, can ever resume drinking of any kind must be rejected in the fact of the research findings. But do these findings, by themselves, mean that the entire disease concept must be rejected? As I have noted in Chapter 2, there are many problems with the disease concept. Nonetheless, I am unconvinced that the findings regarding resumption of social drinking by ex-alcoholics totally undermine it. It could be maintained with a simple modification that the disease in some cases may be reversed and controlled even while drinking. In fact, one major supporter of the disease concept, at least for purposes of treatment, appears to have taken this position, recognizing that "alcoholics can be successfully taught to return to social drinking in the community" (Vaillant 1983:217–218).

That many, probably most, alcoholics who attempt to drink moderately following treatment fail to do so does give some support to the position that once a recovered alcoholic begins to drink again he or she is apt to quickly fall back into excessive drinking. Whatever the reason, once one has developed a pattern of problem drinking he or she remains at a much greater risk of relapsing to that same pattern than does a person who has never drunk heavily. For someone who has been a chronic drunk or who has developed severe problems from drinking and recovered from that, the safest thing, of course, is not to drink at all. Why take the risk? Do the reasons for drinking at a controlled level outweigh the playing-with-fire risk of becoming a dysfunctional drinker again, with all of the heartache and ruined relationships that go along with it? I do not think so. The fact remains, however, that many have taken the risk and succeeded.

There has been less media attention and controversy on this issue of social drinking as a goal of alcohol treatment in recent years. Nonetheless, it remains as a central point of contention, and we can reasonably expect it to continue to generate controversy within the treatment and research community.

Behavioral Approaches in Alcohol Treatment

Behavioral and social learning approaches (under the general heading of behavior modification or behavior therapy) in treatment of alcoholics do not assume that alcoholism is a disease. The heavy drinking, the abuse, and other problems connected with drinking are not treated as merely symptoms of an underlying sickness. Instead, the focus is on the problem behavior itself, as a dysfunctional habit. The goal is to train alcoholics to abstain or to drink in ways that are not abusive or destructive. If the behavior is changed or extinguished, then one is no longer an alcoholic. In Chapter 11, we examined the sources and kinds of conditioning that are involved in alcoholism. But whatever these are, it should be possible to treat alcoholism by reversing the process or changing the conditioning factors. Actions and decisions by the person resulted in the problem drinking, and actions and decisions by the same person can remove or mitigate the problem.

Aversion Therapy. The first behavioral conditioning approach to alcoholism developed was aversion therapy. Aversive conditioning is based on creating an association of the taste, smell, feel, or effects of alcohol with aversive, unpleasant stimuli so that the person comes to experience punishing rather than rewarding effects from drinking. This approach was first tried in the 1930s and was quite often used in the 1940s. Its use declined, however, and was not resumed systematically until the early 1960s (Franks 1963; Sanderson, Campbell, and Laverty 1963). In the earlier years, the treatment relied on nausea-inducing (apomorphine or emetine) or alcohol-antagonistic (Antabuse) drugs to cause people to vomit when they drank alcoholic beverages. If this was repeated enough times, the alcohol itself would produce nausea and the person could not stand to take a drink. Later, electric shock and other aversive stimuli came into use. Aversion therapy has been used with some success to train alcoholics to abstain completely or to drink in moderation. Sometimes the aversion therapy has been combined with *relaxation* and other behavior-modification techniques (Rachman and Teasdale 1970).

The results of aversion therapy have been mixed. Generally, the therapy has been more successful than no treatment or traditional psychiatric treatment. However, the rate of success varies considerably from one group of treated subjects to another. Only in a few instances has the rate of cure reached more than 50 percent. Part of this lack of success is due to the way in which practitioners in this area have applied aversive conditioning therapy and carried out the evaluation research. Chapman and associates conclude that "most instances of behavior therapy have carried over directly the precision of laboratory procedures to the clinic. The treatment of alcoholism is a notable exception. Gross errors are widespread in the literature" (1969:1). The person's motivation to change and willingness to undergo the rigors of aversive conditioning and the number of "booster" sessions are other variables in the success of aversive therapy, but they are not often taken into account in assessment of the treatment (Bandura 1969).

The mixed success of aversive conditioning therapy in treating alcoholism is probably also due to the fact that most programs have not had systematic follow-up to deal with variables, such as social influence, in alcohol behavior. Whatever aversive environmental features that have sustained the heavy drinking in the past as negative reinforcement are not likely to disappear simply because someone has undergone contrived unpleasantness connected with alcohol in a treatment setting. Positively reinforcing features (drinking groups, supportive spouses, drinking friends) are also not likely to lose their potency because the person has undergone aversion therapy. "The major value of aversion procedures is that they provide a rapid means of achieving control over injurious behavior for a period during which alternative, and more rewarding, modes of behavior can be established" (Bandura 1969:554).

Other Social Behavioral Approaches

It is this differential reinforcement approach—rewarding sobriety while punishing alcoholic drinking; reinforcing ideas, beliefs, and behavior supportive of nonproblem drinking; and training to control relapse—which has been used with more success in "broad spectrum" behavior-modification programs. The emphasis has shifted from sole reliance on conditioning the person to have an aversive reaction to alcohol to adding treatment procedures that promote thinking and behavior which is incompatible with heavy drinking. The success rate of these broad-spectrum programs is better than conventional treatment (Hamburg 1975). Since they begin with the same principles of learning, these programs most closely reflect the treatment implications of social learning theory.

Even with consenting patients, infliction of pain, nausea, sickness, and electric shock in order to condition aversion to alcohol in the patient presents some ethical problems. The range of behavioral therapies have been developed partly because of these ethical concerns, partly because of the lack of long-term effect from aversion therapy alone, and partly to provide an alternative model to the traditional disease model. Various kinds of anxiety-management techniques have been used in treating alcoholics. Patients have been trained to relax through biofeedback and systematic desensitization, in which the person gradually becomes desensitized to the cue stimuli precipitating heavy drinking. Problem drinkers have also been given training in how to improve social skills so that interpersonal difficulties can be adequately handled without turning to alcohol. Contingency management, using points, tokens, and social reinforcers for sobriety, has been used in both controlled settings and the community. There is some evidence of the greater effectiveness of these approaches than of traditional counseling and therapy, but there is less strong evidence of lasting effect (Sobell et al. 1982).

The Community-Reinforcement Model. A good example of these alternative social-behavioral programs for alcoholics is the "community-reinforcement" model. This model, using differential reinforcement concepts in social learning theory, was first developed by Nathan Azrin and associates in the early 1970s. It uses reinforcers available in the community such as employment, family, and social relationships to establish and maintain sobriety and socially responsible behavior incompatible with abusive drinking. The idea is to train the patient and family members to arrange social reinforcers and engage in specific behavior in a way that supports sobriety and discourages drinking.

Patients were given vocational counseling (résumé preparation, telephone skills in job solicitation, interview skills, and so on) in the hospital, and as soon as satisfactory employment was found they were released. The first session with spouse and other family members occurred in the hospital, and then all other sessions were in the home after release. These sessions trained patients and family members in how to provide mutual reinforcement for a functioning family relationship, and a specific set of behavior rewarding to each other family member was drawn up. Patients also received behavioral training in developing and improving social relationships with friends that depended on sobriety, not drinking, and were discouraged from associating with problem drinkers. Indeed, a nonalcoholic social club (meeting in a converted tavern) was formed among the patients, family, and friends for regular social gatherings. For the first month after discharge, the alcoholics were visited by a counselor up to eight times and up to twice a month thereafter. During these visits, the reinforcers available from family, job, and social life for abstention were reviewed and problems discussed and resolved (Hunt and Azrin 1973).

The research evaluating this community-reinforcement program has shown (although with small samples) clear evidence of some success. In the first study done, patients in the program were matched with a group who received the standard counseling program in the hospital. Six months after release, the time spent drinking, unemployed, away from home, or back in the hospital was twice as high for the group receiving the regular hospital program for alcoholics as for the community-reinforcement treatment group (Hunt and Azrin 1973).

Later the program was modified to include a "buddy system," group counseling sessions, and a daily reporting procedure. Also, special motivation and training procedures were added for clients to continue taking the alcohol-antagonist drug Antabuse to maintain aversion to alcohol. These included timing the Antabuse administration to a well-established habit such as mealtime, involving the spouse to act as a monitor and helper in remembering to take the Antabuse, and requiring that the drug be taken only in the presence of spouse, peer advisor, or counselor. During the six-month follow-up period, the community-reinforcement group spent only 2 percent of its time drinking compared to 55 percent of the time spent drinking by those randomly assigned to the control group (who received the same housing and hospital counseling services but not the community-reinforcement program). The treatment group did much better than the control group in employment and spending time with the family. None of the treatment group was rehospitalized, while 45 percent of the control group's time was spent institutionalized. These significant differences continued for a two-year evaluation period. All of the community-reinforcement group maintained regular family and social relations sustaining sobriety, and as a group remained 90 percent abstinent in the two years following release (Azrin 1976).

Other variations on the reinforcement therapy carried out by Azrin and others also have proven to be more effective than traditional approaches, even on somewhat larger samples. For instance, the special motivation procedures for sustaining Antabuse medication combined with the community-reinforcement program were found to be more effective than the traditional Antabuse therapy (wherein patients are pretty much left alone to take the drug on their own). (Azrin et al. 1982; see also Sisson and Azrin 1986).

Individualized Behavior Therapy for Alcoholics. Another differential reinforcement approach is that of the Sobells' discussed earlier. One part of the program was in a simulated bar environment in which subjects in training to become moderate social drinkers were hooked up to electrodes to receive electric shock. As long as they leisurely consumed a modest number of drinks within a specified time the shock was withheld, but if they drank more than allowed, a mild shock was administered (Sobell and Sobell 1978). But the treatment was not limited to this modified aversion therapy. Rather, the treatment was a seventeen-session broad-spectrum behavior-modification program to teach the alcoholics to drink moderately. Seventy volunteers from alcoholics in a treatment hospital were divided into two groups, those who wanted to take up controlled drinking and those who were to pursue the traditional goal of total abstinence. Then, within each of these groups, subjects were randomly assigned to the experimental treatment program or to a control group that received the traditional treatment program offered by the hospital. The follow-up evaluation found that the behavior-modification group, compared to the traditional treatment group, had more success in achieving fewer days of heavy drinking; more significantly, they were much more able to sustain controlled, social drinking (Sobell and Sobell 1978, 1984).

Relapse Prevention through Behavioral Self-Management. G. Alan Marlatt and his associates offer another treatment program based on social learning principles. They have developed a treatment model for alcoholism (as well as for drug abuse, obesity, and smoking) based on self-control and self-reinforcement. As we have seen, the disease model assumes that the alcoholic cannot voluntarily control his or her alcohol intake. In Marlatt's approach, alcoholism is viewed as an acquired habit that can be controlled by the person's self-management of relapse. In this model, after abstinence has been achieved, taking another drink is treated as simply a behavioral "slip" or "lapse" that may or may not result in another binge. It does not have to mean that one is completely off the wagon and inexorably sliding back into alcoholism. Rather, it depends on how the person handles the situation. The treatment program, then, consists of training in coping skills and self-management of relapse instances (Marlatt and Gordon 1985).

An example of how this model is applied to alcoholism is the Problem Drinkers' Project (PDP) carried out in a private hospital for treating alcoholics. The program uses a social learning framework in which the emphasis is on behavioral and cognitive factors, with self-help groups and self-reinforcement for sober behavior. This is primarily an outpatient program, although some in the program undergo 24-hour hospitalization. After an initial period of detoxification, clients spend an average of three weeks in a series of groups. In these groups, clients learn to assess the extent and severity of their drinking problems and to identify those aspects of their lives which led up to their drinking problems. They are taught to acquire behavioral skills such as drink-refusal behavior, to engage in alternative behavior, to set rational goals for themselves, and to control the consequences of drinking. They also develop social support systems (friends, family, employers, AA, and other groups). One of the key groups is the "slips group" in which clients and their families are helped to develop the ability to recognize the conditions under which slips will occur, to realize when a slip is about to occur, to avoid slips, and if a slip does occur, to keep it from becoming a full-fledged relapse to problem drinking. In a follow-up study six months after 174 clients had completed the program, the treatment group was abstinent 85 percent of the time and average ethanol consumption had dropped from eight ounces to one ounce a day, although employment had not improved (McCrady et al. 1985).

Tobacco

E F F E C T S   O F   N I C O T I N E   A N D   H E A L T H   H A Z A R D S   O F   T O B A C C O   U S E

The active drug in tobacco is nicotine. There are other ingredients, including polyphenols and alkali nitrates, in tobacco, and its smoke contains many elements such as hydrogen cyanide and carbon monoxide. The nicotine is ingested into the bloodstream through the lungs and the soft tissues of the mouth. As with all other substances, the nicotine's pharmacological action is on the neurotransmitters in the synaptic spaces and the dendrite receptor sites. It initially acts as a central nervous system stimulant and causes release of adrenaline. After the initial impact, nicotine may produce a relaxing effect. Nicotine in the system can cause nausea and dizziness, increases heart rate and blood pressure, suppresses appetite, and decreases oxygen flow in the blood creating shortness of breath.

The severe long-term health hazards of smoking and use of other tobacco products are now common knowledge. Cigarette smoking is the leading cause of lung cancer and a major factor in heart disease. Two out of five cancer deaths can be linked to smoking, and 80 to 90 percent of all lung cancer deaths come from smoking. A whole range of other major and minor maladies are associated with smoking, and there is growing evidence that smoking may harm others besides the smoker. The most direct link to the injurious effects on others is the adversity suffered by the fetus of a smoking mother. Nicotine and other chemicals from smoking that are present in the mother's blood become part of the fetus' blood flow, reducing the amount of oxygen that gets to the fetus. As is true for babies born of mothers using alcohol or drugs, the baby of a smoking mother runs a higher risk of low birth weight, indicative of general health problems. The infant may suffer neurological damage and later in life have behavioral problems and poor reading and math skills. If the mother continues smoking, or if the father smokes, while the child is being reared, the likelihood of the child having health problems such as respiratory illnesses is increased (U.S. DHEW 1979; Ray and Ksir 1987; Schwartz 1987). Indeed, adult nonsmokers exposed to high levels of smoke at home or in the workplace show some effects, although there is not much evidence of harm to persons who are irregularly or casually in the presence of smoke.

Smokeless tobacco today is consumed mainly in the form of moist snuff placed between the cheek and gum or loose-leaf chewing tobacco. Dry snuff which is inhaled through the nose was at one time the preferred tobacco snuff but today is only a tiny portion of the smokeless market in the United States. Oral smokeless tobacco is absorbed through the membranes of the mouth into the bloodstream where the nicotine has the same effects as it does when absorbed through the lungs. Smokeless tobacco is not related to lung cancer, but it carries health risks of its own, including cancer of the tongue, cheeks, gums, and esophagus. It is common for the habitual snuff user to have leukoplakia—white, thick precancerous patches on oral tissues (U.S. DHHS 1986; Ray and Ksir 1987).

SOCIAL NORMS AND PUBLIC POLICY ON TOBACCO

In the past two decades, smoking and other uses of tobacco have become increasingly deviant, socially and legally, in American society. The majority of the population disapproves of smoking (Johnston, O'Malley, and Bachman 1989), and legal regulations have become increasingly stringent. The evidence is incontrovertible that smoking is a life-threatening hazard to those who smoke (over 350,000 smoking-related deaths per year) and presents some health risks to those who are regularly in enclosed areas with smokers. The social disapproval is ordinarily expressed in trying to persuade others not to take up smoking or to quit smoking to avoid these health problems. However, the disapproval has taken on an increasingly strident moral edge to it as social norms and legal regulations have become more intolerant of smokers. Manufacturers and distributors face ever more strict regulation on the advertisement and sale of tobacco products, and smokers face rigorous constraints on where and when they smoke. Local, state, and federal laws, administrative directives, and court decisions have become so restrictive that they stop just short of outright criminalization of tobacco use (Neuhring and Markle 1974; Markle and Troyer 1979; Troyer and Markle 1983). Antismoking groups such as ASH (Action on Smoking and Health) have formed to battle the influence of the tobacco lobby and push for antitobacco legislation and to campaign for the divestment of tobacco stocks by hospitals, universities, and other institutions. Although still largely unsuccessful, hundreds of wrongful death and personal injury suits have been filed against tobacco companies (*Newsweek*, Apr. 11, 1988). The continuing suppression of smoking, the conflicts between smokers and nonsmokers, and the reactions of the tobacco industry have been described as a "war over smoking" (*Time*, Apr. 18, 1988:64–75).

Habitual smoking has become defined by a growing number of mental health and treatment professionals as an addiction more difficult to stop than a heroin habit. In 1988 the U.S. Surgeon General (U.S. DHHS 1988) declared tobacco to be physiologically addictive, and for more than a decade psychiatrists have defined habitual smoking as a "substance use disorder." The diagnostic and treatment language, such as "pathological" and "addictive personality," once reserved for alcohol and narcotics abuse has long since become rountinely applied to tobacco (Harrup, Hansen, and Soghikian 1979).

Many of us have the impression that the health concerns over smoking began with the 1964 Surgeon General's report and that social and political controversy revolving around tobacco started about the same time. In fact, tobacco has been vilified and defended, demonized and vindicated, almost from the very beginning of its use in recorded history. Social norms regarding tobacco smoking have gone from defining it as despicable to desirable and back again. Political and economic interests and groups are always involved in the defining and redefining of tobacco and continue to be prominent in today's changing smoking norms (Troyer and Markle 1983).

> It is clear that the reports that smoking is harmful to health were not the catalysts for the official actions coercing smokers. These official actions were a direct response to pressure-group activities. It also appears, however, that the pressure-group tactics were successful, in part because they were able to use the health evidence. Therefore, it seems that the research reports that smoking is bad for health were a necessary condition, with interest-group activities the sufficient condition for the coercive definitions to emerge. (Troyer and Markle 1983:88)

History of Smoking as Conforming and Deviant Behavior

Tobacco was used by American Indians prior to first contact with Europeans. They introduced European explorers to tobacco, and these explorers brought it back to Europe. By the middle of the sixteenth century, it had become one of the principal trade items from the New World. It was believed to have medicinal benefits, but by the end of the century was widely used throughout Europe as a recreational drug.

Early in the seventeenth century, King James I of England attacked tobacco smoking as evil, harmful to health, a cause of birth defects and insanity, and offensive to religion. He imposed heavy taxes and import duties on it and sought to ban its use completely. It became more and more important to economic development, however, and the laws regulating and criminalizing tobacco use were difficult to enforce. By the end of the seventeenth century and the beginning of the eighteenth century, most of the laws against tobacco use had been repealed. Smoking was again socially acceptable, and tobacco was widely available and used by significant portions of the population at every social class level (Best 1979; Troyer and Markle 1983).

Tobacco use (mainly pipe smoking and dry snuff) became well established in colonial America, but its use did not involve a large segment of the population. In the early part of the nineteenth century, tobacco chewing and cigar smoking become more common, but after the Civil War cigarette smoking began to take over as the most popular form of tobacco consumption. The most significant development was the invention and production of machines that could produce "tailor-made" cigarettes in great quantities. The increased sales and consumption of cigarettes created a social backlash of regulation so that by the end of the century cigarette sales to minors were banned in all states and fourteen states banned all sales even to adults. The Anti-Cigarette League was organized and remained active until the time of World War I.

Cigarette smoking became common among American soldiers and became identified in the public mind as part of the war effort. An economically strong tobacco industry and increasingly effective political lobby of that industry promoted the social acceptability of cigarette smoking (even by women for whom it had been deemed unseemly) and repeal of regulation of the tobacco market. By 1930 all strict prohibition laws had been repealed, and even laws against sales to minors began to be softened and enforcement became more lax. Over the next thirty years smoking became not only acceptable but also desirable for large segments of the population. This movement was helped by the seemingly universal practice of smoking by American troops during World War II and the identification of American cigarettes as the best in the world (coveted even by the enemy). Cigarettes became better than currency in black markets during and after the war. Cigarette smoking was not only a symbol of American superiority, but a symbol of sucess, sexuality, and the American way as well. Smoking was glamorized in movies and magazines and later on television. The tobacco industry became one of the largest advertisers promoting the image of smoking as a sophisticated practice associated with youth, good looks, health, and success.

In the 1950s, dormant concerns about the health risks of tobacco consumption (cigarettes had long been known as "coffin nails") resurfaced along with more research evidence on the links between various illnesses/diseases and cigarette smoking. This evidence was the primary basis for the famous 1964 U.S. Surgeon General's report, which found the epidemiological and clinical findings overwhelmingly to support the link between smoking and a range of health problems, most particularly lung cancer and cardiovascular diseases. The Tobacco Institute (funded by the tobacco industry) argued then and continues to argue that the case against cigarettes (and smokeless tobacco) is only "statistical" and that it has never been shown conclusively that smoking actually "causes" the diseases. Nevertheless, the antismoking groups that had begun to form gained strength from the report. Legal regulations restricting cigarette advertising and health warning labels followed almost immediately; television stations were required to carry antismoking spots. In 1970 the requirement was imposed that cigarette packaging carry the specific warning "The Surgeon General Has Determined That Cigarette Smoking Is Dangerous To Your Health." The next year all television and radio advertising of cigarettes was banned, and in 1972 all print advertising was required to carry the same health warnings as appeared on cigarette packaging. Pipe and cigar smoking also became more restricted.

In the following decade, governments at all levels legislated increasingly severe restrictions on smoking, providing for segregation of smokers in transportation and certain public facilities. The efforts of the tobacco lobbies managed to stop the laws short of outright banning of cigarettes, but the antismoking lobbies continued to score victory after victory in smoking regulations. In the 1980s, the antismoking momentum continued with tightening of advertising and warning regulations. Social disapproval grew, and smoking was banned in public buildings, transportation, and workplaces. In 1984 a new set of rotating warnings on cigarette packages and advertising was required (Troyer and Markle 1983; Ray and Ksir 1987). In 1986 the U.S. Surgeon General released another report on the health dangers of smoking, but this time the emphasis was on the dangers of passive, or second-hand, inhalation of smoke by those in the company of smokers. In that same year, the Surgeon General endorsed a report on the dangers and addictive potential of smokeless tobacco. Legal restrictions on advertisement of smokeless-tobacco products and requirements of warning labels on packages and in advertisements were enacted shortly after that. In 1988 the Surgeon General officially designated nicotine as an addictive drug (although apparently under the newer rather than the traditional concept of addiction discussed in Chapter 2). In 1990 the Environmental Protection Agency officially labeled secondary smoke to be a carcinogen (*Newsweek*, June 11, 1990:59). In 1989 smoking was banned on all domestic airplane flights, and by 1990 virtually all states and hundreds of localities had placed restrictions on smoking (*Newsweek*, June 16, 1990:16–17).

There is little doubt that the social and legal norms on tobacco have undergone enormous change. While still legal and not as severely condemned as illicit use of narcotics, smoking and other forms of tobacco consumption are clearly back in the category of socially disapproved behavior. As the social pendulum has swung back to disapproval of smoking by all age groups, smoking in the teenage years has become even more disapproved. Through the first three decades of the twentieth century, smoking was particularly disapproved as premature, inappropriate behavior for minors. It was considered a sign of delinquent tendencies, and smoking by minors itself was legally defined as delinquency in many jurisdictions. From the 1930s to the 1960s, as smoking became not only acceptable but fashionable for large segments of the populations, teenage smoking was less condemned. By the 1960s, teenage smoking was so widely viewed as nonproblematic that smoking became as "extinct as the tattoo in the literature on delinquency" (Hirschi 1969:168). By the late 1970s, some researchers discounted reports of declining rates of teenage smoking in national surveys on the grounds that they simply reflected a greater tendency for teenagers to falsify self-reports of smoking behavior because it had become so socially undesirable (Warner 1978). Some researchers even pictured smoking by adolescents as in the same taboo category as other drug use (Evans, Hansen, and Mittelmark 1977). This overstates the case, but there is little doubt that the majority of the population, both adult and juvenile, disapproves of smoking, especially by minors.

TRENDS IN SMOKING AND TOBACCO CONSUMPTION

The amount of smoking in the population has reflected the extent to which it has been socially approved or disapproved. Concern about health both supports and reflects this social dimension. The health issue seems insufficient to account for the variations in proportions of smokers by time and place. The principal factor seems to be the extent to which smoking is socially acceptable or disreputable and both formal and informal sanctions are applied to it. During times when smoking is socially accepted and has few legal controls, its prevalence in the population is high; when it is legally restricted and socially deviant, the prevalence rate is low. This pattern is seen in both historical patterns and recent trends.

In 1870, 13.9 million cigarettes were sold in the United States. At that time, per capita consumption was .36. By 1900 sales had increased to *2.6 billion* cigarettes per year and per capita consumption had increased by 3,400 percent! As dramatic as these percentage increases were, the big surge in absolute numbers of smokers came during and after World War I when cigarette smoking became widely accepted and regulations began to be repealed. By 1930 nearly 120 billion cigarettes were sold annually with a per capita consumption of 977 (Troyer and Markle 1983).

These leaps in sales and per capita consumption continued following World War II, reaching a volume peak of *550 billion* cigarettes sold in 1967. The peak of 4,300 cigarettes per capita sales for the adult population had been reached in 1964. At that time, over two-fifths of the adult population were regular smokers. By the end of the decade, annual per capita consumption had declined to less than 4,000. There was a period of increase in cigarette sales in the 1970s; the proportion of the population who were smokers was less, but remaining smokers increased their consumption, partly because so many had switched to low tar and nicotine and filtered cigarettes. From the mid-1970s on, cigarette sales have declined every year. By 1984 the consumption rate had dropped to 3,411 per capita, the lowest level since 1944. Adult and teenage females increased their level of smoking in the 1970s as male smoking was declining. Since then, the proportions of smokers among both men and women have continued downward (Ray and Ksir 1987; Schwartz 1987).

The prevalence of smoking among adolescents increased steadily from the 1950s until the beginning of the 1970s. By that time the majority of those in the 12- to 17-year-old group had experimented with cigarettes. About half as many girls as boys were regular smokers. At that point the prevalence of smoking among boys stabilized but continued upward among girls so that by the end of the decade their rate of smoking equaled that of the boys. Prevalence among both teenage boys and girls has declined since 1977. At the beginning of the 1980s, less than half of the 12- to 17-year-olds had ever smoked. About 15 percent were regular (at least once weekly) smokers, 10 percent were daily smokers, and 3 percent smoked a pack of cigarettes or more a day; and only one in a hundred was classified as a heavy smoker (Fishburne, Abelson, and Cisin 1980; Johnston, Bachman, and O'Malley 1980; Lauer et al. 1982).

Table 13.1 shows smoking trends from 1979 to 1990 as reflected in the high school senior surveys. All indicators of smoking by the seniors show a sustained downward trend. Nearly two-thirds in 1990 had tried cigarettes, but this compares to the three-fourths who had smoked in 1979. Most significantly, the latest findings show that only about one in ten of the graduating seniors have developed a daily cigarette habit of half-a-pack or more. Although

T A B L E   1 3 . 1   *Trends in cigarette smoking among high school seniors*

	1979	1985	1990
Ever used	74.0%	68.8%	64.4%
Past month	34.4	30.1	29.4
Daily	25.4	19.5	19.1
Daily: ½ pack or more	16.5	12.5	11.3

Sources: Johnston 1989; University of Michigan 1991.

T A B L E   1 3 . 2   *Trends in cigarette smoking by age group: 1979–1990*

	1979	1985	1990
12–17			
Ever used	54.1%	45.2%	40.2%
Past year	13.3	25.8	22.2
Past month	12.1[a]	15.3	11.6
18–25			
Ever used	82.8	75.6	70.2
Past year	46.7	44.3	39.7
Past month	42.6	36.8	31.2
26 +			
Ever used	83.0	80.5	78.0
Past year	39.7	36.0	31.9
Past month	36.9	32.8	27.7

Source: NIDA 1989a, 1990a.
[a]For 1979 the figure is the percent only of those who ever smoked at least five packs. In 1977, 22.3 percent of all those in this age group smoked cigarettes in the past month.

there were slightly more daily smokers among the high school seniors in 1990 than in 1988 (not shown in the table), the proportions are down considerably from the over 16 percent who smoked that much in 1979.

Table 13.2 shows that smoking is down among all age groups compared to a decade ago. The table does not show daily smoking, but a 1987 survey in thirty-two states by the Center for Disease Control reported the proportion of regular smokers in the adult population to be 25 percent, varying from a high of 32 percent in Kentucky to a low of 15 percent in Utah (*USA Today,* July 14, 1989).

Table 13.3 shows that there are only small differences in smoking in the proportion of smokers in white, black, and Hispanic populations. Black

T A B L E   1 3 . 3 *Sociodemographic characteristics of cigarette smokers (percent used in the past month)*

	Age Groups				
	12–17	18–25	26–34	35 +	Total
Sex					
Male	12.4%	35.2%	40.7%	32.2%	32.2%
Female	11.2	34.8	33.6	23.0	25.6
Race/Ethnicity					
White	13.9	36.9	37.2	26.3	28.7
Black	5.1	29.5	36.1	35.5	30.1
Hispanic	7.5	28.2	33.6	27.5	26.3
Education					
Less than HS	NA	49.2	58.3	32.9	38.5
HS graduate	NA	37.2	42.4	28.9	33.9
Some college	NA	26.0	32.2	25.9	27.3
College graduate	NA	17.5	18.3	16.9	17.4

Source: NIDA 1989a, 1990b (1988 survey).

smokers tend to smoke fewer cigarettes, but to smoke high-nicotine brands (Schwartz 1987). Smoking is inversely related to education, occupational prestige, and employment so that both males and females in the lower classes are more likely to smoke than are those in the middle and upper classes. Table 13.3 shows that high school dropouts are more than twice as likely as college graduates to smoke. The unemployed are much more likely than the fully employed to be smokers (not shown in the table). From this table we see that among adolescents and young adults smoking by men and by women has converged in the past decade to become nearly equal. In the older age groups, men are still slightly more likely than women to be current smokers (smoke sometime during the past month).

There has been no convergence, however, in the use of smokeless tobacco. Chewing tobacco and using moist snuff have always been and remain nearly exclusive male activities and are especially high among southern whites. Smokeless tobacco is the only tobacco product for which sales have increased and for which prevalence has remained stable or has increased since 1979. Consumption of chewing tobacco and moist snuff ("pinch" or "dip") noticeably increased among teenage boys and young adult males in the 1980s. A fourth of male adolescents have used smokeless tobacco more than once or twice, and more than one in ten have used it in the past year. Over 40 percent of young adult males (18 to 25) have used smokeless tobacco.

The Iowa Smoking Study

These national prevalence rates and trends in cigarette smoking and use of smokeless tobacco are supplemented by surveys in local communities. A study which measures the same variables at set points over time is known as a longitudinal study. Ronald Lauer (a physician and medical researcher specializing in pediatric cardiology), Marvin Krohn (a sociologist), other associates, and I conducted a longitudinal study of secondary school students in a community in Iowa of about 23,000 population. The research was a self-report questionnaire survey of the junior high and senior high school students (about 2,000 each year). Each year, starting in 1980 and concluding in 1984, students attending both junior high schools and the one senior high school in this community were surveyed in the spring semester. Within this overall sample is a panel of seventh- and eighth-grade students who were in the study for all five years. (For additional description of the study, see Lauer et al. 1982, Akers et al. 1983; Krohn et al. 1985; and Akers et al. 1987.)

Are Self-Reports of Smoking Valid? If you ask adolescents whether they use drugs, smoke, or drink alcohol (all of which are illegal for them), will they tell you the truth? This is a question that comes up regarding use of self-report surveys for use of any substance. In the Iowa Study, we gauged the truthfulness of responses to our questions about smoking by matching the answers with the level of thiocyanate (a chemical residue of nicotine) found in saliva samples taken from the same respondents. One may underreport or overreport about his or her own smoking behavior, but one cannot deliberately falsify the presence or absence of residues of nicotine in body fluids. The levels of thiocyanate found in the saliva corresponded closely to the self-reports of the teenagers in the study about their smoking within the last forty-eight hours, how frequently they smoked, how many cigarettes they smoked each day, and how they described themselves as a non-smoker, moderate smoker, or heavy smoker (Lauer et al. 1982; Akers et al. 1983). These findings agree with the results of other studies that show self-reports are valid measures of substance use (Whitehead and Smart 1972) as well as other types of deviant behavior (Hardt and Peterson-Hardt 1977; Hindelang, Hirschi, and Weiss 1981).

Trends in Teenage Smoking and Tobacco Use in the Iowa Study. In the Iowa Study, the proportions of students smoking and smoking regularly (weekly or daily) or using smokeless tobacco increased with grade level. About a third of the respondents had had some experience with cigarettes by the time they were in the seventh grade, but majorities were not reached until the ninth grade. There was no tendency over the five-year period for either a consistent increase or a consistent decrease in smoking either at a given grade level or overall.

The older students smoked more than the younger students, and the chances of smoking increased in each of the cohorts as the teenagers got older. In 1980, 39 percent of the seventh graders were smokers and about 6 percent of them were regular smokers. Four years later, as high school juniors, over 60 percent had at least tried cigarettes and a fifth of them were regular smokers (smoked at least weekly). Similarly, as the original cohort of eighth graders got older, the proportion having smoked at all and the proportion smoking on a regular basis increased so that by the time they were high school seniors, nearly two-thirds had experimented with cigarettes and a fourth had established regular smoking habits.

Among those in the study who were abstainers in grades 7 and 8 in the first year of the survey, 16 percent tried cigarettes the next year. By the last year of the study, when they were juniors and seniors in high school, half of these junior high school abstainers had acquired some smoking experience. On the other hand, 20 percent of those who had reported smoking in the seventh and eighth grades stopped smoking the next year. After that a decreasing percentage reported not smoking in subsequent years indicating a tendency for smoking to stabilize over time.

In contrast to smoking, there was a definite upswing in teenage use of smokeless tobacco over the five years of the Iowa Study. The percentage using smokeless tobacco at all jumped significantly from 15 to 23 percent, and the percentage of regular users nearly doubled (from 1.9 to 3.2 percent). This drop in smoking accompanied by an increase in use of smokeless tobacco raises the question of the relationship between cigarette smoking and use of smokeless tobacco by teenagers. Is the perception that smokeless tobacco is less of a health risk than smoking inducing some teenagers to use moist snuff or chewing tobacco who otherwise would abstain from all tobacco use? Or has the increased use of smokeless tobacco prevented what would otherwise have been an increase in smoking?

Relationship of Cigarette Smoking to Use of Smokeless Tobacco.   Table 13.4 presents the cross-tabulation of cigarette smoking by use of smokeless tobacco for each year in the Iowa Study. This table shows neither that use of smokeless tobacco is substituting for smoking nor that significant numbers of teenagers who would, were it not for snuff, be total tobacco abstainers. What the table shows is that use of tobacco in one form (cigarettes) is associated with the use of tobacco in another form (smokeless tobacco). As the frequency of smoking increases, the chances of using snuff increase. Daily smokers are four to five times more likely than nonsmokers to use smokeless tobacco. Of snuff or chewing-tobacco users, 70 to 80 percent are also smoking

T A B L E   1 3 . 4   *Overlap of smokeless-tobacco users and cigarette smokers*

	1980	1981	1982	1983	1984
Percent of Smokers Who Use Smokeless Tobacco					
Nonsmokers	6.6%	9.4%	10.3%	9.8%	11.9%
Weekly smokers	29.6	31.1	29.4	41.7	44.8
Daily smokers	32.5	33.3	40.2	45.2	49.2
Percent of Smokeless-Tobacco Users Who Smoke					
Nonusers	2.9	29.1	26.0	23.1	17.8
Users	76.1	70.9	74.0	76.9	82.2
N =	2,047	2,051	2,289	2,220	1,382

Source: Adapted from Akers et al. 1987.

cigarettes. Snuff (or chewing tobacco) is a substitute for, or is used to the exclusion of, cigarette smoking for only the minority of smokeless-tobacco users. A majority of smokers abstain from snuff, but daily smokers are about evenly divided between snuff users and nonusers.

S O C I A L   L E A R N I N G   A N D   S M O K I N G   B E H A V I O R

Social learning incorporates a number of variables in the acquisition and maintenance of or refraining from substance use. However, as stated in Chapters 1 and 5, there are four principal concepts in the social learning theory, and these have been incorporated into the research as main sets of independent variables—differential association, differential reinforcement, definitions, and imitation.

Differential association refers specifically to two dimensions. First, it refers to the frequency, intensity, duration, and priority of interaction with others. Second, it refers to exposure to normative patterns shared by others. The interaction and exposure are mainly in family and peer groups, but the individual also may be influenced by secondary groups as well as by media-portrayed situations and norms. From these groups, the person learns *definitions* (attitudes, orientations, and evaluative knowledge) favorable or unfavorable to smoking. It is these same groups which also expose one to behavioral models, *imitation,* and patterns of social reinforcement. *Differential reinforcement* refers to the process whereby behavior is acquired and persists or does not develop depending on the anticipated, past, and present rewards and punishments attached to it and alternative behavior. These may be social or nonsocial, as from the physiological effects of smoking. Pomerleau and Pomerleau point to both social reinforcement and the reinforcing effects of nicotine in sustaining a smoking habit:

> Some of these phenomena can be explained in a straightforward manner within the context of social learning theory. Acquisition of the habit is known to occur under conditions of social reinforcement. . . .
>
> Smoking can thus be conceptualized as a generalized primary and secondary reinforcer, providing both positive and negative reinforcement over a remarkably wide array of life situations. Smoking is also powerfully entrained because of its ability to provide immediate reinforcement: Nicotine from an inhaled cigarette reaches the brain in seven seconds. . . . Furthermore, the habit is greatly overlearned: At ten puffs per cigarette, the pack-a-day smoker gets more than 70,000 puffing reinforcements in a year—a frequency unmatched by any other form of drug taking. Although most smokers recognize that sustained smoking can lead to a variety of unpleasant consequences, . . . these aversive consequences are delayed and therefore have less influence over ongoing smoking behavior than immediate consequences—a situation common to a number of substances of abuse. Unlike alcohol and many other dependence-producing substances, however, not only does nicotine *not* impair performance, but it seems to enhance the capacity of normal people to work and to socialize. There are thus few immediate noticeable negative consequences to interfere with entertainment. (Pomerleau and Pomerleau 1988: 122–123)

Social learning is a complex, ongoing behavioral process, and the sequence of events is variable depending on the particular behavior and individuals in question. Nevertheless, the typical process envisioned by the theory is that individuals interact and identify with family, friends, and other groups in which they are exposed to behavioral models, norms, and reinforcement patterns tending toward abstinence or smoking. The balance of definitions favorable and unfavorable to smoking, combined with imitation and the anticipated balance of reinforcement, produces the initial smoking. After initiation, imitation becomes less important (although facilitative effects of modeling may remain) while the effects of definitions (themselves now affected by the consequences of initial smoking) and reinforcement continue. Differential association has a strong effect in both initiation and maintenance. Those associations are most often formed initially on bases other than co-involvement in smoking.

This is obviously the case within the family (one does not choose his family), and it is also hypothesized to be the typical case with peer associations. However, formation or continuation of peer friendships will be affected in part by one's own attitudes and prior or anticipated parental and peer re-inforcement. Further, after smoking has begun and the consequences accom-panying it are experienced, the associational patterns over which one has any choice may themselves be altered so that the fact that one is drawn to or chooses further interaction with others is based, at least in part, on whether they too are smokers.

Predicting Adolescent Smoking Behavior with Social Learning Variables

This social learning theory was first tested on teenage smoking in the Iowa Study by analyzing the first-year survey. Spear and Akers (1988) found that all of the social learning variables were strongly related to abstinence and frequency of smoking. Next the social learning model was tested with the first three years of the longitudinal data from the Iowa Study to see to what extent social learning variables could predict who would begin to smoke and who would continue or cease after smoking was initiated. Krohn and col-leagues (1985) found that among those adolescents who were smoking in the first year of the survey (T1) the social learning variables measured at T1 and T2 successfully predicted (41 percent of the variance explained) who was still smoking and who had quit at T3, the third year of the survey. However, the social learning model was not very successful in predicting from among ab-stainers at both T1 or T2 who would begin experimenting with cigarettes at T3.

However, when these abstainers were followed until the fifth year, the social learning model did a better job of predicting the onset of smoking and an even better job of predicting who would start at T3 and continue to smoke at T5, when experimental starters and stoppers are excluded. Peer associa-tion was found to be the best predictor. In fact, knowing the smoking behavior of one's best friends in the first year of the study is about as good a predictor of one's smoking behavior in the fourth and fifth years as knowing one's own smoking behavior in the first year. The imitation of parental smoking models, parental attitudes toward smoking, and one's own definitions favorable to smok-ing also had significant direct effects on smoking. It should be noted, though, that there were some technical statistical problems with this model, and con-clusions based on it need to be viewed with caution. With this caution in mind, it can be tentatively concluded that the social learning model was found to predict both initiation (although perhaps not very well) and continuation of teenage smoking.

The Combined Effect of Friends and Parents on Teenage Smoking

Our research on initiation and continuation of substance use among adolescents shows clearly that the most important influence on them is the

T A B L E   1 3 . 5   Parents' and friends' influence on teenage smoking

Smoking by Parents and Friends of Respondents	Smoking by Respondents		
	Never	Regularly	N =
Neither parents nor best friend smoke	75%	1%	522
Parents smoke but best friend doesn't	63	6	543
Best friend smokes but parents don't	27	26	120
Both parents and best friend smoke	16	44	458

Source: Adapted from Lauer et al. 1982.

behavior of peers, especially close friends. But parental influence is also important in the social learning model. Although the influences of parents and peers often counteract one another, they also may point in the same direction. When this happens the combined effect on the adolescent is most powerful, as shown in Table 13.5.

When neither parents nor friends smoke, the teenager is very likely not even to try cigarettes and is almost certain (99 percent of the time) not to be a regular smoker. On the other hand, when both parents and friends smoke, 84 percent of the teenagers have experimented with smoking and 44 percent are regular smokers.

The findings from the Iowa Study of teenage smoking provide additional support for social learning as an explanation of smoking or not smoking. The same variables found to be important in my earlier studies of drug use described in Chapters 3 and 5 are also important in this study of smoking, and the correlations are as high. Moreover, the evidence shows that knowing where the students stand with regard to the social learning variables of differential association, reinforcement, definitions, and imitation in one year allows prediction, with some degree of accuracy, of whether or not they will be smokers in later years.

P R E V E N T I O N   A N D
C E S S A T I O N   O F   S M O K I N G

Several prevention and education programs designed specifically to delay or prevent the onset of smoking have been conducted. These programs, especially those based on acquisition of coping and refusal skills, have been

Smoking-Cessation Methods

The U.S. Department of Health and Human Services has provided the most comprehensive review and evaluation of smoking-cessation methods available, identifying major, somewhat overlapping, categories of approaches to quitting cigarettes (Schwartz 1987). The principal categories, with a few examples of each, are:

1. Self-Care Aids
   a. Instruction books and pamphlets
   b. Products such as nicotine-reduction filters
   c. Computer-assisted self-help behavioral instructions
2. Educational Activities, Clinics, and Groups
   a. Cessation programs in schools
   b. Lectures and cessation education in hospitals and other settings
   c. Withdrawl clinics and groups
   d. Commercial and proprietary programs
3. Nicotine Chewing Gum, Medication, and Nicotine Substitutes
4. Hypnosis
5. Acupuncture
6. Physician Counseling
7. Mass Media and Community Programs
   a. Mass media antismoking messages
   b. Great American Smokeout days
   c. Community programs
8. Behavior Modification
   a. Aversive conditioning, rapid smoking, satiation, shock
   b. Desensitization and relaxation
   c. Self-management techniques, self-monitoring, contingency management
   d. Multicomponent behavioral self-control

among the more successful and have served as models for general alcohol and drug prevention programs, described in Chapter 9, with which they are often combined (see Bell and Battjes 1987; Flay 1987).

Treatment programs for habitual smokers to get them off of cigarettes, on the other hand, typically have not been combined with alcohol and drug treatment programs, although many of the same counseling techniques are used. Rather, a wide range of separate smoking-cessation programs have developed supporting a fairly sizable public and private stop-smoking industry that parallels and partially overlaps with the drug and alcohol treatment industry. There are over 500,000 self-help support groups such as Smokers Anonymous and an unknown number of smoking-cessation clinics and programs. Although cutting down on consumption is the goal in some programs, the almost universal goal is to help smokers quit cigarettes altogether without relapse. Many different approaches to achieve this goal of smoking cessation have been developed (see the box "Smoking-Cessation Methods").

Success of Stop-Smoking Programs

No general category, or specific methods within each category, has been thoroughly studied for effectiveness. But the research which has been done finds that none of these programs have been able to show low relapse rates at one-year follow-ups (Schwartz 1987). It is partly the low success rates of cessation programs that form the basis of the U.S. Attorney General's image, and the popular image, of smoking as a terrible addiction that is nearly impossible to quit. It is common to encounter statements in the popular press such as:

> Nearly all smokers have tried and failed to give up their habit. . . . Very few smokers succeed [in quitting] on the first try, or even the second or third. The relapse rate is comparable to that of heroin. (*Time*, Apr. 18, 1988:71).

This is a false image of smokers; it applies primarily to those troubled enough by their smoking to have entered systematic smoking-cessation programs. By definition, these are smokers who have had the most trouble giving up cigarettes and who have failed on their own to quit. They are not representative of the general population of smokers. It is true that "the majority of smokers have made at least one serious but unsuccessful attempt to stop smoking" (Schwartz 1987:15). Nevertheless, millions of smokers have quit, even though it often takes more than one try, and almost always on their own. The makers of commercial stop-smoking products promote the idea that smoking is an addiction over which the person has no control and which cannot be cured without the product they have to sell. Television, newspaper, magazine, and drug-store advertisements for nicotine gum and other products claim that

> it's not your fault if you can't quit. Cigarette smoking is an addiction, a medical problem. But today, your doctor has a medicine and a program that have helped millions quit more easily and less painfully. (Nicorette advertisement appearing in *USA Today*, July 14, 1989)

In fact, with only an 11 percent "cure" rate, the use of nicotine gum by itself is the least successful of the smoking-cessation techniques (Schwartz 1987). Often the smoker simply substitutes a nicotine chewing-gum habit for a smoking habit or combines the two. The success rate of smoking-cessation programs overall is not very high, about 20 to 25 percent, but there is great variations in success depending on the techniques and groups involved. Those persons going through quit-smoking procedures who have the highest motivation and face the most imminent danger from continuation of smoking, such as cardiac and pulmonary patients, are the most likely to be successful in giving up cigarettes (median of 31 percent and 43 percent, respectively). The most successful methods with the general population of smokers seeking help to quit are some form of behavioral modification (Schwartz 1987; *Newsweek*, Aug. 22, 1988:64; *Time*, Apr. 18, 1988:71; *U.S. News & World Report*, Aug. 1, 1988:59–60; Peele 1989).

One social behavioral approach that appears to have had some success stresses training for self-control and cessation:

> We approach the modification of smoking behavior as a problem in self-control or self-management . . . with a focus on critical situations and on personal self-management skills. . . . The development of skills for coping with relapse-facilitating situations is the major focus of our clinical approach . . . to teach clients an approach to regulating their own behavior and lifestyle. The client is not passively acted upon but is the active agent of treatment. (Schiffman et al. 1985:473)

This program teaches cognitive and behavioral coping skills to control relapse once smoking has ceased so that one slip does not trigger a complete relapse. Clients learn to avoid or escape from situations that have in the past triggered smoking episodes. They learn to distract themselves from smoking and to engage in alternative behavior (Schiffman et al. 1985). The median one-year success rate for behavioral techniques combined with nicotine chewing gum is 29 percent (with about a third of the studies reporting more than 33 percent success). But several behavioral techniques on their own without nicotine gum or other medication have higher cessation rates; for some techniques, half of the studies report at least 33 percent success. Use of the self-care products listed in the first category of the list on page 252 does not seem to work very well. The most effective of all the programs are those that take a multiple-component behavioral approach to teach clients self-management of smoking. These programs have a median success rate of 40 percent with over 65 percent of the studies done on them reporting cessation rates of one-third or higher (Schwartz 1987).

The Most Common Successful Technique: Stopping on Your Own

This emphasis on self-control is well placed because the typical way that people stop or cut down on cigarette smoking is by their own efforts. Self-cessation is the most common way that people give up bad habits of all kinds, and quitting the smoking habit on one's own is the primary example of this (Peele 1988a, 1989). At the time of the first report by the U.S. Surgeon General on the health hazards of smoking in 1964, about 40 percent of the adult population (52 percent of the men and 34 percent of the women) were habitual smokers. Twenty-four years later, when the Surgeon General declared nicotine to be an addictive drug, the percentage of adult smokers had been cut by two-fifths. By 1983 the percent of adult male smokers had declined to 35 percent and the percent of adult female smokers was down to 29 percent. The survey by the Centers for Disease Control in 1987 found that only 25.2 percent of adult men and women had a smoking habit. A 1986 Gallup Poll found that the proportion of adult men and women who had smoked sometime during the past week (31 percent) reached its lowest point in forty-two years (Schwartz 1987).

Some of this reduction is the result of fewer people developing a smoking habit simply by never starting to smoke. But a large part of the reduction has come about because a great many former smokers have quit. The proportion of ex-smokers in the adult population has increased steadily since 1965, and 45 percent of all those who have ever had a smoking habit have quit. The American Cancer Society reports that this has resulted in 40 to 41 million ex-smokers in the United States. *About 95 percent of these people have stopped smoking on their own without receiving any treatment* (Schwartz 1987; *U.S. News & World Report*, Aug. 1, 1988:59; Peele 1989).

There is no way of knowing how much of this prevention of onset and cessation by smokers over the past twenty-five years has come about as a result of the large-scale educational campaigns and various treatment programs. We do not know how much effect has been felt from the increasingly strict legal regulation of smoking or how much has resulted from changing social norms and informal social control. Whatever the causes, containing the smoking problem may go down in history as one of the great successes in the struggle against substance abuse. Tobacco is still the second most often consumed drug in American society, but if the trend continues, regular smokers will become an endangered species. In 1986 the Surgeon General endorsed the public-policy goal of having a "smoke-free society by the year 2000" (*Time*, July 28, 1986:19). We may never achieve such a tobacco-free society, but we appear to be headed toward a time when habitual tobacco smoking will be the activity of a small, deviant minority.

References

Abadinsky, Howard
  1989   *Drug abuse: an introduction.* Chicago: Nelson-Hall.

Abelson, Herbert I., and Fishburne, Patricia M.
  1976   *Nonmedical use of psychoactive substances.* Princeton, N.J.:
          Response Analysis Corp.

Adler, Israel, and Kandel, Denise
  1982   Cross-cultural perspectives on development of stages in adolescent
          drug use. *Journal of Studies on Alcohol* 42:701–15.

Adler, Patricia, and Adler, Peter
  1978   Tinydopers: a case study of deviant socialization. *Symbolic Interaction* 1:90–105.

Akers, Ronald L.
  1970   Teenage drinking and drug use. Pp. 266–88 in Ellis Evans, ed.,
          Adolescents. Hinsdale, IL: Dryden.

  1977   *Deviant behavior: a social learning approach.* 2d ed. Belmont, CA:
          Wadsworth.

  1984   Delinquent behavior, drugs, and alcohol: what is the relationship?
          Today's Delinquent 3:19–47.

  1985   *Deviant behavior: a social learning approach.* 3d ed. Belmont, CA:
          Wadsworth.

Akers, Ronald L.; Burgess, Robert L.; and Johnson, Weldon
  1968   Opiate use, addiction, and relapse. *Social Problems* 15:459–69.

Akers, Ronald L., and Cochran, John K.
>   1985   Adolescent marijuana use: a test of three theories of deviant
>   behavior. *Deviant Behavior* 6:323–46.

Akers, Ronald L.; Krohn, Marvin D.; Lanza-Kaduce, Lonn;
and Radosevich, Marcia
>   1979   Social learning and deviant behavior: a specific test of a general
>   theory. *American Sociological Review* 44:636–55.

Akers, Ronald L., and La Greca, Anthony J.
>   1988   Alcohol, contact with the legal system, and illegal behavior among
>   the elderly. Pp. 51–61 in Belinda McCarthy and Robert Langworthy,
>   eds., *Older offenders: perspectives in criminology and criminal
>   justice.* New York: Praeger.

>   1991   Alcohol use among the elderly: social learning, community context,
>   and life events. In David J. Pittman and Helene White, eds., *Soci-
>   ety, culture and drinking patterns re-examined.* New Brunswick, NJ:
>   Rutgers University Press.

Akers, Ronald L.; La Greca, Anthony J.; Cochran, John K.; and Sellers, Christine
>   1989   Social learning and alcohol behavior among the elderly. *Sociological
>   Quarterly* 30:625–63.

Akers, Ronald L.; Massey, James; Clarke, William; and Lauer, Ronald M.
>   1983   Are self reports of adolescent deviance valid? biochemical
>   measures, randomized response, and the bogus pipeline in smoking
>   behavior. *Social Forces* 62:234–51.

Akers, Ronald L.; Skinner, William F.; Krohn, Marvin D.; and Lauer, Ronald M.
>   1987   Recent trends in teenage tobacco use: findings from a five-year
>   longitudinal study. *Sociology and Social Research* 71:110–14.

Alcoholics Anonymous
>   1976   *Alcoholics Anonymous: the story of how many thousands of men and
>   women have recovered from alcoholism.* 3d ed. New York: Alcoholics
>   Anonymous World Services.

Andrews, Kenneth H., and Kandel, Denise B.
>   1979   Attitude and behavior: a specification of the contingent consistency
>   hypothesis. *American Sociological Review* 44:298–310.

Anglin, M. Douglas
>   1988   The efficacy of civil commitment in treating narcotic addiction. Pp.
>   8–34 in Carl G. Leukefeld and Frank M. Tims, eds., *Compulsory
>   treatment of drug abuse: research and clinical practice.* Rockville,
>   MD: National Institute on Drug Abuse.

Anglin, M. Douglas, and Hser, Yih-ing
>   1987   Addicted women and crime. *Criminology* 25:359–97.

Anglin, M. Douglas, and Speckart, George
  1988   Narcotics use and crime: a multisample, multimethod analysis. *Criminology* 26:197–233.

Armor, David J.; Polich, J. Michael; and Stambul, Harriet B.
  1976   *Alcoholism and treatment.* New York: Wiley.

Austin, Gregory A.
  1978   *Perspectives on the history of psychoactive substance use.* Research Issues 24. Rockville, MD: National Institute on Drug Abuse.

Austin, Gregory A.; Macari, Mary A.; and Lettieri, Dan J., eds.
  1979   *Research issues update.* National Institute on Drug Abuse. Washington, DC: U.S. Government Printing Office.

Ausubel, David P.
  1958   *Drug addiction.* New York: Random House.
  1960   Controversial issues in the management of drug addiction. *Mental Hygiene* 44:535–44.

Ayllon, T., and Azrin, N.
  1966   Punishment as a discriminative stimulus and conditioned reinforcer for humans. *Journal of the Experimental Analysis of Behavior* 9:411–19.

Azrin, N. H.
  1976   Improvements in the community-reinforcement approach to alcoholism. *Behavior Research and Therapy* 14:339–48.

Azrin, N. H.; Sisson, R. W.; Meyers, R.; and Godley, M.
  1982   Alcoholism treatment by disulfiram and community reinforcement therapy. *Journal of Behavioral Therapy and Experimental Psychiatry* 13:105–12.

Ball, John C.
  1967   Marijuana smoking and the onset of heroin use. *British Journal of Criminology* 7:408–13.

Ball, John C., and Cottrell, Emily S.
  1965   Admissions of narcotic drug addicts to public health service hospitals, 1935–63. *Public Health Reports* 80:471–75.

Bandura, Albert
  1969   *Principles of behavior modification.* New York: Holt, Rinehart, and Winston.
  1977   *Social learning theory.* Englewood Cliffs, NJ: Prentice-Hall.
  1986   *Social foundations of thought and action: a social cognitive theory.* Englewood Cliffs, NJ: Prentice-Hall.

Barnes, Grace
 1979   Alcohol use among older persons: findings from a western New York state general population survey. *Journal of the American Geriatric Society* 27:244–50.

Beck, Allen J.; Kline, Susan A.; and Greenfield, Lawrence A.
 1988   *Survey of youth in custody, 1987.* Bureau of Justice Statistics special report. U.S. Department of Justice, September.

Becker, Howard S.
 1963   ed. *Outsiders: studies in the sociology of deviance.* New York: Free Press.
 1967   History, culture, and subjective experience: an exploration of the social basis of drug-induced experiences. *Journal of Health and Social Behavior* 8:163–76.

Bell, Catherine S., and Battjes, Robert
 1987   *Prevention research: deterring drug abuse among children and adolescents.* Rockville, MD: National Institute on Drug Abuse.

Bennett, William
 1990   Should drugs be legalized? *Reader's Digest,* March, 90–94.

Benoit, Ellen
 1989   The case for legalization. *Financial World,* October 3, 32–35.

Benson, Daniel Ray
 1989   Treatment and prevention of alcoholism and substance abuse in the military. Pp. 341–55 in Gary W. Lawson and Ann W. Lawson, eds., *Alcohol and substance abuse in special populations.* Rockville, MD: Aspen Publishers.

Berger, Dale E., and Snortum, John R.
 1986   A structural model of drinking and driving: alcohol consumption, social norms, and moral commitments. *Criminology* 24:139–54.

Berkowitz, Alan D., and Perkins, H. Wesley
 1986   Problem drinking among college students: a review of recent research. *Journal of American College Health* 35:21–28.

Beschner, George M., and Bovelle, Elliott I.
 1985   Life with heroin: voices of experience. Pp. 75–107 in Bill Hanson, George Beschner, James Walter, and Elliott Bovelle, eds., *Life with heroin: voices from the inner city.* Lexington, MA: Lexington Books.

Best, Joel
 1979   Economic interests and the vindication of deviance: tobacco in seventeenth century Europe. *Sociological Quarterly* 20:171–82.

Biernacki, Patrick
 1986   *Pathways from heroin addiction: recovery without treatment.* Philadelphia: Temple University Press.

Blackwell, Judith S.
1983   Drifting, controlling, and overcoming: opiate users who avoid becoming chronically dependent. *Journal of Drug Issues* 13:219–35.

Block, Alan A.
1979   The snowman cometh: coke in progressive New York. *Criminology* 17:75–99.

Blum, Richard
1967   Mind-altering drugs and dangerous behavior: narcotics. Pp. 40–61 in *Task force report: narcotics and drug abuse*. The President's Commission on Law Enforcement and Administration of Justice. Washington, DC: U.S. Government Printing Office.

Blum, Terry C., and Roman, Paul M.
1988   Purveyor organizations and the implementation of employee assistance programs. *Journal of Applied Behavioral Analysis* 24:397–411.

Borgatta, Edgar F.; Montgomery, Rhonda J. V.; and Borgatta, Marie L.
1982   Alcohol use and abuse, life crisis events, and the elderly. *Research on Aging* 4:378–408.

Boyle, John M., and Brunswick, Ann F.
1980   What happened in Harlem? *Journal of Drug Issues* 10:109–30.

Braithwaite, John
1989   *Crime, shame, and reintegration.* Cambridge: Cambridge University Press.

Brantingham, Paul J.
1973   The legal administration of drug abuse control in Britain and the role of the British police. *Journal of Drug Issues* 3:135–43.

Braucht, G. Nicholas; Follingstad, Diane; Brakarsh, Daniel; and Berry, K. L.
1973   Drug education: a review of goals, approaches, and effectiveness, and a paradigm for evaluation. *Quarterly Journal of Studies on Alcohol* 34:1279–92.

Brook, Robert C., and Whitehead, Paul C.
1980   *Drug free therapeutic community: an evaluation.* New York: Human Sciences Press.

Brown, Frieda, and Tooley, Joan
1989   Alcoholism in the black community. Pp. 115–30 in Gary W. Lawson and Ann W. Lawson, eds., *Alcohol and substance abuse in special populations*. Rockville, MD: Aspen Publishers.

Brown, Lee P.
1988   Strategies for dealing with crack houses. *FBI Law Enforcement Bulletin* 57(6):4–7.

Buckley, William F.
1989 An argument for legalizing drugs. *Gainesville Sun*, October 27, 6A.

Bureau of Justice Assistance (BJA)
1988 *An invitation to project DARE: drug abuse resistance education. Program brief.* Washington, DC: U.S. Department of Justice.

Bureau of Justice Statistics (BJS)
1985 *Sourcebook of criminal justice statistics.* Washington, DC: U.S. Government Printing Office.

Burkett, Steven, and Warren, Bruce O.
1987 Religiosity, peer associations, and adolescent marijuana use: a panel study of underlying causal structures. *Criminology* 25:109–32.

Cahalan, Don
1970 *Problem drinkers: a national survey.* San Francisco: Jossey-Bass.

Cahalan, Don, and Cisin, Ira H.
1968 American drinking practices: summary of findings from a national probability sample. *Quarterly Journal of Studies on Alcohol* 29:130–51.

Cahalan, Don; Cisin, Ira H.; and Crossley, Helen M.
1967 *American drinking practices.* Washington, DC: George Washington University.

Cahalan, Don, and Room, Robin
1974 *Problem drinking among American men.* New Brunswick, NJ: College and University Press.

Califano, Joseph A.
1982 *Drug abuse and alcoholism.* New York: Warner Books.

Caudill, Barry D., and Lipscomb, Thomas R.
1980 Modeling influences on alcoholics' rates of alcohol consumption. *Journal of Applied Behavior Analysis* 13:355–65.

Chaiken, Marcia R.
1989 *In-prison programs for drug-involved offenders.* Washington, DC: National Institute of Justice.

Chambers, Carl D.
1974 Some epidemiological considerations of opiate use in the United States. Pp. 65–82 in Eric Josephson and Eleanor E. Carroll, eds., *Drug use: epidemiological and sociological perspectives.* New York: Halsted.

Chambliss, William J.
1988 Dealing drugs in America. Paper presented at the American Bar Association Law-Related Education Leadership Conference, November, Orlando, FL.

Chapman, Robert F.; Garlington, Warren K.; and Lloyd, Kenneth E.
1969   A critical review of learning based treatments of alcoholism. Paper presented to State of Washington Alcohol Research Group, Seattle.

Chein, Isidor; Gerald, Donald L.; Lee, Robert S.; and Rosenfeld, Eva
1964   *The road to h: narcotics, delinquency, and social policy.* New York: Basic Books.

Childress, Anna R.; McLellan, A. Thomas; and O'Brien, Charles P.
1985   Behavioral therapies for substance abuse. *International Journal of the Addictions* 20:947–69.

Clark, Walter B., and Midanik, Lorraine
1982   Alcohol use and alcohol problems among U.S. adults: results of the 1979 survey. Pp. 3–52 in *Alcohol consumption and related problems.* Department of Health and Human Services. Washington, DC: U.S. Government Printing Office.

Clayton, Richard R.; Cattarello, Anne; Day, L. Edward; and Walden, Katherine P.
1990   Persuasive communication and drug prevention: an evaluation of the D.A.R.E. program. In Lewis Donohew, Howard Sypher, and William Bukoski, eds., *Persuasive communication and drug abuse prevention.* Hillsdale, NJ: Lawrence Erlbaum.

Clayton, Richard R., and Voss, Harwin, L.
1981   *Young men and drugs in Manhattan: a causal analysis.* National Institute on Drug Abuse. Washington, DC: U.S. Government Printing Office.

Cloward, Richard, and Ohlin, Lloyd
1961   *Delinquency and opportunity.* Glencoe, IL: Free Press.

Cochran, John K., and Akers, Ronald L.
1989   Beyond hellfire: an exploration of the variable effects of religiosity on adolescent marijuana and alcohol use. *Journal of Research on Crime and Delinquency* 26:198–225.

Cohen, C. I.; Teresi, J.; and Holmes, D.
1985   Social networks, stress, adaptation, and health. *Research on Aging* 7:409–31.

Cohen, Sidney
1979   Inhalants. Pp. 213–20 in Robert I. Dupont, Avram Goldstein, and John O'Donnell, eds., *Handbook on drug abuse.* Washington, DC: U.S. Government Printing Office.

Colasanto, Diane
1990   Widespread public opposition to drug legalization. *Gallup Poll Monthly*, January, 2–8.

Cole-Harding, Shirley, and Wilson, James R.
  1987   Ethanol metabolism in men and women. *Journal of Studies on Alcohol* 48:380–87.

Collins, James J.
  1981   Alcohol use and criminal behavior: an empirical, theoretical, and methodological overview. Pp. 288–316 in James J. Collins, ed., *Drinking and crime*. New York: Guilford Press.

Conger, John J.
  1956   Reinforcement theory and the dynamics of alcoholism. *Quarterly Journal of Studies on Alcohol* 17:296–305.

Conrad, Peter, and Schneider, Joseph W.
  1980   *Deviance and medicalization*. St. Louis, MO: Mosby.

Corry, James M., and Cimbolic, Peter
  1985   *Drugs: facts, alternatives, decisions*. Belmont, CA: Wadsworth.

Covington, Jeanette
  1986   Self-esteem and deviance: the effects of race and gender. *Criminology* 24:105–38.

DeFleur, Lois B.; Ball, John C.; and Snarr, Richard W.
  1969   The long-term social correlates of opiate addiction. *Social Problems* 17:225–33.

DeJong, William
  1986   *Project DARE: teaching kids to say "no" to drugs and alcohol*. Rockville, MD: National Institute of Justice.

De Leon, George
  1988a   Legal pressure in therapeutic communities. Pp. 160–77 in Carl G. Leukefeld and Frank M. Tims, eds., *Compulsory treatment of drug abuse: research and clinical practice*. Rockville, MD: National Institute on Drug Abuse.

  1988b   Program-based evaluation research in therapeutic communities. Pp. 69–87 in Frank M. Tims and Jacqueline P. Ludford, eds., *Drug abuse treatment evaluation: strategies, progress, and prospects*. Rockville, MD: National Institute on Drug Abuse.

De Leon, George, and Rosenthal, Mitchell S.
  1979   Therapeutic communities. Pp. 39–47 in Robert I. Dupont, Avram Goldstein, and John O'Donnell, eds., *Handbook on drug abuse*. Washington, DC: U.S. Government Printing Office.

Dembo, Richard; Grandon, Gary; La Voie, Lawrence; Schmeidler, James; and Burgos, William
  1986   Parents and drugs revisited: some further evidence in support of social learning theory. *Criminology* 24:85–104.

Denzin, Norman K.
1987   *The alcoholic self.* Newbury Park, CA: Sage.

Dequine, Jeanne
1985   Cocaine: the cost to its users is devastating. Cox News Service, August 18.

Dericco, Denice, and Niemann, Joan
1980   In vivo effects of peer modeling on drinking rate. *Journal of Applied Behavior Analysis* 13:149–52.

Dickson, Clarence
1988   Drug stings in Miami. *FBI Law Enforcement Bulletin* 57(1):1–6.

Dickson, Donald T.
1968   Bureaucracy and morality: an organizational perspective on a moral crusade. *Social Problems* 16:143–56.

Downs, William R.
1987   A panel study of normative structure, adolescent alcohol use and peer alcohol use. *Journal of Studies on Alcohol* 48:167–75.

Drug Enforcement Administration (DEA)
1988a   *Drug of abuse: 1988 edition.* Washington, DC: U.S. Department of Justice.

1988b   *Crack cocaine availability and trafficking in the United States.* Washington, DC: U.S. Department of Justice.

Dull, R. Thomas
1983   Friends' use and adult drug and drinking behavior: a further test of differential association theory. *Journal of Criminal Law and Criminology* 74:1608–19.

Dunham, Roger G., and Janik, Stephen W.
1985   Adoption of the Uniform Alcoholism Act and the availability of alcoholism treatment programs: a state-by-state examination. *International Journal of the Addictions* 20:503–18.

Dunham, Roger G., and Mauss, Armand L.
1982   Reluctant referrals: the effectiveness of legal coercion in outpatient treatment for problem drinkers. *Journal of Drug Issues* 12:5–20.

Dupont, Robert L., ed.
1989   *Stopping alcohol and other drug use before it starts: the future of prevention.* Rockville, MD: Office for Substance Abuse Prevention.

Edelson, Edward
1981   The neuropeptide explosion. *Mosaic* 12:15–18.

Eldridge, William B.
1962   *Narcotics and the law.* New York: American Bar Foundation.

Elliott, Delbert S., and Huizinga, David
   1983   Social class and delinquent behavior in a national youth panel. *Criminology* 21:149–77.

Elliott, Delbert S.; Huizinga, David; and Ageton, Suzanne
   1985   *Explaining delinquency and drug use.* Beverly Hills, CA: Sage.

Emrick, Chad D.
   1987   Alcoholics Anonymous: affiliation, processes, and effectiveness as treatment. *Alcoholism: Clinical and Experimental Research* 11:416–23.

Engs, Ruth C., and Hanson, David J.
   1986   Age-specific alcohol prohibition and college students' drinking problems. *Psychological Reports* 59:979–84.

   1987   College students' drinking patterns and problems. *National Association of Student Personnel Administrators Monograph Series* 7:57–68.

   1989   Reactance theory: a test with collegiate drinking. *Psychological Reports* 64:1083–86.

Epstein, Edward J.
   1974   Methadone: the forlorn hope. *Public Interest* 36:3–24.

Evans, Richard I.; Hansen, William; and Mittelmark, Maurice
   1977   Increasing the validity of self-reports of smoking behavior in children. *Journal of Applied Psychology* 62:521–23.

Fagan, Jeffrey, and Chin, Ko-Lin
   1989a   Social processes of initiation into crack. Paper presented to the American Society of Criminology, November, Reno, NV.

   1989b   Violence as regulation and social control in the distribution of crack. Paper presented at a technical review of the drugs and violence project sponsored by National Institute on Drug Abuse, September, Rockville, MD.

Fagan, Ronald W., and Mauss, Armand L.
   1978   Padding the revolving door: an initial assessment of the Uniform Alcoholism and Intoxication Treatment Act in practice. *Social Problems* 26:232–46.

Faupel, Charles E., and Klockars, Carl B.
   1987   Drugs–crime connections: elaborations from the life histories of hard-core heroin addicts. *Social Problems* 34:54–68.

Feldman, Harvey W.; Agar, Michael H.; and Beschner, George M., eds.
   1979   *Angel dust: an ethnographic study of PCP users.* Lexington, MA: Lexington Books.

Finestone, Harold
 1957 Narcotics and criminality. *Law and Contemporary Problems* 22:69–85.

 1964 Cats, kicks, and color. Pp. 281–97 in Howard S. Becker, ed., *The other side*. New York: Free Press.

Fingarette, Herbert
 1988 *Heavy drinking: the myth of alcoholism as a disease*. Berkeley, CA: University of California Press.

Fishburne, Patricia; Abelson, Herbert I.; and Cisin, Ira
 1980 *National survey on drug abuse: main findings*. National Institute on Drug Abuse. Washington, DC: U.S. Government Printing Office.

Fitzgerald, J. L., and Mulford, Harold A.
 1981 The prevalence and extent of drinking in Iowa, 1979. *Journal of Studies on Alcohol* 42:38–47.

Flanagan, Timothy J., and McGarrell, Edmund, eds.
 1986 *Sourcebook of criminal justice statistics*. U.S. Department of Justice, Bureau of Justice Statistics. Washington, DC: U.S. Government Printing Office.

Flay, Brian R.
 1987 What we know about the social influence approach to smoking prevention: review and recommendations. Pp. 67–113 in Catherine S. Bell and Robert Battjes, eds., *Prevention research: deterring drug abuse among children and adolescents*. Rockville, MD: National Institute on Drug Abuse.

Florida Alcohol and Drug Abuse Association Clearinghouse
 1989 Cocaine. *Just the Facts: An Educational Newsletter on Addictions*.

Franks, Cyril M.
 1963 Behavior therapy: the principles of conditioning and the treatment of the alcoholic. *Quarterly Journal of Studies on Alcohol* 24:511–29.

Fry, Lincoln J., and Miller, Jon
 1975 Responding to skid row alcoholism: self-defeating arrangements in an innovative treatment program. *Social Problems* 22:674–88.

Gallagher, Winifred
 1989a Marijuana. Pp. 88–92 in William B. Rucker and Marian E. Rucker, eds., *Drugs, society, and behavior*, 4th ed. Guilford, CT: Dushkin.

 1989b The looming menace of designer drugs. Pp. 96–103 in William B. Rucker and Marian E. Rucker, eds., *Drugs, society, and behavior*, 4th ed. Guilford, CT: Dushkin.

Galliher, John F., and Walker, A.
1977   The puzzle of the origins of the Marihuana Tax Act of 1937. *Social Problems* 24:367–76.

Gandossy, R. P.; Williams, J. R.; Cohen, J.; and Harwood, H. J.
1980   *Drugs and crime: a survey and analysis of the literature.* Washington, DC: U.S. Government Printing Office.

Garlington, Warren K., and DeRicco, Denise A.
1977   The effect of modeling on drinking rate. *Journal of Applied Behavior Analysis* 10:207–11.

Geary, Nori
1987   Cocaine: animal research studies. Pp. 19–47 in Henry I. Spitz and Jeffrey S. Rosecan, eds., *Cocaine abuse: new directions in treatment and research.* New York: Brunner/Mazel.

Gildea, William
1988   Life and drugs in sports fast lane. *Reader's Digest,* January, 49–54.

Girdano, Dorothy D., and Girdano, Daniel A.
1980   *Drugs: a factual account.* 3d ed. Reading, MA: Addison-Wesley.

Glantz, M.
1982   Predictions of elderly drug abuse. Pp. 7–16 in David M. Petersen and Frank J. Whittington, eds., *Drugs, alcohol, and aging.* Dubuque, IA: Kendall/Hunt.

Glassner, Barry, and Loughlin, Julia
1987   *Drugs in adolescent worlds: burnouts to straights.* New York: St. Martin's Press.

Glatt, M. M.; Rosin, A. J.; and Jauhar, P.
1978   Alcoholic problems in the elderly. *Age and Ageing* 7:64–71.

Goldberg, Steven R., and Stolerman, Ian P., eds.
1986   *Behavioral analysis of drug dependence.* Orlando, FL: Academic Press.

Goldstein, Avram
1979   Recent advances in basic research relevant to drug abuse. Pp. 439–46 in Robert I. Dupont, Avram Goldstein, and John O'Donnell, eds., *Handbook on drug abuse.* Washington, DC: U.S. Government Printing Office.

Gonzalez, Gerardo M.
1990   Effects of drinking age on reduced consumption of alcohol reported by college students. *Journal of Drug Issues* 20:67–73.

Goode, Erich
1969   Multiple drug use among marijuana smokers. *Social Problems* 17:48–64.

1970   *The marijuana smokers.* New York: Basic Books.

1984   *Drugs in American society.* 2d ed. New York: Knopf.

1989a   *Drugs in American society.* 3d ed. New York: Knopf.

1989b   The American drug panic of the 1980's: social construction or ob-
            jective threat? *Violence, Aggression, and Terrorism* 3:327–48.

Goodstadt, Michael S.
1988   *Drug education. Guide to accompany videotape.* Rockville, MD: Na-
            tional Institute of Justice.

Goodwin, Donald
1976   *Is alcoholism hereditary?* New York: Oxford University Press.

Gottfredson, Michael, and Hirschi, Travis
1990   *A general theory of crime.* Stanford, CA: Stanford University Press.

Goudie, Andrew J., and Demellweek, Colin
1986   Conditioning factors in drug tolerance. Pp. 225–85 in Steven R.
            Goldberg and Ian P. Stolerman, eds., *Behavioral analysis of drug
            dependence.* Orlando, FL: Academic Press.

Grabowski, John; Stitzer, Mazine L.; and Henningfield, Jack E., eds.
1984   *Behavioral intervention techniques in drug dependence treatment.*
            Rockville, MD: National Institute on Drug Abuse.

Grinspoon, Lester, and Bakalar, James B.
1969   Marijuana. *Scientific American* 221:17–25.

1979   Cocaine. Pp. 241–44 in Robert I. Dupont, Avram Goldstein, and
            John O'Donnell, eds., *Handbook on drug abuse.* Washington, DC:
            U.S. Government Printing Office.

Gropper, Bernard A.
1985   *Probing the links between drugs and crime.* National Institute of
            Justice Research in Brief, February.

Halloran, Richard
1987   Drug use in military drops: pervasive testing credited. *New York
            Times,* April 23.

Hamburg, Sam
1975   Behavior therapy in alcoholism. *Journal of Studies on Alcohol* 36:69–87.

Hansen, W. B.; Johnson, C. A.; Flay, B. R.; Graham, J. W.; and Sobel, J.
1988   Affective and social influences approaches to the prevention of
            multiple substance use among seventh grade students: results from
            Project SMART. *Preventive Medicine* 17:1–20.

Hanson, Bill; Beschner, George; Walters, James M.; and Bovelle, Elliott
1985   *Life with heroin.* Lexington, MA: Lexington Books.

Hanson, David J.
  1980   Drug education: does it work? Pp. 251–82 in Frank S. Scarpitti and
          Susan Datesman, eds., *Drugs and the youth culture*. Beverly Hills,
          CA: Sage.

Hardt, Robert H., and Peterson-Hardt, S.
  1977   On determining the quality of the delinquency self-report methods.
          Journal of Research in Crime and Delinquency 14:247–57.

Hargreaves, William A.
  1986   Methadone dosage and duration for maintenance treatment. Pp.
          19–79 in James R. Cooper, Fred Alman, Barry S. Brown, and
          Dorynne Czechowicz, eds., *Research on the treatment of narcotic
          addiction: state of the art*. Rockville, MD: National Institute on
          Drug Abuse.

Harrup, T.; Hansen, B.; and Soghikian, K.
  1979   Clinical methods in smoking cessation. *American Journal of Public
          Health* 69:1226–31.

Hartford, James T., and Samorajski, T.
  1982   Alcoholism in the geriatric population. *Journal of the American
          Geriatric Society* 30:18–24.

Hawkins, J. David; Lishner, Denise M.; and Catalano, Richard F.
  1987   Childhood predictors and the prevention of adolescent substance
          abuse. Pp. 75–126 in Coryl L. Jones and Robert J. Battjes, eds.,
          Etiology of drug abuse. Rockville, MD: National Institute on Drug
          Abuse.

Hayeslip, David W.
  1989   Local level drug enforcement: new strategies. *Research in Action
          NIJ Reports* 213 (March/April):2–6.

Heien, Dale M., and Pittman, David J.
  1989   The economic costs of alcohol abuse: an assessment of cur-
          rent methods and estimates. *Journal of Studies on Alcohol*
          30:567–79.

Helzer, John E.
  1985   Specification of predictors of narcotic use versus addiction. Pp.
          173–97 in Lee Robins, ed., *Studying drug abuse*. New Brunswick,
          NJ: Rutgers University Press.

Hindelang, Michael J.; Hirschi, Travis; and Weiss, Joseph
  1981   *Measuring delinquency*. Beverly Hills, CA: Sage.

Hirschi, Travis
  1969   *Causes of delinquency*. Berkeley, CA: University of California
          Press.

Hollinger, Richard C.
1988   Working under the influence (WUI): correlates of employees' use of alcohol and other drugs. *Journal of Applied Behavioral Science* 24:439–54.

Hollister, Leo E.
1971   Marihuana in man: three years later. *Science* 172:21–28.

Holyfield, Jeff
1989   Study: collegiate steroid use rises. Associated Press, October 17.

Holzer, Charles E.; Robins, Lee; Meyers, Jerome; Weissman, Myrna; Tischler, Gary L.; Leaf, Philip J.; Anthony, J.; and Bednarski, P.
1984   Antecedents and correlates of alcohol abuse and dependence in the elderly. Pp. 217–44 in George Maddox, Lee Robins, and Nathan Rosenberg, eds., *Alcohol abuse among the elderly.* Rockville, MD: National Institute on Alcohol Abuse and Alcoholism.

Hubbard, R. W.; Santos, J. F.; and Santos, M. A.
1979   Alcohol and older adults: overt and covert influences. *Social Casework: The Journal of Contemporary Social Work* 60:166–70.

Huizinga, David H., and Elliott, Delbert S.
1981   A longitudinal study of drug use and delinquency in a national sample of youth: an assessment of causal order. Boulder, CO: Behavioral Research Institute.

Hunt, George M., and Azrin, N. H.
1973   A community-reinforcement approach to alcoholism. *Behavior Research and Therapy* 11:91–104.

Hunt, Leon, and Chambers, Carl D.
1976   *The heroin epidemics.* New York: Spectrum.

Inciardi, James A.
1974   The vilification of euphoria: some perspectives on an elusive issue. *Addictive Diseases* 1:241–67.

1980   Youth, drugs, and street crime. Pp. 175–204 in Frank Scarpitti and Susan Datesman, eds., *Drugs and the youth culture.* Beverly Hills, CA: Sage.

1986   *The war on drugs: heroin, cocaine, crime, and public policy.* Palo Alto, CA: Mayfield.

Inciardi, James A., and Chambers, Carl D.
1971   Patterns of pentazocine abuse and addiction. *New York Journal of Medicine* 15:1727–33.

Inciardi, James A., and McBride, Duane C.
1990   Legalizing drugs: a formless, naive idea. *Criminologist* 15(5):1, 3–4.

Innes, Christopher A.
   1988   *Drug use and crime.* Bureau of Justice Statistics Special Report,
            July. Washington, DC: U.S. Department of Justice.

Jacobs, James B.
   1990   Imagining drug legalization. *Public Interest* 101:28–42.

James, Randolph
   1989   Hazards of clandestine drug laboratories. *FBI Law Enforcement
            Bulletin* 58(4):16–21.

Jehl, Douglas
   1990   Cocaine supplies down dramatically, DEA says. *Los Angeles Times,*
            July 18.

Jellinek, E. M.
   1960   *The disease concept of alcoholism.* New Haven, CT: Hillhouse
            Press.

Jessor, Richard
   1979   Marihuana: a review of recent psychosocial research. Pp. 337–56
            in Robert I. Dupont, Avram Goldstein, and John O'Donnell, eds.,
            Handbook on drug abuse. Washington, DC: U.S. Government Print-
            ing Office.

Jessor, Richard, and Jessor, Shirley L.
   1977   *Problem behavior and psychological development.* New York:
            Academic Press.

Jessor, Richard; Jessor, Shirley L.; and Finney, John
   1973   A social psychology of marijuana use: longitudinal studies of high
            school and college youth. *Journal of Personality and Social
            Psychology* 26:1–15.

Johnson, Bruce J.; Goldstein, Paul J.; Preble, Edward; Schimeidler, James;
Lipton, Douglas; Spunt, Barry; and Miller, Thomas
   1985   *Taking care of business: the economics of crime by heroin abusers.*
            Lexington, MA: Heath.

Johnston, Lloyd
   1973   *Drugs and American youth.* Ann Arbor, MI: Institute for Social
            Research.

   1989   Teen drug use continues decline. News release from the University
            of Michigan, Ann Arbor, February 24.

Johnston, Lloyd D.; Bachman, Jerald G.; and O'Malley, Patrick M.
   1980   *Highlights from student drug use in America: 1975–1980.* National
            Institute on Drug Abuse. Washington, DC: U.S. Government Print-
            ing Office.

1982   *Student drug use, attitudes, and beliefs: national trends 1975–1982.*
            National Institute on Drug Abuse. Washington, DC: U.S. Govern-
            ment Printing Office.

Johnston, Lloyd D.; O'Malley, Patrick M.; and Bachman, Jerald G.
1988   *Illicit drug use, smoking, and drinking by America's high school
            students, college students, and young adults, 1975–1987.* National
            Institute on Drug Abuse. Washington, DC: U.S. Government Print-
            ing Office.

1989   *Drug use, drinking, and smoking: national survey results from high
            school, college, and young adult populations, 1975–1988.* National
            Institute on Drug Abuse. Washington, DC: U.S. Government Print-
            ing Office.

Johnston, Lloyd D.; O'Malley, Patrick M.; and Eveland, Leslie K.
1978   Drugs and delinquency: a search for causal connections.
            Pp. 137–56 in Denise Kandel, ed., *Longitudinal research on drug
            use.* Washington, DC: Hemisphere Press.

Joint Committee on New York Drug Law Evaluation
1977   *The nation's toughest drug law: evaluating the New York experience.*
            Washington, DC: The Association of the Bar of the City of New
            York and Drug Abuse Council.

Jones, Coryl L., and Battjes, Robert J., eds.
1987   *Etiology of drug abuse: implications for prevention.* Rockville, MD:
            National Institute on Drug Abuse.

Journal of Criminal Law and Criminology
1990   Review of Supreme Court decisions, pp. 996–1085.

Judson, Horace F.
1974   *Heroin addiction: what America can learn from the British ex-
            perience.* New York: Vintage Books.

Kandel, Denise
1974   Interpersonal influences on adolescent illegal drug use. Pp. 207–40
            in Eric Josephson and Eleanor E. Carroll, eds., *Drug use:
            epidemiological and sociological perspectives.* New York: Halsted.

1975   Stages in adolescent involvement in drug use. *Science* 190:912–14.

1978   ed., *Longitudinal research on drug use.* New York: Hemisphere
            Press.

1980   Drug and drinking behavior among youth. *Annual Review of
            Sociology,* 235–85.

1984   Substance abuse by adolescents in Israel and France: a cross-
            cultural perspective. *Public Health Reports* 99:277–83.

Kandel, Denise B., and Adler, Israel
 1982   Socialization into marijuana use among French adolescents: a
         cross-cultural comparison with the United States. *Journal of Health
         and Social Behavior* 23:295–309.

Kandel, Denise, and Faust, R.
 1975   Sequence and stages in patterns of adolescent drug use. *Archives of
         General Psychiatry* 32:923–32.

Kandel, Denise B., and Yamaguchi, Kazuo
 1987   Job mobility and drug use: an event history analysis. *American Jour-
         nal of Sociology* 97:836–78.

Kantor, Glenda K., and Straus, Murray A.
 1987   The "drunken bum" theory of wife beating. *Social Problems*
         34:213–30.

Kaplan, Howard B.
 1975   *Self-attitudes and deviant behavior.* Pacific Palisades, CA: Goodyear.

Kaplan, Howard B.; Martin, Steven S.; Johnson, Robert J.;
and Robbins, Cynthia A.
 1986   Escalation of marijuana use: application of a general theory of de-
         viant behavior. *Journal of Health and Social Behavior* 27:44–61.

Kaplan, Howard B.; Martin, Steven S.; and Robbins, Cynthia
 1982   Application of a general theory of deviant behavior: self-derogation
         and adolescent drug use. *Journal of Health and Social Behavior*
         23:274–94.

Kaplan, John
 1971   *Marijuana: the new prohibition.* New York: Pocket Book.

 1988   Taking drugs seriously. *Public Interest* 92:32–50.

Katz, Jonathan L., and Valentino, Rita J.
 1986   Pharmacological and behavioral factors in opioid dependence in
         animals. Pp. 287–327 in Steven R. Goldberg and Ian P. Stolerman,
         eds., *Behavioral analysis of drug dependence.* Orlando, FL:
         Academic Press.

Keller, Mark
 1958   Alcoholism: nature and extent of the problem. *Annals of the
         American Academy of Political and Social Science* 315:1–11.

 1976   Disease concept of alcoholism revisited. *Journal of Studies on
         Alcohol* 37:1694–1717.

Kepner, Elaine
 1964   Application of learning theory to the etiology and treatment
         of alcoholism. *Quarterly Journal of Studies on Alcohol*
         25:279–91.

Kobrin, Solomon, and Finestone, Harold
1968   Drug addiction among young persons in Chicago. Pp. 110–30 in James F. Short, ed., *Gang delinquency and delinquent subcultures.* New York: Harper and Row.

Kolata, Gina
1988   Experts: kicking crack is almost impossible. *New York Times* News Service, June 25.

Krause, Neal
1986   Social support, stress, and well-being among older adults. *Journal of Gerontology* 41:512–19.

Krohn, Marvin D.
1974   An investigation of the effect of parental and peer associations on marijuana use: an empirical test of differential association theory. Pp. 75–87 in Marc Riedel and Terence P. Thornberry, eds., *Crime and delinquency: dimensions of deviance.* New York: Praeger.

Krohn, Marvin D.; Akers, Ronald L.; Radosevich, Marcia J.; and Lanza-Kaduce, Lonn
1982   Norm qualities and adolescent drinking and drug behavior. *Journal of Drug Issues* 12:343–59.

Krohn, Marvin D.; Lanza-Kaduce, Lonn; and Akers, Ronald L.
1984   Community context and theories of deviant behavior: an examination of social learning and social bonding theories. *Sociological Quarterly* 25:353–71.

Krohn, Marvin D.; Skinner, William F.; Massey, James L.; and Akers, Ronald L.
1985   Social learning theory and adolescent cigarette smoking. *Social Problems* 32:455–73.

La Greca, Anthony J.; Akers, Ronald L.; and Dwyer, Jeffery W.
1988   Life events and alcohol behavior among older adults. *Gerontologist* 4:552–58.

Lang, Alan R., and Michalec, Elizabeth M.
1990   Expectancy effects in reinforcement from alcohol. Pp. 193–232 in Miles Cox, ed., *Why people drink.* New York: Gardner Press.

Lanza-Kaduce, Lonn
1988   Perceptual deterrence and drinking and driving among college students. *Criminology* 26:321–42.

Lanza-Kaduce, Lonn; Akers, Ronald L.; Krohn, Marvin D.; and Radosevich, Marcia
1984   Cessation of alcohol and drug use among adolescents: a social learning model. *Deviant Behavior* 5:79–96.

Lanza-Kaduce, Lonn, and Bishop, Donna
1986   Legal fictions and criminology: the jurisprudence of drunk driving. *Journal of Criminal Law and Criminology* 77:501–21.

Larsen, Donald D., and Abu-Laban, Baha
  1968   Norm qualities and deviant drinking behavior. *Social Problems*
            15:441–49.

Lauer, Ronald M.; Akers, Ronald L.; Massey, James; and Clarke, William
  1982   The evaluation of cigarette smoking among adolescents: the
            Muscatine study. *Preventive Medicine* 11:417–28.

Lemert, Edwin M.
  1967   *Human deviance, social problems, and social control.* Englewood
            Cliffs, NJ: Prentice-Hall.

Lester, David
  1987   Genetic theory: an assessment of the heritability of alcoholism.
            Center of Alcohol Studies, Rutgers University, New Bruns-
            wick, NJ.

Lettieri, Dan J.; Sayers, Mollie; and Pearson, Helen W., eds.
  1980   *Theories on drug abuse.* NIDA Research Monograph 30. Rockville,
            MD: National Institute on Drug Abuse.

Leukefeld, Carl G., and Tims, Frank M., eds.
  1988   *Compulsory treatment of drug abuse: research and clinical practice.*
            Rockville, MD: National Institute on Drug Abuse.

Lindesmith, Alfred
  1938   A sociological theory of drug addiction. *American Journal of
            Sociology* 43:593–613.

  1967   *The addict and the law.* New York: Vintage Books.

  1968   *Addiction and opiates.* Chicago: Aldine.

  1980   A general theory of addiction to opiate-type drugs. Pp. 34–37 in
            Dan J. Lettieri, Mollie Sayers, and Helen Wallenstein Pearson, eds.,
            Theories on drug abuse. National Institute on Drug Abuse.
            Washington, DC: U.S. Government Printing Office.

Lukoff, Irving F.
  1974   Issues in the evaluation of heroin treatment. Pp. 129–57 in Eric
            Josephson and Eleanor E. Carroll, eds., Drug use: epidemiological
            and sociological perspectives. New York: Halsted.

MacAndrew, Craig, and Edgerton, Robert B.
  1969   *Drunken comportment: a social explanation.* Chicago: Aldine.

Maddox, George L.; Robins, Lee; and Rosenberg, Nathan, eds.
  1984   *Nature and extent of alcohol problems among the elderly.* Rockville,
            MD: National Institute on Alcohol Abuse and Alcoholism.

Mann, Peggy

1979   Marijuana alert I: brain and sex damage. *Reader's Digest,*
            December, 139–44.

1980a   Marijuana alert II: more of the grim story. *Reader's Digest,*
            November, 65–71.

1980b   Marijuana: the myth of harmlessness goes up in smoke. *Saturday
            Evening Post,* July/August, 32–43.

1981   Death on the "high" way. *Saturday Evening Post,* September,
            54–55, 114.

1985   *Marijuana alert.* New York: McGraw-Hill.

1988   Dogged crusader against drugs. *Reader's Digest,* March, 102–6.

Maranto, Gina

1985   The truth about cocaine. *Reader's Digest,* March, 95–99.

Marcos, Anastasios C.; Bahr, Stephen J.; and Johnson, Richard E.

1986   Testing of a bonding/association theory of adolescent drug use.
            Social Forces 65:135–61.

Markle, Gerald E., and Troyer, Ronald J.

1979   Smoke gets in your eyes: cigarette smoking as deviant behavior.
            Social Problems 26:611–25.

Marlatt, G. Alan, and Fromme, Kim

1988   Metaphors for addiction. Pp. 1–24 in Stanton Peele, ed., *Visions of
            addiction.* Lexington, MA: Heath.

Marlatt, G. Alan, and Gordon, Judith R., eds.

1985   *Relapse prevention.* New York: Guilford Press.

Marlatt, G. Alan, and Rohsenow, Damaris J.

1981   The think-drink effect. *Psychology Today,* December, 60–69, 93.

Martin, Herbert, and Thrasher, Delia

1989   Chemical dependency and treatment of the professional athlete.
            Pp. 315–39 in Gary W. Lawson and Ann W. Lawson, eds., *Alcohol
            and substance abuse in special populations.* Rockville, MD: Aspen
            Publishers.

McAuliffe, William E.; Feldman, Barry; Friedman, Rob; Launer, Elaine;
Magnuson, Elizabeth; Mahoney, Carl; Santangelo, Susan Ward; William;
and Weiss, Roger

1986   Explaining relapse to opiate addiction following successful comple-
            tion of treatment. Pp. 136–56 in Frank M. Tims and Carl G.
            Leukefeld, eds., *Relapse and recovery in drug abuse.* Rockville, MD:
            National Institute on Drug Abuse.

McAuliffe, William E., and Gordon, Robert A.

1974   A test of Lindesmith's theory of addiction: the frequency of euphoria among long-term addicts. *American Journal of Sociology* 79:795–840.

1980   Reinforcement and the combination of effects: summary of a theory of opiate addiction. Pp. 137–41 in Dan J. Lettieri, Mollie Sayers, and Helen Wallenstein Pearson, eds., *Theories on drug abuse.* National Institute on Drug Abuse. Washington, DC: U.S. Government Printing Office.

McAuliffe, William E.; Rothman, Mary; Santangelo, Susan; Feldman, Barry; Magnuson, Elizabeth; Sobol, Arthur; and Weissman, Joel

1986   Psychoactive drug use among practicing physicians and medical students. *New England Journal of Medicine* 315:805–10.

McCrady, Barbara S.; Dean, Larry; Dubreuil, Edmund; and Swanson, Suzanne

1985   The problem drinkers' project: a programmatic application of social learning-based treatment. Pp. 417–71 in Alan C. Marlatt and Judith R. Gordon, eds., *Relapse prevention.* New York: Guilford Press.

McGlothin, William H.

1979   Drugs and crime. Pp. 357–69 in Robert I. Dupont, Avram Goldstein, and John O'Donnell, eds., *Handbook on drug abuse.* Washington, DC: U.S. Government Printing Office.

McGlothin, William, H.; Anglin, M. Douglas; and Wilson, Bruce D.

1978   Narcotic addiction and crime. *Criminology* 16:293–316.

Merton, Robert K.

1938   Social structure and anomie. *American Sociological Review* 3:672–82.

1957   *Social theory and social structure.* Glencoe, IL: Free Press.

Meyers, A. R.; Goldman, E.; Hingson, R.; Scotch, N.; and Mangione, T.

1981–82   Evidence of cohort and generational differences in drinking behavior of older adults. *International Journal of Aging and Human Development* 14:31–44.

Meyers, A. R.; Hingson, R.; Muscatel, M.; and Goldman, E.

1982   Social and psychologic correlates of problem drinking in old age. *Journal of the American Geriatrics Society* 30:452–56.

Mieczkowski, Thomas

1986   Geeking up and throwing down: heroin street life in Detroit. *Criminology* 24:645–66.

Miller, Judith D.; Cisin, Ira H.; Gardner-Keaton, Hilary; Harrell, Adele; Wirtz, Philip W.; Abelson, Herbert I.; and Fishburne, Patricia M.
    1983   *National survey on drug abuse: main findings 1982.* National Institute on Drug Abuse. Washington, DC: U.S. Government Printing Office.

Miller, J. Keith
    1987   *Sin: overcoming the ultimate deadly addiction.* San Francisco: Harper and Row.

Miller, Ken
    1989   Newest form of amphetamine more addictive. *Reno Gazette-Journal,* November 12.

Mizruchi, Ephraim H., and Perruci, Robert
    1962   Norm qualities and differential effects of deviant behavior. *American Sociological Review* 27:391–99.

Moberg, D. Paul
    1986   The interorganizational political economy of adolescent alcohol and drug services. Paper presented at the meetings of the Society for the Study of Social Problems, August, New York.

Modlin, H. C., and Montes, A.
    1964   Narcotic addiction in physicians. *American Journal of Psychiatry* 121:358–65.

Moore, Mark H., and Kleiman, Mark A. R.
    1989   The police and drugs. *Perspectives on Policing* 11:1–14.

Moore, Nancy P., and Lewis, Gary R.
    1989   Substance abuse and the physician. Pp. 131–37 in Gary W. Lawson and Ann W. Lawson, eds., *Alcohol and substance abuse in special populations.* Rockville, MD: Aspen Publishers.

Mulford, Harold A.
    1964   Drinking and deviant drinking, USA, 1963. *Quarterly Journal of Studies on Alcohol* 25:634–50.

Mulford, Harold A., and Miller, Donald
    1960   Drinking in Iowa IV: preoccupation with alcohol and definitions of alcoholism, heavy drinking, and trouble due to drinking. *Quarterly Journal of Studies on Alcohol* 21:279–96.

Nadelman, Ethan A.
    1989   Drug prohibition in the United States: costs, consequences, and alternatives. *Science* 245:921, 939–47.

Nahas, Gabriel
    1980   *Keeping off the grass*. New York: Pergamon Press.

National Academy of Sciences
    1982   *Marijuana and health: report of a study*. Institute of Medicine.
        Washington, DC: National Academy Press.

National Institute on Alcohol Abuse and Alcoholism (NIAAA)
    1981   *Fourth special report to the U.S. Congress on alcohol and health*.
        Washington, DC: U.S. Government Printing Office.

    1982   Researchers investigating inherited alcohol problems. NIAAA Infor-
        mation and Feature Service, August 30. National Clearinghouse for
        Alcohol Information. Rockville, MD: National Institute on Alcohol
        Abuse and Alcoholism.

    1987   *Alcohol and health: sixth special report to the U.S. Congress from the*
        secretary of health and human services. Washington, DC: U.S.
        Government Printing Office.

National Institute on Drug Abuse (NIDA)
    1985   *Epidemiology of drug abuse: research, clinical, and social perspec-*
        tives. Rockville, MD: National Institute on Drug Abuse.

    1986   Highlights of the 1985 national household survey on drug abuse.
        NIDA Capsules, November. Rockville, MD: National Institute on
        Drug Abuse.

    1988a   *National household survey on drug abuse: main findings, 1985*.
        Rockville, MD: National Institute on Drug Abuse.

    1988b   *Data from the Drug Abuse Warning Network (DAWN): annual data,*
        1987. Rockville, MD: National Institute on Drug Abuse.

    1989a   Highlights of the 1988 household survey on drug abuse. *NIDA*
        Capsules, August. Rockville, MD: National Institute on Drug
        Abuse.

    1989b   *National household survey on drug abuse: population estimates,*
        1988. Rockville, MD: National Institute on Drug Abuse.

    1990a   Overview of the 1990 national household survey on drug abuse.
        NIDA Capsules, December. Rockville, MD: National Institute on
        Drug Abuse.

    1990b   *National household survey on drug abuse: main findings, 1988*.
        Rockville, MD: National Institute on Drug Abuse.

National Institute on Drug Abuse and National Institute on Alcohol Abuse
and Alcoholism (NIDA/NIAAA)
    1990   *National Drug and Alcoholism Treatment Unit Survey (NDATUS):*
        1989 main findings report. Rockville, MD: U.S. Department of
        Health and Human Services.

National Institute of Justice (NIJ)

1984 *Drug use and pretrial crime in the District of Columbia.* NIJ Research in Brief, October. Washington, DC: U.S. Department of Justice.

1987 *Controlling drug abuse and crime: a research update.* NIJ Research in Action reprint of NIJ Report No. 202 (March/April). Washington, DC: National Institute of Justice.

1989 NIJ Report No. 213 (March/April), 7. Washington, DC: National Institute of Justice.

1990 DUF: Drug use forecasting. *NIJ Research in Action.* March. Washington, DC: National Institute of Justice.

Neuhring, Elaine, and Markle, Gerald E.

1974 Nicotine and norms: the re-emergence of a deviant behavior. *Social problems* 21:513–26.

Newcomb, Michael D.

1988 *Drug use in the workplace: risk factors for disruptive substance use among young adults.* Dover, MA: Auburn House.

Nichols, John R.

1965 How opiates change behavior. *Scientific American* 212:80–88.

Nichols, John R., and Davis, W. M.

1959 Drug addiction II: variation of addiction. *Journal of the American Pharmaceutical Association* 45:259–62.

Nordstrom, Goran, and Berglund, Mats

1987 A prospective study of successful long-term adjustment in alcohol dependence: social drinking vs. abstinence. *Journal of Studies on Alcohol* 48:95–103.

Nunes, Edward V., and Klein, Donald F.

1987 Research issues in cocaine abuse: future directions. Pp. 273–98 in Henry I. Spitz and Jeffrey S. Rosecan, eds., *Cocaine abuse: new directions in treatment and research.* New York: Brunner/Mazel.

Nunes, Edward V., and Rosecan, Jeffrey S.

1987 Human neurobiology of cocaine. Pp. 48–94 in Henry I. Spitz and Jeffrey S. Rosecan, eds., *Cocaine abuse: new directions in treatment and research.* New York: Brunner/Mazel.

O'Brien, Charles P.; Ehrman, Ronald N.; and Ternes, Joseph W.

1986 Classical conditioning in human opioid dependence. Pp. 329–56 in Steven R. Goldberg and Ian P. Stolerman, eds., *Behavioral analysis of drug dependence.* Orlando, FL: Academic Press.

O'Donnell, John A.

   1964   A follow-up of narcotic addicts. *American Journal of Ortho-psychiatry* 34:948–54.

   1965   The relapse in narcotic addiction. Pp. 226–46 in Daniel Wilner and Gene Kassebaum, eds., *Narcotics*. New York: McGraw-Hill.

   1966   Narcotic addiction and crime. *Social Problems* 13:374–85.

O'Donnell, John A.; Voss, Harwin L.; Clayton, Richard R.; Slatin, Gerald T.; and Room, Robin G. S.

   1976   *Young men and drugs: a nationwide survey*. Springfield, VA: National Technical Information Service.

Orcutt, James D.

   1987   Differential association and marijuana use: a closer look at Sutherland (with a little help from Becker). *Criminology* 25:341–58.

   1991   Beyond "the exotic and the pathologic": alcohol problems, norm qualities, and sociological theories of deviance. In Paul M. Roman, ed., *Alcohol: the development of sociological perspectives on use and abuse*. New Brunswick, NJ: Rutgers University Press.

Packer, Herbert L.

   1968   *The limits of the criminal sanction*. Stanford, CA: Stanford University Press.

Peele, Stanton

   1985   *The meaning of addiction*. Lexington, MA: Heath.

   1987   The limitations of the control-of-supply models for explaining and preventing alcoholism and drug addiction. *Journal of Studies on Alcohol* 48:61–77.

   1988a   ed., *Visions of addiction*. Lexington, MA: Heath.

   1988b   A moral vision of addiction: how people's values determine whether they become and remain addicts. Pp. 201–33 in Stanton Peele, ed., *Visions of addiction*. Lexington, MA: Heath.

   1989   *Diseasing of America: addiction treatment out of control*. Lexington, MA: Lexington Books.

Pendery, Mary L.; Maltzman, Irving M.; and West, L. Jolyon

   1982   Controlled drinking by alcoholics? new findings and a reevaluation of a major affirmative study. *Science* 217:169–75.

Pennell, Susan

   1990   "Ice": DUF interview results from San Diego. *NIJ Research in Action* 221:12–13. Washington, DC: National Institute of Justice.

Perkins, H. Wesley
1985   Religious traditions, parents, and peers as determinants of alcohol
          and drug use among college students. *Review of Religious Research*
          27:15–31.

1987   Parental religion and alcohol use problems as intergenerational
          predictors of problem drinking among college youth. *Journal for
          the Scientific Study of Religion* 26:340–57.

Petersen, David M., and Whittington, Frank J.
1977   Drug use among the elderly: a review. *Journal of Psychedelic Drugs*
          9:25–37.

Petersen, Robert C.
1980   *Marijuana research findings: 1980.* National Institute on Drug
          Abuse. Washington, DC: U.S. Government Printing Office.

Petersen, Robert C., and Stillman, Richard C., eds.
1978   *Phencyclidine (PCP) abuse: an appraisal.* National Institute on Drug
          Abuse. Washington, DC: U.S. Government Printing Office.

Pittman, David J., and Gordon, C. Wayne
1958   *Revolving door: a study of chronic police case inebriates.* New
          Haven, CT: Yale Center of Alcohol Studies.

Plaut, Thomas F. A.
1967   *Alcohol problems: a report to the nation.* New York: Oxford University Press.

Polich, J. Michael; Ellickson, Phyllis L.; Reuter, Peter; and Kahan, James P.
1984   *Strategies for controlling adolescent drug use.* Santa Monica, CA:
          Rand Corp.

Pomerleau, Ovide F., and Pomerleau, Cynthia S.
1988   A biobehavioral view of substance abuse and addiction. Pp. 117–39
          in Stanton Peele, ed., *Visions of addiction.* Lexington, MA: Heath.

Postrel, Virginia
1989   Making drugs legal will end so-called war. *USA Today*, December 15, 10A.

Rachman, Stanley, and Teasdale, John
1970   *Aversion therapy and behavior disorders.* Coral Gables, FL: University of Miami Press.

Radosevich, Marcia; Lanza-Kaduce, Lonn; Akers, Ronald L.;
and Krohn, Marvin D.
1979   The sociology of adolescent drug and drinking behavior: a review
          of the state of the field: part I. *Deviant Behavior* 1:15–35.

1980 The sociology of adolescent drug and drinking behavior: a review of the state of the field: part II. *Deviant Behavior* 1:145–69.

Ray, Marsh
1964 The cycle of abstinence and relapse among heroin addicts. Pp. 163–78 in Howard S. Becker, ed., *The other side.* New York: Free Press.

Ray, Oakley, and Ksir, Charles
1987 *Drugs, society, and human behavior.* 4th ed. St. Louis, MO: Times Mirror/Mosby.

Reader's Digest, eds.
1987 Can cocaine conquer America? January, 31–38.

Reinarman, Craig, and Levine, Harry G.
1989 The crack attack: politics and media in America's latest drug scare. Pp. 115–35 in Joel Best, ed., *Images of issues.* New York: Aldine de Gruyer.
1990 A peace movement has emerged against the war on drugs, *American Sociological Association Footnotes* 18:3.

Reinarman, Craig; Waldorf, Dan; and Murphy, Sheigla
1989 The call of the pipe: freebasing and crack use as norm bound episodic compulsion. Paper presented at the annual meeting of the American Society of Criminology, November, Reno, NV.

Robins, Lee N.
1973 *A follow-up of Vietnam drug users.* Washington, DC: U.S. Government Printing Office.

Robins, Lee N.; Murphy, G. E.; and Breckenbridge, M. B.
1968 Drinking behavior of young urban Negro men. *Quarterly Journal of Studies on Alcohol* 29:657–84.

Roman, Paul M.
1981 From employee alcoholism to employee assistance: deemphasis on prevention and alcohol problems in work-based programs. *Journal of Studies on Alcohol* 42:244–72.

Room, Robin
1987 Alcohol control, addiction and processes of change: comment on "the limitations of control-of-supply models for explaining and preventing alcoholism and drug addiction." *Journal of Studies on Alcohol* 48:78–83.

Rooney, James
1980 Organizational success through program failure: skid-row rescue missions. *Social Forces* 58:904–24.

Rosecan, Jeffrey S., and Spitz, Henry I.
1987   Cocaine reconceptualized: historical overview. Pp. 5–15 in Henry I. Spitz and Jeffrey S. Rosecan, eds., *Cocaine abuse: new directions in treatment and research.* New York: Brunner/Mazel.

Rosecan, Jeffrey S.; Spitz, Henry, I.; and Gross, Barbara
1987   Contemporary issues in the treatment of cocaine abuse. Pp. 299–323 in Henry I. Spitz and Jeffrey Rosecan, eds., *Cocaine abuse: new directions in treatment and research.* New York: Brunner/Mazel.

Ross, H. Lawrence
1982   *Deterring the drinking driver: legal policy and social control.* Lexington, MA: Lexington Books.

Rowan, Carl, and Mazie, David
1988   The mounting menace of steroids. *Reader's Digest,* February, 133–37.

Royce, James E.
1989   *Alcohol problems and alcoholism.* Rev. ed. New York: Free Press.

Rubin, Vera, and Comitas, Lambros
1976   *Ganja in Jamaica: the effects of marijuana use.* Garden City, NY: Anchor/Doubleday.

Rudy, David
1986   *Becoming alcoholic: Alcoholics Anonymous and the reality of alcoholism.* Carbondale, IL: Southern Illinois University Press.

Sanderson, R. E.; Campbell, Dugal; and Laverty, S. G.
1963   An investigation of a new aversive conditioning treatment for alcoholism. *Quarterly Journal of Studies on Alcohol* 24:261–75.

Sandmaier, Marian
1980   *The invisible alcoholic: women and alcohol abuse in America.* New York: McGraw-Hill.

Scanlon, Walter F.
1986   *Alcoholism and drug abuse in the workplace: Employee assistance programs.* New York: Praeger.

Schiffman, Saul; Read, Laura; Maltese, Joan; Rapkin, David; and Jarvik, Murray E.
1985   Preventing relapse in ex-smokers: a self-management approach. Pp. 472–520 in Alan C. Marlatt and Judith R. Gordon, eds., *Relapse prevention.* New York: Guilford Press.

Schlaadt, Richard G., and Shannon, Peter T.
   1986   *Drugs of choice: current perspectives on drug use.* 2d ed.
            Englewood Cliffs, NJ: Prentice-Hall.

Schuckit, Mark A.
   1977   Geriatric alcoholism and drug abuse. *Gerontologist* 17:168–74.

Schur, Edwin M.
   1965   *Crimes without victims.* Englewood Cliffs, NJ: Prentice-Hall.
   1971   *Labeling deviant behavior.* New York: Harper and Row.

Schwartz, Jerome L.
   1987   *Review and evaluation of smoking cessation methods.* National In-
            stitute of Health, Department of Health and Human Services.
            Washington, DC: U.S. Government Printing Office.

Seeman, Melvin, and Anderson, Carolyn
   1983   Alienation and alcohol. *American Sociological Review* 48:60–77.

Sellers, Christine S., and Winfree, L. Thomas
   1990   Differential associations and definitions: a panel study of youthful
            drinking behavior. *International Journal of the Addictions* 25:755–71.

Sells, S. B.
   1979   Treatment effectiveness. Pp. 105–20 in Robert I. Dupont, Avram
            Goldstein, and John O'Donnell, eds., *Handbook on drug abuse.*
            Washington, DC: U.S. Government Printing Office.

Shaffer, Howard J., and Jones, Stephanie B.
   1989   *Quitting cocaine: the struggle against impulse.* Lexington, MA: Lex-
            ington Books.

Sherman, Lawrence W.
   1990   Police crackdowns. *National Institute of Justice Report* 219:2–6.

Siegel, R. K.
   1984   Changing patterns of cocaine use: longitudinal observations, conse-
            quences and treatment. *NIDA Research Monograph Series* 50:92–110.

Siegel, Shepard; Krank, Marvin D.; and Hinson, Riley E.
   1988   Anticipation of pharmacological and nonpharmacological events:
            classical conditioning and addictive behavior. Pp. 85–116 in Stanton
            Peele, ed., *Visions of addiction.* Lexington, MA: Heath.

Simon, Eric J.
   1980   Opiate receptors and their implications for drug addiction. Pp.
            303–8 in Dan J. Lettieri, Mollie Sayers, and Helen Wallenstein
            Pearson, eds., *Theories on drug abuse.* National Institute on Drug
            Abuse. Washington, DC: U.S. Government Printing Office.

Simpson, D. Dwayne, and Marsh, Kerry L.
1986   Relapse and recovery among opioid addicts 12 years after treat-
        ment. Pp. 86–103 in Frank M. Tims and Carl G. Leukefeld, eds.,
        Relapse and recovery in drug abuse. Rockville, MD: National In-
        stitute on Drug Abuse.

Sisson, Robert W., and Azrin, Nathan H.
1986   Family-member involvement to initiate and promote treatment of
        problem drinkers. *Journal of Behavioral Therapy and Experimental
        Psychiatry* 17:15–21.

Smart, Reginald G., and Liban, Carolyn B.
1982   Predictors of problem drinking among elderly, middle aged, and
        youthful drinkers. Pp. 43–53 in David M. Petersen and Frank J.
        Whittington, eds., *Drugs, alcohol, and aging.* Dubuque, IA:
        Kendall/Hunt.

Smith, D. E., and Gay, G. R.
1972   *It's so good, don't even try it once.* Englewood Cliffs, NJ:
        Prentice-Hall.

Smith, David E.; Seymour, Richard B.; and Wasson, Donald R.
1979   The abuse of barbiturates and other sedative hypnotics. Pp. 223–40
        in Robert I. Dupont, Avram Goldstein, and John O'Donnell, eds.,
        Handbook on drug abuse. Washington, DC: U.S. Government Print-
        ing Office.

Smith, H. J.
1990   Opponents argue the merits of marijuana. *Gainesville Sun,*
        November 3.

Snyder, Charles R.
1964   Inebriety, alcoholism, and anomie. Pp. 189–213 in Marshall B.
        Clinard, ed., *Anomie and deviant behavior.* New York: Free
        Press.

Snyder, S. H.
1984   Drug and neurotransmitter receptors in the brain. *Science*
        224:22–31.

Sobell, Mark B., and Sobell, Linda C.
1978   *Behavioral treatment of alcohol problems: individualized therapy and
        controlled drinking.* New York: Plenum.

1984   The aftermath of heresy: a response to Pendery et al.'s (1982)
        critique of "individualized behavior therapy for alcoholics."
        Behavior Research and Therapy 22:413–40.

Sobell, Mark B.; Sobell, Linda C.; Ersner-Hershfield, Seth;
and Nirenberg, Ted N.
1982 Alcohol and drug problems. Pp. 501–33 in Alan S. Bellack, Michael
Hersen, and Alan E. Kazden, eds., *International handbook of
behavior modification and therapy*. New York: Plenum Press.

Sonnenstuhl, William J.
1982 Understanding EAP self-referral. *Contemporary Drug Problems*,
Summer, 269–93.
1988 Contrasting employee assistance, health promotion, and quality of
work life programs and their effects on alcohol abuse and
dependence. *Journal of Applied Behavioral Science* 24:347–63.

Spear, Sherilyn, and Akers, Ronald L.
1988 Social learning variables and the risk of habitual smoking among
adolescents: the Muscatine Study. *American Journal of Preventive
Medicine* 4:336–48.

Speckart, George, and Anglin, M. Douglas
1987 Narcotics use and crime: an overview of recent research advances.
Contemporary Drug Problems 16:741–69.

Spitz, Henry I., and Rosecan, Jeffrey S., eds.
1987 *Cocaine abuse: new directions in treatment and research*. New York:
Brunner/Mazel.

Spradley, James P.
1970 *You owe yourself a drunk: an ethnography of urban nomads*. Boston:
Little, Brown.

Statistical Abstracts
1983 *Statistical abstracts of the United States*. Washington, DC: U.S.
Government Printing Office.

Steele, Paul D., ed.
1988 Substance abuse and the workplace: special attention to employee
assistance programs. Special Issue of *Applied Behavioral Science*
24:315–469.

Stefanis, Costa; Dornbush, Rhea; and Fink, Max
1977 *Hashish: studies of long-term use*. New York: Raven Press.

Stephens, Richard, and Ellis, Rosaland D.
1975 Narcotic addicts and crime. *Criminology* 12:474–88.

Stewart, R. J.
1989 Prescription drug abuse in Vancouver. *Police Chief* 55:52–54.

Straus, Hal
1989 From crack to ecstasy. Pp. 93–95 in William B. Rucker and Marian
E. Rucker, eds., *Drugs, society, and behavior*. Guilford, CT: Dushkin.

Stumphauzer, Jerome S.
  1983   Learning not to drink: adolescents and abstinence. *Journal of Drug
            Education* 13:39–48.

Sutter, Alan G.
  1970   A hierarchy of drug users. Pp. 666–76 in Marvin Wolfgang,
            Leonard Savitz, and Norman Johnston, eds., *The sociology of crime
            and delinquency*, 2d ed. New York: Wiley.

Taylor, Norman
  1966   The pleasant assassin. Pp. 31–47 in David Solomon, ed., *The
            marihuana papers*. New York: Signet.

Thomas, Jon R.
  1985   International narcotics control: the challenge of our decade. *Police
            Chief* 52:42–46.

Tims, Frank M., and Leukefeld, Carl G., eds.
  1986   *Relapse and recovery in drug abuse*. Rockville, MD: National In-
            stitute on Drug Abuse.

Tims, Frank M., and Ludford, Jacqueline P., eds.
  1984   *Drug abuse treatment evaluation: strategies, progress and prospects*.
            Rockville, MD: National Institute on Drug Abuse.

Tobler, Nancy S.
  1986   Meta-analysis of 143 adolescent drug prevention programs: quan-
            titative outcome results of program participants compared to a con-
            trol or comparison group. *Journal of Drug Issues* 16:537–67.

Treaster, Joseph B.
  1990   Data: cocaine use at a peak. *New York Times* News Service, July 8.

Trebach, Arnold S.
  1982   *The heroin solution*. New Haven, CT: Yale University Press.

  1987   *The great drug war: radical proposals that could make America safe
            again*. New York: Macmillan.

Trice, Harrison
  1966   *Alcoholism in America*. New York: McGraw-Hill.

  1984   "Alcoholism in America" revisited. *Journal of Drug Issues* 14:109–23.

Trice, Harrison M., and Beyer, Janice M.
  1982   Social control in work settings: using the constructive confrontation
            strategy with problem-drinking employees. *Journal of Drug Issues*
            12:21–48.

  1984   Work-related outcomes of the constructive-confrontation strategy in
            a job-based alcoholism program. *Journal of Studies on Alcohol*
            45:393–404.

Trice, Harrison, and Roman, Paul M.
  1978   *Spirits and demons at work: alcohol and other drugs on the job.* 2d
          ed. Ithaca, NY: Cornell University Press.

Trice, Harrison, and Sonnenstuhl, William J.
  1988   Drinking behavior and risk factors related to the work place: im-
          plications for research and prevention. *Journal of Applied
          Behavioral Science* 24:327–46.

Troyer, Ronald J., and Markle, Gerald E.
  1983   *Cigarettes: the battle over smoking.* New Brunswick, NJ: Rutgers
          University Press.

Ullman, Albert D.
  1958   Sociocultural background and alcoholism. *Annals of the American
          Academy of Political and Social Science* 315:48–54.

United States Department of Health, Education, and Welfare (U.S. DHEW)
  1975   *Marihuana and Health: Fifth Annual Report to Congress.*
          Washington, DC: U.S. Government Printing Office.
  1979   *Smoking and health: a report of the Surgeon General.* U.S. Public
          Health Service. Washington, DC: U.S. Government Printing Office.

United States Department of Health and Human Services (U.S. DHHS)
  1986   *The health consequences of using smokeless tobacco.* NIH Publica-
          tion No. 86-2874. Bethesda, MD: Public Health Service, Depart-
          ment of Health and Human Services.
  1988   *The health consequences of smoking: nicotine addiction. A report of
          the Surgeon General.* Bethesda, MD: Public Health Service, Depart-
          ment of Health and Human Services.

United States Department of Justice (U.S. DOJ)
  1983   Inmates admit to heavy drinking before crime. *Justice Assistance
          News* 4 (March):5.
  1988   *Bureau of Justice Statistics Data Report, 1988.* Washington, DC: U.S.
          Department of Justice.

University of Michigan
  1991   Use of crack and other illicit drugs has declined significantly
          among young Americans, but cigarette smoking and alcohol use re-
          main high. News release from University of News and Information
          Service, January 24.

Uzelac, Ellen
  1990   Toad a la mode: a new high for drug lovers. *Baltimore Sun*, February 1.

Vaillant, George
  1983   *The natural history of alcoholism.* Cambridge: Harvard University Press.

Vawrinek, Jeffery J.
1982   First amendment—drug paraphernalia statutes and the Constitution. *Journal of Criminal Law and Criminology* 73:1365–87.

Vogel-Spratt, M., and Barrett, P.
1984   Age, drinking habits, and the effects of alcohol. *Journal of Studies on Alcohol* 45:517–21.

Waldorf, Dan
1970   Life without heroin: social adjustment during long-term periods of voluntary abstention. *Social Problems* 18:228–43.
1973   *Careers in dope.* Englewood Cliffs, NJ: Prentice-Hall.
1983   Natural recovery from opiate addiction. *Journal of Drug Issues* 13:237–80.

Waldorf, Dan; Murphy, Sheigla; and Lauderback, David
1989   Cocaine sellers: self-reported reasons for stopping cocaine sales. Paper presented at the annual meetings of the American Society of Criminology, November, Reno, NV.

Waldorf, Dan; Murphy, Sheigla; and Reinarman, Craig
1988   Social psychological strategies of cessation from cocaine. Paper presented at the annual meetings of the Society for the Study of Social Problems, August, Atlanta, GA.

Warner, K. E.
1978   Possible increases in underreporting of cigarette smoking. *Journal of the American Statistical Association* 73:314–18.

Washton, Arnold M.
1989   *Cocaine addiction.* New York: Norton.

Weeks, James R.
1964   Experimental narcotic addiction. Reprint 178 *Scientific American.*

Weil, Andrew T.; Zinberg, Norman; and Nelsen, Judith M.
1968   Clinical and psychological effects of marihuana in man. *Science* 162:1234–42.

Weisheit, Ralph A.
1990a   Domestic marijuana growers: mainstreaming deviance. *Deviant Behavior* 11:107–29.
1990b   Challenging the criminalizers. *Criminologist* 15(4):1, 3–5.

Weissman, James C.; Marr, Samuel W.; and Katsampes, Paul L.
1976   Addiction and criminal behavior. *Journal of Drug Issues* 6:153–65.

White, Helene Raskin; Bates, Marsha; and Johnson, Valerie
1990   Social reinforcement and alcohol consumption. Pp. 233–61 in Miles Cox, ed., *Why people drink.* New York: Gardner Press.

White, Helene Raskin; Johnson, Valerie; and Garrison, Carole Gozansky
1985 The drugs–crime nexus among adolescents and their peers. *Deviant Behavior* 6:183–204.

White, Helene Raskin; Pandina, Robert J.; and LaGrange, Randy L.
1987 Longitudinal predictors of serious substance use and delinquency. *Criminology* 25:715–40.

Whitehead, Paul C.
1975 The prevention of alcoholism: divergences and convergences of two approaches. *Addictive Diseases* 1:431–43.

Whitehead, Paul C., and Smart, Reginald G.
1972 Validity and reliability of self-reported drug use. *Canadian Journal of Criminology and Corrections* 14:1–8.

Whitehead, Paul C., and Wechsler, Henry
1980 Implications for future research and public policy. Pp. 177–83 in Henry Wechsler, ed., *Minimum-drinking-age laws: an evaluation.* Lexington, MA: Lexington Books.

Wilbanks, William L.
1988a The "monkey model" of addiction: a dangerous myth. Paper presented at the International Conference on Drug Policy, October, Washington, DC.

1988b The new obscenity. *Reader's Digest*, December, 23, 24, 27.

Wilsnak, Richard, and Cheloha, Randall
1987 Women's roles and problem drinking across the life span. *Social Problems* 34:231–48.

Wilson, Catherine
1989 Experts fear new drug "ice" may become "cool" in U.S. Associated Press, October 23.

Winfree, L. T., and Griffiths, C. T.
1983 Social learning and marijuana use: a trend study of deviant behavior in a rural middle school. *Rural Sociology* 48:219–39.

Winick, Charles
1964 Physician narcotic addicts. Pp. 261–80 in Howard S. Becker, ed., *The other side.* New York: Free Press.

1965 Epidemiology of narcotics use. Pp. 3–18 in Daniel Wilner and Gene Kassebaum, eds. *Narcotics.* New York: McGraw-Hill.

Wiseman, Jacqueline P.
1970 *Stations of the lost: the treatment of skid row alcoholics.* Englewood Cliffs, NJ: Prentice-Hall.

Wish, Eric D.
    1990   U.S. drug policy in the 1990s: insights from new data from arrestees. *International Journal of the Addictions* 25:377–409.

Wish, Eric D., and O'Neil, Joyce
    1989   *DUF: Drug Use Forecasting January to March 1989.* National Institute of Justice Research in Action, September.

Wister, Andrew V., and Avison, William R.
    1982   "Friendly persuasion": a social network analysis of sex differences in marijuana use. *International Journal of the Addictions* 17:523–41.

Yablonsky, Lewis
    1965   *The tunnel back: Synanon.* New York: Macmillan.

Yamaguchi, Kazuo, and Kandel, Denise
    1984a   Patterns of drug use from adolescence to young adulthood: II. Sequences of progression. *American Journal of Public Health* 74:668–72.

    1984b   Patterns of drug use from adolescence to young adulthood: III. Predictors of progression. *American Journal of Public Health* 74:673–81.

Young, Alice M., and Herling, Seymore
    1986   Drugs as reinforcers: studies in laboratory animals. Pp. 9–67 in Steven R. Goldberg and Ian P. Stolerman, eds., *Behavioral analysis of drug dependence.* Orlando, FL: Academic Press.

Zimberg, S.
    1974a   The elderly alcoholic. *Gerontologist* 14:221–24.
    1974b   Two types of problem drinkers: both can be managed. *Geriatrics*, August, 135–38.

Zinberg, Norman E.
    1979   Nonaddictive opiate use. Pp. 303–14 in Robert I. Dupont, Avram Goldstein, and John O'Donnell, eds. *Handbook on drug abuse.* Washington, DC: U.S. Government Printing Office.

    1984   *Drug, set, and setting: the basis for controlled intoxicant use.* New Haven, CT: Yale University Press.

Zinberg, Norman E., and Harding, Wayne M.
    1979   Control and intoxicant use: a theoretical and practical overview. *Journal of Drug Issues* 9:121–43.

Name Index

Subject Index